0 250

Hafiz.
Aejaz.

LAWRENCE
AND
OPPENHEIMER

by
NUEL PHARR DAVIS

SIMON AND SCHUSTER   NEW YORK

LIBRARY OF CONGRESS CATALOG CARD NUMBER: 68-19940
DESIGNED BY EDITH FOWLER
MANUFACTURED IN THE UNITED STATES OF AMERICA

To Richard Kluger

CONTENTS

PREFACE

Background as given here was taken from a mountain of print—popular, technical, and governmental—some of it of great interest. But of greater interest to me were the memories of my two subjects told to me by about a hundred of their associates, mostly physicists. Any quotations in the book, unless otherwise attributed, came to me directly from the source cited. One reason for undertaking a book of this sort is the occasion it provides for interviews with figures of our time whose lives have escaped the commonplace. Among those to whom I owe thanks for such interviews are Roger Adams, Paul C. Aebersold, Samuel K. Allison, Gerald M. Almy, Daniel Alpert, Ralph A. Bard, Hans A. Bethe, Raymond T. Birge, Norris E. Bradbury, James J. Brady, Mrs. James J. Brady, Mrs. Bernice Brode, Robert A. Charpie, Lester Coleman, John R. Dunning, John Farmakes, Mrs. Laura Fermi, Hans Frauenfelder, Samuel A. Goudsmit, Mrs. Elizabeth Graves, George Kenneth Green, Leland J. Haworth, William Higinbotham, Roger Hildebrand, A. Llewelyn Hughes, David R. Inglis, Martin D. Kamen, Irving Kaplan, George F. Kennan, L. D. Percival King, Lew Kowarski, Robert Krohn, P. Gerald Kruger, Mrs. Mariette Kuper, Alexander S. Langsdorf, John Lansdale Jr., Mrs. Anna Lavatelli, Leo Lavatelli, John H. Lawrence, John J. Livingood, Stanley Livingston, F. Wheeler Loomis, Leon Love, Ernest M. Lyman, John R. Manley, Wilfrid B. Mann, John Marshall Jr., Anthony Matz, Paul W. McDaniel, Joseph L. McKibben, Edwin M. McMillan, George C. McVittie, Carrol Mills, Seth H. Neddermeyer, Thomas J. O'Donnell, Robert Oppenheimer, Melvin Price, Isidor I. Rabi, Eugene I. Rabinowitch, Leslie A. Redman, Clark S. Robinson, Arthur E. Ruark, R. E. Schreiber, Emilio Segré, Frederick Seitz, Robert Serber, Chalmers Sherwin, David H. Sloan,

9

Ralph Carlisle Smith, Mrs. Ralph Carlisle Smith, Henry D. Smyth, Lewis L. Strauss, Edward Teller, Robert L. Thornton, James L. Tuck, Louis A. Turner, Stanislaw M. Ulam, Frederick T. Wall, Albert Wattenberg, Sam I. Weissman, Eugene P. Wigner, K. C. Wu, Hoylande Young, and Mrs. Ida Zeleny.

Everyone involved in the story of course had his own perspective. None of the people named here would see exactly as I did the pattern of events and ideas that unfolded for me during the course of my work on the book, and some would be opposed.

To the Research Board of the University of Illinois I am indebted for a contribution toward the expense of gathering information. My thanks are also due to the university librarians, to a university technical publications director, Professor E. C. McClintock, and to information officers of the Argonne, Berkeley, Brookhaven, Germantown, and Los Alamos laboratories and the Joint Congressional Committee on Atomic Energy.

N. P. D.
Urbana, Illinois
April 27, 1968

We shall rest, Uncle Vanya.
—Anton Chekhov

1

THE WESTERNER

"Doctor, is it true that from 1943 until recently, at least, you were the most influential scientist in the atomic energy field in this country?" a government lawyer asked Robert Oppenheimer on April 14, 1954.

Oppenheimer did not smile. He was being accused of treason. Under oath, he hesitated. "I think Lawrence had in many ways more influence," he answered.

ERNEST ORLANDO LAWRENCE was an experimental physicist, Julius Robert Oppenheimer a theoretical physicist. The quarter century of their association was an age of personality in physics, as distinguished from the present, which is an age of organization. Theirs were the two strongest personalities. Berkeley, California, was the place they met, worked together, and made their impact on American science.

Lawrence came first, in a hurry, driving fast on U. S. Route 66 in August of 1928 in a Reo Flying Cloud coupé. He was escaping from Yale, where he had taught sophomore physics. "Will you give my boy special help so he will pass the course?" a Yale man's father asked him in late 1927.

"No," said Lawrence.

Expensively tailored, confident and casual, the man smiled. "Do you have a car?"

"No."

"Pass the boy and I'll give you one."

Walking home that afternoon across the campus, Lawrence realized he had actually felt tempted. For the first time he noticed the "Undergraduates Only" sign on a campus swimming pool. "They treat you like a servant," he afterward told another physicist, Isidor Rabi. To relieve his slowly rising anger, he bought the Flying Cloud, almost new, at a price he could not afford. It did not help much.

For Lawrence, Yale was two people, Swann and Zeleny, warm and cold. Lawrence worshiped William Swann, a tall Englishman with theatrically tousled hair and deep lines in his face which he called laugh lines. A rare bird from the Royal College of Science, in London, Swann had dipped briefly across the Great Plains, Lawrence's native habitat, had picked Lawrence up and carried him east. In 1923, as professor of physics at Minnesota, he supervised Lawrence's first graduate year; in 1924, as professor of physics at Chicago, Lawrence's second; in 1925, as professor of physics at Yale, Lawrence's third.

Swann once went down with newspaper reporters into the country's deepest bank vault to measure cosmic rays. He once played the cello for two and a quarter hours to an unhappy national meeting of the American Physical Society. Other physicists called him a fourflusher and envied his sure step in the plush world of foundations, bureaus, and patrons. He was a salesman in need of a good line, and he said he had found in Lawrence "unusual fertility of mind and more than his share of ideas." He published Lawrence's work, got him fellowships and grants for expensive experimental equipment, and persuaded John Zeleny to make him assistant professor of physics at Yale in the fall of 1927. This done, he flitted again to directorship of the Bartol Research Foundation in Pennsylvania (capital $1,666,586) and left Lawrence to cope with Zeleny alone.

Zeleny, chairman of physics, was a big man with a drooping gray mustache and a tranquil face. He blended perfectly into Yale's collegiate Gothic architecture, some of it nearly two hundred years old, which Lawrence detested. Lawrence could not understand him. Zeleny was the son of an immigrant farmer on the northwest plains, and this should have been a tie. But he seemed to have no comprehension of a young man's ambitions.

The memories he liked to talk about at faculty teas were to Lawrence alien and uncongenial. Ever since he had first wandered through the woods gathering wild raspberries as a pretext for hunting the fairy-tale gingerbread house, said Zeleny, he had left his career to chance, never asking for a job or a promotion.

Lawrence had to ask him for a promotion. To keep on with his research at Yale, Lawrence had to have graduate students, a different breed from the undergraduates, and these Zeleny reserved for the senior faculty. A few weeks after buying the Flying Cloud, Lawrence went to his office to talk with him.

Something in Zeleny's tranquil hazel eyes suggested he felt Lawrence had come seeking the gingerbread house. "You can do nothing for Yale" was the way Lawrence interpreted the look to a later colleague. "What is it you want Yale to do for you?" Lawrence was bitter, because he felt his research had already done something for Yale. Experimental physicists were then nibbling at the periphery of the atom, the electron shell. One way of ripping away an electron was with a flash of light by a process called the photoelectric effect. Lawrence had, in a series of experiments, cut the flash down to three billionths of a second, the shortest interval of time that human beings had ever measured. His reports had begun to be listened to with respect at meetings of the American Physical Society. In the world of the undergraduates suffering through a required course, all this was dull Greek. Lawrence had felt his excitement and creativity slipping away from him. Graduate students would be willing listeners and helpers. If he were to get them at Yale, Zeleny would have to promote him to associate professor of physics. He asked Zeleny to do it, and Zeleny said No.

Zeleny's tone was gentle. "Later, in due course, at the proper time," he seemed to be saying; but Lawrence could not wait. He was twenty-seven. American laboratories held firmly, almost superstitiously, to the belief that a physicist must make his mark by the age of thirty. Lawrence too believed it. He came to the wrenching decision that if he could not work at a first-rate university, it was time to try a second-rate one. Two physicists from California—Leonard Loeb and Raymond Birge—had told him the University at Berkeley was trying to build up its physics department. He wrote to them, got an offer of an associate professorship, and resigned at Yale. At the end of the school year in May of 1928, he brought his family—his parents and younger brother— to a tea at Zeleny's. Zeleny talked with them with surprising sympathy about Lawrence's hopes. "Ernest is making a mistake," he said.

Lawrence's father was president of a teachers' college at Springfield, South Dakota. None of the family had seen the country on the far side of the Great Divide. In August, on his way west in the Flying Cloud, Lawrence stopped in Springfield to pick them up and take them with him. They were all big, rugged, good-looking people. Lawrence was the biggest, with shoulders so broad his father and mother had trouble squeezing inside the coupé with him. "Born grown up," his mother called him, and worried that he might give an inferiority complex to his brother John, who sat in the rumble seat.

All showed in their faces a touch of the austerity that comes from growing up on the South Dakota plains. It was most pronounced in the mother, who as she watched the Teton Range roll by could have sat for the central figure in a pioneer group in bronze on the grounds of some state capitol. Very thrifty, very clearsighted, she had taught the boys to be water-savers, to work their way, to move ahead through privations. She used to joke to them that she was afraid their father might come home any day in his shirt, having given the coat off his back to the first panhandler.

Baptist or Episcopalian, join one church or the other, that's all there is here, the father had been told when he got to be somebody in his college town. For the whole family he had chosen the Episcopalian, because he thought it would be more broadening. Even so, in that strict environment he required the family's collusion to slip away from dinner guests for a cigar upstairs where the aroma would not be detected. He also read Horace without too much trouble over either the syntax or the ideas, and he taught the boys that, "dry" laws notwithstanding, there was nothing really sinful about a glass of wine.

Ernest takes after his mother, John takes after his father, relatives used to say, meaning perhaps only that when the younger brother grew up, the family was better off. Ernest had supported himself since his first undergraduate year at South Dakota University; as a medical student at Harvard, John had never had such an idea. Ernest had once felt obliged to pull him up for too much athletics at the expense of his studies.

John had not been offended; nor was he when, west of the mountains, Ernest drove unstopping through a heavy summer rain that soaked him in the rumble seat. Ernest, as always, looked confident and cheerful. But the family knew that Yale had hurt him more than an outsider could guess, and that he faced unknown Berkeley with a troubled mind.

After they arrived, the family stayed on for two weeks, giving such help as they could while Associate Professor Lawrence, very big but very young, tried to make out what was expected of him.

Gray-faced and tired-looking, Edward Hall, the physics chairman, welcomed Lawrence briefly. Most of the orientation Hall entrusted to Raymond Birge, departmental second-in-charge. Birge was a transplanted ninth-generation Yankee, short, wiry, brisk and birdlike. In spectroscopy, which was then turning a microscope on the atom's outer shell, he had a reputation for high achievement. Mercilessly he walked Lawrence back and forth across the hill up which the campus straggled nondescriptly to a breathtaking view of the Pacific Ocean. What he wanted, what Hall and the Department wanted, he kept saying, was men who would be active in research.

This emphasis made LeConte Hall, the physics laboratory, a clean-cut and simple place, comparatively innocent of festering animosities. There were a dozen physicists above the rank of instructor.

Activity in research was almost, but not quite, all that Birge and Hall cared about. Personally and instinctively, the two disliked the stigmata of the foreigner. Central-European, east-European, Levantine: the more obviously a man's background diverged from the Anglo-Saxon, the more they recoiled. "Background makes a difference," Birge used to say, and Hall's views were stricter. To get men who would be active in research, they had been willing to do violence to their feelings. So far their ventures had paid poorly. New hires of this stripe had distinguished themselves less by research than by drinking, or by marriage just before the child was born, or as house guests by retiring for the night without turning down the bed. Still Birge and Hall meant to keep trying. Just three weeks before hiring Lawrence, they told him, they had engaged a gorgeous new exotic. Julius Robert Oppenheimer, a rich New York Jewish merchant's son, was to join the faculty next year.

Lawrence had heard of Oppenheimer ("Say Robert, not Julius," they told him), who had aggravated his discontent with Yale by setting Harvard afire. European physics was in revolution over the discovery that matter was packets or limited trains of waves. To perceive reality was to define the position of particles in terms of wavelike probability distribution. Oppenheimer had brought to Harvard the most definitive and dramatic statement of the new physics that America had yet heard. To a score of packed houses he had lectured with rigorous mathematics and conveyed boiling excitement. "Quantize it!" he had shouted, and his audience had gasped as at a revival meeting.

Birge and Hall looked forward to Oppenheimer's coming with mixed eagerness and dread; Lawrence, when he heard of it, with eagerness alone. He wanted the best possible theoretical physicist at hand for consultation, and he lacked his elders' prejudice. "Protestant, Catholic, Jew, they're all good"—he liked to philosophize about religion, and he might have attended services himself if he had not felt it necessary to be active in research at LeConte Hall on Sunday mornings.

In fitting into the way of life at Berkeley, he got some help from his parents. The touch of the Great Plains in their faces came as a relief to Birge and Hall. "They were good folks," says Birge.

For his principal course, Electromagnetic Theory, Lawrence chose the terrible hour of eight o'clock every Tuesday, Thursday, and Saturday morning. For his lodging he chose the Faculty Club. Thus from sleep to waking, weekends included, he surrounded himself with his work. "You've got to practically crucify yourself if you're going to amount to anything," he explained to a young student assistant, James Brady, whom he had slipped into the habit of talking to at LeConte.

"Lawrence was a good teacher," Birge recollects when asked. "At least we never had any complaints, and that's unusual." Lawrence kept his eye beyond the classroom. Graduate students kindled at his vision of research. The first was Niels Edlef Edlefsen, a very civilized, very unaggressive blond giant from Utah. Edlefsen, LeConte's best laboratory assistant, knew how to put his hands on the smallest bit of equipment, and Lawrence drew happily on his knowledge. He gave Edlefsen the doctoral-thesis assignment of building a gargantuan ultraviolet lamp in a tank of water. They began experiments to prove that deionization—recovery by the atom of a lost electron—occurred at a rate predicted by Oppenheimer in a published paper on wave mechanics.

Edlefsen, a Mormon missionary, brought in two other Mormon students, to whom Lawrence assigned other photoelectric experiments. Brady, even before he had finished his required preliminary courses, began precocious thesis-experiments on the motion of electrons in thin metal-surface films. For still another student, Frank Dunnington of Colorado, Lawrence invented a method of measuring the ratio of an electron's mass to its charge. Dunnington's work, Birge said a decade later, established "possibly the most accurate value we have" for a fundamental constant of nature.

Thus, in the spring of 1929 Lawrence found himself doing well as college professors measure their lives. But time was going by, he was nearing thirty, and so far he had only picked at the periphery of the atom. Massive and tiny inside its veil of electrons, the nucleus remained unassailable. "Like a fly inside a cathedral," he called it at a lecture, never a man to varnish his similes. Physicists all over the world were talking about how to get at it. All agreed that the way was to stand above the roof of the cathedral and drop a hydrogen ion on the fly. Ions—atoms with an electron ripped off—were easy to drop. Being positively charged, they could be made to move toward a negative charge like a falling stone. The problem was to get enough voltage to make them fall fast enough. The nucleus protected itself behind a skin called the Coulomb barrier. To penetrate it an ion must move with an energy of many, many volts.* Lawrence did not know exactly how many. Like most physicists the world over, he thought vaguely in terms of a million. No apparatus in the world could generate such voltage, no insulation could contain it.

A man who lives at the Faculty Club has little to lose from an evening at the library. Lawrence formed the habit of going to it to

_____

* A nuclear physicist who hoped to be both precise and intelligible would say, "Ions must have a very high speed (velocity) in order to give them enough (kinetic) energy to penetrate the Coulomb barrier and for this, high accelerating voltages are required."

meditate on the virgin nucleus and to keep up with the technical journals. One evening there his life was altered. "It is a curious thing," said Birge. "I have never been able to find out the day it happened. He did not keep notebooks then. The best guess is February 1929."*

Overpersistent contributors haunt the technical journals much as they do the letters-to-the-editor columns of newspapers. The experienced reader recognizes their names and automatically skips. Such a contributor was Rolf Wideröe, a Norwegian living in Switzerland—volatile, restless, prolific of articles and ideas, often dubious. Coming upon an article of Wideröe's in the *Archiv für Electrotechnic*, Lawrence skipped the text but looked at a diagram on the first page.†

The diagram showed a pair of tubes set end to end. Through the first tube an ion could be made to fall from the positive to the negative end with an energy of 25,000 volts. The idea was commonplace and the energy contemptible. But at the time the ion passed out of the first tube and entered the second, the charge was to be reversed and the ion given another 25,000 volts of energy. Thus the diagram illustrated the concept of resonance, which, in this context, means giving repeated electric pushes at just the right time to reaccelerate an accelerated particle. The concept was already ten years old, but Wideröe was the first to suggest this specific apparatus.

Lawrence felt a stir of excitement. How many tubes, he wondered, could one set end to end? No limit on the number meant no limit on the speed to which ions could accelerate. He sketched out a series in his mind. There *was* a limit, he decided, at which the ions would spread like a shotgun pattern and hit the tube walls before they reached the million-volt acceleration he wanted.

* Lawrence's own account of the date is unreliable (below, p. 94). Stanley Livingston (see Chapter 2) puts it in the summer of 1929. Brady too says he would have put it a little later than Birge "except that I would not want to go against what Birge says, for he is a careful man."

† "I am only a footnote in history," Wideröe lamented to physicists at a Swiss scientific conference in the mid-Fifties. Though crushed by his loss of Norwegian citizenship on grounds of pro-Nazi collaboration, Wideröe was still prolific. At the conference he mounted the platform to begin a talk. Lawrence sat in the front row. The two rushed together and embraced on the platform steps. This was their only meeting.

He laid down the magazine. Still his excitement intensified. He saw the ions curving round as they fell—a vision as giddy and dreamlike to him as that of the falling moon, which also curved round, had been to Newton. To make the ions go round, all that was needed was to set them moving between the poles of a magnet. More than that, the time it took them to go round would be always the same. An electric push repeated at the right instant would send them spiraling out into bigger and bigger circles, traveling faster each time they went around. The thought was big and new, a fundamental discovery. Here he could see no limit to the speed that could be given them. He wrote down a simple set of equations.

All this happened in a few minutes. Without reading Wideröe's article he walked home to bed. Upon waking next morning, he looked at his notes and found he had told himself $MR\theta = eRH$. The mass of a particle times the radius of the orbit in which it moves times its angular velocity equals the electric charge of the particle times the radius of the orbit times the intensity of the magnetic field. It was still true in the morning light, and so beautiful he had to tell somebody.

"I may have been the first person Lawrence mentioned it to," said Brady. "I well remember the event if not the date, because it was then that I grew up as a physicist. He came bursting into the lab at LeConte, where I was working on another problem, his eyes glowing with enthusiasm, and pulled me over to the blackboard.

"He drew the equations of motion in a magnetic field. 'Notice that R appears on both sides,' he said. 'Cancels out. R cancels R. Do you see what that means? The resonance condition is not dependent on the radius of the circle [and therefore ions can be accelerated to speeds without any apparent limit]. *Any* acceleration!'

"I studied the blackboard. 'Yes, I see,' I answered. 'Looks good.'

" 'R cancels R,' he said again. 'Do you see?'

"I got an idea this was going to go on all day. 'About my problem of thin films,' I ventured. 'I have some questions.'

"He kept repeating that R canceled R, but I persisted. His eyes glazed. 'Oh, that,' he said. 'Well, you know as much on that now as I do. Just go ahead on your own.'

"I had never seen him this way before. He had his problem, I had mine. Each to his own. Nobody really cared. Gave me a terribly lonely feeling. So I grew up as a physicist. Later I told him, and he said his own turning point had come at Yale. Zeleny was taking Robert Millikan, America's most famous name in physics, on a tour of the labs. Lawrence was in the dumps, thinking he hadn't enough brains for physics and ought to get out. Millikan asked so many fool questions and had to try so hard to understand that Lawrence decided he himself wasn't so bad after all, and from that time he had confidence in his career.

"Afterward, when he told me this, it helped, but I was feeling lost when he walked away. He left in a rush, I suppose to tell other people that R canceled R. While the door was closing behind him, I heard a voice from the corridor cadenced in a typical graduate-student whine: 'Gee! You know, the way he flings that door open, he's gonna kill somebody.' "

Through the spring and summer of 1929 Lawrence told a number of physicists how important it was that R canceled R. Their attitude he later summed up at a lecture as follows: "Don't forget that having an idea and making it work are two different things." This they would tell him just before, out of sheer boredom, they changed the subject.

The liveliest talk among them was about Oppenheimer, scheduled to arrive at Berkeley and begin teaching that fall. Oppenheimer's journey was more eventful than Lawrence's. In a sense it began when Oppenheimer met Percy Bridgman at Harvard. Oppenheimer's father had encouraged him to do anything he wanted to. Bridgman convinced him that he wanted to "do physics." The phrase is Oppenheimer's own. It had a special meaning which he developed slowly.

For him Bridgman was a Swann and a Zeleny, a patron and a judge, combined. Treating him as an intellectual equal, the most graduate of undergraduates, Bridgman made physics easy for him. In return Oppenheimer showed brilliant mastery of the most abstruse concepts. Somehow Bridgman kept him from feeling the lack of long preparation which even the best physicist must have before making original advances. It was Bridgman's physics, not his own, that he manipulated at Harvard. "I was Bridgman's caddy," he said later.

Three years younger than Lawrence, he qualified for his bachelor's at Harvard in 1925 at the same time Lawrence received his doctor's at Yale. That fall he went abroad to study at the Cavendish Laboratories in Cambridge. This was the year that quantum mechanics first began to throw its blinding light. "It was at Cambridge," he said, "that I first grappled with solitary physics." Standing at a blackboard, he attempted to do physics, to write down equations for a reality which had not yet been formulated.

Hours passed while he stared with chalk in his hand. He would wake with a start to realize the day had gone in gray silence. For a man who could have anything he wanted, this was not necessarily the wrong thing. But at other times as the hours passed he would hear his own voice telling the blackboard, "The point is. The point is. The point is."

So he felt there must be a point. The blackboard wanted him to define the wave nature of matter, and he was paralyzed by inability either to do it or stop trying. He thought of suicide, then drove up to one of London's higher-priced psychiatrists. After a number of sessions, the psychiatrist presented a diagnosis. "Dementia praecox," he told Oppenheimer. "Your case is hopeless. I can do nothing for you. These visits are dangerous. You must not come to me any more."

The psychiatrist was mistaken. He did not know the verge which theoretical physics stood on, the push it was about to give the world from what that famed astronomer and charming metaphysician Harlow Shapley calls the Cenozoic to the Psychozoic Age. To help his patient, he would have needed to understand how hard it was to make the push.

Trying to escape the blackboard, Oppenheimer went with a friend on a long vacation in Corsica. He was twenty-two years old. Physics had detached him from life. Corsica brought him back with an experience whose details are hard to come by (at a guess there was a European girl who could not marry him). "A great thing in my life, a great and lasting part of it, more to me now, even more as I look back when my life is nearly over," he said long afterward. "My reason for telling you? Those loyalty hearings that the government held on me in 1954. The records printed in so many hundreds of pages of fine print in 1954. My big year, I've heard people say, and my life story complete in those records. But it isn't so. Almost nothing that was important to me came out there, almost nothing that meant anything to me is in those records. You see, don't you, that I'm proving this point to you now. With something important to me not in those records.

"The psychiatrist was a prelude to what began for me in Corsica. You ask whether I will tell you the full story or whether you must, dig it out. But it is known to few and they won't tell. You can't dig it out. What you need to know is that it was not a mere love affair, not a love affair at all, but love."

Sustained by an embrace as calm and lasting as the Mediterranean's, Oppenheimer defeated the psychiatrist. He became able to balance *can* and *must*. "Geography," he said, "was henceforth the only separation I recognized, but for me it was not a real separation."

He went to Göttingen and acquired the competence that must underlie brilliance. Max Born was first his teacher and then his collaborator. He published a series of papers which, though they did not originate quantum mechanics, vastly extended its meaning. His work became known to physicists the world over. Looking back through a mushroom cloud, Born said he wished Oppenheimer had shown less cleverness and more wisdom. But after his fashion Oppenheimer searched for wisdom, which to him as a physical scientist presented itself as the riddle of values not subject to measurement.

"Why do you waste time on such trash?" Paul Dirac asked him irritably a month after he started spending two hours a day studying Dante. Dirac had a great hard bare mind then wholly dedicated to thinking out the mathematics of a negative energy-state which nobody before him had conceived of. Dostoevsky, Proust, and Thomas Aquinas were other indulgences Dirac disliked to see in a colleague who had proved capable of actually understanding and contributing to the Dirac Theory. "And I think you're giving too much time to music and that painting collection of yours," Dirac would say during long walks he took with Oppenheimer for the purpose of persuading him to quit the pursuit of the irrational.

Oppenheimer liked Dirac because Dirac's theory brought him moments of intense happiness and beauty. Neither of the two knew much of the world. The difference was that Oppenheimer, being in love, was attempting a wider synthesis. Into his scale of values he found himself trying to fit another irrational. "I was homesick," he said. There was no use trying to describe the feeling to Dirac, so he described it to young Isidor Rabi from New York.

In Oppenheimer homesickness took the form of distress at the thought that he and his countrymen had had to seek the frontier of physics so far from home. His dream, as Rabi worked it out of him in successive conversations, was nothing less than to make the United States an international center for theoretical physics. Himself no ordinary man, Rabi did not think this preposterous. He judged then, as he does now, that in physics Oppenheimer had the best mind of his generation. "I was never in the same class with him," he says with a matter-of-factness odd on the lips of a Nobel laureate.

After a flare of indignation over the fact that Oppenheimer had not remembered to register as a student, the university authorities at Göttingen gave him a doctor's degree in 1927. He sailed home, lectured a few weeks at Harvard while Lawrence was chafing about being a servant to the Yale men, and then headed west.

Driving a big gray Cadillac, he chose the southern route across the country. The desert struck him as the most beautiful part of the United States. His spirits rose. He began thinking of physics, which about that time had brought him one of his life's happiest moments, symbolized for him as follows:

This was the start of a set of formulas he had discovered for measuring the chance of matter to pass through mass, of an object to get on the other side of an unbroken obstacle without going over or around. The Tunnel Effect, it came to be called—inaptly since the moving object would leave no tunnel. By the Tunnel Effect a huntsman's arrow could pass through the heart of an unwounded deer. X was the chance of any object's getting through, smaller for bigger objects but always computable.

The car had no blackboard, but it had a windshield. The formula may have been superimposed on the glass when, just east of a town near the California border, he ran off the road. A neighborly crowd gathered and heaved the car out of a ditch. He thanked them, drove into town and up a long flight of granite steps and slammed the car against the big courthouse door. No Tunnel Effect. Disarmingly simple, mildly bewildered, the expression on his face set the crowd to laughing when they gathered again. Instead of fining him, they lowered the car into the street, checked its vital points, and told him they hoped he would get to California.

His first destination was the California Institute of Technology at Pasadena. There he walked through the Bridge Laboratory and stood still in the middle of the busiest workroom. Clerks and mechanics gradually began to take notice of him. He had one arm in a sling and looked as though he had not shaved, bathed, or changed clothes in three days. "I am Oppenheimer," he said when he noticed they were staring.

A round-faced, cheerful little man named Charles Christian Lauritsen was bending over apparatus scattered across the floor. He straightened up. "Oh, are you Oppenheimer?" he said. "Then you can help me. Why am I getting the wrong results from this confounded cascade voltage generator I have put together?"

With these details Lawrence's colleagues entertained each other at Berkeley. Oppenheimer stayed as research fellow at Pasadena until the beginning of 1928. He had been offered positions at twelve universities, ten American and two European. Not knowing much about the usual thing, he had accepted assistant professorships at Pasadena and Berkeley with the idea of going north in the fall and south in the spring. But he had no conception of a poor man's need to get started on a career. For the rich young creedless and fetterless Jew, beauty was wisdom. More of it, personal and intellectual, remained for him to explore in Europe, and he said he wanted another year there first. Prestige-hungry, the Institute at Pasadena began listing him in its faculty register in 1928 but does not seem to have paid him any salary until 1930.

There was a physicist in Leiden, Paul Ehrenfest, whose ruthless honesty and zeal for clarity Oppenheimer wanted to acquire for himself. Ehrenfest diagnosed his thinking as original but loose and sent him for tightening to Europe's sharpest mind and tongue, Wolfgang Pauli at Zurich. After a few months, Pauli returned him. Ehrenfest found the looseness corrected and dismissed him, perfected as a thinker though as a man further diminished.

The first cost to him was tuberculosis, an infected spot on one lung. To catch his breath, he spent the summer of 1929 in the Sangre de Cristo Mountains of New Mexico. Their red desolation permanently enthralled him. "I have two loves," he used to say (the third one he seldom talked about), "physics and the desert. It troubles me that I don't see any way to bring them together."

Like Lawrence, he had an admiring younger brother. Frank Oppenheimer had the naïve open heart of a seventeen-year-old who had been sheltered from stress. Almost a professional with the flute, he played for hours on end to Robert that summer. They lived on a little ranch the family had bought for the older brother's convalescence. Later the two began reading the classics and, as Oppenheimer put it, fiddling with horses. Their mother was dead. Their father came to see them but because of a heart weakness could not stay long in the two-mile altitude. At the end of the summer Frank said he had decided that he too wanted to be a physicist.

In September of 1929 Oppenheimer came to Berkeley ready to begin teaching. He and Lawrence liked each other at once. Conversing earnestly, they took long walks together along San Francisco Bay. Mostly they talked about physics. Experimentalist and theoretician, they were fascinated by the unexpected vistas each could open for the other. Soon the social life of the campus furnished a further subject.

Lawrence was not only handsome, single, and rising. He was also the only young physics professor who had a good car. Oppenheimer had disposed of his. Samuel Allison, active in research on X rays, had one, but he had paid only fifty dollars for it, and it was not dependable. Berkeley's scenery and restaurant prices made picnics popular. At a reception, Oppenheimer, displaying as usual wider interests than physics wives were used to, mentioned an East Indian dish which the women identified phonetically as *nasty gory*. It was easy to prepare, he said, and with a bottle of wine made a complete meal. Mrs. Robert Brode, whose husband was active in research on cosmic rays, suggested a picnic and said she would bring fruit for dessert. Oppenheimer agreed to furnish wine and "nasty gory," the Allisons to furnish their bad car, and Lawrence his good one.

They drove across the Bay. Oppenheimer opened a handsome fitted condiment case and mixed up the "nasty gory." It tasted like sweepings from a Bombay gutter. The others finished the wine and fruit and waited for Oppenheimer to notice they had eaten nothing else. He never did; as a recent consumptive who ate by force of will, he thought it natural they would want only a mouthful to test the flavor. "We passed a hot-dog stand about two miles back," Lawrence said finally, and they all drove there, Oppenheimer looking puzzled.

Faculty wives poured invitations on the two bachelors. A hostess recalls that when invited to dinner, Lawrence would bring her bunches of roses—always red roses. She wanted to supply him dinner partners, but when possible he brought his own. When he did, there could be no table talk of campus concerts, lectures and amateur plays. "Hair-raising," she called Lawrence's girls and wondered how he picked them and whether they had even finished high school. So long as they were healthy and good-natured, he did not seem to care. He was always tired from the laboratory. She came to expect him to eat heavily and then turn sleepy.

Lawrence, in fact, selected girls on the basis of whether they cared for movies, which he liked but often slept through. He would also have liked to take them roller-skating. "But I guess it just wouldn't look right to do it here," he philosophized to young Brady in LeConte. "Around a university they expect professors to be dignified. So I only do it whenever I'm in South Dakota with my folks. I'm good, though."

Oppenheimer, by contrast, let his hostess assign him any dinner partner who happened to need an escort. With his affections engaged elsewhere, he maintained a detached chivalry. As for flowers, she remembers white gardenias and a centerpiece that must have required intricate planning with a florist. He talked Sanskrit poetry to her and lent her abstract paintings; one summer for storage purposes, as he put it, he had his grand piano sent to her house. "We all had a crush on Oppenheimer," she says, her face softening even now in reminiscence.

On their walks together, Lawrence and Oppenheimer disagreed sometimes about physics, but never about women. The same ones, they decided, were after them both.

When aroused, Oppenheimer lit cigarette after cigarette. He confessed to Birge that he could not think without one in his hand. Hall, the chairman, confessed that he could not think close to a smoker, especially Oppenheimer, and asked Birge to take care of any departmental Oppenheimer business. Hating cigarettes a little less than he hated inactivity in research, Birge consented. He waited with interest for news of Oppenheimer's impact on the students in his graduate course, Quantum Mechanics. Soon Oppenheimer came to him discouraged. "It's going too slow," he said. "They're not learning. I don't know what's wrong."

Students in the class were mimeographing their notes and selling them, but only to each other. "Since we couldn't understand what he was saying," Brady recollects, "we watched the cigarette. We were always expecting him to write on the board with it and smoke the chalk, but I don't think he ever did." Many of the class trooped in to Birge with complaints. "Went too fast," they told him. "Skipped the connections. We can't follow him. What shall we do?"

Birge told the students to take it easy and took care to show no concern to Oppenheimer. About the third month Oppenheimer began watching faces. His classes became first intellectual dramas and then arenas of total experience in which the students had to be restrained from abjectly submitting every aspect of their lives to him. The reputation of his courses rose, until he became recognized as the best native physics teacher of his time.

"But you didn't get much across to us that first quarter," Brady told him after the war.

"I was talking to myself," Oppenheimer replied.

During the Christmas holidays of 1929, Lawrence made a trip east and saw his brother John, then in his third year at Harvard Medical School. Otto Stern, an experimental physicist from Hamburg, was also at Harvard on a visit. To the two brothers he seemed very old, though he was only about fifty, and very august for his Nobel prize work on molecular beams. Stern did not understand Prohibition. He asked Lawrence to take him to a speakeasy.

The three drank red wine from wet glasses that left intricate red rings on the table cloth.

It looked almost like a diagram. Lawrence lapsed into talk of accelerations in circles of increasing radius. Stern listened without ever giving the usual hint that he would welcome a change of subject. Enraptured, Lawrence drew a design for an experimental apparatus on the cloth. Stern bent to examine it so deliberately that he gave an impression of computer wheels clicking in his head. "Ernest," he said, "don't just talk any more. You must get back to California and get to work on that."

Stern ended Lawrence's long contemplation. Back in Berkeley, he surveyed available facilities. Edlefsen at just that time finished his thesis. Being a laboratory instructor, he stayed at Berkeley to wait for the formalities of his doctor's in the spring. Lawrence decided Edlefsen needed something to do. Once again he drew the design for the apparatus. The two started the laboratory glass blower and the brass fitter to making parts for a model. Lawrence issued no formal announcement of his project. But by this time every large physics laboratory in the world was seeking a way to break open the nucleus of the atom with high voltage. Experimental physicists everywhere began talking of Lawrence's new approach.

In April of 1930 Lawrence presided at the doctoral examinations of Edlefsen and two other graduate students, far more than his share of the seven held in physics at Berkeley that year. Zeleny saw him just after this accomplishment. "Came by on a recruiting trip for Yale, polite but absolutely confident," crowed Birge. "Just couldn't believe it when everybody here turned him down." Berkeley was arriving in science. The National Academy of Sciences, the country's highest scientific body, voted to hold its first meeting west of the Mississippi there in September. A talk by Lawrence on his new accelerator was scheduled to be Berkeley's star contribution.

The Physics Department decided to reward him with a six-hundred-dollar raise to a salary of $3,900 for the next year. Northwestern University offered him six thousand and the headship of its physics department. The physics faculty at Berkeley met to consider matching the offer. Lawrence's seniors had begun to resent his rapid advance. But true to their ideal of activity in research, they voted to make him full professor. This recommendation, unprecedented because Lawrence was so young, went to a budget committee appointed from the whole university. The chairman of the committee was William Popper, aged fifty-six, Old Testament and Hebraic literature scholar. Popper's tight trousers, rusty black coat, stub collar and bushy gray whiskers suggested an out-of-date kind of learning, a fancy inappropriate to the Twenties. His committee rejected Lawrence's promotion unanimously.

Physics appealed and persuaded the administration to set up a special committee to arbitrate. It was headed by Gilbert Lewis, chairman of chemistry. Lewis took pride in having revolutionized his department by making it work with the physicists. Fleshy and balding, usually in shirt sleeves, usually with a cigar in his teeth, Lewis was strongly addicted in the evenings to checker games at the Faculty Club. In daylight he wandered impartially through physics and chemistry laboratories watching experiments and arousing a certain uneasiness with his lit cigar. "You're too conservative," he liked to taunt the physicists. "With all this new knowledge, why don't you invent a time machine?" He was Lawrence's warm friend.

Lewis' committee voted to grant Lawrence the promotion. Popper's committee voted no again. On July 1, 1930, while the university was thus examining its reason for existence, it installed a new president, Robert Gordon Sproul. The Lawrence issue was Sproul's first crisis. Sproul had political charm, the looks of movie actor John Wayne, and an engineering degree which Berkeley physicists were quick to point out did not make him a scientist. It may have given him an idea of science, though, which Lawrence fitted perfectly. He wanted Lawrence to have the promotion.

At first Sproul thought that all he had to do was bring the two committees together again. When he did, the two chairmen faced each other pugnaciously.

"You're hurting the university," said Lewis.

"The younger you are, the higher your salary here," Popper retorted with a bitter edge to his voice. "When you get older, does it go down?"

The committees adjourned, deadlocked again.

Aside from a visit to Northwestern, Lawrence stayed in LeConte building his accelerator. "I think he flew back and forth in three days," said Brady. "When he told me he'd been all the way east to Chicago, I couldn't believe him. He was the first person I knew to make the trip by air."

With him in LeConte, Lawrence had Swann, who, probably at Lawrence's suggestion, was giving a lecture series at Berkeley that summer. "Swann got to the lab about eight o'clock on Sunday mornings," Brady recalled. "From then on, I'd work to the sound of his cello floating down from Lawrence's third-floor office. I thought it sounded pretty. After the war, I asked Lawrence if Swann still played. Lawrence laughed and said, 'Yes, and he's still as full of sour notes as ever.' "

Lawrence avoided talk about the issue on which Berkeley was split. Swann wrote Sproul a letter predicting that in ten years Lawrence would be one of America's ten leading physicists. Sproul called the two committees together again and read them the letter. "If there's one chance in ten that Swann is right, I'm willing to take that chance," he told them. Under pretense of compromise he overrode Popper, still recalcitrant, and awarded Lawrence the promotion. "Wouldn't have gone through except for Sproul," Birge said.

When accepting, Lawrence casually told Birge his impression of Northwestern: "Those people don't know what research means." Birge decided that Lawrence had never intended to leave Berkeley. Lawrence flew east again, lectured a fortnight at the General Electric laboratory in Schenectady, borrowed some electrical equipment, and came home to finish his accelerator.

Sproul in September memorized a welcoming address to the Academy of Sciences, then out of sheer nervousness forgot it when the time came for him to open the meeting. In due course, Lewis introduced Lawrence. A ripple of excitement passed over the audience of scientists. On the platform behind Lawrence was his invention: a four-inch pillbox sprouting arms like an octopus, each joint so heavily daubed with red sealing wax that it was hard to tell the thing was made of glass. It was mounted between the poles of an electromagnet. Transformers, oscillator-tube equipment, and a vacuum pump strewed the floor.

Lawrence turned it on. In the pillbox, hydrogen ions were flung back and forth in an alternating electric field. The magnetic field curved their path and turned it into a spiral. An electrometer showed ions striking a collector with an energy far higher than the voltage of the electric field. This, said Lawrence, was evidence of resonance achieved.

To break into the nucleus of the atom, he went on, ions must be accelerated to about a million volts of energy. A straightforward way to accelerate them would be between two electric poles charged with a difference in potential of a million volts. But because of the high electric fields involved, the difficulties of constructing such an apparatus were obvious. His new method avoided these difficulties. To get a million-volt acceleration in the circling ions, he needed only a bigger magnet, a bigger circular chamber, and an oscillator tube of 10,000 volts potential. "Experiments indicate there are probably no serious difficulties in the way," he concluded.

"SPEED HYDROGEN IONS TO BREAK UP ATOMS," *The New York Times* headlined its story of the meeting. "A new apparatus to hurl particles at a speed of 37,000 miles a second in an effort to obtain a long-sought goal—the breaking up of the atom —was described here today by Professor Ernest O. Lawrence of the University of California."

Lawrence had put Berkeley on the map. "If I ever get a swelled head, promise you'll let me know," he asked Birge. He was still a year short of thirty, the critical time of fruition for American physicists.

2

THE ENCHANTED LABORATORY

In September of 1930 Lawrence entangled his career with that of a student, Stanley Livingston, who came to know him in a special way. "I shall never forget him as long as I live," says Livingston with conviction usually absent from such protests. Livingston needed a thesis project. About the first of the month he called on Lawrence while making a tour of LeConte to see what experimental physicists could offer him.

Having lost Edlefsen by graduation, Lawrence needed someone else to build a bigger model of his invention. He mentioned other projects to Livingston—he was still interested in photoelectric experiments—but pushed this one with intoxicating urgency. Livingston was not a man to be hurried.

"Afterward I went on shopping to several others of the faculty, including Brode and Leonard Loeb, an authority on electrical discharge in gases," he said. "During my talks with them I commented on Lawrence's suggestion and asked their advice." The response he got was cooler than competitiveness for graduate students would justify. The conversation turned into questions on the path of the speeding ions. What difference did the curved path make? Spiral, circle, or straight line, would not the shotgun pattern of ions spread out anyway? How could enough of them be focused in any one place to be worth reaccelerating and finally collecting? "I remember Loeb in particular was quite pessimistic," Livingston recalled.

The invention worked, Lawrence answered when Livingston

went back to him. By temperament Livingston inclined toward
the dark side. But he found that in Lawrence's presence doubt disappeared: "Lawrence was young, he was bursting with energy,
his enthusiasm swept me off my feet."

About the time Lawrence's invention started getting unheard-of
newspaper publicity, Livingston signed up as his graduate student. First, he looked at Lawrence's and Edlefsen's calculations.
Then cautiously scraping superfluous red sealing wax off the apparatus, he examined it painstakingly. After making sure that all
connections were tight, he turned on the power.

The resonance or circular reacceleration which the apparatus
was designed for could at that time be determined only by corre-
lating the voltage of the ions with the intensity of the magnetic
field. Livingston could not make the apparatus work. He decided
it never had worked. Ordinary unreaccelerated ions were arriving
at the collector and electrons were leaving it by photo-ionization.
A slip in mathematics could cause these phenomena to be mistaken for resonance. Going over the original calculations, Livingston looked for the slip and found it. "Lawrence and Edlefsen had
made an error in their calibration of the magnetic field," he said.

A few days later, in *Science* magazine, he read Lawrence's sum-
mary of his talk to the National Academy and was specially
struck by the conclusion that probably no serious difficulty lay in
the way of reaching a million volts. "The confidence of the paper
was based on the error of thinking cyclotron resonance had been
observed," he reflected. "The concluding statement was a sample
of Lawrence's optimism."

Livingston at twenty-five was big, muscular, and tough-looking. He had a share of Lawrence's drive. At Pomona College he
had washed dishes and clerked in a store for his first degree. He
intended to get his thesis done in one year, because that was all he
could afford. In August, only a month before, he had married a
little, thin, dark, intense girl, Lois Robinson, who was to help out
during the year by working in an office. At the same time she
meant to get a master's degree in English literature.

"Before their marriage, I double-dated a good deal with them,"
said Brady. "I wouldn't like to call her snooty, but she didn't go
much for the common touch. She was pretty. Livingston kept telling me she was pretty as a movie star. He was sort of elegant him-

self. The Depression was on then, and he told me, 'Whatever happens I'm not going to lower *my* standard of living.' An aristocrat. Or when you bring up the dishwashing, I suppose a would-be aristocrat."

Brady, who had flair, found Livingston's elegance vaguely pedestrian, vaguely irritating. But the two were intimately accustomed to sharing each other's problems. Livingston was drawn to the tremendous potentialities of Lawrence's invention and at the same time shaken by his private discoveries about it. He did not tell these to Brady, but said he wondered if the project was right for a man who had to finish his thesis promptly. He asked Brady's opinion about taking up one of the easier projects Lawrence had offered.

"You'd better take the big one," Brady advised him. "On anything else you won't get any attention from Lawrence."

"Yes." Livingston paused thoughtfully over the point. "Yes. I'll ride the wave."

LeConte's laboratory assistants were half-envious, half-amused to see him poking glumly at the famous merry-go-round that he could not make go round. Lawrence called it a device for producing high energy without requiring high voltage. Livingston called it a magnetic resonance accelerator. For the proposed new model, Lawrence got him a giant voltage-oscillator vacuum tube tradenamed Radiotron. The "-tron" suggested something fancy and mysterious to the assistants. To annoy Livingston, they formed the habit of asking him what results he was getting on the cyclotron.

For eight weeks Livingston tinkered with the apparatus he had inherited from Edlefsen. "By December of 1930," he said, "I observed the legitimate resonance effect in the glass-vial tube originally used." He believed he was the first man to see it. It was too infinitesimal to prove anything except that Loeb's doubts were well founded. But it freed Livingston to get on with his thesis project, the construction of a more substantial model.

He discarded almost everything but the electromagnet and built a new pillbox of brass. It was four inches wide like the glass one, but precise and different inside. Within it and insulated from it nested the halves of a smaller pillbox sliced down the middle from top to bottom. He called the halves "Dees" because they looked like two capital *D*'s facing straight side to. The alternating electric field was set up in the quarter inch of space between them.

Lawrence emphasized to Livingston that the hollow inside each Dee must be kept free of the electric field. Thus an ion received its push in the space between the Dees, glided through one of them in a spiraling half-circle because of the magnetic field, then when it came out received another push into the other Dee.

To keep the electric field out of the Dees, Livingston mounted a perforated brass strip across the lips of the open side of each Dee. He made it so delicately that it was four fifths holes. Even so, he realized that a fifth of the revolving ions were being stopped each time they got halfway round. He took off the strips and replaced them with fine wires that would constitute less of a barrier.

In March of 1931 with this arrangement he accelerated ions to an energy of eighty-thousand volts with an alternating charge on the Dees of only two thousand volts. The ions were going round about twenty times, picking up speed at each half-revolution.*

* In more detail the cyclotron, which was about as complicated as an automobile, worked as follows:

Hydrogen gas was trickled into the vacuum chamber. There as a first step it had to be converted into positive ions—that is, the protons that constituted its atomic nuclei had to be stripped of their attendant electrons. To break the grip of an electron on a hydrogen nucleus, one only needs to strike the clinging electron with a free electron moving at any speed over 13.5 volts, a feeble energy which is called the ionization potential of hydrogen. A small electric field pulled out free electrons at this energy from a hot filament located between the cyclotron Dees to turn the gas into ions. Lines of magnetic force channeled the electrons away in a stream that did not interfere with the operation of electric and magnetic forces upon the ions.

Commercial 10,000-volt high-frequency radio oscillator tubes gave each of the two Dees alternately a positive, then a negative electric charge. When a Dee was negatively charged, it attracted the freshly created positive ions. The ions plunged into it. Momentum would have carried them in a straight line until they hit the curved metal back of the Dee, except for the effect of the magnetic field. From this arose Lawrence's big discovery. The magnetic field exerted upon the moving ions a force continually at right angles to their direction of motion. Thus the ions were pulled sideways in a curve. Some of them curved all the way round and were already headed back in the opposite direction at the instant that the electric charge was alternated and the Dee they were traveling in became positively charged. These ions moved with increasing speed into the opposite Dee, where the process was repeated. As they gained speed, centrifugal force made them move in wider circles. But traveling faster, they could still cover the longer path in the

The final acceleration and, more particularly, the number of ions accelerated were still too trifling even to hint of any practical use. But Lawrence, his eyes blazing with enthusiasm over Livingston's shoulder, did not see them that way. He ordered an eleven-inch magnet and set Livingston to building a new cyclotron—after fighting the name, the two had begun to accept it—larger in proportion, the third in the series.

"Lawrence stimulated and supported me," said Livingston afterward, a little wryly. Brady, who was crucifying himself over his own thesis project in accordance with Lawrence's prescription, got used to watching a small evening drama. Livingston had a wife whom he had hardly seen since their marriage.

"Well, it's after six," Livingston would say. "Lois said she was planning a big dinner. She told me I had to get home this time sure."

"Just a few minutes," Lawrence would reply. "You told me yourself you were having trouble with the vacuum seal. It shouldn't take long."

Restimulated, Livingston would work far into the night. Vaguely he thought of himself as a permanency among transients whose movements at the periphery of his attention gave him some notion of the passage of time. Most would leave promptly at five, others like Brady a little later, as it seemed to him. Latest would be Lawrence, come back to check on the stimulation. "Had a night on the town," Livingston would think, looking at Lawrence's fresh collar with a sort of dull resentment.

Not even Lawrence could expect to drive Livingston to build the eleven-inch before the end of the academic year. Consequently in early April of 1931 Lawrence broke in on Livingston's concentration with a reminder of something Livingston had almost forgotten. "If you get your doctorate this spring, I can get you an in-

---

same time and would theoretically be reaccelerated a third time, and then many more times thereafter. This was the reason for Lawrence's excitement over the discovery that the time of the ions' revolution was independent of the radius of their orbit, or that R canceled R (p. 19).

Would the ions keep in the same plane (in a flat spiral like a watch spring) or would they become lost by going up or down (in a helix like a bedspring)? The answer, which emerged progressively in the events presented in the rest of this chapter, is recapitulated in the Glossary under "Focusing."

structorship next year," Lawrence said. "But you must get your doctorate."

The deadline for turning in a thesis and taking the required examination was then only three weeks away. "I don't have time to read the background material," Livingston protested.

"Don't worry," Lawrence replied. "We're making history. We can go back to the basic literature any time. Just write your thesis."

Livingston dreaded Birge, a pitiless examiner who was to sit on his committee and who so far had never let human considerations sway him. But the ordeal turned out all right: "When Birge asked me about Rutherford's historic developments in England, I could feel my ignorance showing. I hadn't any time to study the literature. Birge was a precisionist. I'm sure I flunked him [flunked his examination]. Lawrence defended me. There's no doubt in my mind it was Lawrence who got me my pass. To me, this is a marvelous story of friendship between people doing exciting things together."

Though the cyclotron lacked visibly moving parts, everyone called it a machine, and though it was small, Lawrence was making it grow fast. First documentations were Lawrence's premature announcement in *Science* and Livingston's thesis, *The Production of High-Velocity Hydrogen Ions without the Use of High Voltage*. These inaugurated the country's most distinctive contribution to the nuclear age—big-machine physics. It began with a characteristic inaccuracy over the time element. "Around the lab they started calling Livingston the Ninety-day Wonder," recollects a graduate student. "But this was wrong. He didn't have anywhere near that much time to bone up on physics for his doctorate."

Shortly afterward Lawrence went on a long trip east. In Washington, speaking in Livingston's name as well as his own, he addressed the Physical Society. He reported the 80,000 volts of energy now achieved and conveyed an impression of smooth, routine progress. "These preliminary experiments," he concluded, "indicate clearly that there are no difficulties in the way of producing one-million-volt ions in this manner." Next he went on to Cambridge to see a tall blond girl named Mary Blumer whom everyone called Molly. She had a Phi Beta Kappa key from Vassar, she was getting a master's in biology at Radcliffe, her father was a professor at Yale, where Lawrence first met her, but she liked movies, at least when Lawrence took her. This he did night after night in June of 1931 until one night after the show they became engaged in a car Lawrence had borrowed from his brother, then finishing at Harvard Medical School.

"While Lawrence was away courting," said Livingston, "I had time to think." To be of much use as a research tool, the cyclotron would have to produce a beam of several million ions a second. Nothing like this was in sight, either for the four-inch or the unfinished eleven-inch which Livingston was working on. Furthermore, the energy of the ions was far too low in any reasonable projection one could make of the existing design. Each time the ions spiraled outward they gained energy, but each time a good proportion of them would also bump against the top or bottom of the hollow Dees and disappear. If the collector was placed far out to catch the fast ions, there would not be enough of them. If the collector was moved in to catch the slow ones, they would not have enough energy.

All this was what Loeb had pessimistically predicted, and Livingston still had no answer to make to him. Lawrence had stressed the need for keeping the hollow space inside the Dees free of the electric field. But Livingston had increased the yield of ions by replacing the perforated guard with a grid of wires.

In the unaccustomed stillness at Berkeley, Livingston cogitated. "I took the opportunity to strike out on my own. Hoping to get higher intensity, I removed the grid of wires. The intensity then became a hundred times what it was before. When Lawrence returned to Berkeley, he helped me to understand this was a consequence of focusing the ions by means of the electric field inside the Dees."

Ions spiraling up or down were pushed toward a central plane by the newly admitted electric field. The principle, electrostatic focusing, was the second of three fundamental discoveries necessary to make the cyclotron useful. Elsewhere, other scientists were making an independent discovery and application of electrostatic focusing. "About the same time," said Livingston, "it was being developed for electron lenses in electronics." But he had no conscious knowledge of this when he removed the grid of wires.

In July of 1931, Lawrence and Livingston worked on the eleven-inch. The two men did not yet know what it could do, but Lawrence already dreamed of something bigger. Each successive cyclotron had to start with an electromagnet. That of the eleven-inch weighed two tons. Leonard Fuller, chairman of electrical engineering, told Lawrence of one that weighed eighty-five tons rusting away in a storage dump in Palo Alto. Built for radio transmission across the Pacific, it had been made obsolete by the vacuum tube. Fuller, vice-president of the near-defunct Federal Telegraph Company, which owned it, offered it to Lawrence as a gift.

In the Flying Cloud Lawrence and Livingston drove down to Palo Alto to look it over. "It was in bad shape," said Livingston. He thought of all the work required to resculpture and wind the core. Lawrence thought of how he could haul it to Berkeley and where he could put it. Already, the rest of the physics faculty had started to complain that his projects were crowding LeConte's second-floor workrooms. Not even he could have cheerful illusions about what they would say if they saw him trying to hoist an eighty-five-ton magnet in.

While Lawrence pondered this problem at Berkeley, a tall, gray-haired, unpressed eccentric inventor named Frederick Cottrell made a tour of the laboratory. From bulging packets he took a half-dozen pairs of dime-store glasses one after another and through them peered nearsightedly at the two cyclotrons. Cottrell was rich himself and distinguished for a knack of persuading other rich people to give money to science, of which he was the country's best-known patron. "I had the pleasure of conducting him through the physics laboratory and showing him our work on the development of means for accelerating charged particles to high velocities," said Lawrence. "He immediately appreciated the possibilities of the cyclotron principle and with infectious enthusiasm volunteered to help in any way he could."

Lawrence and Livingston took him to Palo Alto to see the big magnet. According to a legend hard to authenticate, Lawrence asked Cottrell to help him raise $500 for haulage. Cottrell replied that $5,000 would be easier to raise, since subsidizers of research judged the respectability of a request by its size.

Cottrell promised to see what he could do and went to Long Beach for a holiday before returning to his headquarters in New York. Lawrence and Livingston put the eleven-inch into operation. For the first time electrostatic focusing was tried out in a machine of usable size. Both men were astonished and excited, Lawrence exactly twice as much. A million volts, a half million volts: the report depended on who made it. Lawrence wrote two letters dated July 20, 1931.

One to Cottrell, Lawrence wrote alone:

I telegraphed you last night asking if it is convenient for me to come to see you Wednesday or Thursday . . . on my way east.

As you have probably surmised, I want to get your advice on the present best procedure toward raising some more money for the high-speed proton experiments. The present developments in the work make it practically certain that we will be able to produce ten- or twenty-million-volt protons when the large magnet and a powerful oscillator are made available to us. With the present setup we have exceeded one million volts and the proton currents are very much more intense than we had expected. . . .

It seems to me that at least $10,000 and possibly $15,000 will be needed to cover adequately the expense of all the equipment needed for the work, and the money must be found somewhere. . . .

It appears that our difficulties are no longer of a physical but of a financial nature.

The other, to the editor of the *Physical Review*, Lawrence and Livingston wrote together:

A method for the production of high-speed protons was described before the National Academy of Science last September. . . . Later before the American Physical Society . . . results were presented . . . and the conclusions . . . that there are no significant difficulties in the way of producing 1,000,000 volt protons. . . .

This important conclusion has now been confirmed. . . . Protons and hydrogen molecule ions having energies in excess of one half million volts have been produced. . . . Currents turned out to be surprisingly large. . . .

There can be little doubt that one-million-volt ions will be produced . . . when the present experimental tube is enlarged.

"Lawrence had the sort of genius which was 'way ahead of time," Livingston explained. Lawrence went east again. At Harvard he made his brother's medical associates uneasy by the way he talked cyclotrons. "Is he going out of his mind?" they asked. He was not. From Cottrell he obtained $5,000 and an introduction to Roger Adams, adviser to the Chemical Foundation, which had been created to subsidize research with money from war-confiscated patents. "Has vision," Adams decided, and he granted him $2,500.

After a stop with Molly at New Haven, Lawrence returned to Berkeley in September for a passionate talk with President Sproul. He needed a home for the big magnet and a few thousands more toward the cost of turning it into a cyclotron. The university was about to tear down a shack just east of LeConte Hall. Lawrence showed in a letter to his family how lyrically he viewed the shack and how well he dealt with Sproul:

. . . The president has turned over a whole building (the old Civil Engineering laboratory) for our experiments and has put at our disposal $3,300 in addition to the $7,500 I got in N. Y. We are getting some more things as gifts, so the $10,800 will be adequate. I'm busy now in the process of spending it most effectively. We are going to have a great year of it. Only time can tell the outcome of our efforts, but I have hopes of doing some really important work in the not-too-distant future. . . .

Though I'm busy I naturally have time to write Molly every other day. Boy, I certainly am in love with her. . . . Molly had her engagement announced at the Lawn Club a week ago Wednesday. Now, I'm hoping she will decide on *next* June instead of a year later!   •

If it weren't for the unusually interesting state of our work I don't know what I would do without Molly! . . .

By the way, get the habit of using the air mail.

To Lawrence invention had been joy; to Livingston the need for it was a curse. The eleven-inch magnet was giving Livingston trouble. True, electrostatic focusing now held the ions flat as a watch spring in the first part of their spiraling course. But about a third of the way out, too many of them began to wobble and disappear. The loss was worse with the eleven-inch than with the four-inch, so the outlook for the twenty-seven-inch was cloudy.

Livingston interpreted the loss to mean there were irregularities in the magnetic field. No amount of truing the faces of the magnet poles ended the problem. Swearing, he gave up trying to make them perfectly flat and instead took an irrational step. He cut paper-thin sheet iron into pieces shaped like the silverfish moth that eats clothing. They were wide at one end and narrow at the other. To him they seemed exclamation points without the period. He laid them atop the pillbox vacuum chamber with the wide end toward the center.

Acceleration increased four times. The ions held their watch-spring path all the way out to the collector and arrived in a stream only a millimeter thick.

This was the invention that completed the cyclotron as the world knows it. The effect was immediately clear; the theory took much longer to work out than had that of electrostatic focusing. "Magnetic focusing came purely pragmatically," said Livingston. "Lawrence and I had not thought of it. I accomplished it by putting in shims of iron near the pole face with the narrow end outward. This had a large effect on small orbits and a smaller effect on large orbits. It was thus strictly empirical proof that cyclotrons had to have a magnetic field which decreased from the center outward. Eventually we realized that this was magnetic focusing."

Lawrence's sparkling eyes, pale blue and a little brighter than human—these are what Livingston remembers when at last he produced a million volts. He brought the eleven-inch, extensively rebuilt, to this peak in February of 1932. By now he was using protons, single hydrogen ions with more penetrating power than the paired molecular ions he had accelerated to half a million volts in July. "I wrote the figure on the blackboard," he said. "Lawrence came in late one evening. He saw the board, looked at the micro-ammeter to check the resonance current, and literally danced around the room."

Lawrence spread the news next morning at breakfast in the Faculty Club. Livingston said: "We were busy all that day demonstrating million-volt protons to eager viewers."

Lawrence and Livingston offered the cyclotron to the world as the best and most effective machine for nuclear research. The cyclotron was now completely dependable, they reported in a historic article in the *Physical Review:* "It is well to emphasize two particular features that have contributed more than anything else to the effectiveness of the method: *the focusing action of the elec-*

tric and magnetic fields, and the *simple means of empirically cor-recting the magnetic field* by the introduction of suitable iron shims."

"TO USE BIG MAGNET TO BREAK UP ATOM," ran an AP lead. "MAY TRY TO CREATE GOLD," said *The New York Times*. The *San Francisco Examiner* sent a reporter out to Le-Conte, and he returned awed.

Two University of California scientists are setting about trying to break up the atom and release its terrific energy. Working only with a two-ton magnet, the scientists, Professor Ernest O. Lawrence and M. Stanley Livingston, say they have been able to penetrate the outer husk of the atom. [This may be a confused reference to ionization experi-ments.] With the greater magnet, they hope to shatter the atom com-pletely with an ultimate 25,000,000-volt impact. What wonders will result, only time can tell.

"Clearly . . . there are no difficulties in the way of producing one-million-volt ions," Lawrence had told the Physical Society in May of 1931 before the two focusing discoveries. Doubters like Loeb had based their objection on focusing. Now that Lawrence had a complete double-barreled answer to the objection, he phrased it himself forcefully: "Consideration of this matter might lead one to believe that it is a requirement impossible to achieve. It is therefore to be emphasized that this requirement has been ob-viated . . . by focusing action of the electric field . . . and by . . . focusing action due to curvature of the magnetic field."

This he wrote in an application for a patent on the cyclotron, which was received at the Patent Office on January 26, 1932. "I claim . . ." he said, in the arrogant style which patent procedure forces on the solitary inventor. He did not mention Livingston.

Of course he did not need to; a graduate student is expected to contribute cheerfully not only his hands but such brains as he has. Lawrence gave the patent to Cottrell, who treated it as a mere symbol of achievement, a free license to all cyclotron builders. In the *Physical Review* Lawrence and Livingston had seemed to have a special relation. Outside it, Lawrence increasingly tended to credit the cyclotron's realization to many undifferentiated hands, to the whole circle of graduate and postdoctoral students enlarg-ing around him. This was good for their morale, but not for Livingston's. He felt a youthful hurt that afterward turned into a lasting bitterness.

"A sorehead" Livingston is sometimes called by other physicists from California. The question of his share in the creation of the cyclotron divides physicists generally. Brady doubts Livingston was first to see resonance, electrostatic focusing, and magnetic focusing. "But even if this were true," he says, "the work was closely supervised by Lawrence. The impression I have is that Lawrence made all the major improvements. I think he worked out the whole focusing problem after the proton beam proved much larger and more intense than he had calculated. I don't think a day went by when Lawrence was in town that he didn't come to the lab to operate the controls.

"I'll have to admit my opinions are just those I picked up from the talk then going on in the lab. Anyway, Livingston seems to me to be afraid he won't get enough credit. He told me he had complained about this to Lawrence. Lawrence told him: 'If you're dissatisfied, you can drop out of the project, and I'll get someone else who can take your place.'"

"A matter of clashing personalities," say physicists who profess impartiality. Most accept Livingston's account. At Berkeley it came to be considered bad taste or worse to discuss the issue. As a result, Lawrence's definite original contributions to the cyclotron after the original idea have become unnecessarily clouded. There is a fuzzy overlap between the limited focusing action at the perimeter of a level magnetic field and the all-pervasive focusing action of a continually declining magnetic field. Of the former, which would not have helped much with large cyclotrons, Lawrence may have planned to make use before Livingston discovered the latter.

As for Lawrence's chilling offer to Livingston to replace him, it is by no means clear how quickly this could have been done. "I stayed on, developing larger and larger cyclotrons," said Livingston. "I was the mechanic—no one else then could do it—and Lawrence promoted the money."

On May 3, 1932, the Berkeley *Gazette* reported:

Dr. Ernest O. Lawrence, world-renowned authority on the atom, will wed Miss Mary Blumer of New Haven, Connecticut, on May 14, in the eastern city, according to word received by friends in Berkeley. Dr. Lawrence left a fortnight ago to attend the meeting of the American Physical Society and read a paper there.

Brady at this time was working on the first research experiment ever attempted with the cyclotron. "It was because I had some free time," he explained. "Lawrence had held me a long while on my thin-films thesis project. Friends told me it was too long." ("He means me," interjected Mrs. Brady. "I told him. I wanted to get married.") "So I went to Lawrence and wailed, 'You could keep me at this for ten years,' and he let me finish and got me onto the faculty of St. Louis University for the next fall. Meanwhile, I was in LeConte with a fellowship and some free time. Livingston was over in the shack working hard on the twenty-seven-inch. But a graduate student named Milton White had got to wondering whether the eleven-inch really *was* accelerating high-speed particles. The only evidence so far had to be deduced from calculations of the magnetic and electric fields. He wanted something more concrete. So he got the idea of seeing whether the cyclotron could accelerate protons fast enough to shoot them through mica sheets of varying thickness. We mounted the sheets around the circumference of a wheel and set it inside the vacuum chamber just in front of the collector.

"Getting this done took us about to the end of July. I was fiddling with an improvement to the proton-injector gun, which had never worked well, just getting ready to shoot protons through mica. I never did. A telegram from Lawrence stopped me cold. It was about two physicists in England. 'Cockcroft and Walton have disintegrated the lithium atom,' it said. 'Get lithium from chemistry department and start preparations to repeat with cyclotron. Will be back shortly.'

"Lawrence was honeymooning on a boat in Connecticut. Must have put into shore somewhere. I showed the telegram to the future Mrs. Brady and said, 'That's what physicists on their honeymoon think about.' "

"It was bad news to me," she recollects. "We'd planned to slip away the first week in August as soon as he did the mica thing. Now this meant we'd have to wait until they'd disintegrated the atom. I wanted to get married."

For Lawrence too it was bad news that he and the United States with such a unique and incomparable tool as the cyclotron could not have been first to penetrate the nucleus. Surprisingly, the English had done it with an old-fashioned conventional voltage generator. "At that time it was generally thought that nothing much would happen in the way of nuclear reactions below about one million electron volts," Lawrence explained in a lecture. "In England Cockcroft and Walton at the Cavendish Laboratory . . . realizing the difficulties of reaching one million . . . with their apparatus decided to try with protons of energies of only several hundred thousand. They immediately discovered lithium and beryllium could be disintegrated with energies as low as a quarter million. . . . We could have done so with our eleven-inch cyclotron almost a year before."

Still the news had a bright side. Now that England had shown what could be done, Lawrence could make a more definite case to Sproul and Cottrell for funds. So far in his drive for bigger cyclotrons Lawrence had neglected other equipment that would be needed to put them to use. "We had the energy for atomic disintegration," said Livingston, "but we lacked the instruments for observing it." Now from Yale, Lawrence brought out a new Ph.D., Franz Kurie, to build a cloud chamber, and another, Malcolm Henderson, a wealthy easy-going native of New Haven, to work with counter devices. Also from Yale, Lawrence summoned a forty-year-old research fellow, Donald Cooksey, to help with Geiger counters. Cooksey, a brooding hypochondriac millionaire bachelor, had been Lawrence's closest friend at Yale. He was glad to come, because he needed someone to tell him what to do. He commuted back and forth across the continent for a year or so, then settled down in Lawrence's shack.

From Princeton in September came Lawrence's most cultured staff member, John Livingood (not to be confused with Livingston), who accounts for his coming as follows: "As an undergraduate at Princeton I majored in philosophy, loved it and went on to graduate work. Then I read in Plutarch how Hannibal crossed the Alps. He split rocks by pouring vinegar in the cracks so his elephants could get over. This gave me a hankering for physics. So I started over and got a Ph.D. in that. By then, after eleven years, Princeton felt like an ingrowing toenail. Berkeley looked new."

From Leland Stanford came Paul Aebersold. The first time he was there he had come to Berkeley for some athletic tryouts. He wanted a look at the country's most celebrated scientific invention. In sweatshirt and gym pants, he trotted up to the little wooden building and knocked on the door. Lawrence opened it, red sealing wax on his hands. "If you want to see the cyclotron," he said, "this is the main part right here. There's a leak in the vacuum chamber."

"So young, so energetic, doesn't know me from Adam but still he *talks* to me," reflected Aebersold and transferred to Berkeley to start his graduate work.

Newspaper stories of the cyclotron had captured the public imagination. Among the crowds trooping through the shack came Telesio Lucci, ex-commander in the Italian navy, exile from Mussolini—a stiff, dark little man. "Lawrence," he said while the graduate students watched with discreet curiosity, "I'd like to work for you. I'll do anything, and I don't want money."

Lawrence put him to work alongside another volunteer, Lorenzo Emo, whom the graduate students believed to be an Italian count and whom they patronizingly referred to as all thumbs, but willing.

"A new kind of laboratory," Lawrence called the shack while thanking Cottrell profusely and artlessly in late 1932. Cottrell's continued gifts, wrote Lawrence, were "virtually responsible for a new kind of laboratory, the Radiation Laboratory of the University of California. One cannot predict what the experiments in the Radiation* Laboratory will bring forth, but it is at least certain

* This was derived from the fact that radiations were Lawrence's stock in trade. Most exciting and distinctive were the radiations that his ion beams produced from targets hit at nucleus-disintegrating speeds. These radiations were of two kinds. The first kind, such as beta and alpha rays, were particle streams. Beta rays were high-speed electron streams that might or might not indicate nuclear disintegration; alpha rays were streams of helium nuclei that, when emitted from a target, always did. The other kind of rays was waves of energy produced by impact of the beam upon a target. The shorter their wave length, the higher their energy and the greater the likelihood that they came from inside the nucleus of the atom. Hence in the early years the enthusiasm of Lawrence's experimenters ran precisely along what is called the electromagnetic spectrum gamut: soft X rays, long wave length, low energy, little enthusiasm; hard X rays, middling wave length, moderate energy and enthusiasm; gamma rays, short wave length, high energy and congratulations!

that the experimenters look forward to the work with enthusiasm."

The Radiation Laboratory was then only the shack and some space shared with reluctant faculty colleagues in LeConte. So far it existed only in Lawrence's mind, a creation free from the cloud of someone else's unacknowledged contribution. To keep Brady an extra month, Lawrence persuaded St. Louis University to let him earn his first pay check *in absentia*. Brady stayed until he saw the chemistry department's finest lithium crystal, which he had demanded with a flourish of the telegram, light up with the bluish glow of nuclear disintegration. "In September of 1932," Sproul proudly reported to the Governor of California, "artificial disintegration was first accomplished outside of Europe in the laboratory of Professor Ernest O. Lawrence. This laboratory has taken the lead, in all the world, in the disintegration of the elements."

During the nights of that waning summer, Brady's fiancée had prowled round and round outside of Le Conte's locked doors. Inside, the experimenters in Room 216 could measure her discontent; first a gentle pebble against the window pane, next a harder one, next a rock thrown recklessly. "I'd better go down and let her in," Lawrence would say with resignation, for then the problem shifted to how to make her sit still on a stool and wait.

Lawrence betrayed occasional signs of wanting to get home to his own bride ("No, just a little longer," Livingston would insist until Lawrence's face turned angry red) but generally he kept her in far better order. She learned early. On her first Sunday at Berkeley she turned up at noon at the house of another faculty member's wife. "Ernest's been at the lab all morning," she said with a bewildered air. "It wasn't like this at Yale. What shall I do?"

Another difference from Yale for her was learning to sleep with the buzz. "The Federal Communications Commission didn't like cyclotrons," recalled Livingood. "More and more often as time went by Lawrence would go to bed nights like a gentleman. But he didn't take the pressure off us to keep working. He kept a table radio at his bedside tuned to the 26-meter band. The cyclotron leaked and broadcast a buzz there. "Whenever the buzz stopped, Lawrence would get on the phone. 'What the hell's the matter?' he'd ask."

Meanwhile, Oppenheimer had got his first graduate student. The way he did it interested the rest of the faculty.

Samuel Allison knew him well. Allison found the fact that Oppenheimer was reading the *Mahabharata* with the chairman of the Sanskrit Department as hard to swallow as the "nasty gory." He watched Oppenheimer warily, looking for signs of the *poseur*.

"At Berkeley there had been a poor half-mad creature in one of my classes whom I'd felt sorry for," said Allison. "He collected street signs and unscrewed the handles on brass fire hydrants. He lived at night and was never seen in daytime. Since he was obviously on the verge of insanity, I'd have a twinge of conscience about him every now and then and try to do something for him.

"Once my wife and I had him and Oppenheimer to dinner. We all talked about how much better things were at night than in the daytime. Oppenheimer explained why he wouldn't teach a morning class earlier than eleven o'clock. He needed the night, he said, to think and work and talk in. The proper hours for the study of physics, he went on, were from two to five in the morning and you couldn't really study physics at other hours.

"The student's face lit up when he heard this. Oppenheimer was an impulsive inviter. 'Come study physics with me,' he said to the student.

"I don't know whether they set a date, but the student went around that very night to the house where Oppenheimer had an apartment. Everything was locked up. But the student had no compunctions. He pried a screen open and crawled through. He groped around in the dark and located Oppenheimer's bedroom. 'Dr. Allison, I found him sound asleep,' the student complained to me. 'Was I right not to wake him?'"

Because Allison left Berkeley in 1930, he did not see the end of this typical Oppenheimer story, which has overtones of the *Mahabharata* concept of Krishna fluting. On the student Oppenheimer conferred lasting deliverance. This was the impulse which Allison had noted. Oppenheimer's invitation was to do physics rather than study it passively. Under Oppenheimer's night tutelage the student wrote a thesis and made internationally known discoveries. Afterward he held high positions in the academic world until the day he died. He was the first stone in the edifice of American theoretical physics that Oppenheimer was constructing.

By asking Oppenheimer the right questions, Lawrence and his experimentalists could have been first to smash the atom instead of second. They did ask Oppenheimer questions, though not the right ones. Brady has lively memories of the way the process worked: "I told Lawrence I had some experimental results suggesting that the temperature of electrons was higher in the thin film at the top of a metal surface than in the underlying metal surface itself. 'Sounds like a good idea,' said Lawrence. 'Let's ask Oppenheimer.'

"We caught him coming to work across the campus and Lawrence told him I had an interesting question. His eyes brightened and I started: 'I've got some experimental evidence that electron temperature is higher in the thin film than in the underlying met. . . .'

"I stopped, because he was putting out a diminuendo murmur: 'No no no no.' When it dwindled to silence, Lawrence and I stared at him and he stared at the horizon.

"Lawrence drew in a deep, exasperated breath. 'But aren't you going to even *listen* to him?' he pleaded.

" 'Oh,' said Oppenheimer, 'that. That's a violation of the first law of thermodynamics.' "

Oppenheimer had yet to learn how mysterious to experimentalists was his commonplace. Lawrence won general admiration by not being fazed. Theoretical and experimental physicists met at weekly afternoon seminars and the Tuesday evening Journal Club. "We called it the Journal Club because we met and digested the journals," explained Livingston. "I remember those were among the few times that experimentalists like me could see Oppenheimer. At other times he was away in his office upstairs busy with his students. We didn't know the language of quantum mechanics, didn't know how to talk to him. Our contact with him was through Lawrence.

"Lawrence and Oppenheimer were very close, very good friends then. Lawrence had one great quality. He didn't give a damn if he asked foolish questions. At the seminars and Journal Club we sat afraid to ask Oppenheimer anything. Lawrence would pop up and ask something silly."

Another of Lawrence's early graduate students was David Sloan, in some ways the brightest and most appealing, the perfect type of childlike inventor. Sloan was building the world's first linear or straight-line accelerators. Wideröe's article had been a description of this device, and Lawrence had given much thought to it while discovering the cyclotron principle. Even before hearing of Wideröe, Sloan had had some idea of building it. He began work without any initial suggestion from Lawrence, but with Lawrence's enthusiastic help at glass blowing. Over the course of years a particular gentleness of feeling developed between him and Oppenheimer, but it was slow in coming. "I wanted high voltage for itself and didn't care about threshold values [i.e., the voltage needed to split the atom]," said Sloan. "During my first two or three years here after 1930, theoretical physics didn't fit much into our work except to stimulate Lawrence. He was our channel. We were so awed by Oppenheimer we hardly dared speak to him. Later I discovered we needn't have been."

At this time in the Physics Department it was Birge's views that counted. "Nobody can be a good scientist unless he understands scientific things and knows when he doesn't," he said. "That came to me very slowly. Geniuses like Oppenheimer get it almost instantly. That's the point. His rate of taking in new ideas and his enormous memory are what distinguish him from merely bright people. There's a huge difference between a genius and a bright person. The reason Oppenheimer knows so much is that it's easy when you learn ten times as fast as other physicists and remember everything.

"Here in our seminars Oppenheimer knew more experimental physics than even the experimental physicists did. He could reel off figures and equations relating to experiments better than any experimental physicist in the room.

"It wasn't long before his work here began to command national attention. [About 1933] I reported to President Sproul that the National Research Foundation appointed just three Fellows in theoretical physics for the year. All three came here to work under Oppenheimer. Berkeley was definitely becoming the leading place in the country."

During the other half of his teaching year, the spring term at Pasadena, Oppenheimer had also been watched. The top physicist and chief figure at California Institute of Technology was Robert Millikan. Small, sturdy, active in church work, Millikan had written twelve books, won a Nobel prize, received twenty-two honorary degrees, and been given fifteen medals. Liberal and tolerant, he admitted sharing humanity's quest for ultimate value. Einstein's wonder at the mystery of conscious life, he said, was a clue to the existence of God. "Science does not disturb the inner spirit," he affirmed.

Forgetfulness of obsolete models keeps us from realizing how famous he was. A little after this time Robert Serber, one of Oppenheimer's students, tried to get a room in a small, crowded hotel without a reservation. "Let him in," he heard the proprietor's wife say. "He's the assistant of Millikan's assistant."

Millikan knew his place in America's heart. Birge once called at his office for a conference. It was disturbed by a secretary.

"I'm sorry, Dr. Millikan," she said, "but there are two reporters outside who insist on seeing you."

"Oh, those damned reporters," said Millikan. "How they pester me!"

Birge later learned Millikan had made appointments for them to come. Millikan's anonymous subordinates saw him in a light different from the public one. "I couldn't stand him," said Thomas O'Donnell, his laboratory mechanic. Always precise, Birge earned his dislike by exposing inaccuracies in his work. A puckish student of Birge's named Edward Condon once wrote a paper for the purpose. "How dare you let such a thing come out of your laboratories? I'll kill Condon if he publishes that," Millikan said to another of the Berkeley faculty.

Birge's attitude toward Oppenheimer furnished the key to Millikan's. A merely bright person hobbling after a genius: that was the way Birge thought of himself when he and Oppenheimer talked physics. Inhumanly predisposed though he was to activity in research, Birge does not pretend to have relished the involuntary self-comparison. Was there not something alien, repulsive, perhaps even peculiarly Jewish in the way Oppenheimer could comprehend and define so much faster? As for Millikan, on this point he had no doubts.

"Millikan loathed Oppenheimer, wouldn't match the promotions we gave him here, and harassed him maliciously," said Birge. Oppenheimer did not complain and may not have known enough about colleges to understand what he had to complain of. Birge remembers a complaint from another source, Niels Bohr, the greatest physicist in Europe: "Visiting from Denmark, Bohr sized things up at Pasadena and talked with me and with the Berkeley administration. Oppenheimer began to stay longer into the spring here. Later he taught the full session at Berkeley and cut his stay at Pasadena to four summer weeks. Millikan just left his name in the faculty register and made him miserable when the chance came."

Lawrence and Oppenheimer were not the only Berkeley physicists active in research in 1933. Birge, that precise man, had long been critical of water. He complained in print that its principal ingredient, hydrogen, weighted $\frac{1}{6000}$ more than all the textbooks said was its atomic weight. Gilbert Lewis, of the chemistry department, who had helped bring about Lawrence's promotion, began looking for what made a million hydrogen atoms weigh more than a million times the theoretical atomic weight of a single one. Columbia University broke Lewis' and Birge's hearts by discovering the isotope deuterium, the odd one-in-five-thousand overweight hydrogen atom, just when Lewis was about to do so. Still Lewis went doggedly on with his investigation. At the start of 1933 he began preparing the world's first usable samples of heavy water (H_2^2O).

Lawrence glued himself to Lewis' shoulder and goaded him to produce faster. He wanted to accelerate deuterium in the cyclotron. All ions known up till then carried the burden of a repellent charge proportional to their mass. The lightest was, therefore, the most effective against the nucleus. Deuterium promised to become an exception. It carried no more repellent charge than an ordinary hydrogen ion or proton, but it had twice the mass and as a projectile might prove twice as effective. In 1932 an uncharged particle called the neutron had been discovered by an Englishman named Chadwick. Scientists speculated that the deuterium ion was a proton and a neutron bound together.

Lawrence kept asking Lewis how much heavy water he had until about the first of March Lewis was able to show him a whole cubic centimeter. It was enough to accelerate, but at this point Lewis proved to be no physicist. Worried about whether he had manufactured a poison, he fed the whole sample to a mouse. It brought no good or harm to the mouse, but to Lawrence it almost brought apoplexy. "This was the most expensive cocktail that I think mouse or man ever had!" he complained.

Lewis began accumulating another sample of heavy water. Livingston and the other research associates continued work on the twenty-seven-inch cyclotron. "We tuned it up slowly to higher energy by moving the collector outward," said Livingston. Often they would try placing the collector too far out and lose the beam.

"Gentlemen, we must beat a strategic retreat," Commander Lucci would then remark sadly. The process was painful. The pillbox vacuum chamber was held together by Lawrence's red sealing wax. When taken apart, it had to be rewaxed carefully. To check for leaks, the wax had to be sprayed with alcohol, and then it would crumble. Everyone including Lawrence spent a good deal of time checking for pinpoint holes and resealing them with a gas burner.

At the center of the pillbox, an electric filament created the ions. The volume or intensity of the beam depended on the amount of current to the filament. It was held in place by a gob of wax, and when it burned out, no one knew exactly where to put the new one. The whole dismantling operation might have to be repeated several times.

"Lawrence loved to sit at the controls," says Aebersold. "It worried the rest of us. He always wanted to see how far he could push the meter up."

Livingood's recollections have the slangy elegance to be expected from a man with a classical education.

"Lawrence would say, 'Damn it, we've got this machine adjusted,' " Livingood recalls. " 'Don't anybody go over the pencil mark I've put on the meter.'

"Then he'd reach for the controls himself. Bingo! Another filament burned out.

" 'Well, I'll go play tennis,' he'd say. 'Fix it while I'm gone.' "

Through such crises the staff suffered until repetition and familiarity made them engineering problems, if only Lawrence had had the money to hire engineers. Late in March, Lewis brought pure science back into the Laboratory in the form of another sample of heavy water. While Lewis sat puffing a cigar and watching thoughtfully, they fed in the deuterium and tuned the beam against a lithium crystal. As before, it disintegrated into helium, but at a rate far faster than anyone had yet seen.

Now truly alchemists, they also converted aluminum, nitrogen, and half a dozen other light elements into helium. The helium nuclei, which are usually called alpha particles, flew off into the cloud chamber in glittering tracks well over three centimeters long. This showed the disintegration was proceeding with unexpected energy. Moreover, the targets also produced a stream of Chadwick's new particle, the neutron, on a surprising scale.

"Deuterium was a time of intense excitement when everything was new," said Livingston. "We bombarded targets with it and observed proton and neutron particles in the highest intensities ever seen by man." If one counted only the deuterium ions that actually hit and disintegrated a target nucleus, more energy was being produced than was consumed. They constituted what physicists call an exothermic system. Lawrence and his staff talked of a new possibility. If one could construct a large enough exothermic system, power might be generated to heat and light a city. Innocently, they did not think what else might be done to a city by such a system.

Their talk of energy from fusion was a thought from the future briefly wrenched out of its time. Of more concern to them were the heavy elements, so far invulnerable to any attack. They turned the beam of deuterium ions against platinum and gold. The instruments they had showed no transmutation. So far as they could tell, the heavy elements still remained invulnerable. Nevertheless, something else of great interest happened. Since platinum and gold were not transmuted, no helium nuclei were to be looked for. But neutrons and ordinary hydrogen ions or protons flew off the targets into the cloud chamber. The tracks they made matched some that had come from lithium. Lawrence and the staff looked at each other in astonishment. Something was still disintegrating.

Since it could not be platinum or gold, Lawrence decided it must be the deuterium ions in the beam. Deuterium was breaking up into neutrons and ordinary hydrogen ions. The process went on against all targets and with energy ranges fairly constant and easy to measure. The most important question about Chadwick's neutrons was their mass. Lawrence's data allowed him to compute it. He came up with a low figure approximately the same as that for a proton. In the abracadabra of the new physics this low figure damned the neutron as being merely a proton and electron combined, rather than a totally new and indivisible building block of nature. In England Chadwick was hemming and hawing on the question, but being human, he could not help liking the better status for his child. Lawrence's tidings, therefore, whenever Lawrence should get around to publishing them, were not likely to ring sweetly in Chadwick's ear.

Everyone in the Radiation Laboratory was under extreme pressure. The Century of Progress Exposition, or 1933 World's Fair, was about to open in Chicago. Along with fan dancers, science was to be the keynote. The National Academy mobilized all the top scientific organizations in the country for an unprecedented two weeks of meetings to start on the day the Fair opened. Naturally there was a great need for discoveries to be announced. Lawrence drove the staff hard so that he could be ready.

This was not quite the sort of activity in research that Birge thought ideal. He had started the whole operation by criticizing water. Like Frankenstein sourly contemplating his monster, he watched the hurry in the Radiation Laboratory. "It bothered Birge, and he tried to poke fun at Lawrence a little," says one of Lawrence's helpers. "Birge was interested in getting the very last decimal point. Lawrence was interested in exploring a brand-new field. Birge thought Lawrence was a young whippersnapper who didn't think things out, and Lawrence thought Birge was a crotchety old lady."

The Radiation Laboratory came through in time for Lawrence to catch a plane to Chicago and help open the World's Fair. He spoke on June 20 and June 24. All the experiments he reported were uniquely his, uncheckable elsewhere, because they demanded a threshold energy of about a million volts. Only he with his cyclotron could command such energy. Transmutation of elements, the wealth of power stored in deuterium, and the breaking down of barriers at the inmost heart of nature were sensationalized in the press. Everyone in the country who could read had a chance to learn of this scientific miracle worker from California. Those who could not read still caught some awareness of Lawrence through comedians' jokes on the radio about what he had done with heavy water. Lawrence marshaled his talks to end on the weight of the neutron. Consequently, the public picked up a vague idea that neutrons might brighten their future—how incandescently they could not imagine.

Not only the public was impressed. "Wonderful!" reporters

were told by Niels Bohr, one of five foreign Nobel prize winners in attendance. Millikan climbed on the bandwagon and became quotable. He declared that in cosmic space, movements of hydrogen ions like those inside Lawrence's cyclotron were probably going on as part of the continuous process of creation. "The Creator is still on the job," he said.

The World's Fair made Lawrence America's most famous native physicist. He was only thirty-two years old. Later the National Academy met privately to elect new members. When Birge loyally proposed Lawrence, Millikan seemed to forget the parallel he had drawn between Lawrence and the Creator. "Lawrence," he said disparagingly, "has developed one of several existing methods for high voltage."

Birge stood up. "He has developed the *highest* voltage," he said.

"Without directly saying so, Millikan did what he could to keep Lawrence out," Birge recalls. "He made a speech playing Lawrence down. Whenever he came to definite misstatements, I corrected them. He wound up by saying Lawrence was too young."

In resorting to this argument even in private, the old master betrayed that he was at last losing his touch. It was a language the Academy would not tolerate. Birge no longer had to fight the battle alone. Edwin Wilson, a Harvard mathematician, rose to set Millikan straight. "If age mattered," he said, "the best age for a member of the Academy would be one year."

Lawrence became the first South Dakotan to get in. Smarting, Millikan henceforth avoided contacts with Lawrence that would remind him of his demotion to second fiddle. Staying away from California sessions of the Physical Society, he mailed or carried his papers to Eastern meetings.

Lawrence's reputation spread beyond the American border. At McGill University in Montreal a young physicist named Robert Thornton finished his Ph.D. that June. A tough, practical, road-building type somewhat like Livingston, he won an international postdoctoral fellowship and wondered what to do with it. He asked John Foster, his thesis director at McGill. "Go to Berkeley and work with Lawrence," Foster told him. "You'll find some very interesting things going on in American physics. It's not by any means dependent on European physics as it used to be ten or fifteen years ago."

Europe too was beginning to take note of Lawrence. Every three years an international conference of the world's best-known physicists met in Brussels. Their travel expenses were paid from a fund set up by the Belgian inventor, Ernest Solvay. As a portent of the new era impending for mankind, the subject selected for discussion in 1933 was the nucleus of the atom. At Bohr's suggestion, Lawrence was invited to be the American representative.

A thrill of pride ran through the Radiation Laboratory. When Thornton arrived in September, he found every mind on the conference. Lawrence was joyfully preparing to leave. "This was Lawrence's first European recognition," said Thornton. "The whole staff went down to the train to see him off. Next morning they got together in the lab and then took off for a kind of two-day picnic climbing Mount Lassen. They were so happy you'd have thought they were all going to talk at the Solvay conference."

Brussels, for Lawrence, meant being closeted in a small room with Bohr, Dirac, Pauli, Rutherford, Chadwick, Irène Curie and her husband, Frédéric Joliot, and a dozen more of Europe's best. When his turn came to speak, he reviewed his deuterium experiments and concluded that they showed the neutron and proton did not significantly differ in mass.

There followed a few minutes of polite small talk on the cyclotron, a sort of intellectual silence while these chill, dreadful un-American minds digested his data.

Werner Heisenberg, one of the inventors of quantum mechanics, broke in to say there was something he could not understand. Why did deuterium fragments bounce off heavy atomic nuclei such as gold and light ones such as lithium with about the same energy? Bohr, who had heard Lawrence's earlier report at the Chicago World's Fair and had had three months to think, said he could not understand it either. Most of the others spoke up to the same effect.

Answering their tone rather than their words, Lawrence said it could not be due to impurities in his targets. He reminded them that to get the reactions he reported one must have a machine developing at least 800,000 volts.

Chadwick was a prim, schoolmasterish little man with a neat tooth-brush mustache and a penchant for exactitude. He made no comment on Lawrence's talk. When his own turn came, he referred to experiments at Cambridge and to theoretical considerations which established a wholly different mass for the neutron than that which Lawrence had assigned it. These, he concluded, indicated that the neutron was not a combination of particles but a unique indivisible particle in its own right.

Irène Curie made the last allusion of the conference to Lawrence's experiments. "What confidence do you put in cloud-chamber measurements of particles recoiling from the heavier nuclei?" she asked Chadwick.

"Not quite conclusive," Chadwick replied with the faintest of shrugs. The conference chairman congratulated Chadwick on his brilliant discussion of the neutron. Lawrence left the conference feeling bad.

'This was one of Lawrence's saddest experiences," said a Radiation Laboratory associate. No blunt statement of Lawrence's mistake was made until a month or two later. Then physicists at the Carnegie Institution in Washington were able to charge up the cyclotron's weak sister, the electrostatic accelerator, to repeat Lawrence's experiments. They found that deuterium was deposited as an impurity in all targets by the beam. Thus whatever element Lawrence had bombarded, he had always been measuring the effects of deuterium striking deuterium. The protons came from one such reaction [$D(d,p)H^3$] and the neutrons from another [$D(d,n)H^3$].

"This hit Lawrence very hard," says the research associate just quoted. "A major factor of the trouble was that it cost us the support of Chadwick. He thought all work coming from our laboratory was a hoax. Lawrence gave the paper too soon. Looking back, I feel that our work was sketchy and almost technically careless. We weren't purifying targets as we should, and we weren't measuring energy ranges as we should. The spirit was a little slapdash."

Lawrence came home and blistered the staff in whose collective name he had spoken. "He thought the reason we had made this mistake was that we hadn't been critical enough of our work. He said that as individuals we weren't taking enough responsibility. 'You are all going along with the group too much,' he told us. 'In the future we must have more individual work and less teamwork.' "

The heart might as well have ordered the hands and feet to

start pumping their own blood. In that enchanted laboratory the Geiger counter was wired to the same switch as the cyclotron. By turning them both on and off at the same time, one could get on with operations faster. This is the reason the big new idea of 1934 had to make its way in from the outside.

On February 20, 1934, the staff was bombarding boron with deuterium ions. That afternoon Lawrence came running through the door waving a French journal with an article by Frédéric Joliot, who had saturninely watched his discomfiture at Brussels without adding to it. "It is now possible for the first time to create radioactivity in certain elements," Lawrence translated haltingly for the staff. Joliot had used a petty apparatus powered by a minute quantity of radium emanations. While writing his article, he had remembered Lawrence and closed with a postscript on what Lawrence could produce that was beyond Joliot's own power. "For example, Nitrogen 13, which according to our hypothesis is radioactive, could be obtained by bombarding carbon with deuterium ions."

Like puppets on a string, the staff changed the wiring of the Geiger counter and swung a carbon target into the beam. Five minutes later they turned off the cyclotron. *"Click . . . click . . . click* went the Geiger counter," said Livingston. "It was a sound that no one who was there would ever forget." Thus the first Nitrogen 13 ever known to exist in the world announced its presence.

The implications for medicine, biology, and the approaching nuclear age were enormous. The staff had often bombarded carbon, but always before had switched off the Geiger counter with the beam. Now they stared at each other with an identical expression on their faces.

"We looked pretty silly," said Thornton. "We could have made the discovery any time."

Livingood, the most highly educated, interpreted most tersely: "We felt like kicking each other's butts."

3

IN THE EVENING, PEACE

MEN SO PERFECTLY ATTUNED with machines gave
visiting physicists an odd feeling. "I encountered the spirit of the
Radiation Laboratory when I spoke on the structure of the nucleus
at some of their seminars," said David Inglis. "Everybody was so
concentrated on producing higher and higher energies that I got
the impression my subject was very foreign to their interests. I
felt almost apologetic."

To most early members of the Radiation Laboratory, the period
following Joliot's discovery furnishes their brightest memories.
"Professor Lawrence has taken the lead in the Western Hemi-
sphere in the creation of radioactive elements," Sproul said in his
annual report to the Governor of California. An Associated Press
dispatch of April 2, 1934, read: "Lawrence and his associates have
created ten new elements. Experiments have been carried farther
than in Paris." Most newspapers ran the story under the headline
"MAKES RADIUM."

"It was a wonderful time," says Livingood. "Radioactive elements fell in our laps as though we were shaking apples off a
tree." The elements or isotopes they created radiated themselves
away much faster than radium; half-lives ranged from a split second to several days. Consequently the headlines that said the Laboratory had made radium were not quite accurate. Conservative
scientists elsewhere declared that there was a fundamental difference between artificial and natural isotopes. Livingood settled the
question by creating radium E from bismuth and watching it de-

61

cay like ordinary radium E into polonium. This awesome feat required a deuterium beam of about six million volts from the constantly improved cyclotron. It could not have been done in any other laboratory in the world.

"I try to live now the way we did in those days," says Sloan. "We didn't need money except for a place to eat and sleep. No forms to fill out. No organization chart. Not even one secretary. Just people working together and a sense of something new, something exciting. Lawrence had a special ability that made everybody in the Lab think, 'He is my best friend.' "

Since 1930, with Lawrence's backing, Sloan had marshaled the staff to compete against the cyclotron with three kinds of linear accelerators. The first one hurried heavy mercury ions through a series of metal tubes inside a long glass cylinder. Each tube pushed them faster, but the beam kept spreading, and this set a practical limit to the number of tubes. No unforeseen laws of nature came to Sloan's aid with a gift of focusing. In 1934 he and a research associate named Wesley Coates built the largest possible accelerator of this kind. It produced about three million volts of energy and soft X rays in the target but no nuclear disintegration.

The second kind accelerated lighter lithium ions. When Thornton came in 1933 he worked about a year on this one with Sloan and Bernard Kinsey, a burly Englishman with a lisp. Kinsey is remembered for his glass blowing. When the tubes broke in the flame, the staff was fascinated to hear him curse horribly in a lisping British accent. This accelerator was also finished and tested in 1934. It produced disintegration, but not on a worthwhile scale.

The third kind of linear accelerator was most interesting. Sloan's problem was how to increase the voltage without running into impossible insulation requirements. It was the same problem Lawrence had faced in 1929, and Sloan in 1932 had meditated on it as intensely. "My mind was disturbed for weeks," he said. Lawrence, who often referred to Sloan as a kind of genius, watched with interest.

"A thought comes to you reassembling what you know in new patterns," said Sloan. "But you have to be struggling beforehand. When you get a new idea, you don't know if it's any good. They all produce the same quickening of feeling—the bad ones are followed by a letdown."

Sloan was still attending classes. One day he stopped taking notes. The thought came to him that acceleration could be doubled if the polarity of the voltage on the ends of each tube alternated while the ion was halfway through. This would mean attaching the tube to a resonating secondary induction coil. One could hang the whole business, coil and all, inside a vacuum chamber and thus get around the insulation problem.

As Lawrence had done, Sloan fell into a dream. "I missed hearing the lecture that day," he said. "I sat and didn't take in a word." No letdown followed this idea. To a 1932 physicist it was as beautiful and promising as had been that of the cyclotron. Sloan explained it to Lawrence. "He was an enthusiastic listener," said Sloan. "He would try to outdo you in seizing the implications and possibilities." This time he was particularly enthusiastic. "Lawrence believed that the double-energy accelerator could surpass the cyclotron in its yield," said Birge.

With the secondary coil Sloan obtained the highest dependable voltage ever set up in an electrical apparatus. But the work of fitting in the accelerator tube and ion source went slowly. Sloan was laboring with it in 1933 when Lawrence diverted him. He told Sloan that the Medical School wanted a more powerful X-ray machine than any then in existence. Though Physics was better off than Liberal Arts, the only real education money in those bleak days went to Medicine. Sloan and Livingston redesigned the apparatus to produce 800,000-volt X rays. Livingston had a half-year's instructorship at the School for his part in the project. "He did all the work and I got all the credit," said Sloan.

The thing was a small lead-walled room with an orifice that looked like the window of a gas chamber. It stood in the center of a larger lead-walled room into which cancer victims were wheeled for pioneering therapy with hard X rays. Through this machine Lawrence made his first important contribution to medicine.

Sloan went back to the task of designing his resonance transformer to accelerate ions. President Spoul reported to the Governor that it could produce "very high-speed ions in currents of far larger size than ever before obtained in any way." But its operation was made sporadic and dubious by engineering difficulties. Sloan tried to think them through on long solitary walks.

One day in 1934 on a hill near Berkeley he fell and broke his back. After a year or two in bed, he was able to get up but could not bend his spine. Lying flat on a dolly, he paddled about the Radiation Laboratory and helped with his specialty, high-voltage oscillator tubes for the new cyclotrons. But he no longer led independent research programs. The view from the floor sharpened his perspective on his more active days. "The thing I remember is the spirit of adventure," he said. "We were seeing the end of atomic physics and the beginning of nuclear physics. Here was a new field opening up. We knew there was something big ahead, something worth working for. Lawrence made us feel that way." Linear accelerators were abandoned until other hands took them up a decade later.

A new generation of physicists began joining the Laboratory. Most notable among them was Edwin McMillan, slight of build, freckled and sandy-haired. Under a washed-out, vacant expression he concealed a first-rate mind and a sense of humor which other staff members found incomprehensible. "Tied a can to my dachshund's tail and tossed her in the creek at a staff picnic," said one of the research associates. "Boisterous. I guess that's what you'd call him."

McMillan had been about to get his Ph.D. from Princeton in 1932 when he met Lawrence, who was on a visit to the Laboratory there. "That's why I came out here," McMillan said. "I wanted to be associated with him." For two years, however, he worked in other parts of the Physics Department before joining the Radiation Laboratory. The group spirit never blinded him; he listened skeptically to the staff's excuses about artificial radioactivity. It occurred to him that they might have been able to separate out the various complex reactions involved even while the cyclotron was still running. "The trouble was that people were using old-type Geiger counters," he said. "When I came, the counters responded only to heavily ionizing particles. My first work was to build more sensitive instruments that would also register other types of radiation. If this had been done before, there would have been a different story."

He and Thornton led the staff in enlarging the cyclotron first to thirty-one inches, then to thirty-seven. Constant technical improvements gradually eliminated the hitches and breakdowns that had made life colorful. Berkeley became the world center for the study of high-energy radiation.

Turned against a beryllium target, the cyclotron produced a stream of ten million neutrons a second. "DEATH RAY," the newspapers first called it and then, toward the end of 1934, "POSSIBLE CURE FOR CANCER." Continual reports of new radioactive elements kept Lawrence in the headlines. Literate Americans saw in him the embodiment of no mean hope. "It is clear that the physicist stands on the brink of great discoveries," *The New York Times* said in an editorial on Lawrence. "Transmutation, the release of atomic energy are no longer mere romantic possibilities. But it is the secret of matter that is of vital importance—the secret held by every star and stone. Fathom that and the cosmos becomes an open book. Truths may be unveiled that we have been seeking ever since we started thinking about the Universe."

The young president of Harvard, a distinguished chemist named James Bryant Conant, wanted Lawrence badly. In 1935 he offered to make him dean at a salary no state university could match. More than that Conant pledged to duplicate every facility which Lawrence had built up at the Radiation Laboratory. On the very day of his arrival, Conant wrote, Lawrence would have $25,000 to spend as he liked.

Berkeley was thrown into another crisis. This time the question was not "What should we do?" but "What can we do?" Birge, chairman after Hall's death, called in Lawrence's warmest friend on the physics faculty, Oppenheimer. The two decided that in dealing with Lawrence they had best not speak frankly. "Both Oppenheimer and I felt that Lawrence was not interested in college administration," Birge said. "Moreover we agreed that he was entirely unsuited for it, but we also agreed we wouldn't dare intimate this to him. We had to find some other line of approach."

Separately they talked with Lawrence. "We really worked on him just in a personal way," Birge continued. " 'Conant can promise,' we told him, 'but he doesn't realize the cost of everything you have here. And even if he can follow through, you'd still lose a year while he duplicates your laboratory and gets it to operate.' "

Sproul, to whom Lawrence was science incarnate, used more

material arguments. He labored with the Regents to get them to match the Harvard offer. As for the $25,000, he persuaded them to guarantee Lawrence this sum each year. It was to be produced by a sort of juggling. Lawrence's salary was raised to about $3,000 more than that of the highest-paid faculty member, and another $17,000 was allotted to him for staff and equipment.

More important, Sproul skewed the academic chain of command by giving the Radiation Laboratory formal status in the budget and Lawrence the formal title of Director. Thus he created an authority within an authority in the Physics Department. "I think Birge tolerated it because he had to," speculated a Radiation Laboratory staff member.

"I had nothing to do with the Radiation Laboratory budgets," Birge said. "Lawrence handled them. I saw them a little, but I didn't need to at all." Certainly the situation was difficult for Birge. Nevertheless he felt the price was not too high to pay for activity in research. "My greatest accomplishment was holding Lawrence here," he said at the end of his chairmanship many years later.

Lawrence's first act, even before the money started coming in, was to put Cooksey on the new payroll as Assistant Director or, in Birge's words, "sort of Lawrence's business manager."

"Cooksey was interesting," says one of the research associates. "Essentially he was a leg man, a fellow who paid attention to details. But he was never made to feel like that. What would he have done with his life without Lawrence? I think he would have wasted it."

Another staff member once heard Cooksey tell Livingston that to him Lawrence was a god. "Throughout history the rich have had a tendency to enslave themselves," Livingston replied caustically. For such tactlessness Livingston may have paid later. Cooksey, who edited Radiation Laboratory publications, scanted Livingston's part in its early history.

With his instructorship expired, Livingston was making about eighty dollars a month as a research associate. He asked Lawrence's help in finding a job, and Lawrence got him two offers, one at Washington State and the other at Cornell in New York. "Lawrence is a Westerner, I am an Easterner," Livingston decided. He took the job at Cornell and there built a cyclotron of his own, the first outside Lawrence's laboratory. He worked with Cornell's leading physicist, Hans Bethe, and discovered what it meant to have time to think. "Thank God I left Berkeley," he said.

In June of 1935 John Lawrence came to Berkeley to spend the summer convalescing from an automobile accident. Hobbling about the Laboratory on crutches, he learned that the physicists had little idea of radiation danger, especially from neutrons, and only made jokes when he tried to tell them. He procured a rat and at his request Aebersold imprisoned it in a box on the side of the cyclotron in a stream of neutrons from a beryllium target. After five minutes they opened the box and found the rat dead. The faces of the staff turned solemn until they discovered Aebersold had forgotten to put breathing holes in the box.

With this humble death the Radiation Laboratory entered a new phase. Lawrence was life-oriented to a degree unusual among physicists. He had always looked up to doctors, and now relished having one at hand who looked up to him. "Very often in history physicists have been assistants to physicians," he said. "But this is the first time I ever heard of a physician working under a physicist."

Lawrence was producing most of the world's supply of neutrons and artificial radioactive isotopes. In conversations of major importance, he and his brother mapped out three main areas for exploration: to use the isotopes for biological research, to treat cancer with them, and to treat cancer with neutrons. The possibilities isotopes opened for research were amazing. Each behaved chemically like its ordinary nonradioactive counterpart; each could be traced through any number of chemical changes with a radiation counter. Hardly any science or industry on earth could fail to discover uses for this new tool. But the most exciting challenge, Lawrence and his brother agreed, was to unravel the most complex chemical processes, those constituting the physical basis of life.

To begin a campaign for funds, Lawrence invited the public to a series of shows in the Berkeley auditorium. Sodium 24 with a half-life of fifteen hours was then the most versatile of his new creations. He began by uncorking a bottle of it near a Geiger counter. Livingood had prepared him so hot a sample that it overloaded the counter and produced only a long embarrassing silence. Lawrence covered by calling Oppenheimer from the audience. "He got me out on the platform and used me as a guinea pig," said Oppenheimer. "He had me put my hand around a Geiger counter and gave me a glass of water in which part of the salt had radioactive sodium in it. For the first half minute all was quiet, but about fifty seconds after I drank, there was a great clattering of the Geiger counter. This was supposed to show that in at least one complex physiochemical system, the salt had diffused from my mouth through my bloodstream to the tip of my fingers and that the time scale for this was fifty seconds."

In the fall of 1935, Lawrence's brother went back to Harvard. Lawrence went with him and with his help made friends with Harvey Cushing, the country's most eminent brain surgeon. Cushing was almost dazed by Lawrence's enthusiasm. "This field of radiation is something big," Cushing said after hearing Lawrence talk. "I think medicine now is at a threshold like the one when I was a young doctor at the time bacteriology was discovered." With Cushing's support Lawrence was made consultant to the Institute of Cancer Research at Columbia and to the National Cancer Foundation, then a branch of the Federal Department of the Interior.

Another of John Lawrence's eminent friends was old Ludwig Kost, a leader in the New York Medical Society. In New York, Kost took the two brothers to the office of the Josiah Macy Foundation. Speaking alternately, Kost and Lawrence sang praises of the new radiations until the Foundation head decided to issue John Lawrence a research grant with which to set up a small-animal research laboratory.

At Berkeley, John Lawrence needed a physicist collaborator to give him a great deal of time. Because of the Depression he was able to get Aebersold. "Some technical people around the Laboratory, including a very brilliant engineer, were on the W.P.A.," said Aebersold. "There weren't adequate outlets for nuclear physicists, so I gave serious thought to biophysics." Aebersold invented a sort of gun muzzle of wax and lead that could bring into line the neutrons produced when the cyclotron bombarded beryllium. Lawrence obtained him a medical-research fellowship.

John Lawrence measured the effect of neutrons successively on fruit-fly eggs, the blood of rats, and cancers he implanted surgically in mice. His tests indicated that, per unit of radiation, neutrons were three times as lethal as X rays to healthy tissue, but four times as lethal to cancers. In this margin was great hope, though glimmering and uncertain as unproved new things always are.

By the end of 1936, Livingston's original twenty-seven-inch cyclotron had been enlarged to the full limits of the magnet. It accelerated deuterium ions to about eight million volts of energy. Lawrence set the staff to drawing plans for an entirely new sixty-inch cyclotron. Almost everyone contributed ideas to its design, but the guiding spirit of its practical construction drifted in with the usual flotsam of sightseers about this time. His name was William Brobeck. "I'd like a job," he told Lawrence. "I'm a mechanical engineer."

A sloppy young man in a T-shirt, Brobeck had a wide grin like Joe E. Brown's which changed to a sneer as he looked at the enlarged twenty-seven-inch. "He saw all sorts of things that people like me had done wrong," said one of the physicists who watched this characteristic Radiation Laboratory scene.

Lawrence, whose W.P.A. genius had temporarily left him to seek paid employment, needed an engineer even more than usual. "Love to have you," he said. "But I can't afford to pay you. I haven't any money."

"Who said anything about money?" Brobeck replied—it turned out that his father was rich. He worked without salary, until wartime regulations required he be put on the official payroll.

Money was the key to the proposed new machine. With it, unknown nuclear reactions could be explored. But its chief·selling point was more neutrons and isotopes for medical research. To build it, Lawrence had to go after the big money.

He had got all he could hope for from the University budget, but he saw an untapped spring in the Regents personally. Most of them belonged to an Elks' Club of the very rich called the Bohemian, which maintained a wonderful rustic lodge on the Russian River fifty miles north of Berkeley. Here, safe from the creeping bourgeois, the Bohemians played traditional boyish practical jokes on one another and sometimes entertained a few of the top University faculty. Invitations were coveted; there was no more intoxicating distinction than to wash dishes at the Bohemian Grove while President Sproul dried them.

Sproul supported Lawrence as faithfully at the Grove as at board meetings. He helped Lawrence to a jovial kitchen-sink intimacy with two of the most influential Regents, John Neylan and William Crocker. They in turn, by canvassing the other members, got Lawrence a unique honorary life membership.

Neylan, corporation counsel for the Hearst interests and angel of the far right in California politics, made himself chairman of a special subcommittee of the Board of Regents to represent the Radiation Laboratory. Crocker was chairman of the Board. A genuine robber-baron's son and one of the world's biggest stamp collectors, Crocker took an interest in San Francisco opera, philanthropy, and cancer research. His health failed in 1937. Just before he died he gave Lawrence $75,000 for a building to house the proposed new cyclotron.

Ground was broken for it in the fall. The W.P.A. made a heavy but less publicized contribution to the building, which was to be called the Crocker Laboratory. At Cottrell's urging, the Chemical Foundation contributed $68,000. Lawrence estimated for the newspapers that he needed $35,000 more.

To help with the advertising, he accepted an invitation from the science fraternity Sigma Xi to make a national lecture tour. The thought of it frightened him. "I am no speaker," he moaned to his brother when the two were on a visit to Yale. John Lawrence took him to Harvey Cushing, exactly the right man to help. Cushing's *Life of Sir William Osler* was the top literary achievement of an American scientist; Cushing's collection of publications on the biomedical aspects of nuclear physics was one of the country's largest. Cushing planned and organized the speech and arranged a tryout for Lawrence at a Yale medical luncheon. The effect was overpowering. "What kind of baby were you?" asked the famous psychiatrist Arnold Gesell, stunned at the combined impact of Lawrence's personality and Cushing's style. The lecture tour was a success. Brady, who was teaching at St. Louis University, watched Lawrence thrill a packed auditorium there with the medical promise of the cyclotron. Afterward Brady told Lawrence how much he had liked his physics classes in Berkeley. Lawrence thanked him, but said that his classroom days were over— "I'm seldom in Berkeley more than two weeks at a time."

For inventing the cyclotron, South Dakota had given Lawrence an honorary degree in 1936. This year Princeton, Stevens Institute, and Yale, where Zeleny was about to retire, followed suit. Cottrell's Research Corporation gave Lawrence a prize, and the United States Surgeon General granted him $30,000 from the National Cancer Foundation. Probably America's greatest honor for a scientist then was the Comstock Award of $2,500 and a medal, given every five years by the National Academy of Sciences. Lawrence received it in October.

General Electric's William Coolidge, a scientist-inventor in the tradition of Edison and Steinmetz, delivered the address. He made it a panegyric on Lawrence's youth. It was youth and not Livingston, Coolidge seemed to be saying, that had got Lawrence focusing. Coolidge trotted out on the stage—he always trotted everywhere—and in a quick, nervous voice reviewed the efforts of the Twenties to set up high voltage in atom-smashing apparatus. "Dr. Lawrence envisioned a radically different course, one which did not have those difficulties attendant upon the use of potential differences of millions of volts. At the start, however, it presented other difficulties and uncertainties, and it is interesting to speculate on whether an older man, having had the same vision, would ever have attained its successful embodiment and conclusion. It called for boldness and faith and persistence to a degree rarely matched."

Time Magazine put Lawrence's photograph on its cover and labeled him "the cyclotron man, foremost U. S. destroyer and creator of atoms."

All these distinctions helped Lawrence tap the pockets of the rich for the additional $35,000 he said he needed for the new cyclotron. Coolidge wrote him a letter of introduction to Lewis Strauss, a New York financier whose mother had recently died of cancer. As a consequence, Strauss had almost unconsciously begun to survey the supply of radium in different American cities. "I was appalled," he said. "Many had none at all. New York's Memorial Hospital had a stock consisting of two or three grams. Even this had to be kept split up so that patients could be treated who were sent in from hospitals where there was no radium. Mostly they were terminal cases, dying people." Memorial's famous director, Dr. James Ewing, told Strauss his frustration. "You know some might live if only I had a bomb!" Ewing exclaimed. "Something to give massive doses, maybe twenty or thirty grams!"

The new high-voltage machines, by creating artificial radio-actives and neutron beams, promised to do more than relieve the shortage of natural radium. At Pasadena, Strauss had subsidized Millikan, whom he thought an insufficiently appreciated leader, to see whether the surge generator, a weak competitor of the cyclotron, could produce useful quantities of radioactives. "Just as radio-iodine is a thyroid seeker, we thought or hoped there might be a specific isotope for every part of the body," Strauss said. "I suppose I had the medieval notion of the fencing thrust, or of a magic bullet that would strike straight at the disease."

Aside from a certain tinge of melancholic sophistication, Strauss talked Lawrence's language. At this time Millikan had him tied up, and he made Lawrence only what he called a minuscule contribution. Lawrence, who never measured his gratitude, thanked him extravagantly. The two formed the habit of looking each other up on their respective visits to New York and California. "My friendship with Lawrence developed into a close friendship between our families," Strauss said.

Less sophisticated but even richer was William Donner of Pennsylvania, a long-headed, dark-eyed man with the bleak planes in his face and the full, hard-set lips often seen in those who have built a fortune in steel. In 1929 a son's death from cancer had widened Donner's world and led him to set up a foundation. In first grief he defined its function as to meet "the need for more and better trained cancerologists," and a little later he also offered its support to "projects designed to preserve the American Way of Life."

Lawrence, the most American of scientists, ideally embodied both objectives. In 1936 Donner paid his first call on Lawrence at Berkeley. How much Donner contributed in 1937 is hard to guess. "He came out here, visited the Radiation Laboratory, and got much interested," says a physicist. "He thought the work was very valuable for medical physics. The Donner Foundation was supposed to make only research grants, not building grants, but in those early days Mr. Donner just decided what it should give.

"A couple of years later, while the sixty-inch cyclotron was being finished in the Crocker building, I was standing in my office door in LeConte. Donner, who was just ending a visit to the Radiation Laboratory, walked by in the corridor, and Lawrence hurried up from behind to catch up with him.

" 'You may think I'm crazy, but I'd like to have fifty thousand dollars for a new building for medical physics,' Lawrence said to Donner. Just like that. Would you have thought it was that simple?

" 'I'll think about it,' Donner replied.

"Next day Lawrence consulted associates and told Donner he needed $150,000 instead of $50,000. Donner gave it to him. By the time the Donner Laboratory was completed in 1941, it probably cost over $300,000, and later another wing was added."

When Lawrence went to New York, he stayed in the penthouse of the richest of all his patrons, Alfred Lee Loomis. It was Loomis who had financed Harvey Cushing's historic brain-wave studies at Harvard and Yale. Besides being a corporation lawyer and executive, Loomis had taken the time and trouble to become a fair-to-middling physicist in his own right. He liked to keep out of the newspapers.

"Mr. Loomis would come out here to Berkeley for several months at a time and work right in the lab with Lawrence," said a senior colleague of Lawrence's. "He knew his physics and was capable of working. You'd never think he was something special, except that he always arrived in a big seven-passenger limousine. His chauffeur just sat in the car the whole day waiting for him. Otherwise he was an awfully nice fellow.

"Lawrence once told me he was one of the ten richest men in the country. Yet nobody knew this. He made Lawrence his protégé and played angel to him all through the years. He gave Lawrence advice about investments, and I imagine Lawrence made quite a bit out of them.

"Nobody knows how much he gave Lawrence directly. But we knew Lawrence had a private fund marked 'Ernest O. Lawrence, Personal' as the checks were signed. It was just given to him to spend. He could do many things, send Radiation Lab people out to other places or bring people here. I obtained some of that money, so I know. I suspect it came from Loomis.

"I think he would give Lawrence a thousand or two at a time, especially for little things the University wouldn't approve. In general, the University doesn't like these private funds because you don't know how people are spending them. But Lawrence could pay right off the bat without having to get permission from anybody. You could trust him not to misuse the money, so there was no problem."

Young physicists dependent on Lawrence's mysterious fund learned with pain how far he could make it go. One of the brightest of the Radiation Laboratory staff in the later Thirties was Robert Wilson, round-cheeked, bubbling, full of original ideas. Lawrence paid him $60 a month out of the fund during most of an academic year, then stopped. Wilson, hungry, asked to be allowed to go home to his parents. Lawrence insisted he stay and keep working. "He's so *unfeeling!*" Wilson complained.

In the first cyclotrons, the beam had had to be used inside the vacuum chamber. Then McMillan had devised a complicated arrangement of electric fields that drew the beam outside like an eerie-looking death ray. This, of course, was necessary for experiments on animals which the two Lawrence brothers viewed as preliminary to actual medical treatment of patients with neutrons. Meanwhile, Wilson and a young chemist, Martin Kamen, had an idea that seemed to reverse McMillan's work.

They guessed there were currents of ions never drawn out of the vacuum chamber and going to waste there. Wilson opened up the chamber, soldered in a target which he wanted to turn into radioactive phosphorus, resealed the chamber, and told other staff members waiting impatiently to get on with their own projects that the cyclotron was now ready for use. As he and Kamen had predicted, the external beam was not impaired. Merely as a by-product, the cyclotron now turned out three times as much artificial radioactive isotopes as before. But Wilson's first experiment got him only curses. He had overlooked what the internal ion currents might do to the solder. They spread it over the inside of the vacuum chamber in a radioactive coating, which the whole staff worked for weeks to scrape off. "Kill Wilson" they wrote on signs they hung on the dismantled cyclotron.

After ordering Wilson to devise a clamp to replace the solder, Lawrence divided the staff into three shifts and ran the cyclotron twenty-two to twenty-four hours a day. He wanted to produce radioactive materials totaling in their effect that of a kilogram of radium, and he came appreciably close to this goal, which would have been fantastic in any other laboratory. He distributed isotopes as widely as he could all over the world. Chemical and biophysical research leaped forward in consequence. Perhaps the most fundamental discoveries in radioisotope tracing were made by the Nobel laureate Georg von Hevesy in Sweden. "I couldn't have worked without those wonderful shipments of radioactive phosphorus," Hevesy told Lawrence on a visit to America. Another laureate, the English physiologist Archibald Hill, toured the Laboratory and said to Lawrence, "Some day people may look back on the isotope as being as important to medicine as the microscope."

Since 1935 John Lawrence had been commuting between Yale and Berkeley. When he came west in the fall of 1937, he was still uncertain about where he wanted to work. Yale listed him on its staff for the second half of its winter session. Rules against nepotism for the time prevented Lawrence from putting him on the University of California payroll. He worked in the Radiation Laboratory without pay for several months, collaborating with a professor at the University Medical School in San Francisco, Robert Stone. Joseph Hamilton, a new M. D., worked with him in Berkeley.

The attitude of the Medical School staff unfolded chillingly. In that year of honors for Lawrence, the Dean of the School gave a dinner in his honor. Most of the doctors present felt that Lawrence's radiation therapy was too new and bold, that it was moving too fast from the laboratory to the hospital. They took pains to disassociate themselves from the spirit of the occasion and from the country's hopes that the Radiation Laboratory would achieve a breakthrough in cancer treatment. One doctor, supposedly making a congratulatory speech to Lawrence, asserted the cyclotron was of no use at all in medicine. He said that the previous work of Hamilton and John Lawrence had been a waste of time. There was a general murmur of approval.

Pushing with all the force of his personality, Lawrence made the Medical School put his brother and Hamilton on its staff. It was agreed they were to work one or two days a week across the Bay. Except from Robert Stone, the welcome they had in San Francisco was scant. Nobody was wanted there, it was made plain to them, without extensive clinical experience, which they lacked. John Lawrence went less and less often. Physicists could tell he was unhappy. Hamilton, a recent graduate of the School, got along with it a little better, but not much.

In January of 1938 John Lawrence was supposed to return to Yale for a half year's work. If he had gone, the Radiation Laboratory's contact with medical research, the source of its nationwide financial support, would have been weakened.

His plans were changed by a personal problem. For several months the brothers had worried about their mother, ill in South Dakota. Now at last there could be no doubt that Gunda Lawrence had cancer. To see what could be done, the brothers arranged an appointment for her at the Mayo Clinic in Minnesota. She was sixty-five and her husband, Carl, who came along, sixty-seven.

After the biopsy and other tests were completed, John Lawrence and his parents met the examining physician in his office. The old couple looked tired and apprehensive, the physician grimly matter-of-fact. "You can live about three months," he said to Gunda Lawrence.

John Lawrence watched his parents' faces turn white. The contemplative part of his mind asked, "Why did he tell them?" while the other part pursued with tremendous urgency the question of what to do.

For almost anyone else, there could have been nothing left but resignation, but the Radiation Laboratory was something new in the world. It had created the Sloan machine for extreme high-energy X rays and the cyclotron with its unique neutron beam. John Lawrence conferred with his brother by telephone, and the two decided to bring their mother to Berkeley.

Her cancer was of the pelvis. John Lawrence put her to bed in the stateroom of a jolting train and stood over her while she bled constantly. At the Medical School hospital he sharply insisted on greater doses of radiation from the Sloan machine than the staff was used to giving.

"I'm sick, John, very sick," she said while being wheeled into the lead-lined room that Livingston had built.

"You'll get better, Mother," he answered, keeping his eyes on the meter.

It also seems well attested that the brothers treated her with neutrons. "This was something highly dramatic and very personal," says a close colleague of Lawrence's who should know. "They dosed her with the neutron beam from the cyclotron. She was the very first to be given neutron treatment. It was kept completely confidential."

At the end of three months, she felt little change. After two years she began to get better. In five years she had forgotten everything about the illness except the love and faith which had surrounded her. There followed a healthy and vigorous old age that did not end until she was eighty-three.

"The cancer never came back," says the physicist just quoted. "So after this there was no question about the medical value of the cyclotron. The story has never been told, but it ought to be." The Medical School did not accept this view. Miracles—inexplicable regressions—occur fairly often among cancer victims. But the two brothers, having staked what they loved, felt there was no question. They began a broad campaign against cancer. With radioactive phosphorus John Lawrence began treatment of patients dying of leukemia and of polycythemia vera, a disease of the red blood cells. For this latter he achieved some indubitable cures.

For one day a week, the twenty-seven-inch cyclotron was used to give other dying patients the treatment first used on Gunda Lawrence. Fast neutrons were projected directly from the beryllium target against the diseased tissues. Physicist Gerald Kruger, a friend of Lawrence's from the University of Illinois, contributed the idea of using neutrons slowed by passage through paraffin and therefore less destructive to healthy surface tissue. Seeds of boron were buried in the diseased spots in which the slowed neutrons produced localized ionizing radiation. Improvements in regulating the beam and measuring the dose went forward constantly.

Published case histories suggest the brothers felt for each patient as they did for Gunda Lawrence. Boldness and a desperate personal compassion set their attitude a little apart from the grim decorum of the Medical School. Cancer specialists there watched coldly, trying to calculate the effective limits on the therapeutic value of isotopes and to decide whether neutrons in comparison with X rays had any therapeutic value whatever.

The Medical School continued to refuse John Lawrence a wel-

come. William Donner surprised him by announcing he was to be
director of the $300,000 Donner Laboratory of medical physics
which his brother Ernest had asked Donner to build. A little embarrassingly, Donner's explanation passed lightly over such distinctions of the new director as his work with Harvey Cushing and
dwelt on the fact that he was the son of a college president. Lawrence, to provide his brother a tolerable official footing, persuaded
the University to set up a Division of Medical Physics in the Physics Department.

At Loomis' penthouse and at the Bohemian Grove Lawrence
had learned how to entertain. In Molly he had a skillful hostess
and in Cooksey, who had married the Physics Department secretary and got over his hypochondria, an adept surrogate host when
he was himself too busy. Cocktail parties at the Lawrence and
Cooksey houses became the national meeting place for great
names in science and finance, the latter often leaving with unexpectedly lighter checkbooks. Guests remaining after a party were
startled to see how the Lawrence house turned into a South Dakota farmhouse: he tired and bluntly giving orders, she a *Haus-
frau* who took them meekly. "Lawrence liked the good life, so to
speak, but not at home," said a Nobel laureate who stayed to
breakfast.

When Lawrence had a choice, instead of cocktails he still preferred red wine, "Dago red" as he liked to call it. Twice a year
he had Aebersold phone Dibiasi's Italian Restaurant in Richmond
to tell the cook not to go home. Then he and the Laboratory staff
would share a night of Chianti, spaghetti and horseplay. They
watched him anxiously, fearing his splendid associations were
drawing him away.

In the mid-Thirties, John Lawrence found his brother and Oppenheimer to be close comrades. "Very similar spirits, very complementary to each other," he called them. The three went often
to Jack's, a restaurant for San Francisco epicures. Lawrence let
Oppenheimer deal with the waiter, took white wine instead of red,
and cheerfully dined on the very last meal his own taste called
for: Chablis and snails or sole Marguéry.

In Lawrence's laboratory a superstition grew up that one of
McMillan's most elaborate radiation counters would work only
when Oppenheimer stood beside it. McMillan snorted at the

earlier experimentalists' view of Oppenheimer as the remote, un-intelligible oracle of the seminars whom only Lawrence dared to interrogate. Oppenheimer undertook no experiments of his own, but he was getting to be at home in the Laboratory. Sloan, the last of the early crew who was still there, noticed the change. As an inventor, Sloan was fascinated by Oppenheimer's attitude toward machines. Looking up from his dolly on the floor, he had ample time to watch.

"I suppose nobody in the world ever completely mastered both the theoretical and the experimental fields except the Italian Enrico Fermi," Sloan said, "but Oppenheimer came very close. He used to joke about knowing nothing of experimental physics. 'Every time I come into the lab I bust something,' he'd say, and this was true for a while.

"But then he began to observe, not manipulate. He learned to see the apparatus and to get a feeling of its experimental limitations. He grasped the underlying physics and had the best memory I know of. Everybody's different problems became clear to him. He could always see how far any particular experiment would go. When you couldn't carry it any farther, you could count on him to understand and to be thinking about the next thing you might want to try."

With Robert Serber and two other students, Oppenheimer studied the impact of a high-energy proton upon the atom's Coulomb barrier, the protective skin around the nucleus. They discovered that after penetration the proton decayed into a neutron and two recently found particles, a positron and a neutrino. Experimentalists of the Thirties knew Oppenheimer best for a discovery called the Oppenheimer-Phillips process. With Melba Phillips, another student, he worked out where the neutron goes when a deuterium ion containing it strikes a target atom. At 2.2 million volts, he computed, the neutron would go through the Coulomb barrier and the proton would bounce off. Thus the deuterium ions, torn apart, would transmute the target element into a heavier isotope of itself. The process worked much more effectively than bombardment with manufactured neutrons. It became the basic method for production of heavier isotopes, especially Phosphorus 32, the staple for treatment of leukemia and other deep cancers.

For Oppenheimer, contributions of this sort to experimental

physics were at most a side interest undertaken primarily because of his friendship with Lawrence. "Quite a guy," Oppenheimer called him. "Between us was always the distance of different temperaments. But even so, we were very close." The attack on the nucleus held little appeal for Oppenheimer in comparison with particle or wave mechanics. "I never found nuclear physics so beautiful," he said.

He liked cosmic rays. He and a student named John Carlson used quantum theory to trace the effect of their striking the earth's atmosphere. Each extreme high-energy gamma ray from outer space, they discovered, must fragment into pairs of electrons and positrons and an additional ray that would repeat the process up to a million times. He drew the conclusion that an unknown particle, which has since been labeled the *meson*, must be present at the beginning of the impact. This theory of cascades or multiplicative showers, shining bright in his mind's eye, was a glimpse of austere beauty that brought him his happiest hours of 1936.

Late in the year something—death probably—terminated the love he had felt to be a great part of his life since his Cambridge days. His world, never so complete as other people's, shrank to physics, his career, and his students.

In physics his thoughts turned to the thermonuclear reactions which had just at that time been postulated to give heat to the sun. What would happen to a star, he wondered, when its thermonuclear life ran out? Eventually complex equations from relativity theory gave him the answer. The star would redden and contract into a heavy nuclear core smaller than the smallest stone. An observer standing upon it would see it fall in upon itself in a single day. In the mathematics of collapsing suns he passed his most nearly cheerful hours of 1937.

As for his career, it demanded no special attention. Though slower and quieter than Lawrence's, his promotions at Berkeley had now brought him near the academic top. He never tested his ability to precipitate a crisis by digging up a job offer elsewhere. To Birge he always said he meant to stay at Berkeley for good. At Pasadena a friend, Richard Tolman, removed a thorn by becoming dean in place of Millikan, now semiretired. As a matter of course, the pick of the country's National Research Fellows came to study under him at Berkeley.

In late spring they migrated south with him for a month or two at Pasadena. Most of them imitated him slavishly, even to a stiff, straddle-footed walk he had. Their arrival in Pasadena was a harbinger of summer. "Here comes the mother hen and all the little chickens," a mathematician there used to observe, checking the calendar to see if they were on schedule.

Study with Oppenheimer was nationally recognized as the way to highest distinction in theoretical physics. At present most of the country's best in the field were taught either by him or by those he had taught. But when Oppenheimer looked at them without the insulation and egotism of a man in love, he discovered they were not happy.

Oppenheimer read no newspapers, subscribed to no popular magazines, and owned no radio. He depended on friends like Lawrence to post him on what was going on in the world. One day in the spring of 1930, he and Lawrence had walked all the way to Oakland. While they were exploring the waterfront, Lawrence had told him of the stock-market crash in 1929. Oppenheimer had not heard of it before. He did not know what it meant—Ahimsa, the Hindu concept of doing no hurt, was so far his only social consciousness—but as the years went by, he found out from his students. They asked him to find them professional employment, and in the face of country-wide retrenchment he often failed, even when he exerted all his prestige. They could not get jobs to support them while in training. He made a will leaving his inherited capital, which brought him in about ten thousand a year, to a Berkeley scholarship fund. They preached radicalism to him. He explored the world of the deprived, finding it as new as Lawrence found the world of great wealth into which his path was currently diverging.

Oppenheimer's guide among the shadows was Jean Tatlock, immaculate and severely tailored, a slim, dark, pretty girl with honest, searching eyes. In her mid-twenties, she was studying for a doctor's degree in psychology. She knew everyone on the Berkeley left fringe. At the start of 1937 Oppenheimer occasionally broke his concentration on collapsing suns by letting her lead him to Spanish War Relief bazaars. Shortly afterward they began to be seen often together at campus lectures and concerts. She had a card saying she was a member of the Communist Party, but he did not think she was much of a Communist. Her motives were mixed and tortured.

Her father, Professor John Tatlock (Episcopalian, Harvard '96, medieval literature, Chaucer concordance), held opposite political views from hers. "I must go pick up my fascist husband and radical daughter," her mother once said when leaving an afternoon party. Tatlock did not care for Jews. Jean formed the same on-again, off-again connection with Oppenheimer that she had with Communism. Sometimes they were engaged to be married, sometimes not. An idealist, rebel, and Electra, she had a darkness in her to which he could not speak as he had to that in his kleptomaniac first student. Long afterward when F.B.I. and Military Intelligence reports on her were read out at Oppenheimer's security hearing, Tatlock's only observable reaction at Berkeley was anger at the publicity, for which he seemed to hold Oppenheimer in some way responsible.

Oppenheimer in 1937 joined a Consumers' Union and an American Committee for Democracy and Intellectual Freedom. With Joel Hildebrand, chemistry chairman after Lewis, he helped organize an Alameda County Teachers' Union. In such groups he discovered a new pleasure which most people take for granted. He learned he could slough off the inhuman standard of communication drilled into him by Pauli and Ehrenfest and relax in loose fuzzy talk or, as he put it, companionship.

The glibbest and handsomest radical talker he met was a young French instructor, Haakon Chevalier. A remarkably gifted linguist and a brilliant translator, Chevalier had ambitions to write a novel. He could cite some awesome precedents; most of that starving decade's art had polarized around the radical left. "The cathedrals were fighting for us all against the demon," observed André Malraux in *L'Espoir*, one of the great literary monuments of the time. A style would be born, said Malraux, from the hope in the faces of marching men—"They will have in common with the painter that underground communion which used to be Christianity and is now revolution." Chevalier translated *L'Espoir* and took Oppenheimer to meet Malraux, who had come to this country on a lecture tour.

Oppenheimer subscribed to the Communist *People's World* because in an odd, unexpected way it taught him to read about ordinary current events. It was not until later that he learned to read *Newsweek* and *Time*. Jean Tatlock encouraged his concern for the Spanish Republic, then fighting the curtain-raiser of World War II. Through a Communist doctor in the university Medical School, Oppenheimer began contributing about a hundred dollars a month to the republican armed forces.

His brother Frank, then getting a doctor's in physics at Pasadena, brought him further Communist connections. About this time, Frank learned of the Depression from an angry, hard-up college-girl waitress. Infantile and direct, he married her, clipped and mailed an application from a magazine, and got back a pale-green card bearing the hammer and sickle and saying he was a member of the Communist Party. Carelessly he put the card in his shirt pocket and forgot it; the laundry returned it in a little cellophane envelope. He invited Oppenheimer and a geneticist named Calvin Bridges to a party meeting at his home in Pasadena. Oppenheimer squirmed with embarrassment; the members, white and Negro, devoted themselves to talk about how to get Negroes admitted to the city swimming pool. Oppenheimer thought this was hopeless; he picked up a sense of guilt but went to no more meetings.

Oppenheimer never became a Communist. His students did at about the same rate as mathematics students, which was higher than that of students in experimental physics. Birge worried about them, but not because of their politics. "New York Jews flocked out here to him and some were not as nice as he was," said Birge. "Lawrence and I were very concerned to have people here who were nice people as well as good students."

Lawrence was connected with the problem because, as the Radiation Laboratory began to dwarf the Physics Department, Birge fell into the habit of checking with him on departmental hires and promotions. He said he found Lawrence's judgment good. They laid down two rules. The first, against inbreeding, stopped Berkeley from hiring its own Ph.D.'s from 1934 until 1940, when one of Lawrence's, August Helmholtz, was put on the faculty. With this they kept out Oppenheimer's graduate students. The second was a congeniality rule directed against what they called bohemians. These turned out to include practically all Oppenheimer's postdoctoral National Research Fellows. Berkeley suffered in consequence. Robert Serber, for example, was an intellectual equal of McMillan's. Had he been given faculty standing like McMillan's in those hard years, the collaboration between the two, already fruitful, would probably have produced even more significant research. "Lawrence didn't like bohemians," said Birge.

When Lawrence cursed bohemians, he was more likely than Birge to have in mind their habits rather than their descent. But in the late Thirties he hired a personnel manager for the Radiation Laboratory, George Everson, who preached a tireless crusade against the Communist-New Deal government. "I regarded him as a bad influence," said a staff member. "He crept in gradually and made himself more and more noticeable. I suppose there was need for anybody at all with managerial experience. He was a man of some means. Lawrence's greatest weakness was a conviction that success and status always meant something."

Young scientists come to outstanding university laboratories to finish their training, then seek permanent faculty employment elsewhere. Staffs turn over about once every four or five years. Lawrence's laboratory, being the country's most famous, had drawn in the largest number of experimentalists, and his private fund enabled him to hold them longer than the two to four years provided by the stingy fellowships and assistantships of that decade. But he could provide faculty appointments only to a selected few. His prestige made it easy for the rest to get on the faculties of other universities, to which cyclotrons were becoming almost as necessary as football stadiums.

Livingood, Sloan, and many research fellows and graduate students left in 1938. Hardly anyone remained from the early Thirties but Thornton and Cooksey. Cooksey functioned more and more as a one-way telephone, Lawrence to the staff members. Thornton arranged them into crews and assigned them the hours they could use the cyclotrons. His influence was sobering. "People get the idea scientists are a bunch of screwballs," Thornton used to say. "That's a lot of baloney." On visits to Berkeley, Brady, who had left in 1932, was struck by Lawrence's increasing remoteness from the newer men. "I got the impression he didn't talk to Thornton and the others about his personal feelings the way he had to me."

Lawrence's task of building took him progressively farther away from the Laboratory's day-to-day life. Flashes of the old informality appeared. Martin Kamen heard him hotly shut up a new man who had thought to strike the right note by ridiculing the New Deal. Nevertheless Lawrence and the Laboratory were changing. "I think the rose glow faded in 1938," said a research fellow.

Lawrence believed it was character rather than intelligence that had made him director of the country's most famous laboratory with hundreds of scientist-employees. "I've got fellows with better minds than I have, and they're better physicists," he said.

In the fading glow two besides McMillan stood out strongest in their own light. First was Emilio Segré, the most famous product of Enrico Fermi's Italian school of physics. In the mid-Thirties Segré had conformed to the usual practice of foreign scientists visiting this country by making a tour of Lawrence's laboratory. The cyclotron was in operation. Segré looked at the meters and allowed his jaw to drop in almost insulting astonishment (his teacher Fermi liked to ridicule big-machine physics). "My God, the thing works!" he said.

McMillan and Thornton had just installed a 37-inch vacuum chamber to replace Livingston's original 27-inch, which lay discarded in a corner. The old chamber had a molybdenum lip, where the ion-beam came out. Segré borrowed the lip and took it back with him to the University of Palermo. In it he discovered element 43, technetium, the first of a set of brand-new elements that cannot exist in nature and must be created by man (the radioactives hitherto discovered had all been isotopes of known elements). In 1959 Segré was to receive a Nobel prize.

"Segré was abrupt and outspoken, but fundamentally a nice guy and a hell of a good citizen," said a chemist, Sam Weissman, who worked with him afterward. Deciding the best he could do for Mussolini's Italy was leave it, Segré in 1938 came back to this country for good and joined the Radiation Laboratory staff. His relation with Lawrence is an extreme example of the change that had set in. "To me Lawrence showed the great virtue of leaving me strictly alone in my work," Segré said.

The other most interesting later accession to the Laboratory was Luis Alvarez, recruited by Birge in 1936. Despite his name, Alvarez was an ash-blond whom visiting Scandinavians mistook for an Icelander. Unlike Segré, he imitated Lawrence by planning new apparatus on the biggest scale, driving construction crews of junior physicists pitilessly and showing himself off to the Berkeley public in a big red open car. "Ambitious" is the usual word with which his fellow physicists characterize him. In the late Thirties he used the cyclotron to produce tritium, the unstable second heavy isotope of hydrogen.

Among the multitude of visitors to the Radiation Laboratory in 1938 was Eugene Wigner, sophisticated and enigmatic, destined to be one of the towering figures behind the creation of the atomic bomb. Such men had a sort of mutual understanding that, when alone with Lawrence, they would not talk the kind of physics they talked among themselves. "Lawrence to me was a very impressive man, a magnificent specimen in every sense, but limited," said Edward Teller. Hans Bethe said, "Lawrence was a tremendous influence on the development of physics, good in that he made people conscious of big accelerators. His enthusiasm for this one instrument of research was marvelous. So was the way he could make big foundations and government agencies give him money. He was not so much interested in the results of research—he left that to others—and in this sense he was not even a good physicist."

Consequently Wigner came prepared to discuss what he considered the next most important subject after physics, but here too he had a sense of being separated from Lawrence as by a pane of glass. "Lawrence invited me to address a colloquium and be a guest at his house," said Wigner. "We talked about the threat of war. He expressed concern, but with an ease and detachment of manner that seemed almost to belie his words."

An urbane Englishman, Wilfrid Mann, had just completed two years as research fellow at the Radiation Laboratory and returned to London to become lecturer at the Imperial College of Science and Technology. Mann was then preparing the most readable writing ever done on the cyclotron, a monograph and an article in *Nature*, England's top science magazine. Lawrence kept in close touch with him. On October 14, 1938, he reported to Mann on developments at the Laboratory and on his view of the Munich Agreement:

DEAR WILFRID: . . . You have been having a very anxious time recently, but let us hope the war clouds have passed and that we have ahead of us *at least a decade* of peace. I don't think it absurd to believe it is possible that we have seen a turning point in history, that henceforth international disputes of great powers will be settled by peaceful negotiations and not by war.

Professor [Maxwell] Ellis [of the University of London] was here recently and happened to come on a day we were treating cancer patients with neutrons. . . . Professor Ellis was much impressed and said that as a result of his day here he has completely reversed his stand as regards building a medical cyclotron in London. He said that he had been rather opposed to the project but now feels that certainly it should go ahead without delay, and I believe he wrote to his London colleagues accordingly. . . .

I do hope that the war scare is over and that you are now busily engaged in normal academic pursuits. . . . Cordially, ERNEST

The cyclotron referred to here as being used in medical treatments was the thirty-seven-inch. The sixty-inch was still under construction in the Crocker building. Even so, Lawrence was beginning to dream of a still larger one.

"Each step of the game was to be a leap upward," meditated staff member Martin Kamen. "The concept had become ingrained in Lawrence long before I got there in 1937. Once it had, I think life was easier for him. He just had to make his cyclotrons keep growing and growing and never stop."

So far, as Lawrence had told Cottrell in 1932, money had been his only limitation. Now he encountered another. It came from the theoretical physicists, who live in a world which seems to ignore both common sense and the evidence of the senses. The annoyance these men inflicted upon Lawrence was weird enough to be worthy of them.

How massive is a moving ion, they asked each other, then agreed that its mass would depend upon its speed. According to the theory of relativity, anything that moves increases in mass relative to anything else that does not have the same movement. This meant that the faster the particles in a cyclotron went around, the more they grew in mass. Of course, the cyclotron grew too, because one might as well say it was spinning round the particles, and so were the physicists who operated it. The trouble was that the magnetic field did not also grow. So there must come some point in the acceleration when the field could not keep on swinging the particles properly around. Obviously this must come before they reached the speed of light, for then they would each have infinite mass and be as hard to swing as the universe.

At Cornell, Bethe had Livingston's cyclotron to play with and a knack for solving incredibly complex problems. He and a young postdoctoral student from Brooklyn named Morris Rose worked out the mathematics of this one. They established the relativistic limit to the speed of particles in a cyclotron. It was a speed far less than Lawrence's dreams.

The mathematics in the published Bethe and Rose papers made them hard to wade through. They might possibly have gone unread except by other theoretical physicists. Chadwick, Lawrence's *bête noire* in England, chose to make this difficult. He restated the limitations in words that should have been clear enough to anybody at all who needed to know what a cyclotron could do:

At first sight it seems that exceedingly high energies might be reached. . . . However, a serious difficulty . . . arises from the relativity increase of mass of a particle with its speed. . . . The particle will not keep in step with the electrical oscillations, that is, there will not be resonance. One could try to adjust the magnetic field so that it increases gradually [outward] . . . but this introduces another defect [defocusing], which may result in complete loss of the beam. It may prove possible to find a suitable device to overcome these troubles, but at the present moment it seems that limits are set to the energies which it is feasible to reach, about 10 million volts for protons, 15 million volts for deuterons and alpha particles.

Chadwick said "feasible," not "possible." By increasing the electric push—putting more and more voltage on the Dees—one could get less and less increase of speed. How much water this sieve would hold is an interesting question that physicists like to argue about, but no opinion of physicists today on the practical limits of energy that Lawrence could have obtained would have pleased Lawrence much more than Chadwick's. The largest machine of this kind in 1960 was at the Nobel Institute in Stockholm. Even with the advantage of technology developed by then, its maximum practicable energy was 22 million volts for protons.

Chadwick's article appeared in *Nature*. Afterward Mann took the curse off with his own *Nature* article, in which he accepted Chadwick's strictures but pointed out the wide use of cyclotrons and concluded with a tribute to Lawrence's imagination and experimental skill. "I am unspeakably grateful," Lawrence wrote to Mann in characteristic words on March 14, 1939, and continued as follows:

I got quite a kick out of the last paragraph, being as it is such a fine compliment from such a valued friend. It is quite all right to mention that we have begun clinical therapy with neutron rays. . . .

As regards the question of the theoretical limit on the maximum producible energies of ions imposed by the relativity condition, I think it well to emphasize the practical remoteness of this kind of limitation in view of the fact that the voltage can be increased many-fold over what has been used up to the present time. For example, on the medical cyclotron we are expecting to operate at about a quarter of a million volts in the dees, and we are already yearning for a larger magnet which would make it possible to produce one hundred million volt alpha particles. On such a larger outfit, we would use a voltage on the dees somewhere between one-half million and a million.

Everything is moving along well here. The [sixty-inch] medical cyclotron is nearing completion, and it is possible that in another week we will be able to turn on the radio-frequency power.

During the summer of 1939, Lawrence brought the sixty-inch into operation and accelerated deuterium ions to an energy of 19 million volts. "It is quite thrilling to see the beam extending out a meter and a half into the air," he said.

The outbreak of war in Europe took Lawrence by surprise. "It affected us here much more than you might think," he wrote Mann on October 16. "It affected us so much that work in the laboratory was almost brought to a halt. Now we are resuming almost normal activities."

For Lawrence, as he explained to Mann, the term "normal activities" could have only one meaning. "I have been swamped with many things, including plans for a new cyclotron. Believe it or not, we are seriously preparing for a 2,000-ton installation designed for the energy range above 100 million volts. We haven't the money yet for this big undertaking, but we have some prospects in this direction."

To promote financial support, Lawrence toured the country giving lectures. "He told how he would need as much steel as it took to build a good-sized freighter, and more power than was used by the entire city of Berkeley," said Inglis, who heard him address the American Physical Society. "Physicists just didn't think that big in those days."

For use in his lectures Lawrence had an artist make a picture of the projected machine shooting out an awesome beam of ions a hundred and forty feet into the air. He gave the artist detailed directions so as to show every feature of the new design. It looked like the old ones, only much bigger. He made a hundred million volts his slogan. "I've looked at some of his old correspondence, and it's always a hundred million volts," said McMillan many years later.

Superficially the proposed new cyclotron seemed a routine next step forward. Actually it was nothing of the sort. Chadwick had cautiously given himself an out by saying that some new device might be found to overcome the relativistic limitation. Lawrence's design shows that he had no such thing in mind. Consequently, Chadwick's statement of the limitation remained as unanswerable as Loeb's objection had been before Livingston discovered focusing.

When ions were accelerated to energies much beyond ten or fifteen million volts, said Chadwick, they would outgrow the cyclotron's control. They would grow too massive to be swung effectively round by any magnetic field, too massive to be pushed along effectively in the delicate rhythm of resonance by any electric field. Lawrence's answer with respect to the magnetic field was a magnet with thirty-seven hundred tons of steel and three hundred tons of copper windings. With respect to the electric field, his plans were similarly large. A million volts, he had said in 1930, was too high a differential to set up in the parts of a machine; to avoid the insulation problem, his invention would impart this atom-smashing energy only to the moving ions themselves. Now, to impart a hundred million volts of energy to the ions, he meant to make the apparatus itself contain over a million volts. Naturally the charged parts of the apparatus would have to be heavy, set wide apart, and expansively insulated from each other.

Most physicists who helped draw up the design now comment on it with a mysterious little chuckle. Alexander Langsdorf (research associate from Washington University in St. Louis): "The plan was to set up nearly two million volts potential between the Dees. They would have sparked and fused. Difficult. [*Mysterious little chuckle.*] But if anyone could do it, Lawrence could." McMillan said: "We were planning to go ahead with floods of radio-frequency power to reach the voltage. And perhaps we would have. [*Mysterious little chuckle.*] Who knows?"

Those who admired Lawrence most and those who admired him least comment most straightforwardly. "Sixty million volts would have been the maximum," says Thornton, one of the former, very liberal with his maximum. 'Megalomania," says one of the latter.

In a sense, therefore, Lawrence's fund drive for a hundred-million-volt cyclotron amounted to a battle with the theoretical physicists. On his side he had passion and energy, many allies among the statesmen of science, and a great laboratory. For those moments when even the boldest spirit is assailed by doubt, he had Cooksey at hand to comfort and reassure him.

In November of 1939 an event occurred that further strengthened his position. Word came that Lawrence had been awarded a Nobel prize for invention and development of the cyclotron.

How much the Swedish Academy knew of Livingston's work cannot be determined .Whether they mentioned his name in their deliberations is a secret that will not be revealed in this century. Secret also is the roster of the American scientists whom they consulted. The chances are that it included Lawrence's allies in the fund drive. One of these was the president of Washington's Carnegie Institution, Vannevar Bush, a smiling, quaintly homespun New England-Yankee engineer. There were also two college presidents, Conant of Harvard and Karl Compton of Massachusetts Institute of Technology, a man whom everybody liked. Even more valuable to Lawrence was Compton's brother Arthur, whom Lawrence had known well since his year at Chicago.

Arthur Compton had taken Millikan's place as America's best-known native physicist next to Lawrence. Like Millikan and Coolidge, Arthur Compton belonged to a special American type of scientist who makes a good deal of his Protestant-rural-pious background. His benevolence was a little ostentatious, his ambition a little insensitive. He was what other scientists call an operator, an influential man in the organizations and quasi-governmental fringes of science. Lawrence was fortunate in having his support.

When the Nobel award was announced on November 9, work in the Radiation Laboratory stopped. Following a plan made in advance, the staff carried Lawrence off to Dibiasi's restaurant. Birge did not approve of the red wine—he called it liquor—with which they meant to celebrate. Consequently, Lawrence did not invite him, but he made other plans for Birge in connection with the honor.

Until then no one had ever received the science or literature award except from the hands of the King of Sweden in Stockholm. Lawrence did not want to go there. Ostensibly he feared the dangers of wartime ocean travel. Actually he feared to lose the month which the trip would then have taken away from his fund-raising campaign. He made an unprecedented arrangement to have the award presented to him at Berkeley by the Swedish consul general. The date for the ceremony was fixed for February 29, 1940.

Ten years before, President Sproul had upset normal university procedures in order to keep Lawrence from leaving. He had done so, he said, on the chance that in ten years Lawrence might become one of America's most important scientists. Thrilled and justified by the coincidence of the date, he agreed to preside. One worry clouded his joy. Hitherto no faculty member of a state university had ever been so honored. Everyone who got within striking distance of the prize, said Sproul, had been hired away beforehand by some private university that could afford to pay a vastly greater salary.

When the threat to Sproul's peace of mind materialized, however, it came from an unexpected but highly appropriate quarter. The University of Texas offered to make Lawrence vice-president, give him freedom to spend his time any way he liked, and pay him a salary of $25,000 a year. Though outside contributions by now averaged twenty times as much, this was equal to the sum which

California budgeted for the entire Radiation Laboratory. Faculty members who heard of the offer spoke of it as enormous.

"But Texas has no reputation whatever in physics," Birge anxiously reminded Lawrence.

Lawrence looked into the offer. The Texas Board of Regents, then trying to oust their president on charges of intellectualism, needed to counteract the bad publicity. "I discovered all they want me for is advertising purposes," Lawrence told Birge after a discreet period of waiting.

Lawrence had no stomach for Texas and no intent to leave California, but some of the administration were allowed to think he might. "We pray this may never happen," said Sproul, who deserves a good deal of sympathy. Lawrence was spurring him to an abnormal effort in expecting him to get state funds to help pay for the hundred-million-volt cyclotron.

In these years Lawrence's health was always good, but in mid-February he caught a slight cold. On Tuesday, February 27, he stayed in bed resting up for the Nobel ceremony on Thursday. The Radiation Laboratory kept on working. Of the discoveries pouring from it in these years, one made on this Tuesday may serve as an example. Kamen and Samuel Ruben, a young chemist, discovered and identified Carbon 14. This is the most important of the peaceful isotopes. Its most spectacular use has been carbon-dating, by which one can tell the age of any ancient object made of such things as wood and leather. More fundamental is its value as the most widely useful tracer in all sorts of biological studies.

On this Tuesday, Kamen and Ruben felt fairly sure they had pinned it down. They gathered up their records and drove out to Lawrence's house to report. Molly showed them up to his bedroom. Lawrence's face lit up when they told him. "Great!" he said. He looked at the records, jumped out of bed, and paced the floor. "This is terrific! Can I get it to the newspapers?"

Kamen and Ruben had expected to put in much more work before publishing. They looked at each other nervously. "I guess so," one said, and the other nodded weakly. Lawrence went happily back to bed and the two found their own way out.

On the stairs they stopped and looked at each other again. "Gee, I don't know," said Ruben. "I have a wife and two kids. One way or another, this may be the biggest thing in my career as a scientist. What if it's wrong?"

Ruben need not have worried about his career. It was to end two years later when he died of poison-gas experiments at a government arsenal laboratory. But neither on this point nor on the authenticity of their discovery could Kamen reassure him. They hurried back to the laboratory to do what checking they could before Lawrence unleashed the publicity.

On February 29 Wheeler Hall auditorium was packed with San Francisco notables, university dignitaries, faculty members, and reporters. The Swedish consul general must have been puzzled by the cross-talk in two short speeches by Sproul and Lawrence. Sproul opened the ceremonies by pleading with Lawrence not to leave California. Lawrence closed them by replying that the hundred-million-volt cyclotron was not properly a technical or scientific problem, but a money problem for college presidents.

The principal address came in the middle. It was by Birge. With many details he recounted the development of the cyclotron. To obtain information he had conferred at length with Lawrence beforehand. Later he was irritated to find that Lawrence had given him the wrong date, 1930 instead of 1929, for Lawrence's first conception of the circular-resonance principle.

Birge repeated this error, but it was not the most striking one in his talk. He described Lawrence's work on the glass prototype model prior to the historic demonstration at the National Academy meeting in September of 1930. "Actual resonance effects were obtained," he said. He did not mention Livingston's contribution to focusing. Birge's speech came to be regarded as the most official source material on the history of the cyclotron. Its statements and omissions established a legend that denied Livingston's share. Lawrence, who listened approvingly and spoke later, said the whole Laboratory was being honored, and he made no reference to Livingston.

Lawrence never looked back except to victories. Birge did look back, and his reflections give a clue as to why he accepted Lawrence's unsound data. Birge thought of the day when Lawrence had asked him to tell him if he ever became swell-headed. To Birge it seemed very long ago. "By the time Lawrence got the Nobel prize," he said, "I wouldn't have dared to tell him anything."

Lawrence finished the speechmaking by asking for gifts to his fund drive. Kamen and Ruben waited in the audience for him to turn the limelight upon them. Birge rose and held back the departing crowd. "Now I have an important bit of news to announce," he said, and the reporters began taking notes again. "A new discovery has just been made in the Radiation Laboratory. . . ."

Lawrence estimated an initial cost of about two cents a volt for each of his planned hundred million. He obtained promises of money from Sproul and the Regents, from Cottrell and the Research Foundation, from Loomis personally, and from other wealthy patrons whom Loomis could influence. The total was not quite half enough, and some of the promises were contingent on Lawrence's raising the other half.

For this he turned to the financial heart of America's scientific establishment, the Rockefeller Foundation. In March he finally completed all the formalities which an application to it required. The Trustees announced that early in April they would hold a session to decide. Lawrence had no certainty what the decision would be. He felt the session was crucial.

Obviously there was the danger they might consult some theoretical physicist who had read Bethe, or some other physicist who had read Chadwick; they might even take it into their heads to read Chadwick themselves. In that case they would learn that Lawrence's project for a hundred million volts was no more practicable than a time machine. Lawrence kept in close touch with his four chief allies, Bush, Conant, and the two Comptons. Karl gave up a long-planned vacation to attend the Trustees' session and urge Lawrence's cause.

The Trustees voted Lawrence $1,150,000. When it was certain that he would get the money, the four met triumphantly with him in the Radiation Laboratory. Cooksey took a photograph of these statesmen of science laughing together as though laughing to scorn the un-American idea of brooks too broad for leaping.

4

ELEVENTH HOUR

By the will of God, says Segré, the fission of uranium remained unknown until 1938. In Rome in 1934 he and Fermi had had the discovery in their hands. In a famous experiment they had bombarded uranium with slow neutrons. An obscure paper came out of Germany shortly afterward reviewing their work. "It said that fission was observed," Segré meditates. "Fermi and I read it and we still didn't discover fission. The whole story of our failure is a mystery to me. I keep thinking of a passage from Dante: 'O crucified Jove, do you turn your just eyes away from us or is there here prepared a purpose secret and beyond our comprehension?' "

What stirs Segré is the consequence if they had not failed. Italy was Fascist in 1934. Developing the atomic bomb and deciding what to do with it would logically have become a problem for Germany rather than the United States.

Late in 1938 Otto Hahn, a modest little chemist at Kaiser Wilhelm Institute in Berlin, risked the wrath of the Ministry of Science. He sent a letter to an old friend, poor faded frightened Lise Meitner, then a Jewish refugee in Sweden. The two were great scientists as well as gallant souls. In his letter Hahn told her that he had identified barium in uranium subjected to a repetition of Fermi's experiment. Thus he enabled her at the beginning of 1939 to announce to the world the theory of fission.

The uranium atom, she said, when hit by a neutron splits into lighter atoms with a loss in mass and an enormous release in en-

ergy. Her nephew, Otto Frisch, made immediate historic contributions to the development of the theory. Physicists everywhere
immediately wondered how many new neutrons were also released by each fission. If there were enough of them, then released
neutrons might split other uranium atoms in a multiplying chain
reaction. The result could be heat for power, as in a steam engine,
or a terrible new explosive for bombs.

All this, as a possibility, was clear to physicists in this country
by the spring of 1939. On March 16, Fermi, who was then at
Columbia, took the train to Washington to warn the military.
("Yes, it would make a better story if he rode the day coach, and
maybe he did, but I don't know," says Segré.) Fermi had an appointment to see Admiral Stanford C. Hooper, technical director
for Naval Operations. Perhaps because of a thick Italian accent
which Fermi was trying to get rid of, the interview yielded little
result.* By late summer, published experimental data from French,
British and American laboratories indicated there probably would
be a chain reaction. Fission weapons and fission motors worked their
way into sensational newspaper stories and then into comic strips.

The first chief of state to take official notice was Roosevelt. He
had an amiable, gifted, and very fluent economic adviser named
Alexander Sachs, whom refugee physicists in this country made
their emissary. On October 11, 1939, Sachs went to the White
House with a letter bearing Einstein's signature. No one knew
whether the Germans were even then preparing to add nuclear
weapons to their war machine. Sachs talked and talked until
Roosevelt's face lit with comprehension. "Alex, what you are after
is to see they don't blow us up," he interposed, damming the flow
with a gesture.

Research projects needed by the Federal government were
undertaken by the Bureau of Standards. Roosevelt made its director
chairman of a Uranium Committee authorized to draw funds
from the Army and Navy. This was a bold move. "Roosevelt went
into it baldheaded with the reckless courage that characterized
him," said Lewis Strauss, a more laconic adviser to Presidents.

Thus the problem of the bomb came to the United States. We

* Details of Fermi's mission to the Navy are given in the beautifully written
Atoms in the Family by Laura Fermi (University of Chicago Press, 1954),
pages 162-165.

seemed to be taking it in our stride, but the appearance was deceptive.

It was six months later, in April of 1940, that the meeting of America's science statesmen took place in Lawrence's laboratory. After reviewing their triumphant strategy for the Rockefeller grant, they talked about the work of the Uranium Committee. Out of respect for the Germans, refugee physicists had persuaded their American and British colleagues to a policy of secrecy on fission research. It did not prevent such men as Lawrence and Arthur Compton from learning anything they wanted to about the Committee's work, but it seemed to give such knowledge a jealously parochial flavor.

Lawrence told Compton that so far as he knew, the Uranium Committee was not making much progress. If it had been, he said, he believed he would have heard of it. Compton agreed. He thought the secrecy policy a mistake and judged Sachs's mission to Roosevelt to be worse than a failure. All this, he said, gave the impression that the fission project was in hand when it was not.

With respect to the Uranium Committee, Compton emphasized that many of its consultants were refugees from Central Europe. They were used to taking directions from a head of government and did not realize that in this country power in scientific matters sprang from a different source. Foundations, he said, were capable of giving far more money to research at its initial stage than government could, and he believed the fission project should have made use of these.

On this last point there was an obvious comparison that Compton refrained from making. At least one of the Uranium Committee's consultants was an unquestioned genius—Fermi, then at Columbia. Smoothly and skillfully he was evaluating the potentialities for a chain reaction of uranium fissioning in a graphite pile. Almost as significant were theoretical studies being conducted by Wigner at Princeton. Materials and equipment that the universities could not supply were to be paid for by the Uranium Committee. Though Roosevelt had set no limit on the funds it could draw, it had requested a 1939–1940 budget of only $6,000. This figure stands in eloquent contrast with the Rockefeller grant to Lawrence for his unfeasible hundred-million-volt cyclotron.

In addition to Fermi, Wigner, and Teller, the Uranium Committee had another consultant, whom Compton probably had most in mind when he spoke of foreign backgrounds. Leo Szilard, also at Columbia, had ghostwritten the famous letter signed by Einstein and thus given the first effective push that set the government moving toward the bomb. But Szilard seemed to assume that a single remote, arbitrary fiat was all that physicists needed to turn them into willing secret tools of the state. By this mistake he earned much ill will. Inside the American republic physicists were a smaller republic. They had their own instruments, such as the National Academy and the National Research Council, for defining values and distributing awards. The prizes they strove for were publication, grants from foundations and university research boards, and government subsidies. Szilard ignored the emotions and politics engendered in the working of this system. Compton, who had a favorable image, was strongly aware that Szilard did not.

What Compton had to say could be summed up to the effect that the project was in the wrong hands. Knowledge and power were separated in a typically American schizophrenia. Lawrence was correct in doubting that the Uranium Committee had got anywhere. The exotic brilliance of its consultants was not enough.

The chairman, Lyman Briggs, from the Bureau of Standards, could not see what was wrong. He was a tweedy, amiable man with a shy smile and a habit of fingering an empty tobacco pipe. Proudest of his possessions was a tiny cube of uranium which he liked to keep on his desk and show to insiders. They remembered it well. One of them was Samuel Allison, then at the University of Chicago. "Briggs used to say, 'I want a *whole pound* of this,' " Allison recalled. "Lawrence would have said he wanted forty tons and got it."

With the problem of the bomb this country was fumbling helplessly. Lawrence told Compton that he would look into it. But he had more to lose than any other American scientist from the shift in the nation's mind toward destruction. All his energy and enthusiasm were focused on the new cyclotron. To house it he planned an eight-sided structure on a hill overlooking the Berkeley campus. The first step was to dig a hole for the core of the big magnet so that it could be planted under the foundations. Into these details he plunged happily. He could not believe that a time must come to stop building.

A physicist from Princeton, Henry Smyth, future author of the celebrated Smyth Report (the official history of the bomb), visited Berkeley in the spring of 1940. "I vividly remember," said Smyth, "that nobody in physics there except Oppenheimer and Segré had any interest in the war in Europe or any conception of how it was going to affect their lives. This came as a great shock to me. It wasn't just a matter of their being on the West Coast; at Cal Tech [California Institute of Technology] I found a totally different atmosphere."

Appropriately, Lawrence's laboratory was then creating the most hateful and damnable substance yet made by human hands. At the announcement of fission the staff felt a wave of purely scientific excitement. Several members used the cyclotron's neutron beam against uranium to repeat and confirm the original Fermi-Hahn experiments. McMillan was curious about both the number of radioactive products and the energy released in their formation. He investigated in the irritatingly simple way that marks most really original work. His material was a smear of uranium oxide inside a stack of cigarette papers. After irradiating this, he found a radioactive product in the smear with a half-life of about two days. Since none had exploded into the stack of cigarette papers, it had not been created by fission. Chemically it was like uranium, but it gave off radiations that showed it was not uranium.

In the nineteenth century, everyone had known with absolute certainty that matter consisted of 92 elements. Chemists had arranged these in a periodic table with the heaviest, uranium, numbered 92, at the bottom of the list. For ten years before 1940, physicists had speculated that there might be other heavier elements beyond uranium. Now McMillan was able to establish the existence of element 93. In the outer darkness beyond Uranus rolls the planet Neptune. McMillan called his find *neptunium*.

Uranium, the heaviest element known until then, had proved fissionable in a chain reaction productive of enormous energy. An obvious speculation was that elements heavier still would be similarly fissionable. Neptunium decayed too fast to be in itself of practical use as a producer of fission energy; the most exciting thing about it was what it became when its two-day half-life was over. Farther into the darkness McMillan glimpsed element 94. He could not tell much about it, except that it seemed long-lived and that it fissioned violently. He called it *plutonium* and published a note on his work in the *Physical Review*. For this he got a Nobel prize.

Lawrence at once began to get a series of sharp reminders that there was a world war going. First, the British Embassy sent an attaché to call on him. Similar work had been going on in England, said the attaché. Nothing had been published, but even the two names, *neptunium* and *plutonium*, had been independently invented there. Everything about them was under British security. Chadwick in particular was concerned and shocked at the disclosure. Through the Embassy, the attaché went on, Chadwick wished to appeal to Lawrence to stop his laboratory staff from giving away secrets to the Germans.

Next, the National Academy formed a committee to censor the scientific journals. One of the first papers they decided to hold back was by physicist Louis Turner of Princeton. McMillan's work of discovery, though incomplete, was enough to show that plutonium was produced in a mass of naturally fissioning uranium. Physicists by now knew that only one uranium atom in a hundred, the rare isotope 235, underwent fission. Such an atom could not be separated by chemical means from the other inert atoms; plutonium, being a distinct chemical element, had the advantage that it could be. As for its fission properties, physicists assumed they would be about the same as those of uranium 235. Turner proposed that plutonium be manufactured in Fermi's reactor pile for use in atomic bombs. Many physicists had the thought about the same time Turner did. The Academy's act of censorship was therefore pointless, except as it gave the proposal a sort of negative official endorsement.

Finally in the summer of 1940 the Uranium Committee turned its attention to Lawrence. Its members asked him to devote his laboratory to plutonium research. They "urged" him, says the Smyth Report. The way this word stands out in the dry, impersonal style suggests they felt helpless and frustrated at Lawrence's attitude.

These intrusions on Lawrence were signs of a new relationship that the nation was establishing with its scientists. At Lawrence's conference on the Rockefeller grant, the most infectious laugh had been Vannevar Bush's. Shrewd and winning, Bush had less science than Arthur Compton, but more intuition about people. At this time Roosevelt lifted him into a place in history. Ostensibly he only made him chairman of another of the proliferating committees—the National Defense Research Committee. But hardly any research is wholly unconnected with Defense. In fact Roosevelt gave Bush carte blanche to apply money and organization to American science. "I was czar," said Bush.

The Uranium Committee became one of Bush's problems, but not the most pressing. Instead of urging Lawrence into it, Bush found an easier way to mobilize him. This was through Alfred Loomis, still another of the April conferees.

Just before the Battle of Britain, Loomis made a tour of English laboratories and found radar their chief concern. They needed extreme short-wave types for night-interception planes and antiaircraft guns. Though the problem had nothing to do with nuclear physics, Loomis engaged Lawrence's interest on his return. English physicists came over to confer with them, and they decided to ask Bush to set up a radar laboratory at the Massachusetts Institute of Technology. Bush was still feeling his way with Yankee caution toward the floodgates of the Treasury. Loomis offered to supply most of the money to get the laboratory started, and Lawrence most of the physicists.

By this time Lawrence's disciples were superintending about forty cyclotrons throughout the country. He got in touch with these young men and persuaded as many as he could to go to Boston. In addition he stripped his own laboratory. Among those he sent off were Alvarez and his former W.P.A. genius-designer. Thus, at last, Lawrence showed the war was coming home to him. But to those he enlisted he argued it was a matter of helping civilization and a friendly ally; to him the United States, like the big cyclotron, still stood safely apart. "We all got interested just to save the British," says his ex-student Ernest Lyman. "Nobody expected the United States would be in the war."

With respect to plutonium, Chadwick's warning and the Uranium Committee's urging had made little impression on Lawrence. He had no idea, he said later, that McMillan's work would lead to the bomb. He put it to McMillan as a duty to quit and go to the Boston radar laboratory. Under the enchantment of Lawrence's personality, McMillan did so just when he was beginning to guess at the properties that made his name for the new element so sinisterly and unexpectedly appropriate.

McMillan left Berkeley on November 1, 1940. He and Lawrence glowed with patriotic self-sacrifice, but other physicists throughout the world were appalled. Once again the British Embassy sent its attaché to call. The message was friendlier than before, but equally sharp. Cockcroft, the attaché told Lawrence, was now heading research into the transuranium elements in England, and he wished to take this unusual means of asking Lawrence to keep it going at the Radiation Laboratory.

Lawrence gave in. His favorite chemist at Berkeley was a young instructor named Glenn Seaborg, who had taken his physics from Lawrence and married Lawrence's secretary. Lawrence made Seaborg head of a team of chemists to carry on McMillan's work. To help with the physics he assigned them his top remaining talent, Segré. These men accomplished the actual discovery (that is, isolation and identification) of plutonium.

How reluctantly Lawrence shifted his laboratory from peace to war is indicated in his annual report to Cottrell's Research Foundation. A considerable amount of work had been undertaken for Bush's committee, he said, but he did not put this first. "The outstanding event this year has been the beginning of the construction of the great cyclotron, designed to attack the domain of energies in the atom above 100 million volts."

No one at Berkeley saw more clearly than Oppenheimer the relativistic limitation that stood in the way of this dream. Physicists called him merciless, because of his way of bringing physics discussions directly to the point and then seeming to lapse into bored reverie. "He did not suffer fools gladly," says Bethe, expressing a common view of physicists that would have astonished many a groping social reformer at Berkeley; for most human error Oppenheimer had large tolerance, but for unsound physics very little.

Consequently, for him in particular Lawrence's latest enthusiasm was a trial. Bethe, who had defined the limitation in the first place, was becoming a good friend of both men. His own tact was adequate, but he doubts how well Oppenheimer's stood up under more continual strain. "Robert could make people feel they were fools," said Bethe. "He made me, but I didn't mind. Lawrence did. The two disagreed while they both were still at Berkeley. I think Robert would give Lawrence a feeling he didn't know physics, and since that is what cyclotrons are for, Lawrence didn't like it."

Since Lawrence had begun to move out into the great world in 1938, the two men had seen each other less often. When together they had spent most of their time talking physics. The hundred-million-volt cyclotron made this a ticklish subject, but they found other ground in which their friendship survived.

Though he had no direct involvement like Lawrence's, Oppenheimer could not help thinking of physics in terms of its contribution to national defense. "Ever since the discovery of nuclear fission, the possibility of powerful explosives based on it had been much in my mind, as it had in that of many other physicists," he wrote in 1954. "We had some understanding of what this might do for us in the war, and how much it might change the course of history." The Nazi persecutions had aroused in Oppenheimer a smoldering fury, and he worried about the spread of the war. Toward the end of 1940 Lawrence began to share both this feeling and Oppenheimer's view of the importance of the bomb. At the same time Oppenheimer began to shed the left-wing enthusiasms that had made much of his thinking alien to Lawrence. At the house of Haakon Chevalier, then a French professor, he heard a Communist Party official defend the Nazi-Soviet pact and found himself listening with stark disbelief. He kept on contributing to Spanish War Relief, though wearily, and did not close his door to radical friends. But he began to withdraw from the drab social life of the extreme left and to become merely a New Deal Democrat of advanced views. He had lost his Communist mentor. Each time when on the verge of a formal engagement to him, Jean Tatlock had shown signs of melancholia and withdrawal so marked as to suggest mental illness. "She needed a psychiatrist," said Sam Weissman, then a fledgling chemist at the Radiation Laboratory. In the early spring of 1939, she made a definite break with Oppenheimer and stopped seeing him.

As usual, when Oppenheimer went south to teach in June of 1939, he spent a good deal of time with Lauritsen and Tolman. At their houses he met an attractive young couple, the Richard Harrisons, whom they talked about enthusiastically. Harrison was a crisp energetic Britisher in his mid-thirties with a medical degree from Oxford. He wanted to practice in California and was qualifying for a state license by interning at Huntington Memorial Hospital. His wife Katherine, whom everyone called Kitty, was a slim, dark girl like Jean Tatlock. Harrison planned to specialize in radiology. Kitty had just that month got a degree in biology from the University of Pennsylvania and come west to join him. It would have been hard to find a brighter, healthier pair with a more promising future.

When Oppenheimer came to know them better, however, he found Kitty was not looking forward much to the solid bourgeois satisfaction of being a doctor's wife. Instead she was dazed. Like Jean Tatlock, she had been a restless searcher, but never a timid one. As for Harrison, she hardly knew him. Behind her lay a transfiguration and grief from which she was only now gradually awakening.

Joe Dallet, her first true love, was dead, and in a way she believed she had killed him. "Would it be interesting to you to meet a Communist?" asked friends planning a New Year's Eve party for her in 1933. She was then a Wisconsin co-ed on vacation in Pittsburgh, daughter of a comfortable middle-class steel-works engineer. Offbeat, unbusinesslike people appealed to her. As a young girl she had eloped with a talented musician, then got an annulment when she discovered he lived by drugs and perversion. Yes, she said, it would be interesting.

Dallet offered her his heart, a five-dollar-a-month apartment in a warehouse, and an unpaid job as office girl at the Youngstown Communist Party headquarters. After finishing her semester at Wisconsin, she came to Youngstown in February and married him.

Communism had little attraction for her except as an altruistic-looking passion of Dallet's. The more she saw of it the less she liked it, but to please him she joined the party and paid dues of ten cents a week. After two years she told him she could not stand the party meetings and the poverty and the mimeograph machine in the office any longer. That made him unhappy, she explained long afterward to an inquisitive Atomic Energy Board, because they still cared for each other. But he agreed she could not go on that way, and in June of 1936 she left him to join her parents, who were then living in England.

Six months later, she wrote him that she would like to come back. He answered that he was glad, but that he had signed up to fight with the Republican army in Spain. She spent ten days with him in Paris while he was on his way there. She begged him to find her something to do that would let her stay with him. A few months later, he wrote that he had found her a job in Albacete. She went to Paris to wait while a frontier crossing was arranged for her, but there a friend of his named Steve Nelson met her and told her he had been killed in action.

To her it seemed he had died for love. She wanted to go on to Spain anyhow, but Nelson said it was impossible and advised her to finish college. She came back to the United States, wandered about restlessly for a while, then settled down to study at the University of Pennsylvania. In December of 1938 she married Harrison. He moved to Pasadena in February, and in June after finishing her course she joined him.

Like her, Oppenheimer had a sense of bereavement. Jean had not gone far to make him forget that a great part of his life had ended in 1936. He told Kitty about it. In the fall of 1940 after knowing him for two summers, Kitty went to Virginia City, Nevada, to establish the fiction of legal residence. Six weeks later he took leave from his classes at Berkeley. On November 1 she divorced Harrison and married him.

This was on a Friday. The following Monday Oppenheimer arrived at Berkeley late in the afternoon and took Kitty directly to Lawrence's house. Molly had prepared supper for them. The Journal Club met that evening. Oppenheimer arranged to attend with Lawrence and leave Kitty with Molly.

Next day was the Presidential election. At this stage in his career, Lawrence was exposed to sharply antagonistic political opinions. Marriage had intensified everything about Oppenheimer, including his new political awareness. During the supper he sang the praises of the Democratic party and the New Deal. Lawrence looked undecided. While they walked from the house across the campus, Oppenheimer electioneered continuously. At the door of LeConte, Lawrence made up his mind. "O. K., I'll vote for Roosevelt," he said.

Any end to one of Berkeley's most eligible and inveterate bachelorhoods would have raised a flutter. There was no blinking the fact that about this one there were special circumstances. Lawrence's cheerfully catholic hospitality and Molly's unfailing thoughtfulness as a hostess helped break the ice. Kitty too showed energy and skill in managing the social duties required of her by her husband's career. But most of the women who had married Berkeley physicists felt that she never quite shared their wifely ambitions or talked their language. Because of what they called their crush on Oppenheimer, they were quick to notice her reserve.

For Communism she had long had a quiet distaste. The frequency with which Oppenheimer was seen at Spanish War Relief rallies and other left-wing affairs continued to diminish. On the other hand, her distaste did not extend to Communists. With Oppenheimer's students, several of whom were in this category, she established cordial relations, and also with at least one reputed Communist on the faculty—Chevalier.

She did not give up her friends. In 1941 she learned that Steve Nelson, who had kept her from breaking down in Paris, was in the neighborhood. He had some vague position with the California Communist Party organization. She invited him to her house. He brought his family, and she and Oppenheimer held a picnic for them in the yard. They talked not about Communism but about his memories of Dallet and the war in Spain.

In physics, Oppenheimer's thoughts turned away from collapsing suns and back to the serenity of cosmic rays. Having traced the showers of electrons and positrons back to a creation from mesons in the upper air, he wondered about the mesons' history. Quantum mechanics indicated a startling initial impact in which time itself was altered. His calculations of the energy involved kept coming out infinite. Finally there began to glimmer in his mind the thought that the particles first reaching the earth from space must be many times more massive than mesons. What they were was a puzzle that he and other physicists could not unravel until after the war, but the succession of questions they raised proved absorbing. He was happy.

The total effect of his situation and Lawrence's was to draw them together throughout 1940. Showing a little less candor, perhaps, than a scientist should, Oppenheimer managed to avoid going on record about the hundred-million-volt cyclotron. Lawrence's fourth child, Robert Don Lawrence, was born on January 2, 1941. Physicists believe he was named for the two of their number whom Lawrence cared for most, Oppenheimer and Cooksey.

Meanwhile, the Uranium Committee continued on its slow and frugal course. It asked Allison to test beryllium as a chain-reaction moderator instead of graphite. He surveyed the country and located a stack of beryllium plates about a foot high at the Anheuser-Busch Company in St. Louis. The brewery officials wanted $120 rent for them. True to the Committee's indoctrination, Allison first haggled, then anxiously wired Briggs in Washington for permission to commit the money.

Bush fretted at the lack of progress. In May he had the National Academy assign a board of its strongest leaders, including Lawrence, Coolidge, and Arthur Compton, to investigate. Their first report spoke of developing motors, radiological poisons, and bombs in that futile order. Perhaps the most important thing about the report was Lawrence's name as co-author on the title page. In helping to make it, Lawrence took a step toward reluctant acceptance of the changed demands on him. Bush asked the board to continue its investigations.

New York was then the center of the Uranium Committee's projects. Lawrence looked them over. They were of two kinds: those that made use of unseparated uranium and those that concentrated on separating out the rare isotope 235. In examining each, Lawrence encountered surprises.

At Columbia University, Fermi was leading the first toward development of a chain-reacting pile. With regard to this work the Uranium Committee adopted a baffling attitude. They valued it as a tremendous scientific achievement, a potential source of motive and electric power, and a basis of theoretical studies of fission. How they were going to use it to make a bomb they did not explain to anyone. Preposterous as it sounds, they kept quiet even to the National Academy investigators, on whose verdict their corporate existence depended.

In March, in Lawrence's laboratory Seaborg and Segré had isolated and analyzed the first pure samples of plutonium. The only way it could be manufactured in usable quantities was in a chain-reacting pile. For a nation facing the threat of war, the manufacture of plutonium was what piles were for.

Lawrence talked with Fermi and ascertained that these connections were obvious, though officially ignored. He pointed them out first to his fellow investigators from the Academy and then to the

Uranium Committee. Its members must have known all this already; nevertheless, in dead-pan style the Smyth Report credits Lawrence with initiating the reactor program's defense purpose in a letter of July 11, 1941.

Because of its speed of fission from fast neutrons, isotope 235 of uranium was the only other thing besides plutonium with a chain reaction fast enough for use in a bomb. It constitutes seven tenths of one per cent of ordinary uranium. Separating it out was the second of the Uranium Committee's basic defense projects.

Lawrence spent a long time going over this work, most of which was also being done at Columbia. At Pupin Hall he met John Dunning, the man who worked hardest at this project and was perhaps the only one who had his heart in it. Dunning was a hairy, bull-necked young engineer-physicist from Nebraska. The Uranium Committee carefully kept him out of their china shop. He had a strange, dreary tale to tell Lawrence.

At the very first news of fission, Dunning had bet Bethe ten dollars that only the isotope 235 was responsible. Alfred Nier, a University of Minnesota physicist, who had discovered this isotope four years earlier, supplied Dunning with a microscopic sample. With this, Dunning confirmed his deductions and won his bet. For the preceding two and a half years he had devoted all his immense energy to finding out how the isotope could be separated on a worthwhile scale.

No way looked easy. Nearly all had to begin with a poisonous, corrosive gas, uranium hexafluoride. Nier had used a mass spectrometer, an apparatus a little like a cyclotron. To produce a gram of uranium 235, Nier would have had to operate his mass spectrometer continuously for centuries.

"Frankly, I dropped Al Nier's approach because I wanted to see a power industry develop," says Dunning. "In April of 1939 I sent Al a diagram of an atomic power plant and wrote to him that this industry was going to be a big thing."

Dunning decided to try diffusing the gas through a series of porous walls. Each time the lighter U-235 would go through a little faster and become a little more concentrated. Though everything to do with the gas was hateful and exasperating, Dunning made preliminary studies that showed the method could work and that it offered promise of big yields.

Late in 1939 he began making pilot tests. They were expensive, and he looked across the campus to where Fermi was happily piling up $3,200 worth of uranium, graphite, and cadmium, the largesse of the Uranium Committee. "That was a fair amount of support," he says with a wistfulness that constitutes the Committee's damnation. "I couldn't get any at all, but I worked on it in the university labs anyhow. I just bought equipment myself—I had some money of my own—and by April of 1940 I was convinced that gas diffusion was *the* method. It seemed so large and vital a thing to me. I estimated that about five thousand successive separations would be needed, and a plant costing three or four million dollars."

The Uranium Committee still refused him money; but it acknowledged the importance of separation by adding to its membership Harold C. Urey of Columbia, the nation's authority on isotopes and the discoverer of deuterium. Urey was a prickly, irritable man. He did not like the gas-diffusion method, and he liked Dunning even less. Believing that centrifuges would offer the key to separation, he obtained a Navy grant to study them.

Dunning now had on the Columbia campus two renowned scientists connected with the project, Fermi and Urey, to whom he could appeal for patronage. "They never would transmit my pleas," he recalls. " 'Interesting, young man,' they'd say, 'but we can never separate U-235 on the scale needed. Don't worry, young man, the reactor piles will take care of the fission problem. We've already got things under control!' "

Even so, in the summer of 1941 the Uranium Committee decided that diffusion and centrifuges were the two best methods of isotope production. It was only an abstract scientific decision of a sort in which they were seldom wrong. With respect to money, they held to their familiar incredible policy. "I still hadn't got a nickel from the government to support our separation work," says Dunning.

He tried going directly to Bush, the czar of science, and to Conant, whom Bush had made his special adviser on atomic matters. "Nobody can build a plant with five thousand separation stages," they told him, "and besides Fermi has things under control."

This was Dunning's situation when Lawrence came to see him at Columbia's Pupin Laboratory that summer. Dunning told Lawrence his woes. Lawrence listened thoughtfully. The two men were in some ways much alike. Both were youthful-looking Westerners, passionate builders, experimentalists whom their colleagues had tried to damn with the epithet "engineer."

If the conversation had occurred six months later, Lawrence could have decided the fate of Dunning's project with a word. But he was not yet what he became, the carrier of the country's nuclear burdens. By now, however, he was a troubled patriot, aware that in these times a hundred-million-volt cyclotron was not enough. He had money which did not need to be squeezed out of the Uranium Committee. Dunning's tale affected him in a logical but surprising way. "You know, my guys are gone off, McMillan and Alvarez and so on," he said. "I think I ought to do something on my own. Magnetism and ion beams are in my field. I've got some big magnets on the hill at Berkeley and my new cyclotron's not built yet. By God, I'm going to try this mass spectrograph thing of Nier's."

Dunning had expected almost any other response. "Why not pitch in with the diffusion method?" he asked.

"Oh, you have those five thousand separation stages," Lawrence answered with absent-minded brutality. "That's millions and millions of holes and a single one the size of a pin will ruin you. I'll try the electromagnetic way."

The Uranium Committee's position was that large-scale electromagnetic separation was impossible. For Lawrence this was not much of a handicap, since they gave nothing to the gas-diffusion method or the centrifuge method, the two they liked. Lawrence went back to Berkeley to study the problem.

Since being created in 1939, the Uranium Committee saw its feeble, dithering, unsavory reputation continually deteriorate. Bush had twice shaken it up by adding new members. The effect was to increase the authority of Briggs, the chairman, the only founding figure to survive. From him incoming new scientists innocently picked up the official attitude toward spending money. Bush in 1940 had made large sums available to the Committee, but Briggs winced with distaste at brash people like Dunning who talked in terms of three or four million. What he liked was to listen to a proposal and say, "This is very important. Let's give this man a thousand dollars."

On the subject of bombs the Committee also tended to wince with distaste. This was the reason Lawrence had to make the first official statement that plutonium manufacture was the defense purpose of the reactor program. The Committee's science was good, but its secretiveness was pathological. New members were not reminded that Roosevelt had created it to study blowing people up. "This aspect was played down," said Allison, who was raised to membership in this summer of 1941. "We weren't told. I thought we were making a power source for submarines."

This attitude was established by the second of the Committee's twin souls, Gregory Breit, a thin-skinned, anxiety-ridden theoretical physicist from the University of Wisconsin. In April of 1940 he had been officially appointed Coordinator of Rapid Rupture. Studies of potential weapons were his province, and his principal concern seemed to be that they should be kept quiet. Talk of bombs aroused in him the same uneasiness that Briggs felt about spending money. "Breit was tightly wound," says another of the new members, "and I think he held up early progress. He was a one-man secrecy drive."

In August, while getting over the shock which Lawrence had caused them, Briggs and Breit received another. Starting later than the Americans, the British had used a brilliant refugee group to move purposefully toward the bomb for the last two years. In many ways they were far ahead. Reaching the end of their war-strained industrial resources, they gathered up their data in a report and offered it to the Uranium Committee.

A prominent British physicist, Marcus Oliphant, brought it across the Atlantic. As spokesman for a nation whose investment of about £50,000 outweighed America's so far, he was in a position to talk bluntly. "He came to a meeting of the Uranium Committee and said 'bomb' in no uncertain terms," Allison recalled. "He told us we must concentrate every effort on the bomb and said we had no right to work on power plants or anything but the bomb. The bomb would cost twenty-five million dollars, he said, and Britain didn't have the money or the manpower, so it was up to us."

Though he had not personally done much bomb research, Oliphant was a forceful speaker and for that reason had been chosen to present the official British position here. Since he could not change the Uranium Committee's leadership, strong words to them did not do much to accomplish his purpose. "You could hardly have picked two people less likely to push anything than Briggs and Breit," said Smyth, who had become a member of the Committee about a month before. Oliphant needed to try somewhere else.

During Christmas of 1937, he had become a friend of Lawrence, who had entertained him at Berkeley, helped him locate steel for a cyclotron, and pronounced him a very fine fellow. "They were as alike as two peas in a pod," said physicist James Tuck. "Oliphant knew a little more physics than Lawrence, but both were energetic developers, essentially promoters."

Oliphant went to Berkeley and repeated to Lawrence what he had said to the Uranium Committee. Seldom has there been a more fateful meeting. About September 1, 1941, as the two promoters talked together, the history of America's atomic project reached a turning point. Lawrence at last saw the full demand that was made upon him by his country. It was the beginning of a new period, in which decisions would bear the stamp of his personality rather than Briggs's or Breit's.

Lawrence telephoned Compton in Chicago and tried to tell him how urgent he felt it was to put an end to the long delays. The outcome of the war, he said, depended on whether Germany or America got the bomb first.

Many scientists had said this before, but never with Lawrence's will and power. His urgency was justified. Many months had been wasted. After the war Szilard estimated the total needless delay in the bomb effort at a year and a half and ascribed most of it to this period just prior to the outbreak of hostilities with Japan. The Uranium Committee could have had all the money it wanted, but it would not ask. It had a specific job, to develop bombs, which it would not work at. Its secretiveness was a paralysis that the physics community saw being inflicted more and more conspicuously on an unhappy few of its members. Time had well come for the nation's most forceful and influential physicist to see what he could do.

The government's organization chart provided that the Uranium Committee should report to Conant, Conant to Bush, and Bush to Roosevelt. The best place to short-circuit the Committee was with Conant. He was to receive an honorary degree along with Lawrence at the University of Chicago's semicentennial celebration the following week. Compton said he would see to it that Lawrence and Conant got together.

On a crisp September night, Compton tells in his book *Atomic Quest*, the three gathered around the fireplace in his house. Mrs. Compton handed round coffee cups and withdrew. Lawrence began to talk. He said bombs could be made of both plutonium and uranium 235. Though his own judgment was against Dunning's choice of the gas-diffusion method, he became Dunning's advocate. Here at least, he said, something real had been done. Dunning had a clear-cut program that needed only money to be realized. Lawrence also urged that the reactor program be set moving toward plutonium production.

Conant's view from above of the Uranium Committee had thoroughly discouraged him. Scientists were needed in other defense preparations, he replied. He said he had advised Bush to kill the project and find the Uranium Committee's physicists something else to work at, such as radar, which was going well.

Lawrence argued, and Compton supported him. Finally Conant looked up from the floor. "Ernest," he said, "you say you are convinced of the importance of these fission bombs. Are you willing to devote the next several years of your life to getting them made?"

Compton says that Lawrence gave a start and that his mouth dropped open. For most other physicists this scene of simple melodrama would have been a challenge to a sacrifice costly only to the taxpayer. Since then, few have been able to help gloating in secret over the dream-money, dream-laboratories, and dream-missions of ultimate dream-importance conferred on them by a frantic government. Lawrence, in contrast, had built solidly for himself during the Depression. Rather than scavenge from the war's burning waste heap, he must throw valuable things upon it. He hesitated.

"If you tell me this is my job," he said to Conant, "I'll do it."

The stages of Lawrence's reluctant commitment were watched with mixed feelings by Oppenheimer. His wife, Kitty, a baby born that August, a new home for them with a magnificent view of the bay, a serene excitement in the study of cosmic rays—these made him happy. On the other hand, many of his colleagues had left to do radar and other defense work. He was alive to the prospect of war. His friend Lauritsen was directing the country's rocket research. He asked Lauritsen if he could help, but Lauritsen did not need him at the time. When the fall semester began, he taught overtime, because so many other teachers were gone.

His brother Frank now became a further tie between himself and Lawrence. The year before, Frank had taught at Leland Stanford and been fired for radical talk. Oppenheimer felt a sharpening of the irritation that Communists in general had begun to inspire in him. During the summer he let Frank stew and worry. For what Oppenheimer judged were three very salutary months, Frank hunted vainly for a new job. Then Oppenheimer asked Lawrence if he could take Frank on at the Radiation Laboratory. "Frank's been in a lot of left-wing activity," he admitted.

Lawrence knew Frank well and was more like him than either was like Oppenheimer. In character the two shared a simplicity sometimes appealing, sometimes frightening. In physics they were both passionate experimenters, disdainful of theory.

Lawrence said he would be glad to have Frank as a Research Associate. "Provided he behaves himself," he stipulated.

Oppenheimer had a talk with his brother. How it went he was obliged to tell over and over again at the 1954 hearings. He had to dredge up not only dialogue but also manner and internal attitude. The printed record of that "damned nonsense," as he termed the hearings, looks like chaos. But from it his memories of the talk can be assembled in lively detail.[1] Frank (so Oppenheimer said he remembered) told him he had withdrawn from the Communist Party in the early spring of 1941.

"Ernest hates political activity, especially left-wing activity," Oppenheimer said. Feeling that his honor was involved, he harshly demanded that Frank promise to leave it alone.

Frank was chastened. "I'll be a good boy," he replied.

The outcome of Lawrence's talk with Compton and Conant in Chicago was that Lawrence should see to the production of bomb materials—uranium and plutonium—and that Compton should look into the problem of actually putting a bomb together. The Uranium Committee was allowed to keep on meeting for a few months longer, but only to rubber-stamp decisions made else-

where. The first of these, between Lawrence and Conant, was to
have Dunning build a pilot gas-diffusion separator on the largest
possible laboratory scale. In October, after waiting two and a half
years, Dunning received his first government money.

Compton tried to find out about the bomb from Breit's subsection
of the Uranium Committee. He could not break their psychological
compulsion to keep the thing a secret. "No help was forthcoming,"
he said. There was no point in manufacturing fissionable material
until one could predict when and with what violence it could be
made to explode. Compton communicated his problem to Lawrence. Since it could not be solved by experiment, Lawrence took it
to Oppenheimer.

Thus at last Lawrence relieved Oppenheimer of a small but
persistent feeling of guilt at making no contribution to the country's defense preparations. "It was not until my first connection
with the rudimentary atomic-energy enterprise," he said, "that I
began to see any way in which I could be of direct use."

In order to prepare an official program that could be submitted
to Roosevelt, Compton called together the Academy investigators
for a final meeting to be held in Boston. Oppenheimer was invited
to attend and answer questions on fast fission, the mathematics of
bomb explosion. He traveled across the country with Lawrence,
listening to him talk of electromagnetic separation and thinking
himself of how the bomb might change the course of history.

For Oppenheimer, the chief result of this meeting was that he
became both Lawrence's and Compton's informal technical adviser. Compton could not do much until Bush could obtain for
him the Presidential go-ahead. Lawrence did not wait. He stopped
over in New York and asked Cottrell's Research Foundation for a
grant of $50,000. Cottrell promptly gave it to him. With this
money he came back to Berkeley, brooding over a decision to sacrifice his smallest cyclotron, the thirty-seven-inch, to get parts
for the world's largest mass spectrograph.

From the beginning he gave his projected machine personality
by endowing it with the name "calutron" (*californiauniversity-
tron*). The calutron bore a haunting resemblance to the cyclotron
from which it was about to spring. First, there was to be a sort of
light bulb filled with the hateful uranium-hexafluoride gas. A
filament and electric field would turn the gas into ions. Through an

aperture these would stream into a big vacuum tank shaped like a single Dee of a cyclotron. There the field of the thirty-seven-inch magnet would bend their course into a rough semicircle. The uranium-235 ions, having less mass and momentum, would move in a tighter arc and could be collected at one pocket, while the worthless heavier ions would drop into another.

Thus Lawrence envisaged the workings of his calutron. As physics goes, no concept could be simpler or more characteristic of him. The drawback was that the biggest magnet working on the biggest ion beam could pull out only an insignificant amount of the uranium 235 needed for a bomb. A real beam that could actually be split and focused might produce an enormous yield. But the stream of ions that would flow into the Dee could be called a beam only by courtesy. The apertures through which the ions would pass would roughly line them up, but no one knew enough about the fundamental theory of ion beams even to make an attempt at focusing. Consequently collection of uranium 235 must always be minute or sloppy; the farther apart one set the two collectors, the smaller and purer would be the two samples.

On these grounds the Uranium Committee had long ago considered and rejected the electromagnetic method except for laboratory studies. For Lawrence, therefore, the situation was typical. He faced it with a burst of renewed energy, seeming to grow younger as he returned to the laboratory after his long excursions into statesmanship and administration.

"The ion-beam separation idea sounded ridiculous," said physicist Carrol Mills, who came to work on it the next year. "Lawrence was youthful, aggressive, personable, and determined to make it succeed. He didn't really give a damn about basic understanding of the work, and he used a backward approach, purely experimental. By ignoring theoretical objections in the field of gaseous-discharge physics, he made many innovations."

About the first week of November of 1941, Lawrence assembled a formidable staff to build the calutron. To help with fundamental planning, he called back Thornton, who had just finished a cyclotron at Washington University. Aebersold and Brobeck took charge of design and engineering. Lawrence made Frank Oppenheimer, who liked to work with his hands, crew chief of the young physicists engaged in actual assembling and testing. The thirty-seven-inch was still kept in the wooden shack which now out of deference to all of Lawrence's new buildings was called the Old Radiation Laboratory. There Lawrence and Frank recharged the atmosphere with the excitement of the early Thirties.

Working like maniacs, the crew finished dismantling the cyclotron and began putting together a calutron on November 24, 1941. By December 1 they had it beginning to show signs of crude operation. Lawrence drove them mercilessly, for he did not know how soon he would be called to Washington to hear Roosevelt's decision, and on that day he wanted something to report.

Bush sent him word to come on December 6. Along with Conant, he and Compton gathered in Bush's office. They did not see Roosevelt, but Bush told them Roosevelt had approved the program submitted after their October meeting. Their orders were to give six months to development, drawing whatever funds they wished from the catch-all Office of Emergency Management. Then in the summer, said Roosevelt, he would make a decision whether the Army should take over the task as a major operation capable of deciding the outcome of war.

Bush and Conant gave Lawrence and Compton free choice about what they wanted to do. Compton kept bomb design. Lawrence by this time had begun to think of himself as a specialist in calutrons. The laboratory reclaimed him. His job, as Conant had laid it out, included all U-235 production. Much to his credit, he divested himself of administrative authority that a lesser man would have clung to. He divided up his kingdom and created two other peers of himself and Compton in the small inner circle of power.

Oliphant had told him that the bomb should be made by the gas-diffusion method. Lawrence felt differently, but he meant to see it tried. He recommended that Urey, who after all was the country's top isotope man, should be made program chief with authority to push this method.

Hindsight has often confirmed the futile Uranium Committee's timid foresight. After the war, the centrifuge was called the cheapest method of separating uranium 235. By this means Oliphant's prediction of bombs for twenty-five million dollars might have been fulfilled. Jesse Beams, a friend of Lawrence and a member of the Uranium Committee since June of 1940, had become the

American authority on extreme high-speed centrifuge separation. He was no administrator. Lawrence recommended that the research director of the Standard Oil consortium, Eger Murphree, be made program chief for engineering with special responsibility for centrifuges and that under him Beams should do the work.

In a quick, casual way men have when they actually want to get things done, these arrangements were suggested and agreed to in Bush's office. Real, as distinguished from formal, authority was to run as follows:

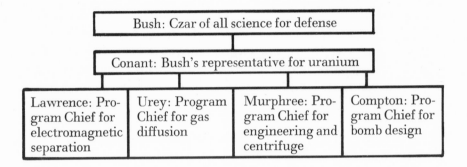

Bush: Czar of all science for defense			
Conant: Bush's representative for uranium			
Lawrence: Program Chief for electromagnetic separation	Urey: Program Chief for gas diffusion	Murphree: Program Chief for engineering and centrifuge	Compton: Program Chief for bomb design

As final evidence of sincerity, they also agreed not to behave like a committee. They decided they would meet once or twice a month for a while but that instead of lobbying for a majority vote, each program chief was to work as hard as he could at whatever he thought most important, whether it was in his program or not. Each one was to confer with Conant at any time he wanted to, and on any subject.

Three details connected with the organizational plan stand out. First, Beams was a silent, unpushing type, and Murphree had begun to show the first signs of failing health. Second, Urey did not care for Dunning, who was doing the bulk of the gas-diffusion work. "He made life miserable for this young engineer," says Dunning. Third, in any group of four program chiefs, Lawrence simply could not help having the most dynamic program. On this day, for example, he thrilled Bush and Conant with an announcement that he could already produce largely purified uranium 235 at the rate of one microgram an hour.

The meeting in Bush's office broke up at noon without any talk of plutonium. This was no oversight. The others were under the influence of Lawrence, and he was still under that of Oliphant. The British had investigated the prospect of getting plutonium from reactors and rejected it as too costly and too slow an operation to be of use in the war. Compton, however, brought it up while having lunch with Conant and Bush at the Cosmos Club. He asked that the development of the chain reaction for plutonium production be added to his program. They demurred a little and then let him have it.

Lawrence did not lunch with them. On that Saturday afternoon, December 6, 1941, there was as yet no military authority that could cripple him by forbidding bomb-project leaders to fly. He went directly to the airport and arrived in Berkeley late that evening, about the time Oppenheimer was coming home bored from a Spanish war-victim-relief rally. On Sunday morning Lawrence hurried to the Old Radiation Laboratory. Characteristically, his announcement of uranium-235 production had inconspicuously used the word "could" rather than "had." At the time he made it, it was still a projection, and he was in furious haste to turn it into reality.

As a matter of course, his staff of physicists also showed up with no quibbles about overtime. "I remember that Sunday," says Aebersold. "We worked all through the day, and that night we ran the first uranium-235 samples on the calutron. They took the form of faint green smudges on the collection box." To Lawrence the sight of them unfolded a vision of vast, strange factories that not even the staff could share. "Extrapolation was Lawrence's outstanding quality," says Aebersold. "He had boundless enthusiasm, and in this he and I were not alike. When I saw the first micrograms of uranium 235, I couldn't envisage, as he could, the miles of electromagnetic separation plants that waited in the future."

When the news of Pearl Harbor came that afternoon, Lawrence did not show much reaction. Several hours later, however, when the calutron had finished its production run, he left the laboratory. It was then surrounded by a fence but guarded only by the campus police. Round and round the fence he walked all night long.

A friend afterward understood him to explain that he did so because he just did not know what might happen. He did not make clear the uncertainty that haunted him, but it brought him a taste for loneliness and darkness. Henceforth when he could he liked to wander about the laboratory grounds late at night. Before a tight system of guards was established in 1942, someone hiding in the dark shot at him. The bullet missed him narrowly. Since he never learned who fired it, the incident remained an ugly irrelevance, meaningful only as it contributed to the tension built up in him by the war.

To George Everson, his reactionary personnel director, he gave orders to make a drive for more staff. He took an active hand himself. During the week after Pearl Harbor, midyear graduating seniors took their final examinations. One of the blithest was a young physics major, Roger Hildebrand, son of Berkeley's chemistry chairman. A restless pacing outside the classroom door disturbed Hildebrand while he finished his last question. "When I went into the hall, Lawrence grabbed me by the shoulder," he says. "It was a most aggressive, physical form of recruiting."

Lawrence marched him to the Crocker Laboratory and took him to the control room of the sixty-inch cyclotron. In Hildebrand the carefree feeling of being through with college courses evaporated fast. "Lawrence told me I was to operate this thing. I was aghast at all the panels of switches and meters. There was a man at the control desk. Lawrence introduced me and left. The man said, 'Hi,' and ignored me. I supposed I was about to get a few years' training, but after twenty minutes of silence the fellow poured out a barrage of instructions for two hours. Then he too walked out, leaving me at the control desk operating the cyclotron."

What Hildebrand was doing was to produce and irradiate artificial transuranic elements for study by Seaborg and Segré. On the afternoon of New Year's Eve, Lawrence judged that Hildebrand had passed his novitiate.

"He came to the control room and took me across the alley to the Old Radiation Laboratory," continues Hildebrand. "Half a dozen people were there under Frank Oppenheimer. Lawrence introduced me to Frank and said I was to work with him. It was the most inspirational experience of my young life.

"They were trying to get a better beam from the calutron, which had just recently been converted from the thirty-seven-inch. No one told me what the process was for, but I learned that if I hadn't figured it out for myself, I'd have been sent back to the other lab the next day.

"Frank and the rest kept intently to their task with an utter disregard of convention and personal comfort. They gave me the feeling that the war was being won in that room. At midnight somebody looked up and said, 'Well, fellows, it's 1942,' and we all went on working."

5
NOCTURNAL CAESARS

For Oppenheimer, Pearl Harbor turned the pages on an old sorrow. To the defeated and scattered Spanish republicans, he had continued to contribute a tithe of his salary through friends in the Communist Party. He and Kitty listened together to the radio as it reported the first war news. "I decided that I had had about enough of the Spanish cause," he said, "and that there were other and more pressing crises in the world."

The bomb project engaged his thoughts in two ways. First, Lawrence drew him into the planning conferences on the calutron. So far as Lawrence would permit him, he brought theoretical physics to bear on the enormous difficulties Lawrence was encountering. To determine the best configuration of the ion beam in the magnetic field, Oppenheimer had a gifted student named David Bohm make a series of calculations that were not very comprehensible to Lawrence's crew of young experimentalists. As a result, however, they found they were able to focus a much bigger beam with Lawrence's thirty-seven-inch magnet. The possibility was opened that a magnet of suitable size might focus more than one beam, and that the yield of separated uranium could be further multiplied.

At the same time, Oppenheimer almost involuntarily kept pondering the questions about fission explosion that he had been asked at the Academy meeting in the fall. Because of the war, these problems could never be solved by trial and error; for him, therefore, they held some of the fascination of purely theoretical physics, and his mind ran on them with increasing excitement. "I began to think more intensively on my own about how to make bombs," he said. "I did some calculations on efficiency, design, probable amounts of material and so on, so that I got into it and knew something about it."

At the beginning of 1942, his role in the bomb project was thus still subordinate and passive. Lawrence and, after him, Compton were the prime movers. Oppenheimer waited until they should tell him what to do. A struggle that took place between them in January had pregnant consequences for him.

The question was where to locate the plutonium-reactor program. By now, on the basis of advice from Oppenheimer and Segré, Lawrence felt that, though big and costly, it might prove the most wholesale process for making bomb material. At Columbia administrative weakness had let rancors grow which dictated that the project should be moved elsewhere. Lawrence wanted it at Berkeley; Compton wanted it at Chicago.

Conant and Bush had given Compton formal authority to decide, but against Lawrence's energy, determination, and prestige, this was not much of a bulwark. Allison, a project leader, watched the drama. "Once I was almost packed to move to California," he said. Since Bush had summoned him to Washington in December, Compton had spent much of his time in train travel from one laboratory to another. Physical strain plus the stress of the impending decision almost broke him down. He backed and filled and on January 15 took to his bed with a fever. Lawrence pursued him into his sickroom. "You'll never get the chain reaction going here," Compton reports him as saying. "The whole tempo of the University of Chicago is too slow."

"None of us except Lawrence realized what could be done with unlimited money," observed Allison. "I think a great deal of credit should go to him for this. But Compton was not far behind. Lawrence set him afire, and once he had, Compton was not afraid of big ideas. He was no mean pusher himself."

Compton steeled his nerves and told Lawrence he was moving the project to Chicago. He bet Lawrence a five-cent cigar—Lawrence smoked, though he did not—that he could have the chain reaction going in 1942. From Bush he drew an authorization to spend about $400,000 at once. This was only the beginning. Allison, who preferred the kind of life he led as a physics teacher, noted wryly how Compton was changing him. "Within a year," he said, "I was ordering a million dollars' worth of material at a time without a qualm."

A day or two after his clash with Compton, Lawrence went back to his calutron. Compton got out of bed and began organizing the installation he had in mind. He code-named it the Metallurgical Laboratory and called Oppenheimer to a conference defining its two programs, plutonium and bomb design.

The Metallurgical Laboratory took shape with quivering anxiety about the German nuclear threat. "I was scared to death," said Allison. The laboratory senior staff was made up largely of refugees with nerves on edge from watching the collapse of nations. Compton did less to calm them than did one of their own number, Fermi, who declared the Germans could not fight a war and build the bomb at the same time. Even so, Fermi had given thought to what country he should escape to next after this one fell. Another leading refugee balked at being fingerprinted. "If the Germans win, they'll use these prints to track us down and kill us all," he protested. He believed the Germans might win; and he could give many reasons for expecting them to have the bomb no later than the end of 1944.*

The most paralyzing anxiety of the new Metallurgical Laboratory, however, did not come from the refugees. At the organizing conference, Oppenheimer spoke on bomb design and had his first encounter with Gregory Breit. The Uranium Committee was by now practically extinct, but Compton had decided to conserve

* Though hurt by loss of refugees, Germany still had a formidable remnant of nuclear physicists. These were headed by the famous Werner Heisenberg, who had publicly urged his fellow scientists to work for Nazi war aims. Through Sweden came rumors that Heisenberg was conducting extensive experiments on the fission process. A refugee named Peter Debye warned American reporters that the Kaiser Wilhelm Institute had shifted its emphasis to uranium research. Production of heavy water for use in reactor piles was known to have been expanded by the Germans in Norway. All this, plus respect for German industrial capacity, aroused strong fear. "In 1941 and 1942," wrote Henry L. Stimson, Secretary of War, "they were believed to be ahead of us." The newest and fullest study of the German nuclear effort is David Irving's *The German Atomic Bomb* (New York: Simon and Schuster, 1968). Interesting also is *Alsos* by Samuel A. Goudsmit (New York: Henry Schuman, 1947), who conducted an official investigation into the German effort for the American government during the war.

what he could from its hoard of knowledge by keeping Breit on as
Coordinator of Rapid Rupture. In April he made Oppenheimer a
consultant of the Metallurgical Laboratory, set him formally
under Breit, and gave him urgent informal instructions to keep
the bomb program advancing. Oppenheimer took tactless delight
in what he called Breit's wonderful title, but when he explored
the situation he had been put in, he found little else to amuse
him.

Breit had two tasks. First, he supervised complex bomb studies
that since 1939 had been farmed out piecemeal to scattered universities. Second, at the Metallurgical Laboratory he held seminars to post the staff on developments of bomb theory that might
guide their plans for plutonium production.

Both tasks were vital. With respect to the first, the holders of
small research contracts were isolated and lonely, cut off from
normal conversation with their faculty colleagues. To work enthusiastically or even intelligently on a compartmentalized detail
of fast fission, each handful of men needed assurance they were
contributing to something useful. Breit was supposed to supply
this, but they did not look forward to seeing him. "Breit was a funny
guy," said a physicist at Columbia. "At that time we had self-im-
posed secrecy, but no real security. Breit made up a list of reports
and articles he felt should be secret. He came through New York
and insisted we hunt up everything on the list that we had in the
laboratory, sign a receipt for each page, and lock them up in a safe.
It took a lot of time. This was typical of his visits. They almost drove
us crazy."

Breit's way with his second task, conducting the seminars, has
also left strong memories. "It was a pity Compton didn't know
enough nuclear physics to get the principles of the bomb over to
us himself," says a junior member of the Metallurgical Laboratory. "Breit was a terrible choice. He was actually capable of
turning a technical problem into a fist fight. When you look back,
you can't feel angry, you just feel a sort of sympathy."

As the second authority after Breit on bomb theory, Oppenheimer struggled drearily. "Breit was always frightened something
would be revealed in the seminars," observed Allison. "Oppenheimer was frightened something would not. I backed Oppenheimer and challenged Breit to cut the censorship. He accused me

of being reckless and hostile to him. I failed. The seminars became uninformative."

Compton, who had become impressed with something firm and bold in Oppenheimer's manner, gave Breit no backing. Breit realized that Oppenheimer stood for the new climate of opinion. He tentatively suggested Oppenheimer visit him on his home grounds at Wisconsin to thresh their difficulties out, and he hinted that Oppenheimer might like to make Wisconsin his base so that they could work closely together. But when the time came to give a definite invitation, Breit simply could not do it. He turned in his resignation to Compton and got completely out of the fission project on June 1, 1942.

Never a man of action, Oppenheimer was thus handed a problem alien to his bent. To some it would have seemed hard to do worse than Breit, and someone had to see that a bomb was ready as soon as there was enough U-235 or plutonium to put in it. Compton asked him to take over Breit's position on a temporary basis. "Although I had no administrative experience and was not an experimental physicist," said Oppenheimer, "I felt sufficiently informed and challenged by the problem to be glad to accept."

At that stage of the atomic project, there was little to work on but theory. Oppenheimer telephoned seven theoretical physicists and asked them to spend part of the summer with him and Serber at Berkeley discussing the bomb. Birge assigned him two dormer rooms at the top of LeConte Hall and had the windows covered with heavy steel netting. A special lock was made with a single key which Birge gave to Oppenheimer. For Birge, Oppenheimer's way with cigarettes brought worrisome thoughts. "In case of fire no one could have got in there," he said.

Inside the netting Oppenheimer handed round to the assembled physicists preliminary studies made by Breit's small contractors and by the British. Everyone agreed that a fission bomb, if it worked, might produce weight for weight several thousand times the blast of T.N.T. They talked of damage from big explosions like that of an ammunition ship at Halifax in 1917.

Next they dealt with elementary aspects of how a fission bomb must look. At the instant before exploding, it would be a uranium or plutonium sphere inside a tight, heavy shell or tamper to reflect back inward the escaping neutrons. These would be produced as in Fermi's projected pile by spontaneous fission, but with the difference that there would be no graphite to slow them down. Before colliding with an atom and thus perhaps producing another fission, the fastest would travel an average distance of ten centimeters. This figure provided a rough, intuitive basis for estimating needed size. Twice a radius of ten centimeters meant a sphere about eight inches thick, less in proportion to the reflecting power of the tamper, more in proportion to inevitable impurities.*

By their calculations, no living creature could ever see such a sphere. It would destroy itself before the eye could deliver an image to the brain. Assembly and detonation must be completed in less than a millionth of a second. Most of the energy would be produced after the sphere and tamper became solid, liquid and gas mixed together as in the primeval chaos.

Consequently, Oppenheimer had to know how much fission would go on when the sphere had reached this state. Bethe, one of the physicists he had summoned, spoke on this hard question. The explosion would begin with a shock wave traveling from the sphere-tamper interface into the tamper and a rarefaction wave from the interface into the sphere, he said with somber poetry. Fluctua-

---

* The ten-centimeter figure came from studies by the British and by Breit's small contractors of what were called neutron cross sections. The *Los Alamos Technical History* (see below, p. 296) describes these cross sections as follows:

"Within the system [*i.e.* the fissioning sphere] a neutron may be absorbed, scattered, or produce fission. The contributions of each process are measured by the corresponding cross sections, or effective target areas presented by the nucleus to an impinging neutron. The total cross section is divided into areas that win, lose or draw (fission, absorb without fission or scatter), these areas corresponding to the relative probabilities of the three processes. If the scattering is not isotropic [*i.e.* in all directions at random], it is also necessary to specify the angular distribution of scattered neutrons. All of these cross sections, moreover, depend upon the nucleus involved and the energy of the incident neutron. Calculation of critical mass and efficiency depends upon all these cross sections, as well as upon the number of neutrons per fission and density of material."

The "elaborateness of the theory involved," says the *Technical History*, made for difficulties of no ordinary kind. The confrontation and solution of these difficulties by Oppenheimer's successive theoretical groups must be taken on trust by laymen as one of the great collective achievements of the human mind. Theoretical physicists in later foreign bomb-development programs were spared from making a comparable effort because they knew in advance that solutions were possible.

tions in density thus caused were not beyond calculation. For the time it took a sphere of minimum size to expand ten centimeters he could roughly estimate the efficiency of the continuing fission process.

This was the first time that a responsible group surveyed the difficulties of making a bomb and laid them out as tasks. Four principal areas of effort became clear: in ordnance, to design a piece of flyable hardware for an available plane; in chemistry, to determine the required purity of materials and the means of getting it; in experimental physics, to work out a method of assembly-detonation; and, above all, in theoretical physics, to measure more exactly the behavior of fission neutrons.

Serber noticed that the conference was going amazingly fast and smoothly. Everybody was contributing something intelligent; nobody was sulking or maundering. Young as he was, Serber had had enough experience to be cynical about meetings, and he found this one was different. He began watching Oppenheimer with puzzled respect.

Edward Teller was another of the physicists at the conference. He had come with a dread associated in his mind with chili peppers. "In 1937 I had had my first contact with Oppenheimer," he said. "It was painful but characteristic. On the evening I was to talk at a Berkeley colloquium, he took me out to a Mexican restaurant for dinner. I didn't have the practice in speaking that I've had since, and I was already a little nervous. The plates were so hot, and the spices were so hot—as you might suspect if you knew Oppenheimer—and his personality was so overpowering, that I lost my voice. I don't know how well I got it back at the colloquium."

Not having seen much of Oppenheimer since then, Teller at the start of the conference watched him with no predisposition to admire. But Teller also noticed that things were going remarkably well. "As chairman, Oppenheimer showed a refined, sure, informal touch," he said. "I don't know how he had acquired this facility for handling people. Those who knew him well were really surprised. I suppose it was the kind of knowledge a politician or administrator has to pick up somewhere."

While he talked and listened, Teller was inwardly gnawed by a special preoccupation. Toward the end of the first week in July he explained it. In doing so he dropped into the smoothly turning wheels of the conference the biggest monkey wrench imaginable. Several weeks before, he said, he and Fermi had lunched together and talked about the heat inside an exploding fission bomb. They had speculated on what one could melt in a fire so much hotter than any yet seen on earth. Going to a large blackboard in Oppenheimer's office, Teller computed the heat buildup. The final figure, he pointed out, was enough to "melt" the Coulomb barrier between light nuclei. More specifically it would fuse deuterium ions into helium. Each pair of deuterium ions thus fused would release about four million volts of energy, five times more than from the same mass of fissioning uranium. Deuterium was cheap and one could wrap as much of it as one liked around a fission bomb. The result, he concluded, would be a superweapon of unlimited power.

The deuterium-deuterium reaction was thoroughly familiar. Lawrence had long ago produced it with the cyclotron during his unhappy efforts to weigh the neutron. Nevertheless, Oppenheimer stared at the blackboard in wild surprise, and the other faces in the room, including Teller's, successively caught the same look. The heat buildup Teller had calculated was enough not only to maintain the deuterium reaction but also another between its reaction products and nitrogen. The nitrogen reaction was part of the solar phoenix, the nuclear-reaction series that keeps the sun hot. By a historic study of this series, Bethe had put to rest the nineteenth-century notion that the universe lives only on heat imparted to it at its creation and therefore is inevitably growing cold. Teller had correctly calculated the heat production of a fission bomb; Oppenheimer saw it, with or without a deuterium wrapper, setting afire the atmosphere of the entire planet, and no one at the conference could prove he was wrong.

Physicists are always exasperated when accused by outsiders of meddling with forces beyond man's puny comprehension. Nevertheless, those in the room were among the world's best, and that is exactly what they felt they had been doing. As soon as it became clear that none of them could refute the implication in Teller's heat study, Oppenheimer suspended the sessions. He decided that Compton ought to know that the program he was directing seemed pointed toward igniting the air and ocean.

A series of long-distance calls turned up the fact that Compton

was vacationing at a lake cottage near Otsego, Michigan. Oppenheimer reached him at the Otsego general merchandise store. In a
distraught voice, Compton later reported to Pearl S. Buck, Oppenheimer spoke to him as follows: "Found something very disturbing—dangerously disturbing. . . . No, not to be mentioned over
the telephone. . . . Yes, we must see each other. . . . Yes, immediately, without an hour's delay."[1]

By this time atomic leaders were forbidden to fly. Compton
gave Oppenheimer directions for getting to Otsego by train and
morning after next met him at the little station. Driving out to a
deserted strip of beach, Compton listened to the story. He decided
that the fission program would have to be abandoned unless Oppenheimer could definitely dispose of the heat question. "Better
to be a slave under the Nazi heel," he summed up, "than to draw
down the final curtain on humanity."

Aside from such wisdom Oppenheimer had little to expect from
his long train trip except that it gave him time to think. He
checked and rechecked Teller's mathematics. The following week
he reconvened the theoretical group. Bethe and the rest had also
done some anxious checking. They confronted each other in one of
the high moments of science history. At such times physicists' faces
seem to shrivel until they become nothing but pairs of eyes, large,
cold, fixed in unnatural contemplation.

Compared with Teller, Oppenheimer had more clarity, less in-
ventiveness. Bethe was something in between. Both surpassed
Teller in mathematics.

They found a mistake in Teller's figures. He had roughly but
correctly calculated heat production in the bomb; he had overlooked certain aspects of heat radiation. Revised calculations by
the whole group made ignition of a deuterium wrapper seem possible but uncertain. How completely they ruled out the possibility of igniting air and water is an interesting question. On this
point Teller, who was there, takes a different view from Compton,
who was not. "We made absolutely certain—I was more deeply
involved in this than anyone else—that no such catastrophe
could occur," Teller says. Compton, on the other hand, told Pearl
Buck that the physicists hemmed and hawed a long time. Then
on his orders, he said, they computed a three-in-a-million chance,
which he felt was low enough to be worth taking.

The discrepancy between the two versions probably arises from the fact that certainty is a state of mind based on not having to depend on someone else's calculations. Allison, who was not there either, sided with Compton. "It was by no means certain," he said. "Earth I never had any questions about. I wasn't quite sure about the nitrogen in the air. I knew the doubts continued still in 1945. At the Metallurgical Laboratory we weren't supposed to tell the younger people. They kept making the discovery for themselves and coming to warn us."

So far as men can who deal with the untried, Oppenheimer's group made certain that the fission bomb would cause no unwanted explosions. Then, moving purposefully under deft control, they evaluated Teller's proposed weapon, which they called the "Super," but which has since become better known as the fusion, the thermonuclear, or the hydrogen bomb.

A fundamental new thought came from one of the youngest conferees—pink-cheeked, soft-spoken Emil Konopinski, a thirty-year-old physicist from Indiana. Since the question was whether the Super would ignite, he asked, why not mix its deuterium with tritium, which had a lower reaction threshold and a higher energy yield? Others objected that to get enough tritium, they would have to irradiate lithium in the reactor piles when and if Fermi and Wigner ever got them going. To do so would vastly curtail the production of plutonium. Even so, said Bethe, tritium could not be ignored in the Super. Some of the deuterium would combine to form it in a secondary reaction, and this might be the deciding factor on whether the primary reaction, once kindled, could be sustained.

For hydrogen-bomb research, guidelines were thus established; they held good for a decade and then broke into the headlines with a curious appearance of being new and controversial. Since such a weapon would have to be built around the outside of a fission bomb, the effect in 1942 was to reemphasize the urgency of the conference's original purpose. As for the fission bomb, Oppenheimer's clear survey of the tasks involved impressed everyone at the conference with a sense of their magnitude. "We first thought it would be a simple thing to figure out this problem, but we soon saw how wrong we were," said Bethe.

No matter how loosely or abruptly the others expressed themselves, they learned to count on the chair to comprehend. "Oppenheimer's great virtue was that he was intelligent," said Teller, not taking into account the queasiness that some of the same physicists had shown under the Uranium Committee and were still to show at places like the Metallurgical Laboratory, where Oppenheimer was not in charge. Inside the conference room Oppenheimer diffused a sort of pain-dispelling glamour. It helped them forget that their calculations were less for the advancement of physics than for the mass incineration of human flesh.

About mid-July the formal conference ended, its members* keyed up by what Oppenheimer called a surer foreknowledge of the potentially world-shattering undertaking ahead. To exploit their entranced enthusiasm, Oppenheimer drew together as many informal studies of bomb theory as he could at Berkeley for the rest of the year. These studies represented one half of his responsibilities. "The other," he said, "was to try to get some sense into the distorted and fragmentary work that was going on in a number of laboratories."

The small contracts were mostly on the experimental side. Since Oppenheimer was a theoretician, Compton asked John Manley to join him in overseeing them. The assignment of authority was vague enough to have given rise to the kind of squabbles plaguing isotope separation at Columbia. But after six frustrating months under Compton, Manley welcomed the chance to work with Oppenheimer. Manley loved physics, had little ambition, and was gifted with a slow-spoken charm. The two made a perfect team.

Together they rode circuit on the small contractors, inspecting and being critically inspected. The stickiest of their visits, to Gregory Breit's home base at the University of Wisconsin, they saved for the last. Here two Van de Graaff accelerators, precise, low-energy competitors of the cyclotron, were being used to study the behavior of neutrons at energies under four hundred thousand volts. The project director, Joseph McKibben, had built the Van de Graaffs while a student of Breit's. McKibben was a square-jawed, blunt young fellow who thought Breit had had a rough deal. "People weren't quite fair to Breit," he said. "He had a lot of irritating, almost traumatic mannerisms, but when the chips were down on a scientific question, he was usually right."

Oppenheimer was prejudiced against the project, and McKib-

* Besides Oppenheimer, Serber, Bethe, Teller and Konopinski, those at the meeting were Felix Bloch, S. P. Frankel, Elred Nelson, and J. H. Van Vleck.

ben was prejudiced against Oppenheimer. At their first serious talk, McKibben studied him unlovingly and noted that he too had irritating mannerisms. "This little Van de Graaff operation doesn't look like much," said Oppenheimer, swallowing nervously and running his fingers through his hair. "It worries me to see good physicists spending their time on it."

McKibben hotly defended his work. Manley interposed that McKibben had a point. At the Van de Graaff's low energy range, said Manley, there was a chance of secondary neutron-fission reactions which had not so far been taken account of in bomb studies. Oppenheimer became interested and, to McKibben's surprise, stopped being nervous.

As the talk went on, McKibben had a sensation of enthusiasm flowing back and forth between him and Oppenheimer, making them both something more than they had been before the conversation began. They laid plans by which the Van de Graaff eventually proved it could indeed fill up an important blank in the knowledge of bomb neutrons. McKibben gave a lingering, regretful thought to Breit, his deposed chief. "Breit was never able to think big enough to delegate responsibility," he concluded. "Oppenheimer did and did it well."

Despite such bright spots, Oppenheimer and Manley found their itinerary progressively discouraging. "We began to notice how very much needed doing and how much the little laboratories suffered from their isolation," said Oppenheimer. "There was supposed to be security; anyway, there was good compartmentalization, and the result was that people did not know what was going on anywhere else. Work was duplicated and there was almost no sense of hope or direction in it. By the fall of 1942, not only the theoretical people but everyone who knew the experimental situation realized that this had to be pulled together."

For several months the problem had increasingly racked Compton's nerves. He backed and filled again as he had done with Lawrence. On the surface, as pushers and promoters, he and Lawrence were much alike, but Compton fell far behind when it came to following through. Compton's jutting jaw, keen eye, bristling black mustache, and crisp manner masked a tendency to vacillation. "Why did he have so much influence?" pondered a young staff member of the Metallurgical Laboratory. "I think it was because he *looked* so much as though he should be an influential scientist." Senior members with more responsibility felt less philosophical. "Compton's decisions were ineffectual," said Manley. "His great mistake was to leave the laboratory to become an administrator. My impression is that he was one of the world's worst."

While Oppenheimer waited for Compton to make up his mind, Lawrence was pushing hard at electromagnetic separation. At Berkeley the only indecisions he tolerated were purely technical, and even for these he lacked patience. "I remember a day when the group I was in got completely stymied," said Carrol Mills. "We tried to solve our problem at a blackboard. Lawrence came in and saw us all staring blankly at a set of equations. His face turned red with anger. 'Get to work,' he ordered."

Lawrence set so fast a pace, the Smyth Report notes dryly, that shrewd guesses had to take the place of adequate research. Security regulations he seems to have valued primarily as a means of stopping time-wasting chatter. "There was a hell of a lot of security for the younger staff members," Mills recollects. "We weren't even supposed to know what element or materials we were working on. I'm sure they still haven't got over the feeling there that they mustn't ask questions. We were supposed to put in sixteen hours a day seven days a week and that was all. Lawrence considered the people in the Radiation Laboratory an extension of his own hands and he didn't feel the need to keep them manicured."

For the young, the roughest leadership can be effective so long as it remains nakedly honest. "Once Lawrence ordered Dennis Gardner and me—Dennis later discovered artificial mesons and died of beryllium poisoning—to build a calutron power source," recalls Roger Hildebrand. "He said we were to get it done in a day and a half. I consider it now a task that should have taken two people several weeks. But we didn't sleep and we improvised and in thirty-six hours we got the power supply going. Lawrence had guessed right about the time. That's where his genius lay—in estimating exactly what was humanly possible. I never knew him to lower a demand. Whenever things went wrong, he'd bawl us out unmercifully, except sometimes when it was very serious. Then he'd just shrug and say nothing. At that time—1942—we all did everything. I remember when I was stacking lead bricks for shielding and Lawrence came and labored beside me a couple of hours. He didn't ask us to do anything he wouldn't."

Despite the fantastic difficulties attendant on the development of the calutron, the basic concept was so simple as to represent patriotism rather than physics. Equally simple, Lawrence's leadership rested on a denial that there are limits to what could be achieved by human effort. The uncanny luck which had hitherto enabled him to keep this belief came to his aid again in the spring of 1942. It took the form of a bitter patriotic sacrifice.

To pull the U-235 out of larger and larger, though still insignificant, beams of ionized uranium-hexafluoride gas, he had so far made use of his thirty-seven-inch magnet. Now he judged he had come to the limit of its power. Unfinished on a slope above the campus he called Cyclotron Hill sat his last giant peacetime machine. Renouncing its promise of a hundred million volts, to him no fantasy, he gave orders for it to be dismantled and converted into a calutron.

Its magnet, far and away the world's largest, had faces fifteen feet wide. Into the big vacuum chamber Oppenheimer's calculations enabled the crew to introduce two ion beams for separation. This calutron Lawrence viewed as his first production prototype and called it Alpha-1. By making appreciable amounts of slimy, bright-green, partially separated U-235, it gave the crew a watchword that measured the state of their morale. "How much gunk?" became the criterion for each day's work.

Alpha-1 turned out enough gunk to look at and analyze but offered little prospect of ever producing enough for a bomb. As a factory prototype it had a vicious weakness. Each of the beams was focused in a field-free region between sets of electrodes of 30,000 and 45,000 volts potential. The whole focusing apparatus, bulky and fragile, stood on insulation outside the vacuum chamber into which it fed. It was always getting out of adjustment. Only a crew of physicists with the knowledge to have invented it could have kept it running.

To get the magnet of Alpha-1, Lawrence had had to undertake the greatest fund drive in the history of American physics. Now in the summer of 1942 he commanded unlimited government dream-money. Casually filling out a requisition form, he ordered another equally gigantic magnet and began constructing Alpha-2. For this he and his staff decided to get rid of an external focusing apparatus. They planned to set up a field-free region inside the vacuum chamber, focus each beam in a straight line, then let it curve as it passed into the isotope-separating magnetic field. Its path took the shape of the letter *J*. Since better use of the magnetic field permitted four beams, Alpha-2 was known as the 4-J unit. Lawrence completed it in December of 1942.

Alpha-2 turned out many times more U-235 than did Alpha-1, though purity was deliberately sacrificed for volume. If one did not count time lost in start-ups and repairs, its production rate of U-235 at 15 per cent pure during its best runs rose as high as a tenth of a gram an hour. But everyone except Lawrence was dismayed at the thought of how many Alpha-2's would be needed to produce enough gunk for the bomb.

Physicists outside of Berkeley took a dim view of the program there and joked about it unkindly. Another electromagnetic process had been invented elsewhere, which in certain purely scientific aspects looked more attractive. It was called the isotron.

In 1940 one of Lawrence's brightest experimentalists, young Robert Wilson, had left Berkeley to teach under Smyth at Princeton. There he and Smyth and a junior crew worked out a brilliant variation on the electromagnetic separation process. By means of radio-frequency oscillators, they were able to create a beam of uranium ions in which the two isotopes traveled in separate bunches. A complexly flickering electric field pulled out only the bunches of U-235. Size for size, such a machine had a potential yield hundreds of times greater than the machines in Berkeley. Everyone assigned to the Princeton project was enthusiastic about it. "Lawrence's calutron simply used raw brute force to pry the beam a little way apart," said one of the crew members, young Leo Lavatelli. "Our method was *elegant*."

In 1942, Wilson and his associates proved that their isotron would work. But by the end of the year it was clear that the United States lacked resources to continue full-scale research on all lines that had been previously developed. Conant and the Uranium Committee announced that the isotron project would be closed down.

Lawrence was program chief not only for the calutron but for all other electromagnetic separation processes. At the start of 1943 Wilson came to Berkeley with the hope of persuading Lawrence to urge a reversal of the decision. Though he had found Lawrence unfeeling about money, Wilson was attached to him and believed he could make him see the isotron's virtues. When Wilson arrived, Berkeley was struggling desperately with the unfinished Alpha-2. Lawrence took him on a tour of the laboratory and gave him the treatment reserved for visiting celebrities.

Comparing the pressures now with those he had known in his own years at Berkeley, Wilson had come prepared to argue with a harassed executive. Instead he found Lawrence sure, relaxed, at ease.

He also found that a large, competent team had made great progress on the engineering problems of incorporating the long-familiar calutron principles into plans for a production plant. By contrast, he had barely established the validity of the isotron's principles. In terms of a practical plant, the isotron was clearly a year or more behind.

Wilson came home to Princeton convinced that the isotron should be abandoned, that its staff should be set free for other bomb duties. Whether the Princeton project could have shortened the war will never be known. "It was never sufficiently tried," says Smyth. One of the most sophisticated of all leading physicists, Wigner, was briefly resting at Princeton from his work with the pile at Chicago. He observed with interest the effect of Lawrence's spell. "Wilson felt no disappointment whatever," he said. "To me it was a wonderful sign of Lawrence's leadership that he could persuade such a man willingly to give up so bright and basic an idea."

A few months earlier in the fall of 1942 the Army had begun preparing to take over the industrial side of the program in accordance with Roosevelt's schedule. Conant and Lawrence and the other program chiefs wanted to decide everything they could for themselves before the Army intruded. Lawrence invited them to meet with him in mid-September at the Bohemian Grove. In this luxurious atmosphere they threshed out the question of what plants to build.

As might be expected, Lawrence's calutron easily got first place in the allotment of funds. Only the impracticable Alpha-1 had by this time been completed, but after a fashion it was running and the other competitive methods were still only possibilities. "I remember President Conant telling me that he was truly thankful for the electromagnetic process, for it would surely work," said Lawrence long afterward. His memory was that the conference voted him 125 million dollars (others remembered the figure as 30 million) to begin building at once the first of a series of vast calutron plants at Oak Ridge, Tennessee.

Favored second and third for the big money about a year later were the plutonium pile and the diffusion process. No one present liked the latter, not even Urey, its program chief. Still they knew that Dunning, a strong though absent voice, would howl unless they kept it on. The centrifuge project was canceled at this meeting. Murphree, its chief, was too sick to stand up for it with the sort of leadership America demanded. "I've always thought the centrifuge method died largely because of the personalities involved," said Smyth. "Murphree's illness kept him from being much of a promoter at the time, whereas Lawrence and Dunning were promoters par excellence."

Having thus decided the fate of unknowing multitudes, Lawrence keyed himself to face the military leader who two days later was to take the surviving programs under his command.

This leader, Colonel Leslie Groves, then had charge of all Army construction, including that snuggest of new military bases, the Pentagon. Since January the nuclear project and its potential plant requirements had demanded increasing amounts of his attention. He loathed it. First, it had not yet shaken off the taint of the Uranium Committee. Second, to him it did not look big; he estimated its total budget for the war would come to hardly more than the money he spent every week. Third, he knew little of physicists and what he knew he did not like. On September 17, 1942, a bad dream came true for him. With a sinking heart he sat in the office of his superior, Major General W. D. Styer, and listened to orders to drop everything else and devote himself to the atom.

At forty-six, Groves was a blunt, shrewd soldier, calculatedly impolitic though not unpolitical. In his revealing khaki shirt and breeches, he looked like an overfed boy. He ate too much. Among the secrets in his office safe was always a box of chocolates which he required a trusted aide to keep replenished. He had a streak of boyish imagination in him which he masked under a harsh, aggressive manner.

Feeling that physicists could best be awed by military rank, he put off meeting them for a few days until a promised promotion to brigadier general came through. Meanwhile, with deepening disgust he studied their plant-construction schedule and decided they had based it on unproven dreams about the three surviving processes. On their nuclear specialty he never hesitated to pronounce judgment. "They had lots of theories," he declared later, "but they didn't know anything. We didn't know, for example, whether plutonium was a gas, solid, or electric."

To physicists a man capable of speaking such stern, authoritative nonsense was not likely to prove a very congenial type. Groves began his scientific contacts with Bush, who in a frightened flutter wrote Conant, "I fear we are in the soup." Moving out into the field, Groves had a depressing conference with Urey in New York and a so-so one with Compton in Chicago. Then he continued west to see Lawrence.

At Berkeley, Lawrence was still struggling to put Alpha-2 together. In the unrealized hope of pilot-modeling an industrial plant, he had organized the most critical work of the Radiation Laboratory around a series of control cubicles like the pulpits of a steel mill. On October 8, 1942, the staff, sick of groping in blind alleys, was flurried by rumor that a real Army general was coming through to inspect them.

Young Hildebrand, whom Lawrence had now aged visibly, was then in charge of taming the hateful caprices of uranium-hexafluoride gas. "One difficulty with the calutron was heating the UF_6," he says. "There's a time lapse in the response of the gas to the ion source. To keep the right adjustment, you have to change the power and the heating. I was trying for a light, quick response.

"When Lawrence led General Groves through the lab, I was down on the floor fiddling with a big gas container. All around it like the stripes on a barber pole I had wrapped calrods. You know, those stainless steel rods with a heating coil inside that they used to have on electric kitchen stoves.

"General Groves turned out to be the kind of man who always wanted to make an intelligent comment when he should have kept his mouth shut. He looked down at me and my big container as if he owned us.

" 'Do you expect to get enough water through those little tubes to do a proper cooling job?' he said.

"I was appalled. My mouth dropped open and I started to protest—'But, General—'

"Lawrence shut me up and towed him off. I watched them walk away along Cubicle Corridor. Lawrence exuded a sort of buoyant confidence. Everything was going very badly, but Lawrence was saying things were never better. Groves believed every word he said."

In Lawrence, Groves had at last met a scientist after his own heart, a man who seemed to regard their common task as a simple one that only needed to be pursued with desperate energy. Rabi, a detached observer by reason of his commitment to radar work, watched the interplay of personalities with disinterested curiosity. Groves was naïve, and sensitive when physicists talked above his head. Lawrence had none of the conceit which caused too many of them to do this. "I think the reason Groves and Lawrence got along so well together," said Rabi, "was that in some fundamental ways they were alike."

For Groves, Lawrence's laboratory stood out as the bright spot in a dingy empire. Elsewhere the atomic project, which the Army had code-named the Manhattan District, was giving him trouble. His authorization had been only to build and run whatever plants the scientists told him to. Here was the rub. They would not tell him. One of the three programs, gas-diffusion separation of U-235, was stalemated by a fight between its chief and his subordinates. Boorish and thin-skinned, Urey had given Groves no satisfaction. "Dr. Urey, who was the head, violently opposed it," Groves recalled later. "He said it couldn't possibly work." Dunning, its only backer, ranked so low on the organization chart that for Groves even to confer with him was doubtful etiquette.

The other program, plutonium, started to slip from Groves's hands as soon as he grasped it firmly. With Compton's approval, he had contracted with the duPont company to construct and operate the plutonium-producing piles. Compton changed his mind and urged cancellation of the contract. The duPont officials wanted out, on the grounds that they had been given the most absurd of the three programs. To show them that this was not so, Groves invited them to appoint duPont scientists to a special committee by which all the programs would be evaluated. Committees had continually proliferated about the fission project, but this one was different.

It descended on Berkeley late in November of 1942. For Lawrence it proved the sorest trial since he had taken up the country's nuclear burdens. Upon it he poured out the intoxicating charm and dynamic leadership that had won over such diverse figures as Conant, Robert Wilson, and Groves. It responded poorly. Its duPont members kept it on the scent of dull facts, not of men. A medical researcher in the biological aspect of the program noted the strain upon Lawrence with a physician's eye. "Ernest was awfully worried," he said. "He felt a terrific pressure on him to make electromagnetic separation go, to sell it to the committee on the basis of his confidence."

The committee recommended support be given first to Urey's program and second to Compton's. As for Lawrence's, the members did not believe it could supply bomb requirements. Consequently, they recommended that only enough of it be retained to produce experimental samples of U-235.

To Groves the blow was as staggering as to Lawrence. Something anarchical and un-American in the thought of transferring support from a leader like Lawrence to a nonleader like Urey made Groves recoil. In his dilemma he rose to a lonely height of leadership.

Next to Lawrence, Dunning in New York watched with keenest suspense. "Groves stood on touchy ground," he said. "The electromagnetic project lacked official government approval. It never did get it." After searching his soul, Groves came to a decision. He confirmed Lawrence's plans to begin building electromagnetic plants at Oak Ridge in February of 1943 at a cost of 125 million dollars. Eventually he spent 544 million on Lawrence's program, far the largest item in the Manhattan District's two-billion-dollar budget.

Thus, Lawrence won the grimmest role that money could buy at the crux of history when physics was impinging negatively on human life. But he had no thought of killing. Birge had at this time been given clearance as a help in holding together some semblance of an active Physics Department. "The bomb will never be dropped on people," Lawrence told him. "As soon as we get it, we'll use it only to dictate terms of peace."

By bold acts like this one with respect to Lawrence, Groves gripped and dominated the fission project in a way not envisaged in his directive. Physicists in general frothed with resentment. But in Bush and Conant, Groves was happy to discover what struck him as intelligent humility. Bush agreed to relinquish the fission part of his science tsardom to Groves; and Conant, who had ruled it under Bush, skipped nimbly down to become Groves's adviser.

In history's dreary record of closed minds triumphing over more open ones, Groves will score drearily high for this achievement. Nevertheless, he was not a commonplace man. When he encountered the physicists, the transforming shock wave moved in more than one direction. On Groves's first visit to Berkeley in October of 1942, Lawrence embodied for him his idea of a scientist. By the time he left, his idea had begun to stretch a little.

As he walked with Lawrence down the quasi-production line of Cubicle Corridor, Groves drew reassurance from Lawrence's quick, confident answers. Alpha-1 and Alpha-2 and the yield of partly separated U-235 looked like the biggest stride yet made anywhere. In his mind's eye Groves tried to project how far the goal of a detonating bomb lay ahead of its only visible rudiment, the faint green smears of gunk.

"How pure will it have to be?" he asked.

Lawrence did not know. But the question was of a type for which he had a ready answer. Explaining that fission from fast neutrons could still be studied only theoretically, he suggested that Groves ask Oppenheimer.

The name reminded Groves of other business he had at Berkeley, and he took the elevator to the third floor of LeConte Hall. Inside the steel netting, Oppenheimer traced for him the path of a fission-born neutron in a mixture of U-235 and U-238 and evaluated its chances of setting off another fission before it escaped or was absorbed. He talked without jargon and made the subject astonishingly clear.

By this time, Groves had got used to watching nuclear physicists obfuscate and squirm away when he asked what seemed the simplest sort of questions. Like Lawrence, Oppenheimer proved a striking exception. Toward nuclear physics he tended to be as irreverent and narrowly demanding as Groves himself. Instead of making it his life's work, he simply wanted to build a bomb as soon as he could and then get back to the serene beauty of cosmic rays.

When Groves congratulated him on being intelligible about the bomb, Oppenheimer made the reply that he made to everybody in those days. "There are no experts," he said absently. "The field is too new." For Groves a dilemma of his strange command had been how not to truckle. With these words Oppenheimer helped solve it. They uncorked a stream of questions that had been rising in Groves's mind since his first contact with the atom.

Physics was not his sole impediment to communication with physicists. Another was of his own making. Immediately upon taking charge, he had ordered each of the many specialized crews in each of the laboratories to keep their colleagues ignorant of their work. This policy he called compartmentalization. He enforced it not only for security against espionage but also because he simply wanted to make the physicists stop talking. "There was just too much of scientific interest," he explained, "and they would just be frittering from one thing to another."

The unique central seat that he thus reserved for himself had discomforts which he found Oppenheimer could cushion. To Groves, Oppenheimer amounted to more than an avowed nonexpert whom he could consult without deference. Though nominally Compton's man, Oppenheimer was in fact a homeless theoretician to whom Groves could talk about the different laboratories without letting one in on another's secrets. In explaining why he unbosomed himself to Oppenheimer of confidences that he kept from Lawrence and Compton, Groves is hard to follow—"Maybe because Dr. Oppenheimer agreed with me, and particularly because of other questions that were raised, I came to depend upon him tremendously for scientific advice on the rest of the Project, although I made no effort to break down my compartmentalization." Rabi, distantly watching Groves trample through his own complicated jealous paradoxes, found a terser explanation. "Oppenheimer handled him beautifully," said Rabi, "and it wasn't always easy."

To do it, Oppenheimer demonstrated either inhuman cunning or an even more inhuman lack of any cunning at all. Physicists who dispute his character agree that there is no middle ground. He functioned for Groves like a marvelous encyclopedia, an idiot savant with no perspective of self-interest to sophisticate his answers. When all Groves's bristles were soothed down, he was able to look at Oppenheimer and see that he was unhappy.

Groves wanted to know why. With uncanny detachment Oppenheimer analyzed his own troubles, speaking of them as though they were a stranger's. He had failed to pull together the scattered small projects assigned to him. The theoreticians conferring at Berkeley had accomplished something, but not enough. Physicists in his part of the Manhattan Project had lost all sense of hope or direction. Everyone agreed they could find it again only when they all worked side by side in a special laboratory concerned solely with bomb design. Though for its senior staff Oppenheimer firmly rejected Groves's fetish of compartmentalization, Groves listened with a stirring of imagination. "Groves was very much interested from the beginning," Oppenheimer said.

On his way east Groves pondered the idea and from Chicago wired Oppenheimer to rejoin him. There he squeezed Oppenheimer, himself, and two of his subordinate colonels into a compartment of the Twentieth Century Limited. In a voice too low to be heard by the Pullman porter in the corridor, he put further questions. While the smoothly clicking rails assured their unconscious minds that the dream side of war was not so bad, Oppenheimer framed his answers. Yes, he agreed, it could be a remote laboratory where bomb physicists could be separated from other physicists in the project and surrounded and watched by the Army. No, there was no reason the senior staff should not be dressed in uniform and sworn to military discipline. ("I would have been glad to be an officer," he said later as though puzzled at someone else's foible. "I thought maybe the others would.") With mounting enthusiasm they talked for eight hours.

Groves realized he would have to decide about the bomb laboratory sooner than he had thought. The three program chiefs, lacking central control, had already bought the vast tract of land at Oak Ridge for factory sites. Their three laboratories were putting out pseudopods there with the vague idea that these in turn would give birth to an ordnance laboratory and make use of the rest of the tract as a proving ground. This would not do, Oppenheimer insisted sharply. Bomb design involved such tremendous unknowns that it could not wait on manufacture of material but must be concurrent and in a sense controlling.

Out of Oppenheimer's talk emerged a shadowy figure, faceless but demanding. The director of the new laboratory would have to stand at the center of the Manhattan Project, gather all its products in his hand, and preside at their thunderous consummation. Who should it be? The appointment had hung fire too long, Oppenheimer said, while the scientists waited through the spring and summer for someone like Groves to take charge and decide. Groves promised to look into it.

He held a round of conferences with Project leaders and listened to their recommendations. Some light can be thrown on what these were. Compton, by whose default the problem had fallen on Groves, offered little help outside a discussion of Oppenheimer's status. This, he told Groves, was merely that of a temporary caretaker. He emphasized that he had made Oppenheimer no commitment. As for the directorship of a bomb laboratory, his choice was Carl Anderson of Pasadena, a Nobel prize winner. But the prestige of the project had been too low, and Anderson had turned him down.

Groves formed the impression that the director would be expected to have a Nobel prize. Nothing in the inhumanly impersonal orientation given him by Oppenheimer had altered an almost unconscious assumption in Groves's mind that the director should be an experimental physicist. If Groves could have appointed anyone he wanted to he would have unhesitatingly selected Lawrence. But he felt that without Lawrence's drive and leadership electromagnetic separation would collapse and even the Radiation Laboratory might not survive.

Next best to Lawrence was whoever most enjoyed his confidence. Groves talked with Lawrence, and Lawrence told him he thought Edwin McMillan, then doing radar work at Boston, was the man for the job. Checking with Oppenheimer, Groves found that he strongly approved. By these two recommendations McMillan became the logical choice. Groves went to see him. Measured against the terrible responsibility of the directorship, McMillan seemed so sure of himself, so confidently competent, so *young*. This much of what Groves felt he conveyed to others; perhaps also a reckless sense of humor may have led McMillan to the sort of jokes young Hildebrand would have made if Lawrence had not shut him up. "Not quite right for it," Groves decided.

There remained as a resource for Groves the possibility of getting an original recommendation out of Oppenheimer. The difficulty, Oppenheimer reminded him, was in finding a physicist whose energies were not already totally committed to war research. Otherwise, he could have named Rabi, Jerrold Zacharias of Hunter College in New York, and a long list of other outstanding men. As it was, he gave his vote to Wolfgang Panofsky, of Pasadena, an experimental physicist with strong theoretical leanings.

Panofsky was a little younger even than McMillan, and no less irrepressible. Comparatively obscure, he was no straw man. All physicists who knew him respected him, and his reputation for breadth and brilliance has since steadily risen. Nevertheless, Groves began to feel that as long as he had got down to considering theoretical physicists he might do better with the devil he knew. To a man of Groves's character, Oppenheimer's very lack of executive drive and experience was in some sense a qualification. The trouble, Groves realized, was going to be with security.

6

MOON AND SAND

SINCE THE BEGINNING OF 1942, Oppenheimer had been under investigation. F.B.I. and Army Intelligence agents had swarmed about him compiling an enormous dossier. In April he had filled out a questionnaire that awed and galvanized them. How they saw it is suggested by a feeble joke they later claimed he had made about it, though he thereafter had no memory of making it. "I am not a Communist," he is reported to have said, "but I have probably belonged to every Communist-front organization on the West Coast."[1] This questionnaire dealt with past activity. What he had been doing lately provided them slimmer pickings, but nothing they chose to neglect.

First there was the matter of his brother Frank and his radical-minded students and ex-students at Berkeley. He continued to associate with them, urging with what some of them considered tiresome fluency that they forget politics and concentrate on war research.

Second, there was the pink-tinged Federation of Architects, Engineers, Chemists and Technicians. Since 1941 it had been trying to move into Lawrence's laboratory in place of the defunct Teachers' Union to which Oppenheimer had belonged. Some of Oppenheimer's ex-students were interested. So was Berkeley's distinguished dean, Joel Hildebrand, father of one of Lawrence's brightest young physicists. Oppenheimer and Hildebrand held a meeting later in 1941 or early in 1942 to talk about whether a Berkeley branch would be a good thing. A chemical engineer named George Eltenton came from the Shell Development Company laboratory nine miles away in the town of Emeryville to do the promoting. A forceful man, Eltenton used the speech and manners of the British upper class to develop an outlook he had acquired during five years in Russia. At Shell he said he had already helped set up a strong Federation chapter which was making scientists conscious of their responsibilities as an élite of labor. Oppenheimer disliked him and opposed the idea of having the Federation in Berkeley.[2]

Third was Kitty Oppenheimer's friend, Steve Nelson, whom she had entertained at an outdoor supper on an autumn day in 1941. Burly, red-faced, scarred and tough-looking, Nelson was a hard-core Communist very different from the chatterers whom Oppenheimer had consorted with during his radical years. In 1941 Oppenheimer had noticed that Nelson and Kitty talked not about Communism but about Joe Dallet. Nelson had spoken to her with rough poetry of bereavement and love. Oppenheimer had been moved. "Good guys," he termed Nelson and Dallet to a perplexed investigator. In 1942 he let Kitty entertain Nelson once more in her back yard, with Frank and his wife the only other guests. Frank noticed that this time too there was no talk of Communism.

Fourth was Jean Tatlock. Since casting loose from Oppenheimer in 1939, she had floated up and down on tides of religious exaltation and reforming idealism, but always with a steady drift toward melancholia. Her family lived around the corner from Oppenheimer's new home on Eagle Hill. She had talked with him only about twice a year, usually in the presence of Kitty, of whose character her own was a dim image.

Even so, it was important to her dwindling sense of reality to know he was there. During the winter of 1942–43 she had to begin taking psychiatric treatment. In the spring she sent him word that she was desperate to see him. Faculty friends told him she was getting worse. For a long time Groves kept providing him with so many exciting new realities of his own that he had no time for her, but finally in June of 1943 he made an appointment to see her. "I felt I almost had to," he explained at his loyalty hearing.

Late in the afternoon of June 9, he walked across the hill to the house of her parents, about whom reports of this incident keep silence. He had a reservation to leave Berkeley for Los Alamos on the evening train, but his appointment ran longer than he had expected. Security agents who shadowed him crept restlessly about behind their cover of shrubs and checked their watches. He stayed the night and missed his train. Nowadays Americans in their darker moods may think government dossiers contain everything. But since the agents found no chink in the draperies to look through, the only word on what went on inside must come from Oppenheimer. "We did not talk of Communism," he said under interrogation in 1954. Next morning he was seriously behind schedule and decided to break the strict rule not to fly. Jean drove him to the plane and he never saw her again.

F.B.I. and Army Intelligence supervisors mulled assiduously over all these activities of Oppenheimer's. They wrote a series of analyses tending to show that this kind of work attracts a special breed of men the world over. To understand the peculiar romanticism of their compositions is worth a little trouble. For example, the "this office" whose opinions are to be quoted here was Lieutenant Colonel Boris T. Pash, Chief of Counterintelligence Branch, Western Defense Command and Fourth Army. "In view of the fact that this office believes that subject still is or may be connected with the Communist Party, and because of the known interest of the Communist Party in the Project, together with the interest of the U.S.S.R. in it, the following possibilities are submitted for your consideration," Pash wrote from San Francisco to his superior in the Pentagon.

The "still" and "connected" show some imagination, but nothing compared with Pash's formulation of the possibilities. He foresaw two of them. One was merely that Oppenheimer might pass on the Project's secrets through an intermediary. Pash did not think much of this; he labeled it "B." In "A" his imagination took flight. Though carefully larded into the verbiage, Pash's romanticism, worthy of Fu Manchu, is visible to anyone who wants to look for it: "A. All indications on the part of Communist Party members who have expressed themselves with regard to the subject lead this office to believe that the Communist Party is making a definite effort to officially divorce subject's affiliation with the Party, and subject himself is not indicating in any way interest in the Party. However, if subject's affiliation with the Party is definite and he is a member of the Party, there is a possibility of his developing a scientific work to a certain extent, then turning it over to the Party without submitting any phase of it to the U.S. Government."

For compositions of this sort Groves was the ultimate reader. He viewed them with a good deal of sympathy. "There was never from about two weeks from the time I took charge of the Project any illusion on my part but that Russia was our enemy," he said, "and the Project was conducted on that basis." In addition to becoming what he termed a thoroughly practical nuclear physicist, he also quickly declared himself an expert on security. This was probably a good thing, because it led him to look with a fellow craftsman's eye at the bricks with which men like Pash built their towers. "I think I was thoroughly familiar with everything that was reported about Dr. Oppenheimer. And that included, as it did on every other matter of importance, personally reading the original evidence, if there was any original evidence. In other words I would read the reports of the interviews with people. In other words I was not reading the conclusions of any security officer. The reason for that was that in this Project there were so many things that the security officer could not know the significance of that I felt I had to do it myself. Of course, I was criticized for doing everything myself."

In the security trade bricks not yet erected into towers are technically known as unassimilated data. Their most formidable collector, the F.B.I., guards them from the public eye. Few of us can know much of them except as we have uncomfortable memories of what spleen has led us to say about an investigated neighbor. Consequently, the best way to get an idea of Groves's primary reading is to look at one of the F.B.I.'s live-wire respondents.

Wendell Latimer, a gaunt, acidulous man then forty-nine, was chemistry head at Berkeley. As an assistant director of Lawrence's laboratory, he had charge of purifying submicroscopic samples of plutonium from the cyclotron. Though he stood five-feet-nine, his bald head swelled and gleamed so massively that Lawrence's staff thought of him as a typical science-fiction dwarf. He liked to put his right heel on his left knee, lean far, far back in his chair (surely he must be going over this instant), waggle a wet-ended cigarette from one corner of his mouth to another by lip movement alone, and deliver himself of startling opinions. One of these was that his value to war research had doomed him to die in an enemy

prison camp—not German, but Russian. What made him truly a
find for the inevitable investigator was that he also believed there
was something unnatural about Robert Oppenheimer.

His feeling was more interesting than Pash's, because he had a
better inkling of its nature. His words were rambling and obscure.
Until the F.B.I. gives up its dead file, they can only be seen in
chronologically relevant excerpts from testimony he swore to a
decade later. Since Oppenheimer had first set foot on the Berkeley
campus, Latimer said then, he had tried to analyze him, using
normal faculty contacts for the purpose and going once to his house
for cocktails. His reason was that he felt Oppenheimer projected a
sort of aura or influence by which those around him were oddly
affected. "He has been a most interesting study for years," Latimer
said. "Unconsciously, I think, one tries to put together the elements in a man that make him tick, where this influence comes
from, what factors in his personality give him this influence. I am
not a psychoanalyst. I can't give you any picture of how this thing
developed, but to me it was an amazing study, just thinking of
these factors."

The flurry over Groves's first visit to Lawrence's laboratory had
been given a peculiar turn by Groves's disappearance inside Oppenheimer's steel netting. Among the security-cleared, this had
been heightened by rumors of the two men's subsequent close
relationship. On Groves, Latimer expressed himself clearly: "He
seemed to be following the Oppenheimer line." Any idea that
Groves might be controlling, Latimer declared, was ridiculous because of Oppenheimer's great gifts. "I know these things were
simply overwhelming to Groves. He was so dependent upon his
judgment that I think it is reasonable to conclude that many of
his ideas were coming from Dr. Oppenheimer."

A strangeness in such triumphs fascinated Latimer. "I studied
this influence that Dr. Oppenheimer had over other men," he re-
iterated insistently. "It was a tremendous thing." Looking both
deeply within at himself and without at his subject, he felt maddeningly close to an epiphany. "There were elements of the mystic
in his apparent philosophy of life that were very difficult to understand. He is a man of tremendous sincerity, and his ability to convince people depends so much on this sincerity. But what was back
of his philosophy of life I found very difficult to understand." Com-

munism, Latimer implied, fitted in somehow. "His associations at Berkeley were well known, the fact that he had Communist friends."[3]

Silent language is usually the clearest. With the blue, concentrated glare from behind thick steel-rimmed glasses, with the wet, faintly obscene mouthplay with the cigarette, Latimer spoke more directly. Communism, though he saw his own death in it, was for him only a timely stalking horse. Any procurer for a medieval burning chamber could have caught his drift.

Hard facts about the times we live in often escape us. If a man has a suitable compulsion and if he persists long enough, ours are good years in which to fix on another man a charge of demoniac possession. What the perplexed investigator at the turn of 1942–43 could make of Latimer is not known. Later investigators regarded him highly. As for his fellow chemists, an appraisal by young Sam Weissman, also at Lawrence's laboratory, seems worth considering, though oversimple and overclean. "I knew him," said Weissman. "He was nuts. He thought he was a manipulator of men and science."

This comment of Weissman's would represent a typical bit of unassimilated data if it had come from an F.B.I. dossier. As for that compiled on Oppenheimer, J. Edgar Hoover after the war looked through what Pash had had to go on for his romance and said he saw nothing serious.* Pash sent the thing to his functional superior in the Pentagon, Lieutenant Colonel John Lansdale, intelligence chief for all fission work.

An implacable anti-Communist, Lansdale had recently clashed with his own very highest superiors to keep former officers of Spain's Abraham Lincoln Brigade from getting commissions. "You are ruining people's careers and doing damage to the Army," Lieutenant General Joseph T. McNarney told him; but he would not shut his mouth until the matter was settled by a direct order from Roosevelt.

Pash's was only the strongest of a number of adverse reports that Lansdale received on Oppenheimer. Everyone in Intelligence besides himself, he discovered, wanted Oppenheimer put out of the Project. Since the beginning of 1942 the case had been a chronic

---

* See below, p. 274.

worry to him. Lansdale's hunger was more sophisticated than that of most security agents. A lean, leathery man of thirty, he had ruined his complexion during a youth spent riding and hunting under the Texas sun. At the end of his teens, which had been a long slaughter of coyote and deer, came moments of disgust at the thought of killing. His upbringing was leisurely and casual; before coming west, the Lansdales had been Maryland gentry. A military tradition in the family had sent him to V.M.I., a legal tradition to Harvard Law School. All this set some restraint on the lower reaches of his imagination and gave him some notion of the timeless, unseasonable, humbly obstinate virtue of good manners. Unlike his subordinate intelligence officers, he thought of himself as a lawyer and had no ambition to make security a career.

At the very start of the war, when Lansdale's commission was still brand new, Conant had borrowed him from G-2 and sent him to Berkeley to do an investigation of the physics laboratories. Make it surreptitious, Conant had said, but on the train Lansdale reflected that no one had told him how. Obviously it would involve lying, so he tried his hand at this on seatmates in the smoker. One of them turned out to be a Berkeley law professor who lectured him about a six-week refresher course there for practicing lawyers. "Exactly what I'm going out to enroll in," Lansdale said with a flash of inspiration. "What with my left-wing views, I feel I must get into the Army and fight Hitler. But first I need more law study —I've just started practice—so I won't be lost when I come out."

Moved, the professor wrote him introductions to all sorts of people on the campus. Lifelong distaste for academic types helped Lansdale put down a little queasiness. For two weeks he infested Lawrence's laboratory. Several of its members owed the eventual ruin of their careers to the notes he made, which set Security to monitoring their activities.[4] Cooksey, whom he liked best, was the only physicist to scent anything fishy about him. Lawrence he also liked, but Lawrence was in too much of a hurry to give him any time. A large but legitimately explainable portion of the names in his black book were Oppenheimer's ex-students; as for Oppenheimer, Lansdale did not like him but felt occasional twinges of admiration to the point of awe when in his presence. After considerable hesitation, he left Oppenheimer's name off his list.

During the next year he somehow kept in mind that despite the clamor for damning documentaries, what the country needed might be a bomb. Comparisons helped. Compton, for example, could not get security clearance either; once he had flirted with the Teachers' Union. To a man who knew him well, the thought of Compton involving himself in a dangerous conspiracy was ludicrous. "You can hardly put your finger on a scientist or university professor or people who get into civil affairs," Lansdale mused in 1954, "you can hardly find one anywhere who is now in his fifties or so that has not been on at least one list which was later determined to be subversive or have leanings that way." Instead of welcoming a wide-open hunt, he narrowed it with what to men like Pash would have been a killjoy definition: "A Communist is a person who is more loyal to Russia than to the United States."

One must not mistake Lansdale for a white knight nor assume that the jugulars into which he bit—another story—were guilty. But when he went back again to Berkeley, he dealt as directly as he could with the Oppenheimer family. He talked with Frank, and Frank failed his test. Lansdale decided that Frank might well have once been a Communist strictly defined. But the simplehearted, hard-working younger brother knew only Lawrence's secrets; he knew nothing of Oppenheimer's studies on the bomb. Besides, there were worse Communists in Lawrence's laboratory, and special procedures were being set up to deal with them. The more intelligent Intelligence agents were showing the first signs of a certain nonchalance about what their enemies, the Russians, learned of the electromagnetic process.

Lansdale talked with Kitty and came back to talk and talk again. Sometimes he was in her parlor and sometimes—after twenty years his memory is vague—perhaps in the back yard, where she had fed Steve Nelson. He remembers that eventually she gave him a martini. "Not the kind to serve tea," he deduced from the way she handled her glass. "Probably never served anybody tea in her entire life." Flushed and pretty, not cordial, Kitty made little pretense of entertaining him socially, yet never showed him the door. "Hates me and everything I stand for," he decided. For his part he let her see she might have reason. To him she was at least a former "Communist Organizer" (his term for mimeograph operator) and ex-wife of one or more Communists including a "Commissar" (his term for any Spanish army volunteer).

To his dry Texas drawl she replied in throaty murmurs, answering all questions with an eagerness that surprised him. He knew her parents had had money from Pennsylvania steel. Listening, he decided they must have been cultivated and poised and assured, not grubbers. Cold hatred mixed with contempt he could have understood in her, for that is what he would have felt, and in pride he sensed they were akin. Instead she burned with an anxiety to persuade, and that seemed out of character.

"She was playing a part," he decided. "As we say in that lingo, she was trying to rope me, just as I was trying to rope her. The thing that impressed me was how hard she was trying. Intensely, emotionally, with everything she had. She struck me as a curious personality, at once very frail and very strong. I felt she'd go to any length for what she believed in. The tactic I fell back on was to try to show her I was a person of balance honestly wanting to evaluate Oppenheimer's position. That's why our talks ran on so long.

"I was sure she'd been a Communist and not sure her abstract opinions had ever changed much. But feelings were her source of belief. I got the impression of a woman who'd craved some sort of quality or distinction of character she could attach herself to, who'd had to find it in order to live. She didn't care how much I knew of what she'd done before she met Oppenheimer or how it looked to me. Gradually I began to see that nothing in her past and nothing in her other husbands meant anything to her compared with him. I became convinced that in him she had an attachment stronger than Communism, that his future meant more to her than Communism. She was trying to sell me on the idea that he was her life, and she did sell me."

While at work, Lansdale differed from other Security agents in keeping his mind more on security. He tried to fit this fixation of Kitty's into a forecast of Oppenheimer's potential behavior. One may think such an effort difficult to the point of absurdity. Still it was better that he should try than the grimy G-2's in the junior commands, and he had observed a very definite peculiarity in Oppenheimer to which his findings on Kitty seemed relevant.

Nobody at all has ever said Oppenheimer did not keep a still tongue in his head about government secrets. But like everyone else who ever dealt with him at length, Lansdale had made the

exasperating discovery that he had no prudence. Normal people
can be counted on to smile or frown, snub or invite, elbow or yield
in accordance with a sensible strategy to get on in the world or at
least not drop back. Deprived of this orientation by a defective education, Oppenheimer replaced it with an intellectual-moral-aes-
thetic criterion of his own devising. On the minus side it involved
him in such contradictions as favoring Ahimsa (or nonviolence)
and wanting to build the bomb. On the plus side it won from a
seemingly random selection of his acquaintances the sympathy
which so puzzled Latimer.

Lansdale diagnosed the trait as social unpredictability. Kitty's
small, fierce person, he decided, would be a bulwark against it.
"She saw he must have no far-left connections," he says. "No one
could have guarded him better. With his character as I read it,
she was going to provide us as good security as anyone could get."
More formally he explained himself under oath and subject to
cross-examination in 1954. "It was my belief that her strength of
character—I think strength of character is the wrong word—her
strength of will was a powerful influence in keeping Dr. Oppenheimer away from what we would regard as dangerous associations."

He talked with Oppenheimer as often as he could catch him
doing nothing in a lounge or dining car on the train. ("All the
big shots kept buzzing back and forth," groused young physicist
Alexander Langsdorff, not reflecting that free deluxe transportation was the smallest amenity on the dream side of war.) Oppenheimer was not a security risk, Lansdale decided, not even a calculated risk of the sort it is wisdom to incur.

By this time Lansdale had begun to follow what Latimer called
the Oppenheimer line. It cleansed his imagination except for hot
flashes that he could recognize and control. On one of their inces-
sant train trips he and Groves picked at the healing scab.

"What would you do," he asked Groves, "if it turned out that
Dr. Oppenheimer was not loyal?"

Groves too was cleansed, but not to the point of becoming a dull
conversationalist. "I would blow the whole thing wide open," he
replied, no doubt with a certain joy.

Of Oppenheimer's utter trustworthiness Groves and Lansdale
could not convince any Intelligence experts but each other. Be-

neath them the security pot bubbled rebelliously until July 20, 1943. Then Groves slammed the lid down. He ordered his staff (Lansdale was technically part of G-2 high command) to issue clearance "without delay irrespective of any information which you have regarding Mr. Oppenheimer."

Long before that, of course, in late 1942, he had made his own brilliant and difficult decision. The circumstances do him the highest credit. By his own account he went around again to the country's science administrators specifically challenging them to accept Oppenheimer or name a better bomb-laboratory director.

Characteristically, Groves had a little more support than he remembered, and he gained it in a characteristic way. "After a fashion Groves did consult me, mumbling and musing," said Allison, then director of the Metallurgical Laboratory under Compton.

"I know Oppenheimer's got a bad reputation from his past," Groves told Allison. "But I think he'll live it down. In a thing like this I suppose I have to . . ."

Groves trailed off into an internal meditation. The two men gazed blankly at each other while Allison tried to make up his mind whether his opinion was being asked. "I approve, certainly I approve," he said to be on the safe side.

As for Lawrence, he took Groves's rejection of McMillan with good grace. In a sense Oppenheimer was almost as much his protégé. "Lawrence was a man who'd place his confidence in people, say, 'This is so,' and have few afterthoughts," said Rabi. "He placed his confidence in Oppenheimer." Unlike the security agents, Lawrence thought the war was against Germany and Japan; Oppenheimer's past radicalism he regarded as of no interest and no relevance. Curiously, he saw a different problem: that Oppenheimer, not being a builder, might have to be taught administration.

Lawrence approved the appointment with two stipulations. First he wanted the new laboratory to be an administrative extension of the University of California. Second, if Oppenheimer should ever say he could not build the bomb, he and Compton must be allowed to take over and apply all their resources to doing the job themselves.[5]

Lawrence had first brought Oppenheimer into the Project. For this second stage of Oppenheimer's career in it Lawrence later said he felt responsible. At the time he told his brother, "We're going to try to get Robert Oppenheimer for director." He spoke with such a serious, determined air that John Lawrence took him for the prime mover in the matter.

Disdaining Groves as a hidebound egotist, physicists nowadays often point to Oppenheimer as an opposite type, representative of themselves. It is odd that they did not do more to help Groves decide. Lawrence and Allison were among the exceptions to a generally sulky inertia which Groves encountered. "Groves's choice of Oppenheimer was very unexpected," says Rabi. "To most physicists it came as a great surprise."

Such surprises to the physics community were Groves's way of keeping himself dominant over them. To keep from preening, Oppenheimer did not need to hear Groves tell with sincere tactlessness how unenthusiastic they were. When asked in later years how he got the job, Oppenheimer would answer, "By default," and remind the researcher what an unpromising job it looked to be. "The truth is," he would reflect, "that the obvious people were already taken and that the Project had a bad name."

About November 1, 1942, as soon as Groves made the appointment definite, Oppenheimer's travels intensified. Groves still insisted on compartmentalization. Oppenheimer would not consider having it in his laboratory. The solution, they agreed, was to find exactly the right location. A good deal of the time when others in the Project wondered what they were talking about, they were talking about geography. Frontiersmen are seldom quite rational. Not too far below the conscious level each wanted a bit of earth to match a feeling he had in his bones about the work to be done there. Ostensibly they began looking for a spot where bomb physicists could speak freely and other physicists in the Project could not listen.

First they examined a site on the eastern slopes of the San Bernardinos. Groves foresaw physicists slipping away across the hills to teas and seminars with their colleagues at Pasadena. He feared that a fence high enough to stop them would attract attention. "Not remote enough," he decided. Briefly they considered the High Sierras and the north edge of Death Valley, then took the train to New Mexico.

There one of Groves's officers had tentatively picked a site. He drove them north from Albuquerque into an oppressive cul-de-sac overhung by walls of rock. It had water and isolation but no view. "Depressing to the personnel," Oppenheimer ventured. "Lacks room to expand in," said Groves.

Oppenheimer knew the land well. His little ranch in the Sangre de Cristo range was on the other side of Santa Fe, a long way off by Eastern standards. But on vacations he was used to riding every trail from the ranch that a horse could follow for days on end.

Before the war while roaming the Pajorito Plateau to the north of where he and Groves now stood, he had come upon a solid-looking adobe house. It turned out to be a tearoom, perhaps the world's loneliest, kept by an old, withered, unpublished poetess named Edith Warner. With the aid of an even older Indian servant named Tilano, she fed him, and he spent the afternoon with her. A few miles from where she lived rose a red mesa spotted with cottonwoods and cut off from the plateau by a canyon. Persistently at the least hint of dampness, a rainbow curved down to the canyon floor so that one could stand at the edge and look for the pot of gold directly under one's feet. To Oppenheimer, old Edith seemed the genius of the place and the place itself the heart of the desert country he loved and could not combine with physics, his other love.

All this he remembered while Groves was shaking his head. He suggested they drive on up the road about thirty miles and look at the mesa, which because of its cottonwoods was called Los Alamos. Much wear on springs and nerves at last brought them to the top of it. Nothing human was there except a boys' school run down by wartime restrictions. Water was scarce. Access was literally terrible. Perhaps because of his liking for the desert, Oppenheimer took little account of these disadvantages. Less clear is how much perverted insight Latimer showed in terming Groves a follower of the Oppenheimer line. To determine whether Groves looked with bewitched eyes at the vast, empty mesa, one can only examine the words he used to describe it when he later found them: "This is the last stand of free men."

Groves chose the site for his bomb laboratory only a few days after choosing its director. The two steps came so close together as to suggest a doubt whether it was Oppenheimer or the mesa he was appointing. Not so much was involved as one would think.

Relative to the whole scattered Manhattan Project, the appointment looked small. Oppenheimer lacked the administrator's hunger, which is as keen in its way as the security agent's. If John Manley had not been his junior partner, he would probably have made an interesting effort to build the bomb with thirty men.

This was the total staff he had in mind in October. Manley made the figure grow by slow, reluctant jerks. "All through the last of 1942 I kept needling him to get things organized," said Manley. Knowing administration and hating it, Manley longed to finish his chore and get wholly back into physics. Specifically he wanted an organization chart, but not the kind that the born administrator spawns incessantly. Each time he put in the needle, Oppenheimer took to the road on a painful selling job.

His prospects were the country's best physicists and chemists, his offer a chance to work in a Godforsaken place on a project with a bad reputation. "There was great fear that this was a boondoggle, which would in fact have nothing to do with the war," Oppenheimer said. Whether he intended it or not, his tactic was glamour. At Princeton, for example, after recruiting Robert Wilson he talked with Leo Lavatelli and a half dozen of Wilson's other young assistants. "We were already security-cleared because of the electromagnetic separation thing at Princeton," said Lavatelli. "He put it to us that this was the great challenge, the heart of the mystery we had been working on. He spoke with a kind of mystical earnestness that captured our imagination. All but one of our group signed up to go with him."

Wives were a disagreeable discovery. Any physicist or chemist at that time had an unlimited choice of jobs to keep him out of the Army. Wives liked cities and private-industry money, which Oppenheimer could not match. "Shall we brief them on the bomb?" he and Groves pondered; after a little hesitation they decided not to. The result was that wives knew everything except exactly how much to admit they knew. The hardest fact to make them swallow was that once they set foot in the desert, Security would not let them leave as long as they stayed married.

Oppenheimer recognized it was his duty to indoctrinate them, but when he tried, he relapsed into the nervousness that McKibben had noticed. There would be special quiet housing facilities for "the unmarried couples," he said, making jabbing gestures with a large pipe to which the cigarette shortage had reduced him. They deduced that he meant the childless couples, noticed that his tweed jacket though wrinkled was perfectly tailored, and mentally classified him as the poetic type. "We shall all be one large family doing vital work inside the wire," he told them.

Manley was based in Chicago, Oppenheimer in Berkeley. Consequently, the needle had to be applied by long-distance telephone, and security kept Oppenheimer vague in his replies. Manley worried until he could no longer stand it. In mid-December of 1942 he took the plane to Berkeley—not being an official program leader, he was allowed to fly. "It was the most miserable kind of weather all the way," he recalls. "I was still sick as a dog when I walked into Oppenheimer's office and interrupted a dreamy mathematical conversation he was having with Emil Konopinski. Though he greeted me, I wondered if he really knew I was there. Then he picked up a paper from his desk and handed it to me.

" 'Here's your damned organization chart,' he said.

"I checked through it and saw it not only covered big names in physics like Bethe and Segré but also practical things like organic chemistry and stock control. Somehow it moved me to discover how much my needling had done to bring so abstract and theoretical a figure down to the business at hand. About the stockroom, for example, I don't suppose anyone but a physicist would understand. He had got Dana Mitchell of Columbia for it, absolutely the country's best. I still don't know how he did it or what persuasion he used."

By this time Manley too had become a follower of the Oppenheimer line. More worldly-wise physicists involved in the undertaking still had pangs of common sense. "Just before Christmas of 1942 Oppenheimer asked me to come and help plan the preliminary layout on the Mesa," said Allison. "An officer was supposed to meet us in Santa Fe with a car. After looking all over town, we finally located him very high in a bar. Fortunately he had an enlisted man to do the driving.

"The officer sat in front. I knew what the ride would be like, so I kept my eye on him. We crossed the Rio Grande with the car wheels hanging over the edge of the road. He sobered up at once and began cautioning the driver. It was interesting to me, because I didn't know danger could have this effect on a drunk. If I hadn't been there before, I expect I might have been too scared to notice. Oppenheimer seemed to have his mind on physics.

"On the Mesa he and I sat down and planned the laboratory. He showed me what he called an organization chart for a hundred personnel. I looked at it and felt sure something was wrong, but I didn't know what.

"The best I could do was poke at random. 'Where are the shipping clerks?' I asked.

"He gave me a thoughtful, sympathetic look. 'We're not going to ship anything,' he answered.

"I completely underestimated the size of the installation, but not so much as he did. We always knew there would be a splinter group for the bomb. It drifted vaguely through my mind that this might instead become the center of the Project. I thought the idea of a desert center was a mistake. It would have looked more sensible to me to put it in a big industrial district. Certainly it would have been more sensible economically, but there was Oppenheimer's love for that country."

To Allison the affair of the Mesa seemed characteristic Oppenheimer. He felt it was of a piece with exotic predilections for the *Mahabharata*, "nasty gory," and physics at night. In this he was correct. But as in his evaluation of the way Oppenheimer got his first graduate student, there was a point that ever so slightly eluded him. Common sense may not always be the surest way to uncommon achievement. In groping toward ultimate weapons, it now seems fairly clear, physicists could be helped by a limitless view of red cliffs and pale-green arroyos.

This fact was by no means apparent at the end of 1942. Allison was the gentlest of the Mesa's critics. Even after hearing Oppenheimer talk of its beauty, many of the security-cleared formed an impression of something weird and deathly, a symbol of the abnormal demand that had changed their lives. Acute and glib in Chicago, Leo Szilard was then making himself a thorn in Compton's dignified side. When Oppenheimer showed up on a recruiting trip, Szilard briefly turned his attention to the Mesa. "Nobody could think straight in a place like that," he asserted to his associates at the Metallurgical Laboratory. "Everybody who goes there will go crazy."

Through the first of 1943 Manley continually forced Oppen-

heimer to lengthen his organization chart. Toward the end of
March recruits began converging. "I came out from Princeton with
a machinist who told me he had been born in Hightstown, New
Jersey," said young Lavatelli. "The farther he got from Hightstown, the more homesick he acted. When we were almost there we
drove across the Sangre de Cristos. 'Look at those beautiful hills,'
I said. He stared at them with his mouth slack and his face so white
I could almost see it reflecting their red glow. 'What a terrible
place!' he said. 'My God, who can work out here?'

"I felt happy that we were getting out of the Eastern crowds,
but his homesickness just broke like a dam. He tried for two
months, then gave up and went back to Hightstown."

Physically, Oppenheimer's affair with the Mesa began with a
defilement. Since December three thousand construction workers,
themselves miserable in trailers, had systematically accomplished
this with rough lumber and building paper. By the first of April
they had mostly finished a main building, five laboratories, a machine shop, a warehouse, and a set of barracks and barrackslike
apartments. Bumping shoulders with them in their shoddy and
characterless creations, scientists struggled to set up a cyclotron
from Harvard, McKibben's Van de Graaffs from Wisconsin, and
chemical apparatus from Berkeley. To the scientists, the construction crews showed themselves as remote and unsympathetic as
the Mesa. Working to specifications laid down once and for all by
the military, they would not change even the location of a shelf
or enlarge a door to let a bit of machinery through.

Oppenheimer had moved out from Berkeley on March 15. "I
went to Los Alamos when they opened it up," said Major Ralph
Carlisle Smith, a chemist and Project patent lawyer. "It was a hell
of a mess. You just didn't have anywhere to do anything. You
wanted somebody to gripe to and you'd see this pork-pie hat bob-
bing toward you across the Mesa, and then the pipe and the
scrawny little guy in the wrinkled suit. His shoes would be covered with that damned sand, but on him somehow it didn't look
so alien. When you talked to him everything slid back into focus
and you remembered what you were there for. This was the impression you got at the time. Afterward when you thought about
it, if you were like me, you had a sense of having been in contact
with urgent fantastic brilliance and tremendous power."

Personnel began drifting in until, on April 15, the new laboratory formally began operation. General Groves was on hand to orient the staff with a limp, chill handshake ("Like a dead fish," said Major Smith. "I think that's one reason so many half-smart civilians here never appreciated him") and a short lecture. "Groves gave us a pep talk," said McKibben. "It seemed to me he was trying to impress everyone with what he knew." Response was generally poor because of a true rumor that Groves had wanted to bugle the physicists out of bed at daybreak for antiparachutist drill. Older hands among them dissuaded him. "You could see clear across the Mesa and for miles and miles beyond," said Allison, who had come down from Chicago for the occasion. "I thought it was the unlikeliest place in the world for parachutists."

Oppenheimer ran into such varied problems of morale as to obscure the fact that he had one unvaried policy for dealing with them. This was to do what he could to let every scientist on the Mesa know what he knew.

To inaugurate this policy he put Serber forward as his spokesman at a lecture series beginning on April 15. The physicists had assembled to do their listening in what was called Main Tech. They avoided referring to it as the administration building, because of a healthy bias originating from Oppenheimer. He had his office there, but so did the other theoretical physicists. Newcomers who expected something like an industrial design and development laboratory were surprised at the juxtaposition. Serber completed their orientation.

A lean, dark, inconspicuous wisp of a man, Serber hated dramatics. While talking he stumbled continually over his words and swallowed impatiently as though he had dust from the Mesa lodged in his throat but felt his subject too trivial to justify a sip of water. Nevertheless, he held his audience. "He wasn't much of a speaker," says one of those present. "But for ammunition he had everything Oppenheimer's theoretical group had uncovered during the last year. He knew it all cold and that was all he cared about."

Serber's remarks were afterward mimeographed and distributed to every scientist who worked there. Younger ones in particular prized their copies and still like to quote from them. Highlights suggest the atmosphere which Oppenheimer had decided to create on the Mesa.

The U-235 bomb, said Serber, would have a critical mass of 15 kilograms under ideal conditions, the plutonium bomb 5 kilo-grams. Manufacturing plants at Oak Ridge and Hanford, Washington, would supply the fissionable material, but the bombs would have to be devised before, not after, its arrival at Los Alamos. To turn out enough for either kind of critical mass, these plants would require about two years. Los Alamos must have the bombs ready by then without a day's delay.

The first task, he continued, would be to find out whether such a thing was really possible. At the moment he could see two reasons why it might not be. First, no one had counted the number of neutrons per fission in fast chain reactions as distinguished from the slowed ones in the Chicago pile, which had achieved a chain reaction in December of 1942. Second, no one had clocked the interval between fast fissions. If the number were too small or the interval too great, Los Alamos could close up shop. These were preliminary questions about U-235, which so far existed only in minute impure green smears. As for plutonium, no one could absolutely prove it existed at all, much less give its fast or slow neutron count.

Difficulties of this sort, Serber predicted, would give way and reveal still greater difficulties ahead. The practical consequence of the time limit for designing the bombs was that Los Alamos must get its information the hard way. To wait until adequate quantities of U-235 and plutonium were on hand to experiment with would prolong the war. Such experiments as could be undertaken would be of two kinds: detail and integral. An example of the first would be to measure the neutron number of an infinitesimal speck of plutonium that the Metallurgical Laboratory promised to send. Integral experiments would have to be "let's-pretend" studies of dummies built up within a framework of theory. Theory, so far the only developed part of the program, would have to dominate. Los Alamos, he made clear, would have to be that contradiction in terms—a pure research laboratory with a production schedule.

Later, he said, he would get down to cases on bomb construction and then give the floor to experts and specialists. First, however, a few additional figures might be of general interest. Weight for weight, the U-235 bomb would embody fifteen million times the explosive energy of T.N.T. By radioactivity it would kill within a radius of a thousand yards. By blast it would destroy within a radius twice as great. Plutonium should do better. At the northeast corner of the Mesa, in Building Y, machinery was being set up to make and test liquid deuterium. This, poured over a fission bomb once they got it, might produce a thermonuclear or fusion bomb with explosive energy weight-for-weight five times greater still. The possibility was interesting, he observed, because deuterium was plentiful enough to provide blast without limit. As for blowing up the earth by igniting the atmosphere, all calculations were against it. Still, he said, the true scientist should consider every possibility, including that of being mistaken. So many computations were involved that one had to admit a statistical probability of an error lurking somewhere among them unrecognized. The chance of an unexpected end for human affairs he would put at three in one million. It had to be deduced so tenuously that one might as well apply it to both the fission bomb and the more violent thermonuclear. All the figures he had given so far, he said, were theoretically derived and should be accepted as at best only approximate.

The dry, stumbling voice stopped, the dark face turned toward a window rattling in the wind, and the greenish eyes rested on the sands of the Mesa. Caught leaning forward in their chairs, the audience raised an excited murmur. "So there really is to be no compartmentalization here" was the gist of what they said to each other. Satisfied with the effect Serber had produced, Oppenheimer broke the long pause. Tomorrow, he said, Serber would pick up again and introduce a series of conferences on specific construction problems.

The easiest way to make a bomb, Serber resumed next day, would be to shape most of the critical mass into a sphere with a hole or deep groove running through it. Then from some sort of gun one could fire the remaining lump into the hole. If the lump moved at the right speed, before it came out on the other side the whole thing would explode. If the lump went in too slowly, the bomb would fizzle by pre-detonation. If it went through too quickly (there was less chance of this), the bomb would fizzle by post-detonation.

Without the fast-neutron count and clocking he had mentioned yesterday, he said it was hard to tell what the right speed should be. Still, on theoretical grounds fast neutrons should breed as fruitfully as slow ones and at an interval of about a hundred-millionth of a second. Not many generations would be needed for a good, efficient explosion. Consequently, it seemed best to have the gun fire the lump at a two-thousand-foot-per-second speed. When the experimental count and clocking were done, this figure might have to be changed. But in the meantime design of the gun could not wait; Oppenheimer had decided that at Los Alamos no part of the program could wait on any other part. Compared with college laboratories, the tempo must be posthaste. Any scientist who felt uneasy about work done or decisions made on the basis of assumptions or incomplete data could lay the responsibility on Oppenheimer.

So far, Serber went on, he had been talking about the gun for the U-235 bomb. The plutonium gun was a tougher problem. All that was known was that theoretically the chain reaction of plutonium should be faster, so the projectile must be fired at higher speed. How much higher no one could say for sure; the best guess was half again as much, or three thousand feet per second. Design of this gun would likewise begin at once.*

Approaching his wind-up, Serber listed other possibilities. A bomb might be made of mixed plutonium and U-235. More than two pieces might be fired together. Assembly might be by autocatalysis, chemical dissolution of barriers holding the pieces apart. An initiator, a calculated radioactive adulterant, might be needed to start the chain reaction at the most desirable billionth of a second. For all the bombs, complex questions of required purity and configuration of target, projectile and tamper (U-238 would fission with violence but without chain reaction) must be urgently

* While being pushed together to form a critical mass, each of two subcritical fissioning masses reacts increasingly to neutrons sent ahead by the other. Plutonium was known to be unlike U-235 in that it emitted much alpha radiation while decaying naturally. Alpha radiation in turn was known to beget additional neutrons in subcritical and near-critical masses of plutonium. The effect, it was known, would vary widely with chemical impurities so incredibly minute that they could never be eliminated from any sample of plutonium (nobody will ever make anything absolutely pure). Consequently by comparison with U-235, as two subcritical masses of plutonium neared each other, it was expected that they would grow more violently and unpredictably unstable. The gun would therefore have to be faster.

explored. Theoretical physics would coordinate, but no scientist should hesitate to express an idea or hang back from working at it for fear it might prove a blind alley.

On this note Serber finished delivering what he called his Primer. After him spoke a succession of physicists, chemists, and explosive experts. Oppenheimer encouraged listeners to talk back freely. Decompartmentalization quickly began bearing fruit. "You could never tell where ideas would come from," said Major Smith, who had to keep some rough track of them for the sake of his documents and patents file. The U-235 gun, regarded as prototype for the plutonium gun, was first to profit. Its target would be screwed to its muzzle. It would only need to fire once; wear on the barrel would be no problem (this thought took a surprisingly long time to come out). With fins and outer casing, the bomb must be kept short enough to hang under the biggest new warplane, the B-29. Length would be seventeen feet, thickness less than two. Gradually the thing clothed itself, first with a concrete image, then with a personality. The earliest of the mortal apparitions to haunt the Mesa, it acquired a name, the Thin Man, whose origin no one now at Los Alamos can account for.*

Meanwhile a flesh-and-blood thin man, Seth Neddermeyer, sat in the crowd repressing a feeling that something was wrong. Neddermeyer was good at repressing his feelings. Tall and bony, sensitive and reserved, he followed the lectures with his jaw clamped on a dead cigar butt and with his gray eyes seemingly turned inward. A touch of gray in his bushy hair (at thirty-six he was almost seven years older than the audience average) set him a little apart from his seatmates. They did not find him very outgoing. "Neddermeyer was shy," said another Mesa physicist, William Higinbotham, himself a life-of-the-party type.

With Oppenheimer he was on more familiar terms than with most of the others there. At Pasadena, Oppenheimer had been one of his teachers. Then in the late winter of this year when he was in war research at the Bureau of Standards in Washington, Oppenheimer had telephoned him from Berkeley. With Manley not

---

* The most likely conjecture is that the Thin Man was named by a physicist who had cultivated his imagination at the movies. William Powell and Myrna Loy had recently made popular a film series based on a Dashiell Hammett novel of that name.

in hearing, Oppenheimer had forgotten the damned organization chart and talked as one nonbuilder to another. "I'm engaged in a little project involving about seventy-five men," he had said. "Would you be interested?"

Pleased, Neddermeyer had said yes, and Oppenheimer had come to see him at the Bureau. Walking in the guarded grounds, Oppenheimer had delighted him with a definite invitation. He was glad to escape from unpromising proximity-fuse work at the Bureau, glad to be in the desert, glad to share in the excitement and creativity of the packed conference room. But he could not fully share. Compared with the intuitive leap his mind was tensing for, the mental processes of the others looked tame and conformist. Phrases of Serber's echoed in his memory with the order and emphasis unaccountably changed. "Serber had said something about using the mathematics of spherical distribution for treating the shockwave," said Neddermeyer. "To me it seemed connected with making the shockwave spherically symmetrical. Yet when I tried I couldn't remember Serber speaking of that. I remembered instead his mentioning the possibility of making the gun fire a mass into a solid backstop of tamper."

These were the impressions Neddermeyer had of his own thoughts in the sequence in which they rose out of his unconscious. Spherical distribution was a routine concept of higher mathematics. Spherical shockwave was a nonsense expression. As for backstops, none should be needed to stop the moving mass, since it should explode before it got to them. Meaningless phrases pointlessly linked: perhaps this is the way any discoverer's account of his moment of discovery would sound. Creative people, psychologists speculate, are those who can tolerate a little brief disorder in the id. Neddermeyer's thoughts had no order that he could see. Putting them in order meant trying to perceive the alien logic of the order in which his unconscious had spewed them up. For a long time Neddermeyer could not do it.

After Serber spoke, Fermi, Rabi, Allison, Bethe, and other notables spoke. Neddermeyer did not interrupt as Oppenheimer had encouraged listeners to do, but his inward preoccupation made him increasingly restless. He talked of it to table companions at coffee breaks. Lecturers changed from physicists to chemists to ordnance experts. One of the latter—all that Neddermeyer could afterward

recollect of him was that he looked young—raised his eyebrows at
the way the word *explosion* had been tossed about. *Explosion*
would not do, he said, to describe the chemical violence that would
drive together the parts of the critical mass in a fission bomb. *Explosion* meant driving *apart*. The proper word for driving together
was *implosion*.

His talk framed pictures already forming in Neddermeyer's
mind (physicists nowadays do not usually think in pictures). Neddermeyer was seeing spheres of uranium and plutonium squeezed
like an orange. Squeeze hard enough on anything hard and it will
behave as though it were soft. Squeeze it unevenly and it will dent
at some places, bulge at others. Squeeze it very evenly and very
hard, and then what will it do? "I remember thinking of trying
to push in a shell of material against a plastic flow," said Neddermeyer, "and I calculated the minimum pressures that would have
to be applied. Then I happened to recall a crazy thing somebody
had published about firing bullets against each other. It may have
had a photograph of two bullets liquefied on impact. That is what
I was thinking of when the ballistics man mentioned implosion.
At this point I raised my hand."

For Los Alamos people, memories of what he said then and later
are mixed together and hard to separate. He was trying to define
implosion, a far different concept to him from what it had been to
the ballistics men. *Implosion* to him meant squeezing a subcritical mass in upon itself from all sides at once. The effect would
be somewhat like that of the collapsing suns Oppenheimer had
brooded about before he met Kitty. The purpose would be to bring
the nuclei of the subcritical mass so close together that they would
all begin to fission about the same time. Thus the subcritical mass
would suddenly become critical, and one would have a new kind
of bomb, an implosion bomb.

Neddermeyer now understood why his unconscious had ob-
truded on him the phrase "spherical shockwave." To make such
a bomb, one would have to set off innumerable chemical explosions around the outside perimeter of a spherical subcritical mass.
All the explosions would have to go off so nearly simultaneously
as to produce a symmetrically converging shockwave. It would
have to be so uniform and so violent as to produce a degree of
compression hitherto undreamed of. When Neddermeyer raised

his hand and started to speak, he was still groping for words with which to define his concept of implosion.

"The gun will compress in one dimension," Manley has the impression he heard him say, though Neddermeyer does not recall using these exact words. "Two dimensions would be better. Three dimensions would be better still." Shorter travel, faster assembly was the reason he gave. Even a sphere of solid metal, he asserted, could be compressed if a layer of T.N.T. were set off around it. Thus better bombs could be made from smaller critical masses of uranium and plutonium.

Haltingly Neddermeyer ("a very mild sort of guy and a very poor salesman," says Higinbotham) worked himself into an argument with the best scientific brains the country could concentrate on its most urgent need. Many impracticable things would be desirable if they were not impracticable. In this sense everyone could see that it would be desirable to compress uranium and plutonium uniformly. In the final analysis, Neddermeyer could not add anything to this commonplace. Measured against their own, the conference leaders found his information and mathematics skimpy. Under other names at other conferences, implosion had been touched on before, though never so persistently. "Neddermeyer faced stiff opposition from Oppenheimer and, I think, Fermi and Bethe," said Manley.

Compared with the ordnance experts, however, these three were enthusiastic. "What do you know about explosives?" the former asked Neddermeyer. When he candidly answered nothing, they grew very polite. His concept of implosion seemed almost against nature, they said and made a transparent effort not to show they felt he was raving.

After a first reaction of outraged sanity, Oppenheimer leaned back watching thoughtfully and taking no further part in the baiting. Even now, when asked about the discussion, those present tend to smile and apologize for a sense of comic incongruity which kept them from seeing that history was being made. James Tuck became absorbed by the implosion question when he arrived at the Mesa a little later. Tuck was perhaps the first person who cared much about defining how Oppenheimer had responded when implosion was first formally proposed to him. "His attitude was 'Haven't we got enough trouble without *that?*' " says Tuck. "But he didn't say, 'Don't do it.' "

"I don't remember much about what I said at the conference that day," says Neddermeyer. "I do remember that Oppenheimer listened. After it was over he talked with me." In Oppenheimer's office the war seemed closer and uglier. Oppenheimer looked tired. Neddermeyer had an impression of a man racked and haggard, alive to a crushing responsibility. "He must make it all work," he reflected. "He must pick things that will work."

Implosion too changed and lost the charm of a thesis to be defended. "This will have to be looked into," Oppenheimer said. He told Neddermeyer he was making him Group Leader, Ordnance Division, Section E-5, Implosion Experimentation.

War research, he intimated when Neddermeyer showed little joy, could not be like college research. With the bleak sympathy of one instinctive nonadministrator for another, Oppenheimer educated him. "Use as many men and as much equipment as you can," he said. Implosion was a dark and difficult prospect, Oppenheimer continued—in his opinion, too difficult to be of any value in the war. But Neddermeyer must prove the contrary. He handed Neddermeyer this paradox as though it brought him a little relief from his own burdens. His face grew younger and lit with a teasing grin. "If you can do it, I'll give you a bottle of whiskey," he promised.

From him Neddermeyer also obtained approval of his plans, which were simple in the extreme. First Neddermeyer went to a government arsenal laboratory to see how explosives were handled. Then with a supply of RDX, which he had learned to call peanut butter, he fired steel cylinders into the air and measured their time of flight. From this he computed the temporary denting that must have occurred in them when they took off. "Crude," said the handful of physicists who gave themselves any concern about implosion. "Noisy," said everyone else on the Mesa, more feelingly. A Governing Board on which Oppenheimer tried to dump administrative duties relegated this work to an arroyo well south of Main Tech. "They didn't exile me," protests Neddermeyer, glad to find something to smile about in the grim, heartbreaking role to which his originality had condemned him.

Anywhere else he would have probably felt less at home. His talent was only a little farther out than that of most of the individualists whom Oppenheimer was trying to put at ease on the Mesa. "Here at great expense," physicists say General Groves told his military staff, "the government has assembled the world's largest collection of crackpots." Be patient, be tolerant, Groves preached, but he found the practice not so easy.

Groves's difficulty was that the Mesa did not see him as he looked to many other people in the Manhattan District. From the Mesa he obtained information, elsewhere he passed it on. Elsewhere he was authority incarnate. Dynamic and unquenchable, he drove contract-corporation heads, construction engineers, and plant production managers relentlessly toward goals which he understood and they did not. On the other hand, on the Mesa he had to play the less congenial role of knowledge seeker, often from scientists with a tactless sense of humor.

At his urging Oppenheimer had strengthened himself on the practical side with an assistant director from industry, Edward Condon, then in charge of research at Westinghouse. Heavy, square-hewn, deceptively slow-moving and dignified, Condon was at heart still the puckish bohemian who had long ago tormented Millikan. Every effort of Groves's to show him who was in command ended in low comedy. Worse still, the slyly glinting brown eyes and the slyly curled lips seemed to follow Groves about with an expression of utter incredulous fascination and distaste. Groves decided Condon had no other occupation. "He didn't do what I term an honest day's work," Groves asserted, still smarting ten years later.

Groves too could hurt, and with harsher weapons. First he used austerity. "No frills," he shrugged when Condon wanted to enlarge the school planned for personnel children. Next he managed to involve Condon in a reprimand about compartmentalization. Though complicated, the story is worth following, because it illustrates the difficulties under which Oppenheimer was struggling.

It began when, in preparation for the conference, Oppenheimer journeyed to Chicago to ask for a speck of plutonium as soon as possible. To underline his urgency he explained to Compton what he meant to do with it. He would have been spared the trip if the chiefs of the three production programs had attended the conference, and Condon wondered why they did not. "To me," he wrote Oppenheimer, "the absence of such men as A. H. Compton, E. O. Lawrence, and H. C. Urey was an unfortunate thing, but up to that time in your office last Monday I had put it down simply to their being too busy."

In Oppenheimer's office Condon learned better. Groves was his teacher. Though Groves had acquiesced, he had squirmed while Oppenheimer broke down compartmentalization inside the Laboratory. To compensate, he made himself furiously strict at the perimeter. In this way he could also compensate for a more fundamental distress, that of being reduced to second fiddle. "It irked him to feel how completely he had got himself under Oppenheimer's thumb," says a scientist who declines to be quoted by name, "so every now and then he would do something that would cause Oppenheimer trouble or embarrassment just to show he could."

This was the background of the scene in Oppenheimer's office. Groves made three points. First, not even Lawrence, Compton, or Urey was to be let in on the business of the bomb laboratory. Second, he resented Oppenheimer's telling Compton. Third, he also blamed Condon as well as Oppenheimer. "I was so shocked I could hardly believe my ears," wrote Condon.

Groves's reason for including Condon in his censure was that, not being able to stand him, he suspected him of somehow putting Oppenheimer up to the guilty act. Condon felt this was the last straw and resigned. "I always thought it was because he thought the project would fail," said Groves, cheerfully unaware of how he might himself tend to put such a notion into a man's head. Oppenheimer let Condon go; it would have been very hard, perhaps impossible, to do anything else, though Condon was a brilliant physicist lost. Graver still was Oppenheimer's loss of freedom to coordinate the work of the production plants directly instead of through Groves. Afterward Groves consented to a very limited amount of interlaboratory communication. But sitting above a succession of harassed local military commanders, he made the Mesa his headquarters for controlling the entire scattered Project. To pass on information, Oppenheimer was often obliged to tutor him. To get information, he was often obliged to depend on the vagaries of what Groves thought worth relaying.

Besides directing the Mesa, Oppenheimer had to continue to recruit scientists for it and procure difficult materials and hardware. To do so, he often traveled to other project installations. At these after the Condon incident he made a fetish of secrecy about the bomb. Curious scenes resulted. "Once Oppenheimer came to the Met Lab [Metallurgical Laboratory] shop to confer about something he wanted made," recalls Thomas J. O'Donnell, shop superintendent. "He looked, first casually, then very closely, at a piece of apparatus we'd been fabricating.

" 'Where's it for?' he asked.

" 'Either Berkeley or Los Alamos,' I told him.

"His face got white, he didn't say anything for a minute, then he hit the ceiling. Acted real mad. Turned out the fabrication was secret inside stuff about the bomb—this wasn't hard to guess—and he hadn't ordered it and didn't know anything about it. I expect he thought he'd come on a big leak in the security wall they had around that place out there."

Groves showed no such concern as he had over Condon. In the course of time Oppenheimer discovered why. To keep as independent as possible, Groves was secretly checking with Alvarez at the Mesa on Oppenheimer's secret plans. Hearing from Groves that Oppenheimer needed to have the apparatus fabricated, Alvarez had merely given the order to O'Donnell. Since the explanation could not be overt—this would have defeated Groves's purpose—Oppenheimer could never be sure what to expect from Alvarez.

In many respects Oppenheimer was still an ignorant man. He had no good ground to doubt that Groves was merely initiating him into the universal folkways of top management. Insofar as he thought it would help build the bomb, he remade himself to conform. Hitherto strong instinct had led him to pass his life among the waxy faces of the night people. Now he rose at dawn and, while the other physicists slept, sat clearing his desk at Main Tech of paper work.

Diverse as the changing colors of the Mesa were the problems that the Governing Board and other buffer organizations let sift through to him there. How could one allocate too few Indian maidservants among too many wives suddenly turned *mem-sahib?* How could one make the penny-pinching Project finance office in California see that to measure the penetrating power of high-energy radiation Dana Mitchell really had to have a thick disk of gold, not lead? How could one maintain morale in a shop of machinists who all wanted to escape the wartime labor freeze by getting fired? And most naggingly and specifically, how could one handle the case of the speeding physicist?

To keep the Mesa's children from being run over on the roads,

Oppenheimer had had a committee set up traffic regulations. Its report hit his desk with the ugly immediacy of a spitwad in teacher's eye, a challenge to his right to tell anybody anything whatever. Owen Chamberlain, the committee complained, drove too fast. They had warned him, then fined him, and he had refused to pay the fine. What should they do next? Try without legal authority to take away his driver's license? Expel him from the Mesa? Post a guard of mothers along his route to work?

Chamberlain was a potential Nobel laureate too valuable to lose, Oppenheimer was an ex-speeder himself, and the committee's expostulation hinted a trace of the busybody. After mulling over these complexities as long as he felt he could, Oppenheimer summoned Chamberlain and glumly surveyed the gangling callow arrogance that confronted him across his desk. "Owen Chamberlain," he said in a formal tone utterly devoid of sympathy, "it's time for you to put up or shut up. You ought to pay that fine."

Chamberlain paid and stayed, though not very cheerfully, and Oppenheimer turned his attention to another unacclimated physicist. Edward Teller was as much an individualist in his way as Neddermeyer, though never a shy one. "Before my wife came out to join me I stayed in a bachelor dormitory," a young physicist recalled. "One evening I was sitting in the lobby waiting to get into the showers and then go to bed. Teller wandered in and started talking about classified data. That was my very first contact with him. I thought decompartmentalization wasn't meant to go this far, but of course he was too big a shot for me to correct. I got into the showers and then he came hobbling in and took off his leather stump—he'd lost part of a foot in a streetcar accident—and kept chattering secret stuff in a very loud voice.

"There was no telling who might happen to overhear him. Besides anybody in the shower stalls, the place was bound to have some kind of cleaning people, though I admit you never saw much sign of them.

" 'We're not inside the Tech Area fence,' I heard myself telling him. 'Hush!'

"He goggled at me. It turned out he had a very loud, high-pitched giggle, which I now heard for the first time. 'Aren't we all a big happy family here?' he said.

"Teller's giggle sounded imbecilic if you weren't following his mental track closely. Gradually I came to associate it with his being derailed from some intense inward concentration. I remember afterward he taught quantum mechanics on the Mesa and I sat in the class. He wrote down a sign wrong about magnetic vector potential and kept using it wrong. It was so exasperating that I forgot I was a student. 'Good God, Man!' I broke in. 'It's the other way!' He stopped talking and responded first with the goggle, then with the giggle."

Superficially Teller and Neddermeyer were opposite types. A younger colleague who thus bluntly forced himself on Neddermeyer's attention might well have been rewarded with a freezing "Let me finish." The giggle, by contrast, showed that Teller was not seriously bothered. He could be counted on for warmth and kindness in nearly any situation. Instead of clinging to one lonely premature fixed idea, he was the kind of man whom other physicists characterize as having an idea a minute, usually wrong. Nevertheless, after a few months the two men's careers on the Mesa became roughly parallel.

The thermonuclear bomb seemed then a hopeful possibility not too much beyond the Mesa's wartime assignment of bombs from uranium and plutonium. Making it his particular province, Teller became a familiar figure at the liquid-deuterium or cryogenics plant, Laboratory Y. Physicists there vividly remember the way his gentle smile illuminated the place, especially during coffee breaks. Watching him stir the entire group's sugar ration into his coffee cup, they wondered how a man could be so genuinely friendly and at the same time so ruthlessly self-absorbed. "Lovable and selfish," concluded a junior student of character at his other headquarters, Main Tech.

Oppenheimer had designed the Mesa's administrative machinery with a view to making unconventional thinkers feel at home. Bethe, his chief lieutenant and head of his Theoretical Division, was well qualified to help him do so. "Bethe impressed me as a man of outstanding power and insight, always showing sympathy and poise, never seeming to get excited," said physicist Llewelyn Hughes, whom Oppenheimer brought from Washington University to replace Condon. Nevertheless, Bethe choked up and got excited when reporting on his relations with Teller. "He was on my staff. I relied—I hoped to rely very heavily on him to help our work in theoretical physics. It turned out that he did not want to cooperate. He did not want to work on the agreed line of research that everybody else in the laboratory had agreed to as the fruitful line. He always suggested new things, new deviations. He did not do the work which he and his group were supposed to do in the framework of the Theoretical Division. So that at the end there was no choice but to relieve him of any work in the general line of development of Los Alamos, and to permit him to pursue his own ideas entirely unrelated to the World War II work with his own group outside of the Theoretical Division. This was quite a blow to us."

Teller wandered about the Mesa projecting a confident, uncannily hypnotic assumption that only the thermonuclear reaction was worth working on. Other physicists could not tell whether he knew or cared about the little circle of bewilderment and disrupted schedules that moved with him. "It would take a flock of psychiatrists to understand Teller," philosophized Allison, then shifting his base from Chicago to the Mesa.

Oppenheimer did not conduct the Mesa's harmonious anarchy by telling other physicists what to do. His way, instead, was to listen and restate so precisely that everyone's ideas seemed by their own motion to find their proper place in the program. Superficially, the process looked like government by committee except that it went on so swiftly. A physicist would have an idea, tell it to Oppenheimer, be rewarded with instant flashing comprehension, and set to work at once in the warm glow of a star pupil appreciated. All this usually took place at public meetings. Should Oppenheimer have appeared to suppress or overlook any significant proposal, morale would have collapsed. Consequently, to impose a new order on the Mesa, Teller had only to stump him in physics.

Conversely, if Teller meant to be taken seriously, he must go to bat with his ideas and let his colleagues see whether Oppenheimer could field them. Game time came at any meeting he and Oppenheimer attended, but most spectacularly on Tuesdays. On these evenings all scientists inside the fence were invited to assemble in Main Tech for a free exchange of ideas. For Teller it was the weekly moment of truth.

The genial enigma with the cold eyes showed his most human

side in these encounters. He remembered the chili peppers with which Oppenheimer had paralyzed him at their first meeting. More breathtakingly, he remembered the blackboard in Oppenheimer's Berkeley office on which he had miscalculated heat loss. Now as time went by he had important new discoveries to announce about the thermonuclear bomb. The effect, he found himself agreeing with Oppenheimer, was to indicate that it would need tritium in quantities not producible during the war. Whenever he stood up to address Oppenheimer, mathematics seemed to resolve every question adversely to his purpose.

Worst of all for Teller, at the Tuesday sessions Oppenheimer showed no awareness that his direction of the Mesa was being challenged. Nothing irked him but faulty computations, and even then he contented himself with suggesting the appropriate correction. Also present was the chemist Sam Weissman, who had observed Oppenheimer at the Berkeley seminars. In comparison with those days, Weissman decided that Oppenheimer was getting soft.

"During the continuing thermonuclear discussions," said Weissman, "I remember Teller's getting up to make a speech. He started out by saying he would give only qualitative factors. But when he warmed up, he laid out a few calculations which showed he had actually forgotten the factor of C^2, the velocity of light. I suppose that for a profusely inventive man any sort of figures could sometimes seem like a straitjacket.

"Oppenheimer looked musingly at the blackboard as though it had opened a new philosophical concept for him. He seemed to be pondering what sort of reasoning could operate with an error of a million per cent. 'This idea of dealing only in qualitative factors makes an interesting approach,' he said, 'but should we go so far as to treat the velocity of light as unity?' "

To every trade its own jokes. Weissman could not tell whether Oppenheimer meant to make one, but the rustle in the audience showed he had done so. Teller seemed to confirm the fact by a response far different from that he had shown in the showers. Weissman noticed no giggle, but a convulsive start and a whitened face. Except by the outlandish logic of the emotions, pain remembered is no index to the depth of a wound. Alienated by scars deep to superficial, Neddermeyer, Condon, Alvarez, Chamberlain, and

Teller would constitute suitable authorship for a negative minority report on Los Alamos.

The content of the majority report began to accumulate as work progressed through the fall and winter of 1943. Despite an agonizing slowness in delivery of U-235 from Oak Ridge, the Thin Man developed nicely. Serber's idea that the fissionable projectile could be stopped by a tamper instead of being allowed to pass through proved feasible. Together with other suggestions, this permitted the Thin Man to be cut by half its length into a more efficiently vicious Little Boy. Not enough information could be developed about plutonium to warrant a similar economy, but design progressed smoothly for its faster gun. The Metallurgical Laboratory delivered the promised speck which, though too minute to reveal much else, confirmed Serber's opinion that the neutron number of plutonium would turn out to be at least as high as that of U-235. This meant that the projectile speed previously decided on for the plutonium gun should prove satisfactory.

A peculiar problem arose at the payroll office, where reports came in on daily hours worked by the scientific staff. Groves had set up the system not to pay overtime but to keep down absenteeism. Group leaders duly supplied the data without reasoning about the purpose. The payroll office did not know what to do with work reports ranging up to a preposterous and unreimbursable eighteen hours a day.

"At five o'clock every afternoon the Military Police closed up the labs," said Lavatelli. "Apparently they didn't have orders to throw us out, but they did have orders to lock up the supplies. We sawed around the locks on the stockroom doors and just stayed and worked. We kept a refrigerator full of milk, beer, and sandwich stuff because everybody was pretty hungry by four in the morning, our usual quitting time. After a while whoever was directing the M.P.'s caught the spirit of the thing and stopped replacing the locks."

Gluttons for work may not be much more attractive than other gluttons, but those at Los Alamos had at least the aesthetic justification that each was only trying to please himself, not an employer. "I suppose the situation resembled that at Lawrence's Berkeley lab from the point of view of hours put in," says physicist Carrol Mills, an alumnus of both places. "The difference was the atmosphere. There you did whatever task they assigned you and learned not to ask why. Here you asked what you liked and at least thought you did what you liked. There the pressure came from outside. Here there didn't seem to be any pressure."

The contrast with other Project installations was more obvious. In New York, antagonism between Urey and Dunning made *esprit de corps* a drollery. From Chicago and Oak Ridge, where the Metallurgical Laboratory had set up a branch, much of the work and many of the best scientists gravitated to Los Alamos. Those who stayed lost research momentum and revived the spirit of the defunct Uranium Committee. They devoted their excess energy to picking hostilely at Compton, the duPont company, and the very notion that their brains had been commandeered for a military use. Ultimately, of course, they must be given credit for remaining sane while the Mesa went mad with bomb fever in accordance with Szilard's prediction. But the atmosphere, Allison complained to Oppenheimer, was not exhilarating.

Before settling down on the Mesa, Fermi commuted several months from Chicago. The contrast between the Mesa and the Metallurgical Laboratory seemed to fascinate him. As at Chicago, he found the German threat was taken very seriously on the Mesa. "We had information in those days of German activity in nuclear fission," said Oppenheimer. "We were aware of what it might mean if they beat us to the draw in the development of atomic bombs." The difference was that the Mesa reacted to the threat with élan instead of anxiety. "When anyone mentions laboratory directors," Fermi philosophized to Segré, "I think of directors and directors and Oppenheimer, who is unique." Fermi also philosophized directly to Oppenheimer. "After he had sat in on one of his first conferences here," Oppenheimer recollected many years later, "he turned to me and said, 'I believe your people actually *want* to make a bomb.' I remember his voice sounded surprised."

If the Mesa were a simple story, this comment would be the sort to dwell on in compiling contributions to the majority report. But at this time the Mesa was giving Latimer in Berkeley new cause to brood. He decided Oppenheimer was making pacifists of the chemists he sent him. What baffled the self-appointed unpossessed inquisitor was that they shared the Mesa's general eagerness to build the bomb. Two simple facts might seem to account for the contradiction: the director was a Jew, and he believed in Ahimsa. Thus he might unconsciously convince his associates that the bomb was the only form of Ahimsa (gentleness) that one could teach to the builders of Auschwitz and Belsen. But such an explanation could not satisfy Latimer. He went on brooding. In him Oppenheimer had no ordinary enemy. The majority report should not stop until it gives some inkling of what Latimer sensed and disliked on the Mesa.

"If you go around asking those of us who were here then about the job Oppenheimer did during the war," says physicist Raemer Schreiber, "the chances are you're just going to hear the word 'magnificent' over and over. Always that same damned monotonous word. I doubt you're going to get anywhere finding out what it means." Schreiber now leads nuclear-propulsion research at Los Alamos. Built like a center for the Green Bay Packers, he has a tough businesslike face that looks incongruous against the fantastically beautiful view outside the window where he keeps his desk.

"The way I felt about Oppenheimer," he meditates, staring thoughtfully at the Mesa. "Well, I'd spent a year measuring tritium-beryllium cross sections without knowing what for. When I got here in July of 1943, Oppenheimer handed me a copy of the Primer that explained it. 'If you need any equipment, see Dana Mitchell,' he said. I was used to wrangling for weeks to get an oscilloscope. Mitchell just gave you what you wanted as though he had a list of it made up beforehand. 'If you need anything else, see me,' Oppenheimer said. And you could. You could always talk with him. I think that's why the work never seemed frustrating. He gave you a sense of urgency and made you feel that what you did was important. But I expect you've heard all this before, and I don't think it goes far to explain what was special about the way he ran this place."

Physicist Norris Bradbury, now director of Los Alamos, has a sensitive, kindly face like Adlai Stevenson's and an even more awesome view of canyons and deserts outside his office window. "Magnificent! That's the exact word. Why? Well, I'm no deep thinker," he said as though someone had called on him to do some deep thinking. "Of course, Oppenheimer could understand everything, and there were some hard physics problems here to understand. When I was a student at Berkeley, I knew him as a lecturer, at first not a good lecturer, impatient and demanding. But even then he was a sort of genius, knowing more about more things than anyone else I knew. Here I've seen him deal incredibly well with what looked like dead-end situations technically speaking. It was not that his decisions were always correct. But they always opened up a course of action where none had been apparent. They were made with a sense of dedication that moved the whole laboratory. Don't forget what an extravagant collection of prima donnas we had here. By his own knowledge and personality he kept them inspired and going forward. With very few exceptions, they felt that what he had decided they had decided and that therefore the official course of action deserved all their support."

"Magnificent!" says Serber. "It makes you wonder why such an enormous scientific talent never won a Nobel prize, though I suppose no one of the discoveries he worked out by himself in Berkeley could be called really outstanding. But he could understand anything. One thing I noticed: he would show up at innumerable different meetings at Los Alamos, listen, and summarize in such a way as to make amazing sense. Nobody else I ever knew could comprehend so quickly. And along with this, he developed tremendous tact. There was a big advisory council that gave Los Alamos the appearance of a democracy just because he handled it so well. Everybody was convinced that his problems were the urgent and important ones, because Oppenheimer thought so."

"Magnificent," says Condon's successor, physicist A. Llewelyn Hughes, making the usual point about understanding. "It was not by skill in human relations that he kept Los Alamos moving, but by wisdom. We trusted him. He was completely honest in a way that in the long run made him completely vulnerable. As for his physics, he maintained a continuing high level of contributions, but this is not so much what wins one a Nobel prize as a single isolated achievement."

"Magnificent," says Bethe, repeating the point about understanding and emphasizing the diversity of problems raised by the bomb. "A physicist like Fermi would delight in solution of a single problem. I admired him to idolatry, but there is another type of mind which is equally needed. Oppenheimer was more interested in the general idea and whole field of physics. He worked at physics mainly because he found physics the best way to do philosophy.

This undoubtedly had something to do with the magnificent way he led Los Alamos."

Perhaps the most familiar scientific visitor who never finally made his home on the Mesa was Rabi. Alien in black suit, black homburg and (a false but persistent legend has it) black patent-leather shoes, he would arrive at the guest lodge carrying a black rolled umbrella. "It hasn't rained in months," Oppenheimer, Bethe, and Allison would say in greeting. At that moment, insists the legend, it always began to rain. Rabi would put up his umbrella and the other three would get wet on the long trek to Main Tech. "They called me the Rainmaker from Hoboken," he declares proudly.

"Magnificent," he says. "I take it you want something from me besides dry talk about how well he handled committees and besides my belief he was the best native physicist of his generation. He worked very fairly, very hard, he was not in the least a dictator, and except by a few he made himself deeply respected, even loved. There was something else. The Mesa as he created it has enlarged the most unexpected variety of careers in science. A certain magic, romance, devotion, causes people who were there to remember it as the most significant period in their lives."

Watching Los Alamos grow, Fermi correctly predicted that by the end of the war it would be home for three thousand scientists. Almost every foreign accent was heard, including that of Niels Bohr, whose English was sometimes hard to distinguish from his Danish. Night after night under the desert moon, Bohr walked the sands with Oppenheimer and urged him to remember he was not there to settle details of personnel or engineering but to get solutions to fundamental problems in physics. Roosevelt and Churchill, without much consultation with anyone else, decided to enrich the babel with a British mission. Toward the start of 1944 the catholic Mesa began echoing the clipped patois of men in Bermuda shorts.

The British contributed to all phases of the program, at first most particularly to hydrodynamics, a mathematical description of the hell at the interface between the inward and outward shock-waves of a detonating bomb. Among the hairiest of the younger knees and most robust of the younger talents were those exhibited by James Tuck, age thirty, from the University of Manchester. A few years after the war, Tuck was summoned back to the Mesa by

Teller and Lewis Strauss to lead research toward control of the thermonuclear reaction for peaceful purposes. This was probably hard luck for him, since it now seems he was saddled with a typically American crash drive into the impossible. But Tuck gives one the impression that he can do it if anybody can; meanwhile, he is amply paying for his keep with serendipity. He has an open, fearless face like that of an honest workingman who has never had to learn the bourgeois's defensive cunning. "I am a prejudiced person" is the way he puts it, meaning in British collegiate jargon that he is unprejudiced. Incongruously, Tuck's laboratory is known on the Mesa as one of the places where the flame kindled by Oppenheimer during the war years now burns brightest. "Tuck is not an administrator, he's an assimilator," says McKibben. "Talk with him. He'll make you see how Oppenheimer ran the Mesa."

Tuck likes the Mesa's fences and badges. They make him think of an aristocracy of talent rather than of Auschwitz, where badges were needed to distinguish those who fed the furnace from those who were fed into it. Tuck prizes what he calls Western civilization and judges Oppenheimer's Mesa to have been a culmination of it.

"The most exclusive club in the world," he says. "At the very start, Oppenheimer killed the idiotic notion prevalent in other laboratories that only a few insiders should know what the work was about and that everyone else should follow them blind. I, an almost unknown scientist, came here and found that I was expected to exchange ideas with men whom I had regarded as names in textbooks. It was a wonderful thing for me, it opened my eyes. Here at Los Alamos I found a spirit of Athens, of Plato, of an ideal republic.

"The ignorant think Oppenheimer originated the bomb. Of course this isn't so, but his contribution was magnificent. Few people in the United States know this place that he created and what it has done. It's a story that ought to be told. Nowadays I read in the papers that this should be made an ordinary town, with no gate and three movie houses. I've never seen a place less ordinary. So many people doing a damned difficult job wresting the secrets from nature. Oppenheimer had to concert the fullest effort of the best minds of the Western world. Los Alamos is a phenomenon unique in history.

"By the grace of God the American government got the right man. His function here was not to do penetrating original research but to inspire it. It required a surpassing knowledge of science and of scientists to sit above warring groups and unify them. A lesser man could not have done it. Scientists are not necessarily cultured, especially in America. Oppenheimer had to be. The people who had been gathered here from so many parts of the world needed a great gentleman to serve under. I think that's why they remember that golden time with enormous emotion."

7

MIDNIGHT

Physicists who brought their wives to the Mesa promptly found two rocks in the marriage bed. "I'm a prisoner," ran the feminine complaint. "Nobody can leave here except on official business, and women don't have any. And that's not all. The way that Security man looks at me, I could swear he's read something intimate I wrote to Mother about how insistent you are and how difficult it is for me with no bathtub." Officially, letters were supposed to be free of censorship. Though husbands pooh-poohed at first, wives maintained that this freedom was actually a policy of entrapment. Quasi evidence mounted on the Mesa into an overwhelming emotional certainty. The Governing Board protested to Oppenheimer, who protested forcibly to Groves, who investigated and issued a denial nobody believed. "If that's the Security man's job, you can at least make it *dull*," the stymied women told their husbands. As a result, censorship became official and with everybody on guard the letters became less interesting.

To most people on the Mesa, Security was Captain Peer DeSilva. Stern views on the sacrifices demanded by war made him ruthless in scanning letters and forbidding travel. Two years out of West Point, he had the bold, aquiline good looks of the actor Gilbert Roland and a coldly correct military bearing. He was twenty-six but seemed older, says Lansdale, and five feet nine but seemed taller. Like the physicists, he became a student of Oppenheimer's character, with the advantage that he could read his mail.

"In the opinion of this officer," he wrote to Pash, his superior in San Francisco, "Oppenheimer must either be incredibly naïve and almost childlike in his sense of reality, or he himself is extremely clever and disloyal." Aside from the last word, DeSilva's range of possibilities agrees fairly well with the physicists'. "Oppenheimer was a curiously simple man," says Tuck, who was also simple. DeSilva unhesitatingly plumped for the opposite alternative. By the lives they lead, people define the words they use. DeSilva's conduct on the Mesa throws some light on what he meant by "naïve" and "clever."

"One evening DeSilva knocked on my door," says the physicist who lived closest to him. "He stood inspecting me as though not sure he'd come to the right place. He was a very handsome, smooth, icy gent.

" 'Thank you, no, I can't sit down,' he told me in a curt emotionless voice. 'My wife and I don't get on. She's leaving me. I'll have to find bachelor quarters. Eggs and butter in the refrigerator. For you if you want them.'

"He dressed up and drove his wife to the railroad station. A month later she reappeared. The rules against visiting away from the Mesa were really strict. DeSilva may have been the only man who got around them at this early time. Deliberate? Sure, but you couldn't prove it. He was too slick."

"The writer wishes to go on record as saying that J. R. Oppenheimer is playing a key part in the attempt of the Soviet Union to secure, by espionage, highly secret information which is vital to the Soviet Union," DeSilva wrote Pash on September 2, 1943. Russia in fact put two spies on the Mesa: brilliant, tormented Klaus Fuchs of the British Mission and loathsome David Greenglass, a machinist who later sent his sister to the electric chair by pretending he had told her scientific secrets of which he in fact had no inkling. But these men Security ignored ("Inexcusable," said Lansdale), perhaps because they could not be connected in any way with Oppenheimer. DeSilva was reacting partly to events at Berkeley shortly to be related, partly to the spirit of Oppenheimer's Mesa. Like the physicists he found this spirit unique, but unlike them he hated it.

It is the opinion of this officer [DeSilva told Pash] that Oppenheimer is deeply concerned with gaining a world-wide reputation as a scientist, and a place in history, as a result of the Project. It is also believed that the Army is in the position to allow him to do so or to destroy his name, reputation and career, if it should choose to do so. Such a possibility, if strongly presented to him, would possibly give him a different view of his position with respect to the Army, which has been heretofore one in which he has been dominant because of his supposed essentiality. If his attitude should be changed by such an action, a more wholesome and loyal attitude might, in turn, be injected into the lower echelons of employees.[1]

Thus DeSilva dreamed of forcing the Mesa to respect him, and in the same words skillfully hinted to Groves, his ultimate reader, a means of rising to first fiddle. For himself his strategy paid well. During the war he rose from lieutenant to lieutenant colonel. On April 11, 1945, he left the Mesa for wider horizons. A letter he then sent to the man whom he had called a spy suggests what the terms "naïve" and "clever" meant to him:

Dear Oppie [older friends called him Robert], Upon my transfer from the project, I want you to know of my sincere appreciation of the support and encouragement which you have personally given me during my service here. In spite of your more urgent problems and duties, your consideration and help on matters I have brought to you have been gratifying and have, in fact, contributed much to whatever success my office has had in performing its mission. . . . My service at the project and my association with you and your fellow workers are matters which I shall remember with pride.[2]

As this letter implies, Oppenheimer took some trouble to make the Security people and their attitude palatable to the Mesa. Astonishingly, he kept down parlor-pink talkativeness, not by suppressing it but by making it unfashionable. Here only would physicists grow restless and drift back to work when a colleague declaimed too wordily that the blind forces of nationalism did not deserve so terrible a weapon. Given better listeners, Fuchs and Greenglass might have talked till they caught DeSilva's ear. DeSilva would probably have been happier at the other laboratories, where spies instead of being lonely and professional mingled congenially with loud but harmless radicals.

In the opinion of Security, for example, Lawrence at Berkeley was unwittingly running a sort of boardinghouse for both types. His Radiation Laboratory, America's second-greatest scientific establishment after Los Alamos, had an authentic Communist cell. Out of curiosity twenty-five-year-old Computer Technician Robert Davis attended a few times at the start of 1943. Half a dozen fellow employees, he found, would assemble joylessly with half a dozen vacant-faced girls, psychology majors with thick glasses, to talk about the Negroes in the South. One evening Steve Nelson came and lectured jesuitically on why they should favor Chiang Kai-shek against their own cobelievers in North China. In April Lawrence lent Davis to the Mesa, where the general madness to build the bomb obliterated these interests from his memory.

The cell, however, continued. Four alleged members, Giovanni Rossi Lomanitz, Max Friedman, David Bohm, and Joseph Weinberg, were ex-students of Oppenheimer's.* Glib, strident, and not very presentable, they all look alike in retrospect but were not. Bohm was a gifted physicist. Lomanitz was allegedly the liveliest party member and recruiter, almost matching in zeal the inevitable government plant, probably a woman who had not yet been allowed to publish her memoirs. He also helped spark a new and successful effort to set up the Federation of Architects, Engineers, Chemists, and Technicians in Lawrence's laboratory. One cannot prove a negative, but with all the Army Intelligence and F.B.I. agents that surrounded these men, one can come as close as need be. Bohm, Lomanitz, and Friedman betrayed no trust to anyone.

Weinberg was a different type. One night in March of 1943, says the House Un-American Activities Committee, Weinberg went to Steve Nelson's home and dictated a complicated formula, which Nelson wrote down and carried to the Third Secretary of the Russian Embassy. Agents outside Nelson's house watched through binoculars, and what the Committee calls a highly confidential informant inside recorded the conversation. Pash, Zindle, Rathman, Murray, and Wagener are among the litany of names

---

* Allegation was by the House Un-American Activities Committee in 1949, and each man refused to answer on grounds of self-incrimination. It may well be they did so for other reasons than that they had actually been Communists. But a long and laborious, though necessarily incomplete, check of newspapers and government documents reveals no subsequent denial by them. For details of their later history, see page 358, note 3 to Chapter VII.

of Security people who got the goods on Weinberg. He kept on passing information to Nelson and they kept on watching him throughout 1943 and probably throughout the war. All these people reported later to the Committee as they had done more immediately to Lansdale, of whose evaluation one may feel less squeamish. "We proved to our satisfaction that he gave information to Steve Nelson for money," Lansdale says.[3]

Instead of arresting Weinberg and Nelson, Security decided to get rid of Lomanitz by drafting him into the Army. To follow the wheels turning within wheels that ground out this decision, one should take Security as meaning Pash reporting to Lansdale reporting to Groves. For Lomanitz, Security was the Army Engineers' Area Office in Lawrence's laboratory. It told him he was being released because his work was no longer essential. Lawrence told him it was essential and gave him a statement to this effect. Condon, who was now at Lawrence's laboratory, interceded with Oppenheimer to give Lomanitz another such statement. Oppenheimer did so on the grounds that he would have to lend Lawrence a man to replace Lomanitz. Both Lawrence and Oppenheimer expressed keen concern. With their two statements Lomanitz, a good soapbox orator, inflamed his local draft board to the point of rebellion against its national headquarters.

Nuclear physicists were by then the country's scarcest labor commodity. Lansdale expected that Oppenheimer would claim for the Mesa any undesirable who might be pried out of Lawrence's laboratory. Besides, he felt that Oppenheimer, what with his marriage, his brother, and his pink background, was in a sense the cause of all his troubles. He decided to pay a visit to the Mesa. "For goodness' sake," he said to Oppenheimer on August 10, 1943, "lay off Lomanitz and stop raising questions." During a series of conversations, Oppenheimer said his policy was to use any physicist who had a suitable outlook and who kept his mind on his work. This would include ex-Communists, he said, but not Communists.

Lomanitz was dangerous, Lansdale replied, but instead of telling about the cell, he remarked that Lomanitz was being indiscreet to outside Federation officials about his work. All the other Project installations except the Mesa were plagued with similar organizations, Lansdale declared cunningly. Oppenheimer alone had kept them out. What would he suggest to help Lawrence's laboratory clean up the Federation? The secrets of the Radiation Laboratory, he went on, had definitely been betrayed to the Russians, and therefore such dubious things as the Federation could not be tolerated. "Information is streaming out," he said sorrowfully.

Oppenheimer thought himself a complex personality, but Tuck was right in calling him simple, and in such conversations there was much to disturb a simple man who wanted to build the bomb. Having DeSilva as a specimen always under his eye and not being a complete fool, he could feel little security about the security provided by these immaculate dream-soldiers. Now it seemed obvious that the best of them could not prevent espionage at Berkeley.

At Berkeley, Lawrence too was learning about Security. Since he was even less prepared, his lessons hurt more. Shades of the political spectrum were still all dull gray to him. When talkers on his laboratory staff tried to spin out a distinction, he shut them up. Against other talkers he defended himself differently. "In 1943 Lawrence and Urey came often to Oak Ridge to watch their production plants go up," said Smyth. "When Compton moved out from Chicago, he invited his fellow program chiefs and me to dinner at his new home. Afterward everyone talked shop and Lawrence grew quite animated. Then the conversation switched to politics and became to me more interesting. Lawrence promptly went to sleep."

"I took a date over to the San Francisco symphony one night," says a younger physicist on Lawrence's staff. "Next day he told me to stick to my work and stop wasting time on such things. Music, art, philosophy, literature—these were impediments he'd dropped in the race to get ahead, even the literature of physics, I think, when it was not directly at his point of effort. And perfectly all right too, until toward the end of the war he'd got so big the question was: who was going to educate him? About the Communist scare, for example. For a long time he stood completely apart from it. Naïve and humanitarian, he grieved more than anyone else at the loss of a good worker when Groves started surgery on his payroll."

"Oblivious?" says Lansdale, his most respectable teacher. "Yes,

I reckon that's the word. He just didn't believe in the stuff I was working on. His personality was completely different from Oppenheimer's. Outgoing, always in a great hurry, simply not concerned about security problems. But he tried. He wouldn't just agree with you to hush you up. He was willing to learn."

It is not quite correct to say that before Lansdale began orienting him Lawrence had no ideas at all about security. But by a specialist's standards these were peculiar. Leftists were not the only unsavory talkers in Lawrence's laboratory. As men with scientific training became harder to hire, George Everson, his employment manager, became increasingly important and outspoken. To listen to him gave older physicists a dizzy feeling that America might welcome her own side's defeat. "He said that the United States had three enemies, Stalin, Roosevelt, and Hitler, in that order," mused one of the internationally famous staff members. "This during the war. Incredible!"

"Eversole and I sometimes traveled together to recruit at the hiring booths of the American Physical Society in other cities," said another senior associate. "He was a man who liked to drink and get mellow and hold the floor at cocktail parties. Lawrence thought this trait should be watched very carefully. He asked me to check on it when we were out of town."

Security, Lawrence learned in 1943, had nothing to do with his vague uneasiness about Eversole ("Never heard of him," says Lansdale). Wringing reluctant consent to draft Lomanitz was Lansdale's first step in educating Lawrence. ("Nobody yelled louder," says Lansdale.) Next, Lansdale persuaded Lawrence to fire another member of the Federation local's executive board, the young alleged Communist Max Friedman. Once Lawrence had committed himself by these acts, his attitude began a massive change. "He got furious at the guys that had joined the union," says one of his staff. "Sure it was a lousy union, but he wouldn't have cared if it had been the best. By the end of 1943, you felt it might cost your job to say anything good about it. He really stamped it out."

Not being a member, Weinberg was unaffected. Copies of reports he was allowed to sell the Russians are still locked in F.B.I. files. With what aim Weinberg and George Eltenton were being manipulated is a more significant topic than anything Weinberg could tell the Russians. But if he stuck faithfully to Lawrence's own point of interest, his liveliest reports were probably on hardware. Berkeley's most impressive exhibits were its pilot-model production machines. Though housed on the campus, these belonged in legal theory not to the Laboratory but to the Tennessee Eastman subsidiary of Eastman Kodak. At Oak Ridge this company was to operate duplicates that four other companies were constructing. Tennessee Eastman kept a training cadre at Berkeley to study each new model.

"In June of 1943 General Electric shipped XAX-2 out to Berkeley for Eastman to get familiar with," says Lester Coleman. "Though supposed to be the first commercial model of Alpha-2, it was still full of bugs. I was a young Eastman engineer operating the thing and tinkering with it on the night shift. That's how I came to know Lawrence. Eastman had a set of buffer executives who pretty well kept Lawrence entertained at a higher level when he visited the day shift. But at night they went to bed and left us unprotected.

"Lawrence would come in and stand beside me and watch the dials. I'd be sitting at one of the control panels with my fingers spread out trying to adjust two or three knobs simultaneously with each hand. Since XAX-2 belonged to Eastman, Lawrence couldn't say, 'Let me run it.' I expect that question had been threshed out on the day shift. But if you took your hands off the controls, Lawrence would put his hands on them. Before you knew it, you'd be edged off the stool and Lawrence would be there in your place. In fifteen minutes he'd get the machine to purring beautifully, actually operating beyond the capacity it was designed for. Then he'd hurry out. Two minutes later, first one insulator would rupture, then another, and the machine would blow up. His purpose, of course, was to test it to destruction to see where the next model needed strengthening. The ruins he left in his wake, which included me, didn't interest him."

In planning his first Alpha, Lawrence had hoped it could turn raw uranium into bomb material in one operation. No matter how hard he pushed men and models, he could not make them deliver with the purity Oppenheimer and his bomb group had determined was needed. At about the time Los Alamos was opened, Lawrence ordered the creation of Beta to refine Alpha-2's product. The first Beta had the same four J-shaped ion beams as

Alpha-2, but smaller and of lower current density. The magnet was as big. Consequently, Beta's resolution was finer, its product purer. Since it had nothing to feed on but Alpha-2's miserly reluctant yield, the fact that its own yield was much slighter seemed no handicap.

During the summer of 1943, Thornton and one of the most junior physicists in his crew tinkered boldly with Beta. Hitherto the four J-beams had plunged in parallel into the vacuum-chamber receiver and been swung in unison by the magnetic field into their respective collectors. Now Thornton and his helper designed an immense new vacuum chamber. Each ion beam entered almost parallel with the chamber rim, and at the point where magnetism swung it inward another beam entered and seemed to follow its original course. By making the receiver oval, Thornton was able to set eight J-shaped beams to following each other, each veering in toward its collector just before it overran the next. This idea, which Thornton called the Race Track, was the Laboratory's most original since Lawrence had first thought of using the mass spectrograph for mass production.

For his machines Lawrence commanded the most spectacular concentration of industrial power this country had yet seen. Besides Eastman and General Electric, he was able to draw almost at will on three other great corporations, Westinghouse, Allis-Chalmers, and Stone and Webster. At his bidding a multitude of scientific representatives from these firms gathered to collaborate with his staff in Berkeley. For their production designs he got them authorization to use fifteen thousand tons of Fort Knox silver as magnet windings in place of copper. Each firm's representatives, like Lawrence's own staff, had theoretically separate responsibilities. But throughout most of 1943 and 1944, everyone worked higgledy-piggledy on Beta. Lawrence's physicists tried desperately to stay ahead of the corporation physicists. As for engineering, no one could form a clear idea of where it began and physics left off.

A disarmed B-25 bomber shuttled mixed gaggles of technical men back and forth to Oak Ridge, where unfinished production Betas were being continuously torn down and reconstructed. "Despite our fantastic, tremendous Oak Ridge machine shops," says an engineer there, "some of Lawrence's scientists could listen to our problems and show up on the next trip with specialized fabrications that were beyond us."

On leaving Berkeley, scientists were warned to quit referring
to the slimy green end of their endeavors as "gunk." Should talk
with uncleared Oak Ridge personnel turn awkward, they were
told, the correct thing was to hint the product was a new kind of
synthetic rubber. At the end of its production run, each giant Beta
had to be taken apart and painfully scraped out to produce sometimes less than a pinhead of slime. Consequently this explanation
was received at Oak Ridge with universal indignation. Hugging
their racist chains, the simpler workmen from Tennessee and Ala-
bama whispered to each other that the slime was a concoction of
Eleanor Roosevelt's to turn Negroes white.

Compared with that at Berkeley, the industrial scientists' invasion of Compton's Chicago Laboratory had been far more modest. But at Chicago it had produced sulks, rebellion, and intrigue.
Lawrence prevented anything of the sort at Berkeley by bluntly
demanding that everyone keep his mind fixed firmly on improving calutrons. "Watch your tongue or you'll be in the Army" was
a standard joke of old hands orienting new ones.

Lawrence also took care that academic scientists should not
compensate for their lower pay by a show of condescension to their
industrial colleagues. "He was very skillful at keeping the two
groups in harmony," said Weissman, who saw a good deal of the
mixing process before leaving for Los Alamos. "At meetings I used
to admire the way he always stepped in and headed off our people
before they could sneer at the industrial guys' dumbness."

Academics vaguely suspected Lawrence of identifying himself
with the big-corporation outlook. They would have been surprised
at the thoughts of the corporation physicists who spoke and listened with alert, urbane, expensively tailored poise. One of them
was thinking about the chairs. "At my first meeting I noticed the
room was pretty much like a classroom, with a blackboard and
straight-backed wooden seats," said a corporation physicist. "There
was one big difference. Facing sideways between the board and
the class was a handsome red-leather easy chair. Lawrence sat
down in it, leaned back and looked us over. There were about two
hundred of us. At a nod from him scientists including Nobel prize
winners would pop up docilely to recite or go to the board. They
stuck with care to the points he wanted covered.

"When they all rose together, I thought I must have missed
hearing the bell ring. The Laboratory had a refreshment room

where we went for a coffee break. Next to the coffee urn was a cabinet with paper cups and spoons on top. Underneath was a red-enameled drawer, which happened to be half open. Inside I could see a china cup and saucer and a silver spoon. On the drawer was a label 'Reserved for the Director.' After my coffee, I reached for a cigar and then noticed a sign 'No Smoking by Order of the Director.' You could get permission, I was told, because the Director himself sometimes smoked and didn't mind others smoking so long as it didn't become too general a thing."

To an interposition that the chair and the drawer emanated more from Cooksey than Lawrence, who was probably only responsible for their being red, the corporation physicist replied, "Well, maybe." His attention was diverted to the question of lines of authority at the Radiation Laboratory. He reached for pencil and paper. "The Organization Chart was a daisy. I mean that literally. Here, I'll show you:

"It's not drawn to scale, because for every man in the laboratory you'd need a line running directly to the center circle, which was Lawrence. Your assistants might disappear any day. Lawrence had no intuition he ought to consult you before taking them away. They weren't formally assigned to you, and to keep them from getting attached to you they were rotated frequently. Sometimes Lawrence would give the transfer order direct, but more often he'd pick up the phone and say one word to Cooksey, who functioned more like an *ame damné* than an executive.

"It's true that some physicists at the Radiation Laboratory had status and some didn't, but the way you got it! Good heavens! In 1943 at my corporation laboratories I was working on a successful research project unrelated to the bomb. When I was about three-quarters through, the vice-president in charge of research came and asked me how I'd like to spend some time at Berkeley with Lawrence.

" 'Fine,' I said. 'In two or three months the project here will be wound up so I'll be ready to leave.'

"He looked disturbed. 'You'll need to leave in two or three days,' he said. 'Lawrence says he's fed up with the contingent of physicists we have out there now. He wants new blood. I wouldn't ask you if I could help it, but do this for me, will you?'

" 'No,' I said.

"He took me to see the corporation president, who told me the same story. My plane landed me in California air-sick on a Sunday morning. Some of our disapproved contingent stood waiting at the runway with a worried, subdued look on their faces. They showed their Berkeley indoctrination by rushing me straight to the Radiation Laboratory to meet Lawrence. Within two hours I had a mop in my hand and a bucket at my feet and was swabbing out the decks of the calutrons. So far as I could tell, this work was to be permanent. A day later I located some rubber boots. A fortnight later the vice-president flew out to see me.

" 'This is a great job you are doing for us here,' he said. 'Lawrence likes it. The president wants you to know we appreciate it.'

" 'No,' I said.

" 'Look, I've got some good news for you,' he said. 'Remember that electronics patent you turned over to us last year? The corporation is sending you a check for it.'

" 'No,' I said.

"He looked at me searchingly. 'A great big check,' he said. 'I know how you feel.'

" 'No, you don't,' I said. 'If you did, I know what you'd do. Lawrence wants Ph.D.'s. The corporation has plenty of good janitors. Why don't you give half a dozen of them honorary Ph.D.'s and send them out here? Lawrence would never know the difference.'

" 'Oh, he would, he would,' he said. 'He wants our finest. You know the corporation has its code, and I never thought we'd ask anything from you but basic research in physics. But I must make it explicitly clear: you're here not to play a professional role as the corporation has always understood it, but to play ball with Lawrence. If he tells you to stand on your head, please, please do it. Lawrence is in a position to exert power over the corporation, and he keeps in touch with the president by telephone. But there's more than that. At the corporation headquarters, we can't see too far into these nuclear developments. But for the war effort, for the nation, we feel you've just got to keep Lawrence happy.'

"After this conversation, I began studying the way Lawrence reacted from day to day. He would walk through the Laboratory and ask people at random how their work was going. If they answered him sleepily or uncertainly or pessimistically, he'd frown. If they went into detail, he'd look impatient. He liked quick, confident, uninformative replies.

"Under me a mop-and-handyman crew was aggregating, all Ph.D.'s, of course. I pondered what would be best for them to tell him. From the early cyclotron days the Laboratory had inherited a set of catch phrases as well as a perpetual furtive debate on whether Lawrence or Livingston had been the inventor.

" 'When Lawrence asks how you're doing,' I told my crew, 'look alert, smile, and say, "Sparking at the lower Dee!" '

" 'What does it mean in terms of our work?' they asked.

" 'Nothing,' I said. 'That's why you say it.'

"They tried it on him, and his face lit up. Overnight my status changed. One day I was myself crew or certainly no more than bos'n's mate. Next day I was definitely an admiral. Partly it was because I spread high morale—that is, insulated him from the facts about his work. Partly it was because I'd shown him I realized he had me where he wanted me, cheerfully doing whatever he said. Power—personal power—was what concerned him. He must have known that I was inwardly still his critic, but he just didn't give a damn. Several times he invited me to transfer from the corporation to Berkeley for good.

"You must remember that in 1943, when I first knew him well, he was at the height of his career. Organized scientific effort in this country had been shaped by his big machines and by his personality. The pattern he had set gave him no more incentive to rest and think than he gave his lowest deck swabber. But he was not then a troubled person; he had no doubts about being the rightly chosen leader.

"Was he a physicist? Not so much as he had been, more than he was going to be. He had put us into this way we have of hunt-

ing in wolf packs, which is now our greatest weakness and sus-
ceptibility. Engineering and instrumentation were taking up more
and more of everybody's time in government-supported research.
Except at Los Alamos, the percentage of physicists actually doing
physics as it used to be known was constantly declining. It was
lowest at Berkeley. At the center of his daisy Lawrence embodied
a demand for results, a stubborn, unfaltering demand that was not
based on insight into physics but on a kind of crazy confidence. I
would call him a physicist of the zeroest order."

As Lawrence concentrated increasingly on hardware instead of
ideas, the physicist just quoted saw him approaching zero. Physicists at the very top of the country's nuclear war effort could not
afford time for such subtle views of mind and character. Instead
they looked at the hardware. Eugene Wigner, himself the designer
of stupendous, insufficiently chronicled hardware for plutonium
production, visited Lawrence in 1943. Within the limits imposed
by compartmentalization they discussed the status of the three
separate manufacturing programs.

"Everything seemed maddeningly slow to me," says Wigner,
"especially the completion of plutonium-producing reactors, the
part of the project of which I was in charge. I complained at
length to Lawrence about how slowly my work was going.*

" 'I'm convinced your reactors are absolutely essential,' he replied. 'You must produce the plutonium and I must produce the
U-235. The third program, gas-diffusion separation, will not succeed. It should be discontinued.'

"I remember this because it was a historic mistake on his part.
His program was the only unsuccessful one. Perhaps I should say
competitively unsuccessful. It did make samples, and I believe the
material for the first U-235 bomb did move to Los Alamos from

* At Hanford, Washington, at this time, on two hundred miles of govern-
ment-sequestered land 60,000 inhabitants of a tar-paper city were building a
mammoth plant in which plutonium-producing reactors were to be worked
by 7,000 duPont employees. At Oak Ridge, in addition to the electromagnetic
plant, the gaseous-diffusion plant was being constructed with a working
force which was to total 25,000. Measured in men and dollars, the government's nuclear effort went overwhelmingly into these plants. Here executives, engineers, technicians, workmen skilled and unskilled, and clerks
performed the functions usual to their vocations. The physicists and their
laboratories constituted only the minute nerve centers by which the sprawl-
ing effort was being marshaled toward the unknown.

his Oak Ridge plants. But that's a criterion that's not as simple as
it looks."

Long obsolete, the calutron is a memory that physicists close to
Lawrence cannot even now discuss dispassionately. "The electromagnetic process had its place, which was to separate samples
of isotopes for experimental purposes," says one of the Radiation Laboratory's better known alumni. "Lawrence's personality
was simply too big for this. To keep his program in the center of
the stage, he never failed to think up cute devices like using the
Fort Knox silver for bus bars. I doubt he was still unpolitical in
1943; he certainly wasn't in his maneuvering to get money. That's
why so much of the Manhattan Project's two billion dollars was
wasted. Lawrence just personally made the money go the way he
wanted it to go."

Conant, then Groves's adviser, had happily relied on the calutron, when he himself was in control of the project, as the most
certain road to the bomb. But for his own adviser Conant selected
the clearest and most ruthless mind in the project—Fermi—and
from him could not help getting a different view. "Privately
Fermi ridiculed the whole idea of the calutron," said Allison.

Groves was perhaps the world's hardest man to advise when it
came to making him see he had backed the wrong horse. But a
pipeline to the thinking of most of the physicists outside Berkeley
was thus opened to him. As a result, in 1943 he adopted an interesting and characteristic position. The calutron, he decided, was
on the one hand the quickest way for a nation to win a war, but
on the other hand he did not much care what his enemies the Russians learned about it. His testimony in 1954 makes it brutally
clear that as early as 1943 he had judged Lawrence's process to be
primitive and as a military secret not worth much. Hence his nonchalance about traitors in the Radiation Laboratory.

On Weinberg [he swore in 1954] I would like to emphasize that
the information he passed on was probably with respect to the electromagnetic process, and with respect to the fact that we were engaged in a big effort, because that is all that he knew legitimately. He
may have known some things illegitimately, and I am sure he did. We
were never too much concerned about that; because I personally felt
that while the electromagnetic process was a process, while it was of

extreme importance to us during the war, and we saved at least a year's time by doing it, that it was not the process we would follow after the war. That is one of the reasons why we put silver in those magnets, because we knew we could get it out.

Security moves in mysterious ways. On his visit to the Mesa in August of 1943, Lansdale said nothing about Weinberg's treason, but instead remarked that Lomanitz, in his conversation with outside officials of the Federation of Architects, Engineers, Chemists and Technicians, was being indiscreet about his work. To recruit for the expanding Mesa and to keep Groves posted, Oppenheimer continued his rounds of universities and of the other Project installations. At the end of August 1943 he arrived at Berkeley with the cares implanted by Lansdale.

Oppenheimer disliked the Federation, but many reputable physicists did not and still do not. Despite Lomanitz' participation, it had about the same aims and methods as any other vertical union. The one sinister difference was its sponsorship from the Shell laboratories, and Oppenheimer had reason to think this needed attention. He called briefly at the campus security office to ask whether it would be all right for him to have a talk with Lomanitz. The young lieutenant in charge there, DeSilva's counterpart, gave permission, but repeated that Lomanitz was dangerous. About to leave, Oppenheimer was reminded of Shell. A man there named George Eltenton should be worth looking into, he said, for word had got around to physicists that he wanted to supply classified information to the Russians.

Borrowing Lawrence's office, Oppenheimer sent for Lomanitz. In 1942 Lomanitz had promised he would cut himself off from the left wing and concentrate on physics. In the ensuing scene, as Oppenheimer reconstructed it under questioning during his security hearings[4] in 1954, Lomanitz now repudiated his promise, admitted lively Communist sympathies, and brassily asserted he was being framed not for these but for his activity as a union man.

"You aren't being framed," said Oppenheimer, irritated to the point of inaccuracy, and he dismissed him.

While Oppenheimer sat mentally abandoning Lomanitz to Lansdale's mercies, a secretary brought word that Bohm and Weinberg wanted to see him. They came in with anxious faces. Bohm said he was a Federation member but not a Communist; Weinberg, whose true loyalty was to the dollar, said he was an ex-Communist but not a Federation member. For both of them, they said, Lomanitz' insulting termination showed what was ahead. How could they be expected to keep their minds on their work? Should they resign now and be done with it?

The Theoretical Section in which Lawrence's program was weakest showed signs of dwindling fast. "I think you should stay on," said Oppenheimer. "Abide strictly by security regulations. Keep out of any kind of political activity. If you do this, I promise you have nothing to fear."

This assurance did not seem to help them much. Their faces did not clear up and they continued to linger anxiously. Six months at Los Alamos had given Oppenheimer a touch of executive brusqueness. He telephoned down to Cubicle Corridor and persuaded Lawrence to come up to the office for a few minutes. To Lawrence he reviewed the conversation, repeated his assurances, and asked Lawrence to confirm them.

Lawrence at this time hated the thought of losing Lomanitz, could not afford to dispense with any more physicists, and did not understand what all the trouble was about. "Yes, yes," he said impatiently and hurried back to Alpha-2.

He had reason to hurry. Alpha-2 and its glimmering half-developed successors constituted a continuing crisis of effort for him. For Oppenheimer they constituted a continuing crisis of judgment. The tremendous buildings then going up to house them at Oak Ridge represented to Oppenheimer not decisions made but decisions that must be made. In accepting from Groves the assignment to build the bomb, he had tacitly accepted responsibility for allocating through Groves the part that Lawrence's machines must play in making bomb material. It was this mounting burden that brought him to Berkeley. By comparison, his recruiting here was a minor task and the business with Security a fleeting distraction.

Security, however, was not through with him. The lieutenant whom he had talked with telephoned Pash in San Francisco. Next day Pash came to the lieutenant's office and sent a request to Oppenheimer to see him there.

"This is a pleasure," said Pash feelingly and switched on a concealed wire recorder. He had already recommended Oppenheimer's dismissal on grounds that he would invent the bomb and tell the Russians, but not his countrymen, how it was done. Now at last Pash had the prospect of something more to go on than intuition. "I don't mean to take much of your time," he said but took enough of it for a conversation of about five thousand words. What he wanted was a list of Oppenheimer's friends who had been approached to supply information to the Russians. What Oppenheimer wanted was to alert him to Eltenton, about whom Pash seemed to know nothing and in whom he showed little interest. The conversation therefore rambled. To the man who thought in terms of Cells, Secret Formulas and Highly Confidential Informants, Oppenheimer tried to communicate the physicists' outlook on security:

"My view about this whole damn thing, of course, is that the information we are working on is probably known to all the governments that care to find out. The information about what we are doing is probably of no use, because it is so complicated. I don't agree that the security problem on the project is a bitter one if one means by the security problem preventing information of technical use to another country from escaping. But I do think that the intensity of our effort and our concern, uh, the international investment involved—that is, information which might alter the course of the other governments."

Anyone who chats unaware into a recorder usually makes his sentences more loosely complex than those of literary dialogue. Conversely, the aware party usually addresses posterity. Only once, when Oppenheimer convinced him fast fission was no mystery to foreign physicists, did Pash forget himself.

"Oh," he said blankly, for the moment deflated and ingenuous.

By refusing to talk about setting a watch on Eltenton, he goaded Oppenheimer into asserting that through an innocent busybody professor not connected with the Project, Eltenton had indirectly approached two or three physicists. The professor, shocked, disapproving and garrulous, Oppenheimer continued, had delivered himself as follows: "An interview could be arranged with this man Eltenton, who had very good contacts with a man from the [Russian] Embassy who was attached to the consulate who was a very reliable guy—that's his story—and who had a lot of experience with microfilm work, or whatever the hell."[5]

Both the physicists who had been approached and the professor himself were in agreement that such an interview would be treasonable, Oppenheimer said, and for this reason the only name he judged proper to mention was Eltenton's.

By harping on the name, Oppenheimer was making himself a bore. Pash could not set a watch on Eltenton. Suspects are a government security organization's vital stock in trade. Eltenton was providing employment to a large crew of F.B.I. men who followed him, cultivated him, and made him their pigeon. For Pash to intrude would mean a clash with J. Edgar Hoover, so fiercely jealous that even Groves, who liked to do everything himself, had been obliged to come to an arrangement with him. Between them these two had decided what they wanted Eltenton to know and tell the Russians, just as Groves alone had decided in Weinberg's case. Intoxicated with the happiness of investigating without being investigated, Security people do astonishing things. Not only little people like Pash and DeSilva were intoxicated, but also Security's very top authorities in this country, Hoover and Groves. These two were playing a dangerous game by permitting Weinberg and Eltenton to traffic with the Russians.

Oppenheimer would have done well to try to fathom these complications before he took it into his head to help Security. Pash, without contradiction, restated as three the two or three physicists Oppenheimer said had been indirectly approached by Eltenton. Aside from this modest gain the interview whetted rather than sated Pash's hunger.

Lansdale's memory of what happened next diverged sharply from Security's written records. These show Oppenheimer a fortnight later consenting, if ordered by Groves, to name three physicists indirectly approached by Eltenton, and Groves declining to give such an order. Lansdale's memory was that Groves gave Oppenheimer his word not to tell and that in exchange Oppenheimer had said that besides himself there was but one physicist involved, his brother Frank. Groves thus got the information he wanted but could not divulge it without breaking his word. This Lansdale learned (so he afterward remembered) because Groves told him. Groves sought to acquit himself for the breach of his own word to Oppenheimer by pledging Lansdale in turn to absolute secrecy. Meanwhile, beneath Lansdale the Security organization began frantically combing Berkeley and Los Alamos payrolls for three physicists who had failed to report a temptation to treason. True, Oppenheimer had insisted to Pash that no one's behavior had been sinister but Eltenton's. Security showed its disbelief by blocking a transfer-promotion of one falsely suspected Berkeley physicist to Oak Ridge. For a simple man who gives his word and keeps it, the position in which Lansdale found himself was not very satisfactory. Instead of telling his subordinates in Security, Lansdale decided to tell the F.B.I., the only people who could do anything about Eltenton. He went to their Washington headquarters and recited the story to the professionally inscrutable faces of E. A. Tamm, a chief assistant of Hoover's, and Lish Whitson, Hoover's Communism expert. "Nothing could be clearer in my memory than going over at night and talking to Tamm and Whitson," he said in 1954.

The great day when the F.B.I. gives up its dead file is worth looking forward to. We shall then learn not only what bastards everybody used to be but also whether, besides naming himself and Frank as the physicists, Oppenheimer named Professor Haakon Chevalier as the garrulous busybody intermediary. This last bit of data did not reach the security organization, its records show, until December 13, 1943. Perhaps because its hunt for the three mythical physicists was upsetting the laboratories, Groves then ordered Oppenheimer to tell Security what he had told him in confidence three months before.

Partly from vanity, partly from cunning, Groves made his testimony incoherent in 1954. It was clearest on his feeling about the subversive effort that had alarmed Oppenheimer. "He was doing what he thought essential," said Groves, "which was to disclose to me the dangers of this particular attempt to enter the Project, namely, it was concerned with the situation out there near Berkeley—I think it was the Shell Laboratory at which Eltenton was supposedly one of the key members—and that was the source of the danger to the Project, and that was the worry." In contrast, Groves viewed the situation as an opportunity. The Russians were bound to want a bomb as soon as this country exploded one in war. Groves seems to have hoped some high commissar would allocate the last five hundred million dollars of an exhausted economy to building calutrons; after all, we had paid out that much. This looks inescapably like the reason he would not let Security or the F.B.I. shut down Eltenton's school for subversives. "I would rather have it there where I would know it," he said. "Of course, after the war I brought it to the attention of various friends in the Shell Oil Company and I believe that group was cleaned out in twenty-four hours."

Whether privately Communist or not, Frank Oppenheimer was minding his own business and working hard. So far as Security's host of witnesses can prove a negative, he had no contact with the Berkeley cell. Neither Oppenheimer nor Groves saw any use naming him to Security. Oppenheimer named himself and Chevalier, as he could not avoid doing. A brassy talker like Lomanitz, Chevalier had the greater smoothness one would expect from an authority on Anatole France. The F.B.I. kept him shadowed but did not approach him overtly until the war was over. He was first surprised, then aggrieved at their repeated visitations. The F.B.I. passed on much of what it knew about Chevalier to the House Un-American Activities Committee and to the California miniature HUAC, the Tenney Committee. "Communist associations" was then a fashionable phrase, and by exposing Chevalier's, these two committees did much harm to his career. He blamed Oppenheimer.

By his trip to the Mesa in early August, Lansdale had set all these complexities unfolding. In the autumn, with his hunter's instinct sated, he decided it was time to let Oppenheimer concentrate more fully on the development of secrets worth stealing. He went back to the Mesa and had his longest interview with Kitty. In guarded, cunning terms he outlined the types of situations in which he judged Oppenheimer was likely to need a nursemaid. She listened grimly and at last gave him a shot of bourbon as a tacit pledge between enemies who respected each other. During the rest of the war, Oppenheimer provided Security with nothing further to go on in backing its intuition that he was a Russian agent.

Not being interested in amusing the Russians, Oppenheimer took a simpler view of the calutron than did Groves. Oppenheimer cared only about its ability to fill the belly of Little Boy, the uranium-235 bomb, on schedule. The crunch came in the spring of 1944. By then Beta had been perfected, the complete layout of calutrons at Oak Ridge had been blueprinted, and total foreseeable yield of uranium 235 computed. It was not enough.

Theoretically this was none of Oppenheimer's business. Under his direction McMillan, then at Los Alamos, had supervised the design of Little Boy. Complete with dummy slugs of beryllium, it stood ready and waiting for its deadly filler. Oppenheimer had thus finished this half of his double assignment, except that he did not have a bomb that would actually explode.

The outlook for the entire project at this time was desolate. Urey's program was sunk in a dreary quandary about what material to use for the porous diffusion barriers. Plutonium, though only an insignificant driblet had arrived at Los Alamos, was beginning to look as unmanageable as a bad dream.

Physicists noticed a tendency in Oppenheimer to grow sharp and merciless at conferences. For the first time he let glimpses of driving anxiety mar the serene atmosphere he had established on the Mesa. Already thin as a rail, he lost weight. Thinking his health might break, Groves asked Conant and other advisers to make up a list of possible successors. They could not name a single man whom Groves considered acceptable both to himself and to the Mesa's physicists.

Oppenheimer intruded into the affairs of the Radiation Laboratory by taking a hard look at the electromagnetic process. "For nearly a year the electromagnetic plant was the only one in operation," says the Smyth Report. "Therefore the urge to increase its production rate was tremendous." It fell short most obviously in Alpha; Beta had a good deal more capacity than Alpha could feed. Searching for a means to help Alpha, Oppenheimer surveyed the country's scientific resources, of which he probably had a wider knowledge than any other physicist.

At Berkeley he had taught theoretical physics to a young research associate of Lawrence's named Philip Abelson. Brilliant, opinionated, and talkative, Abelson had moved on in 1940 to the Naval Research Laboratory in Washington. There he had devised a plan for steam-heating one side of a column of uranium hexafluoride and cooling the other. From the hot side, he correctly conjectured, U-235 could be picked up in a concentration about twice that in natural uranium. Theoretically the product could be recycled, doubling its enrichment each time. In September of 1940 Abelson reported the scheme to Briggs and Breit. Characteristically they gave him a cautious blessing but no money and in replying took care to play down the vile subject of bombs. After a while they stopped answering his letters. Abelson was left feeling direction-less and completely isolated from the project. Thereafter, as the only Ph.D. in a crew of six, he worked with Navy funds to produce fuel for a hypothetical nuclear-powered submarine. Through no security lapse of any sort, but simply because his Washington installation was in purview of foreign diplomats, the Germans got wind of his project (it was the only part of the American nuclear effort they learned about). Outside the Navy, no one paid him much notice but the Nazi intelligence organization and Oppenheimer.

By 1944 Abelson had two columns of plumbing forty feet high leaking noisy clouds of steam but actually enriching uranium. They were cheap to build, though the heating bill each month was almost as large as the Pentagon's. "I think Abelson was worth a little more emphasis than he got in the Smyth Report," says physicist Arthur Ruark, a consultant of Abelson's at the Bureau of Standards. "If someone in authority had decided to put the nation's coal mines to work, Abelson's process alone could have met Little Boy's requirements."

Oppenheimer had no authority over uranium separation, but by 1944 he felt a deep responsibility for making the whole project go. In violation of the security-compartmentalization rules, he went to look at Abelson's steam columns. He estimated that two thousand of them feeding Lawrence's calutron process could theoretically double its yield. In accordance with the rigid executive structure Groves had set up for the Project, Oppenheimer suggested to Groves that he should ask Lawrence about this proposition.

Lawrence at that time felt an utter emotional conviction that however much or little of the bomb isotope was produced, he alone would produce it. Groves's questions shocked him with the first intimation that he was being coolly weighed and judged in quarters beyond his influence. Through him the shock transmitted to his subordinates inside the Radiation Laboratory was equally profound. "Oppenheimer says the direct cycle is no good" was the way Carrol Mills heard of Groves's proposal.

Even so, no difficulty with respect to physics was involved, and Lawrence felt confident he could handle the mere engineering problem. He accepted the steam plant into his system and Groves built it at Oak Ridge in three months' time. Spewing crazily at a thousand leaky joints, it began operation in the fall of 1944. Lawrence began feeding its yield into his calutrons. Alpha dealt with raw uranium by splattering most of it aimlessly over its insides and refining a tiny fraction in the beam. The clean-up job after each run had not been excessive, because a certain amount of waste was permissible. The steam plant's 2 per cent pure U-235 was too precious for that. Lawrence instituted stringent cleanliness requirements for maintenance men at Oak Ridge. Next arose the problem of what to do with such of the steam plant's product as could thus be collected after passage through Alpha. Beta was designed to take raw uranium purified in Alpha to about 10 per cent. Now Alpha's product had a purity of nearly 40 per cent. This was too low to put into a fission bomb, too high to put into Beta without fundamental rebuilding of the existing Oak Ridge plant.

Judged by the frantic criteria of war, however, the steam plant was not wasted. During 1944 Oppenheimer found another use for its product and, himself tormented by anxiety, imposed another torment on Lawrence. At the start of the summer, gas-diffusion scientists stopped wrangling with Urey and got down to business in large-scale tryouts of different kinds of diffusion barriers. The enormous gas-diffusion plants at Oak Ridge showed signs of beginning to produce. Unlike Lawrence's batch process, this one was a cascade. It could accept and give back U-235 at any stage of purification up to the highest of which it was capable. Any 2 per cent isotope that Lawrence could not use was easy to feed into it.

In the late spring of 1944, most physicists were still skeptical about gas diffusion. Facing his Little Boy crisis, Oppenheimer anticipated the general swing of opinion by several months. He intruded again into the calutron cycle. At his suggestion Groves proposed to Lawrence that the diffusion product be fed directly into Beta. Through Groves, Oppenheimer in effect commanded Lawrence to correlate his program with Urey's. Thus he threw Lawrence into fantastic difficulties. Some were due to Groves, some to the strange situation in the diffusion program, and some to Lawrence's own character. In the first place, Groves would not let Oppenheimer play top dog by threshing out practical details in discussions with Lawrence behind his back. In the second place it was hard to learn what was going on in the diffusion program and hard to believe what one learned. "Compartmentalization and security kept news of our program from filtering in to Ernest and his Laboratory," says Dunning. "But more than that, we didn't even tell Urey. We had to keep him out as much as we could. I remember in early 1945 he made a valiant effort to make the thing fold up. He deeply resented the fact that none of the things he wanted to do during the war were followed up."

In the third place, Lawrence's confidence in the superiority of his own program could not be easily shaken. "Ernest knew that if gas diffusion would go at all it would go big," says Dunning. "Finding out that it did was a great shock for him and the people with him. His realization was not one of those things that suddenly dawn. It took time."

Once it began to operate, the gas-diffusion plant poured out 10 per cent pure uranium 235 many times faster than the Alphas could. In February of 1945 the Alphas became obsolete except for a special model Lawrence was trying to modify for the steam plant.

At the same time, Beta began struggling to digest the gas-diffusion plant's product. To keep compartmentalization and prevent the physicists from getting above themselves, Groves assigned the task of coordination to his top military subordinate, Colonel Kenneth Nichols, the Oak Ridge commandant. For Lawrence's staff the result was confusion. Each Beta had to have an ion-beam configuration and a collector system specifically designed for intake of a specific concentration of uranium 235. So far as Lawrence's staff could tell, the purity of their intake material veered unpredictably.

Under Lawrence, Thornton at Oak Ridge bore the brunt of the difficulty. Coping grimly with a series of surprises, he grieved at the effect on his beloved machines. "Their life was dependent on the concentration of the stuff fed into them," he says. "You needed to know, and you didn't. When they reached 10 per cent at the gas-diffusion plant, that was when it was desirable to feed into us [into the Betas]. But they would deliver at 20 to 25 per cent. This would require substantial changes in our machines. We needed a contact outside the contract [i.e., better communication between programs]."

Lawrence and Dunning made signals to each other through Nichols and Urey. The gas-diffusion plant was coming up fast, pressing hard at the calutron's heel. A new agreement was reached that the calutron would take over at 25 per cent. In mid-1945 this figure became a formal limitation on the gas-diffusion plant, which could have delivered at higher purities. From the calutron, uranium 235 at an average purity of 85 per cent was collected and packed into a small lead-lined box. Periodically an F.B.I. man would show up at Oak Ridge and make a little ceremony of thrusting the box under his trench coat before catching the train to Los Alamos. By July 25, 1945, he had delivered fifty kilograms. This was enough for Oppenheimer's physicists to test, transform into shining slugs by chemical separation of the metal from its halogen salts, and fabricate into the nuclear component of a single uranium-235 bomb. The bomb itself, Little Boy, had already been shipped to the island of Tinian in the Pacific. It waited at a bomber base there for the dummy slugs inside it to be replaced with real ones of uranium. At Los Alamos physicists paid scant heed to Little Boy's departure. Preoccupied with the problem of their other bomb, with plutonium and implosion, they regarded Little Boy as already history. For a year the only question about Little Boy had been whether there would be enough uranium 235 to fill its belly.

All of this uranium 235 underwent final processing in Lawrence's calutrons, but by July of 1945 it did not need to. Little Boy required uranium 235 that would be 85 per cent pure. By July the gas-diffusion plant could by itself deliver at this purity without any tortuous detour through the calutrons. Lawrence could not believe it. "He was never much concerned about actual production operations at Oak Ridge until early 1945," says Lester Coleman, who had been transferred there by Eastman the fall before. "Then he got interested for a very special reason. He wanted to make our process competitive with gas diffusion."

As usual, Lawrence made his most colorful efforts on the night shift. "He liked to wander through the big plants at Oak Ridge looking for inefficiency," said a supervisor. "You know, we were working in the most intense magnetic fields ever known. Any guy he came on that had metal on him would be slammed against the wall and stripped of his suspender clips or whatever it was that Lawrence saw. The other thing he hated most was catnaps. Those plants were a quiet, processing sort of place with nothing much to do at night but check the gauges every now and then. 'I wasn't asleep,' a technician complained to me. 'I just looked that way because there was no point in moving around. Why did you let Lawrence bawl hell out of me?' "

Caught up in Lawrence's passion, the Radiation Laboratory staff labored to close the gap. They designed the 16-J development, a Beta that would have produced at half the cost of those in operation at Oak Ridge. But by mid-1945 when the 16-J's could have been built, not even this improvement would have been enough. "The gas-diffusion people just didn't need our process any more," Coleman summed up elegiacally. Lawrence finally gave up. "I think his admission did not come until the summer of 1945," says Dunning.

Like all of Lawrence's struggles so far, this one had been against nature and therefore essentially noble. A good deal can also be said for it on the grounds of seeming practicality. As a batch process, it seemed to promise quicker if more limited returns than gas diffusion's awesome cascade. "I looked on it as a backstop," says Dunning. "For a long time I couldn't guarantee diffusion would work. It was too big, too new." Before making a full effort to grapple with the big and new, the planners might seem justified in taking time to set up a backstop. This in fact is what they did. "Diffusion went into construction a year after us, then into production the next year, and then in the next it superseded us," says Coleman.

Dunning was two years ahead of Lawrence in his initial detailed proposals. He lost this lead before the war, because, unlike Lawrence, he commanded no material resources that would have let him go ahead without the Uranium Committee's support. He would have regained the lead much faster, certainly in 1944 rather than in 1945, if the duPont-inspired review committee's 1942 recommendation had been carried out (see above, p. 142). In that event his program would have had priority over Lawrence's and the war might have been shortened. On the other hand, except for Lawrence's energetic contribution, the government's uranium program might have produced no bomb at all before the war was over. In backing his own belief and program, Lawrence sabotaged no one else's. Such blame as history may assign for misdirected priorities will rest on the general body of American scientists who tended to make the calutron their private joke during the war. Oppenheimer's restraint about it broke down during the crisis of filling Little Boy's belly. "We have made a terrible scientific blunder," he told Groves. The blunder was partly due to the indirectness with which Lawrence and Oppenheimer were obliged to communicate, but the words "we" and "scientific" were hardly accurate. "I would rather not have it talked about by anyone here," Groves remarked at Oppenheimer's security hearing ten years later, "because it reflects to a certain extent on the wisdom of another scientist."

At the same time that Oppenheimer struggled with the uranium crisis in 1944, an even more serious one was weighing upon him. As soon as he could project the yield from his coordination proposals, he forgot U-235 and concentrated on plutonium. It looked hopeless.

The first hint that plutonium might give trouble came in January of 1944 while the fast-gun bomb for it was being finished. Unrelated studies toward an abortive uranium-hydride bomb suggested plutonium manufactured in the reactor piles might prove different from the sample speck the Metallurgical Laboratory had submitted for testing in 1943. With deepening anxiety Oppenheimer waited four months for the piles to produce. The first driblet arrived in late June and confirmed his worst fears, which centered around plutonium's high neutron background, its continual natural emission of neutrons. Any mass of it, no matter how small, emitted many times more neutrons than did an equal mass of uranium. In the first plutonium that reached Los Alamos, the speck supplied by the Metallurgical Laboratory, the source of these neutrons had been traced to alpha radiation, itself also released in plutonium's natural decay process. Neutron background arising from alpha radiation had been seen as a formidable difficulty that would require the plutonium gun to be half again as fast as that for uranium 235.

Theoretical studies meanwhile, however, had suggested that plutonium produced in reactor piles might have a neutron background far higher than could be accounted for on the basis of alpha radiation. The first driblet from the piles proved this view correct. The plutonium thus produced had too high a neutron background to be used in the gun. No two pieces totaling a critical mass could be put together. If one were fired against the other at any possible speed, both would vaporize and pre-detonate before they could meet to form a critical mass.

The cause was a trace of the isotope plutonium 240 created in the main body of plutonium 239 by the neutron flux of the piles.

The more efficiently the piles worked, the more of the evil isotope they would mix with their product. Segré on the Mesa isolated a few molecules. Fermi, his former teacher, displayed them with a sort of fatherly pride that made other physicists long to take a club to him. "It was the nastiest stuff you can imagine," said Manley. "To get it out of the plutonium 239 would have taken at least another Oak Ridge, and of course that was out of the question."

The plutonium bomb was probably the uncanniest problem that organized governmental research had ever groped with. For Oppenheimer it was inextricably mixed with the problem of Neddermeyer, who like True Thomas could see into the land of faerie but could not tell in any mortal tongue what he saw. "Not fast enough," Neddermeyer had said of the Thin Man in April of 1943 without being able to give any acceptable reason.

Late that summer Neddermeyer had reported on his experiment of firing steel cylinders into the air. He spoke at a seminar of all cleared scientists. When he came to relating time-of-flight data to the elastic compression produced by implosion, his talk seemed to bog down. His audience stirred restlessly. "I think the general feeling was expressed by an uninhibited whiz-kid named Richard P. Feynman sitting in the back row," recalls a listener. "Being a pal of Neddermeyer's he knew any honest opinion would be taken the right way. So he waited till Neddermeyer got through with his talk, then held up his hand. 'It stinks,' he said."*

Neddermeyer's immediate superior was the leader of the ordnance division, William Parsons, a stern, dignified Navy captain, the third most important administrator at Los Alamos after Bethe. Parsons' way of defending his implosion-crew chief was worse than Feynman's criticism. "With everyone grinding away in such dead earnest here, we need a touch of relief," Parsons said. "I question Dr. Neddermeyer's seriousness. To my mind he is gradually working up to what I shall refer to as the Beer-Can Experiment. As soon as he gets his explosives properly organized, we will see this done. The point to watch for is whether he can blow in a beer can without splattering the beer."

At the same time accurate and uncomprehending, this statement

* Feynman was awarded a Nobel prize in 1965 for discoveries in quantum mechanics that helped solve difficulties in measuring the interaction of charged particles.

of the implosion principle became a standard joke on the Mesa in late 1943. Oppenheimer did not laugh. Even before the first somber inklings about plutonium came in, he and the other theoretical physicists accepted Neddermeyer as an authentic seer. The only question was from how far in the future had come Neddermeyer's troubling visions. If they were from beyond the war, they could have only academic interest. In so far as he could without slowing gun development, Oppenheimer shifted laboratory orientation toward implosion. "His position was that he just did not know," said Neddermeyer.

The fascinating point about Neddermeyer to theoretical physicists then and to ordinary people now is that he did not know either, yet he behaved as though he did. "I think my objections to the plutonium gun were subconscious," he said. "I don't think I had plutonium in my mind except maybe at the very back of it. I worried vaguely and never articulated anything."

Neddermeyer had to correlate fission rates, heat, neutron paths, internal and external pressures, and changing configurations of a tempered sphere as it collapsed under a series of blows from without. The sheer complexity of the problem attracted the Mesa's chief mathematical consultant, John von Neumann, a plump, round-faced, smiling genius with an eager curiosity about nearly everything. During the fall of 1943 he analyzed it as an intellectual exercise. "I made a simple theory that worked up to a certain level of violence in the shockwave," said Neddermeyer. "Von Neumann is generally credited with originating the science of large compressions. This is true with respect to the organized research of the project itself. But I knew it before and had done it in a naïve way. Von Neumann's was more sophisticated."

Neddermeyer used Oppenheimer's offer of unlimited men and facilities to the extent of recruiting a crew of half a dozen. With one of these, young Henry Linschitz, he applied a new method for observing implosive effects. The two mounted a movie camera at the end of a stubby hollow steel cylinder and took photographs looking down the inside edge in the light of the explosion itself. "You could actually see the half-inch cylinder wall going in," he said.

It did not go in evenly. Behaving as a liquid under the impact, it squirted in irregularly where the shockwaves peaked. Von Neu-

mann estimated that a squirt moving five per cent faster than the
collapsing wall could cause an implosion bomb to fizzle by pre-
detonation. No one could think of any way to prevent this. It even
seemed unlikely that the war would last long enough for von
Neumann to perform all the calculations needed to verify his estimate. This was the situation in early 1944, when the first fore-
bodings arose about the plutonium gun. Made brash and un-
English by the Mesa air, young Tuck stood up at a seminar and
proposed to his seniors the idea of the explosive lens. Sculptured
and layered, it would burn here and there at different speeds to
produce symmetrically converging shockwaves. (Neddermeyer had
thought of it but not communicated it outside his group.)

Oppenheimer grunted with real pain at the proposal; it doubled
difficulties already monstrous. Nevertheless, he set the laboratory
to work on it. To handle the mathematics he had von Neumann
import the most advanced calculating machines then developed.
To handle the explosives he imported the chief American authority
in the field—peppery, conceited, energetic George Kistiakowsky
from Harvard. When Kistiakowsky found out what he was supposed to do, he was scandalized. "Dr. Oppenheimer is mad to think
this thing will make a bomb," he said, and he clung to this view
throughout the next twelve months.

As the bad news about neutron background began gathering in
early 1944, all eyes on the Mesa gradually turned toward Neddermeyer in puzzled reappraisal. "Well, your stuff looks pretty good,"
Feynman told him at a seminar, meaning that every other prospect
for the plutonium bomb looked even worse.

For Oppenheimer, the drama of Neddermeyer vindicated took
place against a background that stilled in him any impulse to ap-
plaud. He could extrapolate his receipts of fissionable material for
the next year of 1945. Victory in the war might well require more
than the flourish of one or two bombs. General Marshall thought
nine might be needed. In that case even if Oppenheimer's coor-
dinating proposals succeeded, he would not have enough U-235.
"Plutonium can be obtained in the [Hanford reactor] factory very
much cheaper than pure U-235 can be obtained by isotope separation," said Wigner. "An almost unlimited quantity of plutonium
could be made in not too many years, enough for a very large
number of bombs."

Looking ahead into 1945, Oppenheimer could see a date when war deaths would become his responsibility. "We had the feeling —perhaps wrong—that a hundred thousand lives, maybe more, might depend on whether this thing was ready August 1, September 1, or October 1," he said. Consequently Oppenheimer took less interest in congratulating Neddermeyer than in reorienting a large part of the laboratory around him. The trouble was that Neddermeyer did not seem to want it. He had his crew of six, he was now making precision photographs of collapsing cylinders and hemispheres, and this was what he liked.

"Use more men and move faster," Oppenheimer told him.

"I'm no operator," Neddermeyer replied. "Never was."

In resisting Oppenheimer's efforts to turn him into an executive, Neddermeyer was right again. But Oppenheimer had integrated hundreds of other brilliant minds into the harmonious madness of the Mesa, and he could not see why Neddermeyer should be an exception. "He became terribly impatient with me in the spring of 1944," said Neddermeyer. "I think he felt very badly because I seemed not to push things as for war research but acted as though it were just a normal research situation."

That spring most cleared personnel on the Mesa gave some thought to implosion. It became the main activity of the Ordnance Division. Inside this, Oppenheimer set up an Implosion Steering Committee and made Neddermeyer chairman. Under him Kistiakowsky succeeded to leadership of his Implosion Experimentation Group, which now constituted only a small portion of the physicists in Ordnance attacking the problem. Personal and technical difficulties arose, says the official record, so Oppenheimer switched Kistiakowsky to chairman and Neddermeyer back to group leader.

No one at Los Alamos cared enough about invidious distinctions to take this game of musical chairs seriously, Oppenheimer least of all. But in his driving anxiety to speed the plutonium bomb, he exerted a hypnotic influence on Neddermeyer's thought and the direction of his work. "In the early experiments which my group and I did, we used small, very thick-walled cylinders and hemispheres," Neddermeyer said. "The geometry was very easy and we were sure that the compression would go. But immediately things got hot, Oppenheimer edged us toward thinner walls of larger diameter and toward a harder push for maximum compression. This got us into extreme idealistic geometries and into experiments of a very unfavorable kind."

During the summer of 1944, Oppenheimer came close to despairing. He foresaw enough plutonium by the next summer to let him test-detonate only a single actual bomb. If it did not work, the plutonium would be spattered by the chemical explosion, and he would have to try to recover as much as he could. As a symbol of hopelessness he ordered Jumbo, a twenty-five-foot steel flask. By mounting the implosion inside Jumbo, he hoped to make the plutonium easier to scrape up after the fizzle.

At the same time he lost the luminous clarity which now makes so many scattered scientists homesick when they think of the Mesa. Scenes with Neddermeyer have left the latter a very different dominant impression. "Oppenheimer lit into me," he says. "A lot of people looked up to him as a source of wisdom and inspiration. I respected him as a scientist, but I just didn't look up to him that way. I didn't look up to him. From my point of view he was an intellectual snob. He could cut you cold and humiliate you right down to the ground. On the other hand, I could irritate him. Did he do a magnificent job at Los Alamos? Yes, I would say an excellent job."

About August 1, Neddermeyer summed up the results of his work. "At a seminar I gave my calculations of the pressures obtainable in the center of a cylinder or sphere. By then it was clear that you could get large sectional impressions [blast a large part of a sphere so violently in upon itself as to produce in the center the extreme pressures required to make the subcritical mass of the sphere suddenly become supercritical]. On the other hand it was not clear how you could live with the jets or squirts which would cause pre-detonation. The picture I drew was black."

Oppenheimer became serene again. He had brought himself to the realization that no matter how many lives were lost in the war, it was time to stop tormenting Neddermeyer. Implosion, he saw, required getting so many nearly uncontrollable factors right that in terms of normal scientific effort it was impossible. But the Mesa offered more than common resources. "The best laboratory in the world," he proudly termed it to a Congressional investigating committee. In August of 1944 he transformed it ruthlessly. Every scientist except Teller and a few engaged in refining the Little Boy slugs was put on an hour-by-hour schedule of work on implosion. "It was taken out of my hands entirely," says Nedder-meyer. "The laboratory was completely reorganized and I was left out, off in a corner working by myself as I should have been."

During his bomb career, Oppenheimer continually surprised those closest to him by the quiet firmness of his executive decisions. Administratively this one was right; aesthetically it would have been better to have kept on nagging Neddermeyer. Oppenheimer was capable of feeling a poet's regret, which he soothed with the knowledge that Neddermeyer, though now only a detail, was an important one. The technical problems that Oppenheimer dis-tributed among a thousand gifted scientists are too complicated to be recounted here. Neddermeyer's corner may serve as an example.

One of the half-dozen greatest difficulties of the plutonium bomb was how to record events inside experimental mock-ups as they imploded. Four methods used were X rays, measurements of mag-netic-field changes, electrical-conduction measurements, and gam-ma-ray measurements from a short-lived radioactive adulterant, lanthanum 140. To Neddermeyer at a seminar, Oppenheimer sug-gested a fifth, the betatron. The microsecond bursts of radiation this produced, he said, not only could penetrate an imploding sphere but also could make a timed record of the stages of change inside it. Neddermeyer's reply lived up to the uncanny reputation he had established on the Mesa. The thing to do, he answered, was to put a betatron on one side of the explosion and on the other side a cloud chamber in which radiation could be trapped and photo-graphed.

To most physicists at the seminar, talk of setting off fifty pounds of T.N.T. between two such fragile instruments sounded grotesque. To Oppenheimer it was a mere bit of routine in his task of co-ordinating the country's best scientific minds. In this case he was implementing a casual suggestion he had picked up in the course of a conversation with the betatron's inventor, Donald Kerst. Ned-dermeyer, in turn, was presenting a midnight reverie on another conversation. "I hadn't thought of the betatron in connection with implosion until I heard Oppenheimer propose it," he says. "As for the cloud chamber, Bob Wilson from Princeton first suggested it to me. I couldn't believe he was serious about using the thing with explosives, and I discouraged the idea. Then later it came to me at night that this was the way." Shock-mounted in blockhouses a few yards apart, the betatron and the cloud chamber worked well together, as did Kerst and Neddermeyer. Toward the end of 1944, data from them along with much other data gave Oppenheimer confidence to throw away Jumbo, the steel flask he had ordered when he believed implosion would fizzle.

The winter wore on, punctuated by monotonous trial explosions echoing continually louder from test stations outside the big fence. Inside, the new animal life of that part of the desert tried to make itself at home. Groping to possess the strangeness of the Mesa, it recoiled in commonplace huddlings. Among other things Oppenheimer's experiment proved that, when suitably sheltered, the very highest I.Q.'s breed as fast as the lowest. Many physicists claim to remember General Groves standing beside a rocketing birth-rate chart and saying, "This has got to be stopped."

Scenting the dry, sharp Mesa air with stale milk and diapers, physicists created a shortage of these latter at the Post Exchange and complained that Groves was behind it. "You could get ikons and mezuzahs and all kinds of fancy crap like that," said Weissman, "but you couldn't get diapers." Most bitterly physicists complained of the diaper service. A young wife had undertaken to run it as her patriotic bit. Even her friends, she discovered, had joined a whisper campaign against her on the grounds that (1) she was too slow and (2) she was making a fortune. Hurt, she at last simply walked out, leaving a mound of soiled diapers to molder and ferment beside a frantically ringing telephone.

Kitty Oppenheimer was one of those caught short. Though she had entered the spirit of things sufficiently to have her second child on the Mesa, she was never well up on Mesa gossip. Weeks after closing shop, the proprietress happened on Kitty in the street. Unless the service improved, Kitty implied with cool terse politeness, she might reluctantly be obliged to take her patronage elsewhere.

Most physicists and their wives wanted to feel it was the desert they liked, not just the fences and free food and warmth and security. Oppenheimer dined once a week at Edith Warner's tearoom. Everyone else wanted a reservation there because it was hard to get. Once they had got it, they often canceled. There was nothing to do there but eat, look at the Indian rugs and woodwork, and note how visibly Edith's health was failing. Having foolishly set prices that made her no money, she was unable to hire other servants to help Tilano.

Physicists and their families squabbled with the Military Police and used them for baby sitters, complained of the water supply and wasted it because it was free, pretended to like the Zuni corn dances and found them intolerably dull. What they really liked was their own dances, square and ballroom, and amateur theatricals and just parties and flirtations and social cabals. They complained continuously and reveled astonishingly. "We on our high mesa top thought we could live it up forever, and the mere thought of returning to a sane and prosaic civilian life sounded flat and dull," says Mrs. Robert Brode in her delightful *Tales of Los Alamos*. "We were having the time of our lives."

In this part of Mesa life the Oppenheimers shared slenderly. Kitty told friends that looking after her husband, working in the biological laboratory, and caring for her baby constituted to her mind a full contribution to the Mesa. "I will not play the Director's Wife," she said. Social activities therefore revolved around Mrs. William Parsons, whose husband about this time was promoted to rear admiral.

Oppenheimer measured his evening appearances. For a performance of *Arsenic and Old Lace* he accepted a role which did not require much study, that of a corpse carried up from the cellar. He made a point of attending a fixed quota of large parties. Women who had known him in California and who now only saw him at these found him socially changed. A few days before one party, such a friend sent him a newspaper clipping reporting that Jean Tatlock had cut her wrists and died in a bathtub. At the party he approached his informant and said only "Thank you." She could not see any difference from the usual melancholy indulgence with which he thinly disguised nervous strain keyed to the mounting intensity of the trial explosions. Hostesses were secretly glad that it was his custom to leave early.

When he went home, he would read himself to sleep over John Donne's *Holy Sonnets*. Poor Jean, equivocal and apologetic even as a ghost, had awakened in him a sense of grief long dormant but never extinguished. She shared timidly in a sort of epitaph he found in Sonnet XVII for the girl in Europe whom he had loved for eight years:

> *Since she whom I lov'd hath payed her last dett*
> *To Nature, and to hers, and my good is dead*

> *And her soul early into heaven ravished,*
> *Wholly on heavenly things my mind is sett;*
> *Here the admyring her my mind did whett*
> *To seek thee God.*

Oppenheimer believed that his mind and will were set on heavenly things. The Mesa as he saw it merged physics not only with the desert but also with Ahimsa, an austerer love. The German nuclear threat was dissipated for him by intelligence reports toward the end of 1944.* He was not much affected; he had always believed that he had a higher purpose than to beat the Germans. To him the monotonous trial explosions that shook the Mesa betokened a greater explosion to come—one that would shake mankind free from parochialism and war. He sustained the Mesa with this faith, hauntingly formulated for him by Donne:

> *Batter my heart, three-personed God, for you*
> *As yet but knock, breathe, shine and seek to mend.*
> *That I may rise and stand, o'erthrow me and bend*
> *Your force to break, blow, burn, and make me new.*

For the overthrow, the future test-detonation of the implosion bomb, he needed a more forbidding desert than that around the Mesa. Such a place he selected in southern New Mexico. Ninety miles of sand and lava, it had been called the Jornada del Muerto by the first Spanish wanderers who had crossed it. To the actual test site he ordered constructed in its heart, he gave the designation Trinity.† "This code name didn't mean anything," he ex-

---

* The German bomb effort began well in 1939–40 with impressive projects for separating uranium isotopes and constructing reactors. Heisenberg helped nuclear physicists overcome a Nazi prejudice that their specialty was un-Aryan. By late 1941, Göring and Himmler would have liked to place all resources of the government behind a massive bomb effort, but could not, because of increased demands from the fighting front. The bomb program degenerated into factions of squabbling scientists before a self-sustaining chain reaction could be achieved. British fears disappeared in the summer of 1944, American fears a few months later. The story of the German effort and of allied intelligence about it is detailed in David Irving's *The German Atomic Bomb* and Samuel Goudsmit's *Alsos*. (See footnote on p. 125 above.)

† "We don't say Alamogordo the way the public does," Los Alamos physicists say patronizingly. "That was the name of a town clear on the other side of the mountains from the test site. Oppenheimer named the test Trinity, and that's what we've always called it."

plained in 1960, wiser after fifteen years of watching for signs of mankind's renewal. "It was just something suggested to me by John Donne's sonnets, which I happened to be reading at the time."

When the mask of conviviality and administrative confidence grew too heavy for Oppenheimer, he had a place to go for deeper quiet than even Kitty could provide. Near the Mesa's southeast fence was a building which he had officially named Omega. He had designed it for experiments that most physicists watched with a cold flip of the heart and a face briefly drained of emotion.

Omega housed critical-assembly tests loosely and collectively referred to by cleared personnel as the Dragon. Here, for example, a neat mechanism dropped a uranium-hydride cube through a hollow structure of the same material. Heating $2°C$ a millisecond, the cube set off a burst of 10^{12} prompt neutrons. It fell too fast to proliferate the delayed neutrons which would have made the whole assembly a sort of weak, fizzling bomb. Once it overheated, paused slightly, and set off a burst of 10^{15} neutrons. Observers in the room sensed a fleeting blue ionization in the air and in themselves a mental discomfort afterward hard to talk about.

Such mechanically controlled, comparatively routine experiments were not the reason parts of Omega were so specially quiet. The true Dragon to the Mesa's mind was embodied in the work of Louis Slotin. Serber had, long before, predicted the critical masses of the two kinds of bombs. A thousand practical developments had since made him seem alternately wrong and right. Now sitting between a Geiger counter and a neutron monitor, Slotin made the next-to-last verification. His materials were glittering curved segments of the actual bomb metal. He poked them together on top of his desk with a screwdriver.

The task was dangerous, suitable for a bachelor leading a crew of a half dozen other bachelors who leaned over his desk to watch in utter silent fascination. Taking their cue from him, they became a rather morose set. A thin, short, blue-bristled man who usually looked in need of a shave, Slotin at age thirty-one had dark circles under his eyes, which contrasted oddly with the heavy tan of his sunken cheeks. He seldom spoke with much animation except about the Dragon and about his other interest, the extrapolation of blast and radiation casualties.

Slotin resembled Oppenheimer's first graduate student at Berkeley but needed a more difficult deliverance than from night and kleptomania. Next to Oppenheimer the physicist who studied Slotin's character most attentively was Fermi. Omega was split in two by a beaverboard partition. On one side was the cold silence of the Dragon; on the other a crew of Fermi's bustled in warm, noisy friendship about a beautiful moderated reactor called the Water Boiler. This too was a critical assembly, but it was as cheerful as a teakettle and, aside from its contribution to fission mathematics, as peaceful. Here Fermi came to relax from theoretical physics and the administrative burdens Oppenheimer had managed to saddle him with (for example, Teller). Fermi's one discomfort was the thought of Slotin beyond the partition.

Fermi disliked the way Slotin's eyes gleamed when he talked of tickling the Dragon's tail. "There's something about the man that outrages me," Fermi told an intimate. What it was, Fermi said, he did not know, except that he found it anarchical, reckless, disturbing. Fermi had a hard clear mind which liked to wrestle with only limited questions, such as the behavior of slow and fast neutrons and high-energy particles. Slotin's behavior angered him by raising a question of a different order. To deal with it, he took the Water Boiler crew on week-long hikes to the Sangre de Cristo Mountains each time Slotin scheduled an assembly.

One of humanity's most ungrateful instincts is to dread not only the frontier but also the frontier guard. Around his desk in addition to the faces of his crew, Slotin could see other faces, at first German, then Japanese, then merely human. Whether one of them was his own or Fermi's was for him an insignificant detail. True knowledge is in the emotions. In its frustration at having become the physicists' test animal, the human race should find a certain comfort in the thought that Slotin knew what he was doing. He could not have passed the most elementary personality-profile test of the kind now routinely used in government and industry. By giving Slotin responsibility and by going to relax in spiritual rapport with him in Omega, Oppenheimer too outraged present-day administrative standards. His reason, of course, was that he wanted to build the bomb. If he had employed only sound, wholesome organization men for his project, Los Alamos would still be designing impressive remote-control machines with which to check its first implosion assembly.

"Our mission was to interpose no day's delay between the arrival of the material and the readiness of the bomb," said Oppenheimer. At the start of 1945 he set July 20 as the target date for both types. For Little Boy this meant only that he expected then to have enough uranium to load it and turn it over to the Army. It was much simpler than the plutonium bomb, and the calculations for it were much cleaner and more confident. The chief question about it was the supply of uranium needed for it. Since there was a war on, he told Groves, the Army had best accept it untested. For the implosion bomb this was his planned test date. It meant that the Mesa must break through a series of prohibitive-looking difficulties.

Oppenheimer made up a timetable and began checking successive stages off. In February, essential physics research done. In March, full-scale lenses fabricated (these were a system of chemical explosives designed by Tuck to realize Neddermeyer's dream of a spherical shockwave imploding symmetrically inward toward its center). In early April, multipoint electric detonator system completed. Before the united effort of the laboratory, each deadline fell away smoothly but did so in a way that made the ultimate uncertainty more haunting. First, in order to work, each detail had to be constructed to near-impossible perfection, and second, each specialized experimental verification of implosion efficiency fell ominously below theoretical predictions. Were the problems first faced by Neddermeyer being solved well enough to make an effective implosion bomb? Each physicist on the Mesa would have given a different estimate of the chances, all would have agreed that the answer was uncertain.

Few ripples from the outside world disturbed the Mesa's concentration. On April 12 the radio brought news of Roosevelt's death. Physicists drifted toward the door of Main Tech with no business there except to digest a sense of change and loss. When about fifty had gathered, Oppenheimer decided that work was being held up and sent word round to the various buildings that anyone who liked might come for a brief memorial observance. Standing beside the flagpole, he made a five-minute talk, impromptu but not unthought or unfelt. Physicists remember it now as the moment that brought them closest to the strangeness of the Mesa. "It was beautiful," says Bradbury, squirming a little with instinctive dislike of using such a word. "By that I mean it was simple and moving with nothing fancy about it."

Oppenheimer's source materials, which he did not list for his audience, included Ahimsa (viewed as "love"), Raj ("passion"), and Attwa ("spirit"). From the *Bhagavad-Gita* he took a text which as he remembered it ran, "Man is consubstantial with his faith and his father." It is a pity that Latimer, the analyst of his philosophy, was not there to listen to him. This would have been Latimer's best chance to judge whether he was sustaining the Mesa by an ideal more catholic than that of Western civilization, which Roosevelt had died defending. No one took down a copy, which in any case would not preserve much of what he conveyed to the physicists herding unquietly in the sand under the desert sun. "He spoke very quickly in a very low voice, seeming to communicate not in words but in thoughts," says Higinbotham. "The effect was inspiring, but afterward you couldn't remember how it was produced."

On May 1, Oppenheimer checked off completion of the initiator. A major scientific achievement, this was a device for creating a strong neutron source at the precisely required instant. It worked by suddenly mixing alpha-radioactive polonium with another material which would support the alpha-radiation neutron-production reaction. A week later, he checked off the first test explosion of a complete lens system.

Long expected, the German surrender made little impact on the Mesa. "Everyone worked harder," Oppenheimer said. Llewelyn Hughes, who had by now straightened out the Personnel Department after Condon's leaving and had gone home to Washington University, found more time for reflection. "The German surrender meant the bomb would be first used not on the white but on the colored peoples of the world," he said. "It looked to me as though this country was going to make a bad start in nuclear arms."

Such misgivings were seldom voiced on the Mesa, but when they were, Oppenheimer, engrossed in the technical problem, had an answer of sorts with which to silence them. "He wanted to get the thing made and tested so that at least the civilian scientists in the Project would know what it could do," says Weissman. "He didn't want it to become a secret of the military which they could use to control the government with after the war."

On June 12 two full-size plutonium hemispheres were delivered to Slotin in Omega. Slotin checked them for neutron multiplication,* then stored them in the thickest-walled building available, an old icehouse belonging to the boy's school. This he did in accordance with an arrangement by which the Mesa tried to rid itself of some obscure responsibility. He was scheduled to retain them formally in his possession until on the night of their detonation he should pretend to hand them over to the secular arm, the Army, on the Jornada del Muerto. If he had poked them all the way together, they would have been about the size of a pair of small cupped hands. The hollow in the center would have been less, and this fact brought Neddermeyer his final anguish on the Mesa.

Under Oppenheimer, Bethe had had responsibility since the previous August for delineating the implosion bomb's theoretical parameters. Bethe had accepted this hard task as part of what he felt was a continuing lifelong demand on him to change the way his mind worked. When he had left Germany in his youth to study with Fermi at Rome, he had discovered that he was a bulldog, remorselessly thorough and slow. He did not like to think of himself in this way. To get to physics' good places, he decided, he must not creep along the low road of mathematical proof; to move at all, he must move faster. Consequently, shaping the plutonium hemispheres to meet a rigid deadline typified the madly uncongenial labors he welcomed as a cure for his habit of mere logical thinking.

"Though Bethe is slow-spoken to the point of irritating some people, his mind works smoothly and quickly, but not intuitively, nor in bursts of activity," says a colleague. The extreme pressure of the deadline required bursts of mental activity, and Bethe produced them. Under himself in turn he selected a young Canadian, Robert Christy, to give day-to-day guidance to the experimental designers.

* Slotin sat at his desk amid a clutter of radiation counters. He laid the bomb-metal pieces on his desk top far enough apart to be out of range of each other's neutrons. Then with a screwdriver he slowly pushed them together. As he did so each piece responded to neutrons from the other by emitting more neutrons. The effect was a progressive multiplication of neutrons that if charted would appear as an ascending curve. Slotin did not push the pieces all the way together. He stopped as soon as in his mind's eye he could extrapolate the ascending curve into the vertical straight line that would stand for neutron multiplication in a detonating bomb.

Christy, with Bethe as his mentor, kept abreast of calculations by the entire Theoretical Division, which established the bomb's configuration. Bethe and Christy worked brilliantly together, obtaining experimental feedbacks enabling them to leap intuitively over many mathematical impasses at a time. When they finished their design journey in June of 1945, they found that it had led them back again to Neddermeyer, whose way was to go instantly from A to Z without knowing how he did it.

"Just before Trinity, Kerst and I got betatron-cloud chamber results on a mock-up of the actual design to be used," said Neddermeyer. "I noticed it assembled into a solid sphere with a hollow only at one end extending into the middle for the detonator source [initiator]. The pieces were small and very thick-walled. This was a sore thing to me. I had made similar proposals before the reorganization of the lab, and Oppenheimer had pushed me toward thin walls and large hollows. After the reorganization, Christy had moved back the other way till he got to a solid sphere again."

To the hurried historians of the Nuclear Age, there should be a clue to the meaning of their period in the feelings of the bomb builders. Next to Oppenheimer, those at Los Alamos chiefly responsible were Fermi, Bethe, and Neddermeyer. Disappointingly, the first two like almost everyone else on the Mesa let Oppenheimer take protective custody of their emotions. They worked fast and cleanly with never a personal display of feelings like Slotin's obvious longing for the Freudian death slip. Neddermeyer, by contrast, stood alone. The way he felt should therefore be of significance to anyone willing to give him a thoughtful hearing. Merciless and humble, he is always his own harshest examiner: "I didn't go to Trinity. Kerst and I were busy trying out a new idea of ours, the chronotron. No. That wasn't why I didn't go. At Los Alamos they called it the Christy bomb. The *Christy* bomb! I stayed home. Really I hoped the goddam thing wouldn't work."

It was seven days after the final driblet of plutonium arrived at the Mesa that Slotin put the hemispheres away in the icehouse. The other components of the Christy bomb were scrambled together ready for testing on July 16, four days before the deadline Oppenheimer had set long before.

At Los Alamos, physicist David Inglis, editor of the laboratory's technical reports, also regarded the term "Christy bomb" as something of a misnomer, but for a different reason than Neddermeyer's. "If any one man was responsible for the bomb, Oppenheimer was," says Inglis. "I think it was the hardest technical job that had ever been done up to that time." As Oppenheimer's neighbor in Main Tech, he watched his weight go down again from a cavernous 130 to a skeleton 116 and wondered where he got all the war-rationed cigarettes he had started chain-smoking again. "Oppenheimer was not only the administrative head of the laboratory but also the technical head, and this double burden—I was there, I saw it—was a miracle of a performance. The duty and devotion to country—I can't describe to you the pressure the man was under."

At the Trinity test site, Oppenheimer had had scores of physicists moving through rigidly detailed rehearsals for the past three months. On May 7 they had stacked a hundred tons of T.N.T. on a twenty-foot tower, fired it off, and learned with dismay how badly laboratory recording instruments worked under field conditions.

This work was being supervised by physicist Kenneth Bainbridge, the official test leader. For Oppenheimer most of the purely technical decisions about the bomb were now in the past, except what to do if it fizzled. At the test he realized that he would be an observer while other physicists did the work. All that he could do on the Jornada del Muerto was to maintain that abnormal climate of alacrity that had distinguished Los Alamos from all other laboratories. "I must remain conscious" was the way he defined his function to himself when he thought of the approaching night of the detonation. To ease the strain on him, Groves summoned the two people outside the Mesa who cared most for him—his brother Frank, then struggling with Beta at Oak Ridge, and Rabi from the Radiation Laboratory at M.I.T.

After his fashion, Frank found a way to take on himself a little of Oppenheimer's burden. He became safety aid to Bainbridge, who gave him a jeep with which he visited the scattered test installations, energetically checking and rechecking for overlooked precautions. "You might have thought this would irritate people, but the way he went to work had the opposite effect," says McKibben. "I was assigned to timing and metering instruments. Frank caught me fiddling with a heavy wooden casket of them at a little station 800 yards west of the planned point zero. He looked the casket over, got a shovel, and started throwing a big mound of sand around it. He was a simple, earnest guy, and the load of worry he carried around—I suppose he had caught it from his brother, whom I couldn't understand so well— somehow made the rest of us feel better." Becoming in a peculiar sense Oppenheimer's surrogate, Frank toured the Jornada del Muerto and soaked up anxieties from which he could in turn deliver himself only in his dreams. "Seventeen thousand yards southeast of point zero was a base camp where we bunked," recalls Lavatelli, one of the test crew. " 'Good God man, don't do that!' I heard Frank say in his sleep. Then he woke up screaming."

"Frank turned into one of the prime worriers of all time," says Rabi. "That was how he tried to keep Robert well. As for me, I was invited just because Robert liked me. He'd asked me to join his project as experimental physics director and I'd refused because of my radar work. Now he was under a tremendous strain and I was supposed to watch him and look after him."

From Los Alamos, Rabi rode south through the desert to the test site in dubious military transportation. "The Army," Allison recalled, "had provided us a bunch of horrible beat-up old wrecks." Into the baking noon of mid-July on the Jornada, said Allison, Rabi stepped out with rubbers and umbrella. There Oppenheimer told him his first piece of business would be to put a dollar into the betting pool. A hundred physicists, he explained, had backed their guesses on the violence of the test bomb in terms of tons of T.N.T. Ignoring those of certain atmospheric-ignition enthusiasts, whose mathematics left him cold, he went on, bets had covered a tonnage range from just above zero to just below eighteen thousand. Officially as director he had taken the position that yield would be about five thousand tons. Unofficially and personally, it had made him feel better to bet on three hundred tons, which practically speaking would be a fizzle. From all this Rabi deduced that he was expected to put his dollar on zero, but physicist Lee DuBridge, who had come with him from M.I.T., got in ahead of him and he was obliged to take eighteen thousand.

"You will room with me," Oppenheimer said. "Change to desert clothes. One reason we picked this spot is that it won't rain here. Naturally I have checked with the meteorologists."

This conversation probably took place in the afternoon of Thursday, July 12. "No sooner had I changed," Rabi declared, "than it began to rain cats and dogs."

On Friday Rabi went with Oppenheimer to an abandoned four-room shack close to point zero. There Slotin mounted the hemispheres inside a capsule that held them just far enough apart to keep them from multiplying each other's neutron emissions. To become a bomb all they now lacked was the explosive lens assembly. This was a thick rind of intricately carved smokeless powder that would first blast the hemispheres together and then compress the solid metal to sudden supercriticality. To be near the capsule from now on involved a certain amount of danger; no one could say how much. Not wishing the project to suffer too much loss in any one accident, Groves had elected to preside at forward operations by deputy. Representing him in the shack was Thomas Farrell, a young brigadier general in the Army Air Force. Pink cheeks, lively blue eyes, and a gushy stage-Irish charm that Groves liked made him an opposite human type from Slotin.

His own eyes gleaming, Slotin pointed to the capsule and told Farrell to touch it. Tamper-coated with uranium metal, it had a size and shape something like a watermelon. Surprised to see it so small, Farrell put his hands on it—the tamper coating made it safe for him to do so—and felt the thing was warm. At some point in the higher levels of his nervous system, he recalled later, the sensation turned into a thrill of realization and dread.

"The receipt," said Slotin, and Farrell signed it as from the Army to the laboratory.

Point zero was a hundred-foot open-work steel tower. On Saturday, Rabi went there with Oppenheimer and saw twenty or so physicists and Army personnel gathered under a canvas roof covering the tower base. The weather was hot, cloudy, and humid. Oppenheimer, who had not himself changed to desert clothes, was the only one wearing a coat. Too emaciated to sweat, he had kept on his familiar sloppy tweed suit, which now fitted him like a tent.

Slotin had brought the plutonium assembly, and Kistiakowsky, the explosive-lens assembly. The task at hand was for Robert Bacher, a slow-spoken, level-headed physicist from Cornell, to supervise the insertion of one inside the other, then mount the whole apparatus in a corrugated-iron shed on top of the tower. Bacher's crew attached the plutonium assembly to a chain hoist and started to lower it into the lens assembly. It would not go. Someone established that its temperature was too high.

Oppenheimer, Bacher, and Kistiakowsky put their heads together. The question was where the unexpected heat had come from. If it was from the plutonium's internal radioactivity, nothing could be done. If it was from the heat of the desert, why had not the lens assembly acquired it and expanded accordingly? Slotin's eagerness, it turned out, was responsible. He had had the hemispheres brought down to the hot Jornada del Muerto from the high cool Mesa almost a full day before Kistiakowsky brought down the lenses. During this time they had absorbed the additional heat.

As soon as this fact came out, Bacher rested one assembly on the other a few minutes to equalize their temperatures, slid them together with a click, and hoisted the now-completed bomb to the platform atop the tower.

A light, intermittent drizzle started. Rabi got into a poker game with Bacher's crew, who played poorly and snarled at him about the weather. Oppenheimer conferred with meteorologists at the tower, rode with them to a distant plateau, where they made additional observations, then went back to base camp. There the leader of the Water Boiler crew, Percival King, looked alternately at him and his own chief, Fermi, the other most significant figure at the test, with a view to comparing their attitudes. "Oppenheimer, who had so much more responsibility, struck me as keyed up to the last degree of strain and tension," he said. "Fermi, on the other hand, seemed not to have a care. Experiment, like that we did at the Water Boiler, was always his way of relaxing from theory. To him I would judge this was just another experiment. I think he was getting a kick out of it."

One of Fermi's traits that caused his colleagues to rank him in the genius class was his knack of extrapolating problem solutions that hid just beyond the range of mathematical proof. On the next day, Sunday, July 15, he gave a chilling demonstration. It began with a graceful compliment to Oppenheimer. If the bomb failed to go off, Fermi said, no one else could ever do better to make it go off, so Oppenheimer and the laboratory would have proved implosion impossible, and this would be the best of good news for mankind. Less obvious and more interesting, he went on, was a point about atmospheric ignition: long study of the possibility had put him in a position to handicap the odds on two contingencies. "I invite bets," he said, "against first the destruction of all human life and second just that of human life in New Mexico."

Groves listened frowning. He had got up a series of press releases to cover all the eventualities he could foresee. The most drastic was that Oppenheimer and the other physicists who were to man the forward station would be wiped out; this he planned to explain by a statement that they had accidentally touched off an Army ammunition dump while enjoying a holiday at Oppenheimer's ranch. Now Fermi exasperated him by raising a contingency for which he was unprepared to account. He decided that Fermi was merely making a bad joke out of a desire to relieve tension. A good many of the senior physicists present felt that Fermi was not merely joking.

Hot and steamy, the drizzle intensified and a south wind blew languidly. Physicists gathered around Oppenheimer to bandy a dreary new word of the twentieth century—*fallout*. A cloud of radioactive debris, they kept telling him, might drift over Amarillo or Albuquerque and be dumped by the rain before it could dissipate or decay. Groves thought they were besieging Oppenheimer to put off the test. He watched with rising annoyance until at six o'clock he could stand it no longer. Leading Oppenheimer into an empty office, he told him to keep calm and said he was summoning the meteorologists for a quiet conference.

Someone had to decide as to what weather conditions the people of Amarillo and Albuquerque should stake their lives on. Groves willingly undertook to do it. An omen for the coming nuclear age was that he began by dismissing the meteorologists whom he had called in. "Since it was obvious that they were completely upset by the failure of the long-range predictions, I soon excused them," he explains. "After that it was necessary for me to make my own weather predictions—a field in which I had no special competence."

Luckily for Amarillo and Albuquerque, Oppenheimer continued to rely on the chief meteorologist, Jack Hubbard. He, Oppenheimer and Farrell had long planned to constitute themselves a triumvirate to decide whether to keep to schedule. None of them wanted a postponement. Oppenheimer told Groves that during the middle of the night they would decide whether to fire the bomb at four o'clock the next morning or to hold off an hour or so until just before daylight. Relieved, Groves advised Oppenheimer to go to bed, but Oppenheimer replied he did not feel like sleeping. At midnight he woke up Groves, who had had no trouble sleeping himself, and drove with him forward to the control station at south ten thousand.

At the base camp and at a number of other observation points ringing the perimeter, physicists who had completed their part of the preparation lapsed into immobility. "For the first time in I couldn't remember how long, we had nothing to do," says Lavatelli. "It was a curious sensation. We drank coffee, wandered to the mess hall for some chow, and listened to an FM radio link with the other points. Around two o'clock a feeble little argument which we couldn't follow seemed to get under way at the control station where Oppenheimer had gone with Groves. 'His Nibs wants it this way,' Oppenheimer's voice broke in, and they stopped talking there."

At point zero McKibben lay on a bedroll in the sand beside the tower. After watching him fully arm the bomb except for the closing of a few safety switches, Bainbridge and Kistiakowsky had left him there since about midnight. Out of sight in the dark, Hubbard and two Army sergeants roved the vicinity sending up weather balloons. Occasionally faint flashes of lightning let McKibben see the tower platform above his head. Here, invisible except to his mind's eye, nestled the bomb. Dressed in the housing that had been left at Los Alamos, it would have been black, egg-shaped, five feet wide, nine and a half feet long, sprouting incongruous tail fins at the narrow end. Stripped, it looked like a peeled orange of five dural segments bolted together to make a sphere fifty-nine inches across. Inside this, its five kilograms of plutonium ticked away their half-life of 24,400 years. Because of its shape, physicists referred to it in writing as Fat Man and in talk with a sort of nervous, pushing overfamiliarity as Fat Boy.

McKibben had been selected for his vigil because he was a dour, utterly dependable, no-nonsense type. Looking up at Fat Boy, he thought it would be a fine thing to drop it on Japan; how could one understand the attitude of people like Kistiakowsky, who had professed to have some qualms on the subject? But the word "qualms" reminded him of Fermi, who had used it in his bland

1

survey of the prospect for atmospheric ignition. The fact was, McKibben told himself, that no one could say for sure what Fat Boy might do. So there was no use thinking of that. He rolled over to face away from the tower and went to sleep.

The trouble was that Kistiakowsky kept coming back from the control station bringing his damned qualms with him. "Go away!" McKibben would tell him, wondering why he had never discovered before that Kistiakowsky's face was not really human. Instead of going, Kistiakowsky connected a garden hose to some unexpected reservoir of qualms and turned it on him. McKibben woke in a gushet of rain, already disappearing, and looked up at the tower, alone except for what poet Frances Davis calls the half-life that did not sleep but would teach others to sleep. The dream had been uneasy, he admitted to himself, but being awake with Fat Boy was not much more fun. He rolled over and slept again until at a quarter to five he felt a hand on his shoulder. Bainbridge was shaking him. "Better get away from here," Bainbridge said. "We're going to shoot this thing off."

Daybreak was still almost an hour away. With Bainbridge and Kistiakowsky dogging his movements, McKibben got up and threw shut the last safety switches. They turned on a powerful light to signal that the bomb was ready to fire. Everyone now began to move briskly; the tower had become a poor place to linger. Collecting two armed guards, they mounted separate jeeps on the theory that even with Army transportation, three simultaneous breakdowns were unlikely. In a careful tight little procession they drove back to the control station, a concrete blockhouse with a single doorless opening facing away from the bomb. Squeezing into it, the arming party found it already filled with physicists, Army personnel, and psychiatrists whom Groves had decided the physicists would need to calm them down. Groves himself was not there. As soon as he had seen the signal light, he had withdrawn to the base camp and left Farrell behind as his deputy.

Oppenheimer glanced at McKibben to see whether he had kept his composure, then faded into the background. By an arrangement characteristic of the Mesa's administrative simplicity, the last man away from the bomb was also to be the man who would actually fire it off. McKibben took charge of the control panel.*

* The traits which caused McKibben to be selected for his role have made him slow to talk about it. Even such excellent accounts of the test as Rob-

Standing beside him, Allison spoke into two microphones link-
ing the control station by wire and radio to the other observation
points. "It is now twenty minutes to zero," Allison said. He continued the count-down at five-minute intervals. At the back of the
crowd, Oppenheimer wandered silently in and out of the unframed
opening, looking for new stars in the clearing sky.

"Five minutes to zero," said Allison. McKibben checked to see
that movie cameras he had asked for were properly set up, then
turned on a battery of photoflood lamps. "Since I didn't know exactly what was coming, I wanted to be sure my skirts would be
clear regardless," he said. "By recording every flicker of the nee-
dles, I could be damned sure."

Next to McKibben stood a youthful physicist with the job of
opening a panic switch to cut off McKibben's control panel in case
something went wrong. "What if I just say this can't go on and
stop it?" he broke in, turning to Oppenheimer.

Oppenheimer studied the young face blinking and grinning at
him in the glare. "Are you all right?" he asked coldly. Sobering,
the face turned back to the control panel. Oppenheimer slipped
again into the background and repeated to himself that he must
remain conscious.

"Four minutes to zero," said Allison in a flat robot voice. No one
moved until his announcement of forty-five seconds, when Mc-
Kibben turned on an automatic timer. Even so, at ten seconds
McKibben had to throw a final manual switch.

"Ten . . . nine . . . eight . . ." Allison droned. McKibben,
finally done with his work, looked away from the control panel,
trying to make out the dark blockhouse opening through the glare.

For Allison, not done yet, the seconds stretched out interminably. He had in fact been counting down for six months. "Be chief
cowpuncher of a no-red-tape committee to keep Fat Boy moving
on schedule," Oppenheimer had told him. "Break up organizational inertias. Ride herd on division heads. See that they get the
job done on time." It was a ticklish assignment; the reason Oppen-

---

ert Cahn's in the *Saturday Evening Post* (July 16, 1960) skimp on him, and
Groves's published recollections ignore him entirely. Since a Military Police
officer at the test had a similar name, it should perhaps be noted that the
man here referred to is always Dr. Joseph L. McKibben, physicist from
Wisconsin.

heimer had chosen Allison for it was that no one resented him. "Fatherly" is the way Mesa physicists describe him, adding with singular unanimity that he was a good physicist and an honest man.

Now that Allison had got Fat Boy done on time, he was reflecting that he did not know what it could do. Opinion on the Mesa was evenly divided on whether it would produce a worthwhile blast. Allison was thinking partly of this and partly of Fermi's qualms. Like McKibben he shared them fully, but they had taken hold of his viscera in a different way. For him it was no justification to say he had done what someone had told him to do; what right had he to participate in an experiment that might kill off the human race?

"Zero," he said.

Facing the door, McKibben noticed a glare that was brighter—much, much brighter—than that of the photoflood lamps. Still, the pupils of his eyes were already fully contracted. He was able to check the meters of the control panel and tell they were all in order. There was a thunderous noise, a minute of silence, and then some sort of excitement going on around Oppenheimer. Since it was evidently congratulatory, McKibben felt he need not concern himself with it. He had been up for a very long time, he suddenly realized, and the nap he had taken under Fat Boy had not done him much good. He went outside to glance at a purple-veiled fireball that everybody had begun talking about, briefly added his own congratulations to those being showered on Oppenheimer, then started looking for a place to lie down.

General Farrell had started to pound Oppenheimer's back and found that Kistiakowsky, a repentant doubter, had got in ahead of him. "Excitable Russian!" thought Farrell, and began pounding Allison's back instead.

"Wonderful, wonderful!" he exclaimed to Allison. "What a wonderful thing that you could count backward at a time like this!"

"Still alive," Allison was musing to himself. "No atmospheric ignition." The psychiatrists, he also noted, needed somebody to calm them down. Meanwhile there was Farrell. The popping blue eyes and the flushed neck inside the khaki collar started new qualms coiling up toward Allison's cerebrum, but for the moment

they did not get there. He walked out to join Oppenheimer, who
was now on the sand gazing at the fireball. Someone calculated
that there were a thousand billion curies of radiation inside the
bright ionization veils with which it had cloaked itself in the
atmosphere.

The best note on Oppenheimer's bearing in the blockhouse is one
which *New York Times* reporter William Laurence obtained later
that day from observers there whom he was careful to keep anonymous. According to them, Oppenheimer's face was tense and
dreamy—withdrawn—until the moment that it was lit by reflections from the sand. Then it relaxed visibly.

He himself told what he believed he was thinking. The glare he
found very white, illuminating in ghastly detail every hummock
and mesquite bush for miles and miles all the way south to the San
Andreas Mountains. Fey with adrenalin like a drowning man, he
had plenty of time to observe and to try to integrate. The problem
was whether Krishna, who is in everything, was in this inhuman
light. The *Bhagavad-Gita* seems to say, though Gandhi denied it,
that it is all right to kill in war provided one does not spare kith
and kin. Better than anyone besides Slotin, Oppenheimer knew the
light was death; this did not matter too much to him provided it
was also Krishna. How could one tell? Compassion and beauty
were Krishna's tokens. To hear Krishna speak was to become
Krishna, who long ago had reassured a reluctant royal swordsman
that he was both the slayer and the slain.

While the light faded, not abruptly for him, Oppenheimer became conscious again that he was not alone in the blockhouse. "A
few people laughed, a few people cried, most people were silent,"
he said. "There floated through my mind a line from the *Bhagavad-Gita* in which Krishna is trying to persuade the Prince that he
should do his duty: 'I am become death, the shatterer of worlds.' I
think we all had this feeling more or less."

By their eyes and eardrums physicists could tell at once that
Fat Boy's violence was something new to human capabilities. "We
felt the world would never be the same again," said Oppenheimer.
While searchlights picked at the faded fireball and re-created it as
a huge ghostly cloud in the night sky, preliminary instrument reports indicated blast had far exceeded the official hopeful expecta-
tion of five thousand tons. From the blockhouse roof Oppenheimer
watched the cloud feint frighteningly north. A little after dawn it

turned east in the direction it had been expected to take. He and the other physicists went back to the base camp.

Allison started to lose himself in the crowd there with something of the relief of a man escaping from too much Shakespeare. The farther one got from Oppenheimer, he was realizing, the easier it was to think undirectedly. He bumped into Groves, who gave him a solemn look and said, "This is the end of traditional warfare."

"This is the end of traditional warfare," Allison parroted. But the pat wording—had Groves rehearsed it?—the crisp military tone, the stiff spine and the overfed khaki waistline all set him to thinking of Farrell's congratulations. What sort of men, he meditated, could be filled with wonder at the mental processes involved in counting from ten to zero?

On the verge of an abysmal revelation, Allison searched desperately for a civilian face. The first he saw was that of Conant, whom he usually called Jim but to whom he now spoke as to a very old man. "Oh, Mr. Conant!" he wailed, his voice infantile and betrayed." They're going to take this thing over and fry *hundreds* of Japanese!"

When Oppenheimer had left the evening before, the two most carefree physicists at the base camp were Fermi and Rabi. Between the flash and the airwave, Fermi had amused himself by dropping bits of paper which enabled him to estimate the blast correctly at twenty thousand tons. Afterward, however, he had received congratulations on this amazing trick with a moody languor quite different from his usual childlike zest for small compliments. His idolatrous Water Boiler crew insists his decline in spirits was simply due to what they call the "itis": diarrhea from too many enchiladas eaten en route. But the fact is that on that day, as he afterward made clear in confessions to his wife about the difficulty of driving home to the Mesa, he had had a bellyful of experiment.

As a consultant, Rabi had shared the Mesa physicists' responsibilities but not their tension. He judged Oppenheimer to be at the core much tougher than Groves or anyone else in authority who worried about him. Consequently casual in his nursemaid duties, he had made no demur at Oppenheimer's leaving him behind at the base camp. There at five o'clock he had lined up with the others to plump down in a curious obeisance: flat on the sand, backside up, feet toward Fat Boy's distant tower.

When the blast came, he was surprised at the response his body made. After a minute he noticed with a scientist's habit of observation that gooseflesh appeared on the backs of his hands. It was not like watching an ordinary explosion scaled up. "The experience was hard to describe," he says. "I haven't got over it yet. It was awful, ominous, personally threatening. I couldn't tell why." Dawn found him still in reverie as he watched the blockhouse party approaching from a long way off across the sand. Oppenheimer parked too far away for Rabi to see his face, but something in his bearing brought Rabi's gooseflesh back again. He moved like a confident stranger, darkly glittering, at ease, in tune with the thing. "I'll never forget his walk," says Rabi. "I'll never forget the way he stepped out of the car."

8

THIS GRAY MORNING

THROUGHOUT the Manhattan Project generally, physicists felt let down by the German surrender. They picked more fretfully at their leaders, especially Compton, and brooded aloud with new unrestraint about the folly of bombs against Japan. "I think the hotbed of this discussion was in Chicago rather than Los Alamos," said Oppenheimer. "At Los Alamos I heard very little talk about it. We always assumed that if bombs were needed they would be used." Trusting as lambs, Mesa physicists were content to let him say "we." William Higinbotham, for example, was an individualist whom nature had destined to lead humanitarian oppositions, but not on the Mesa. "The tempo was too high," he explains. "Also, Oak Ridge and Chicago and some other places all thought they were fighting their administrations. It's a great tribute to Oppenheimer that there was nothing like this at Los Alamos. I formed a steering committee to speak up for the scientists as employees. Oppenheimer sometimes listened to it, sometimes gave it information. About using the bomb, he didn't ask for a vote, but he invited comment. I'm sure people went to his office. As for me, at the time I would have favored it."

As usual, the heart of the opposition was Szilard in Chicago. As a leader Szilard was handicapped by gross impatience. For an associate the trait is symbolized by a conversation he once overheard between Szilard and a Security officer at Oak Ridge.

"Why can't you be a good American?" the officer asked, half exasperated, half appealing.

"Like who?"

"Well, like me."

"*Ugh*. No."

Szilard tried to see Truman to get him not to drop the bomb but was shunted off to James Byrnes, incoming Secretary of State. The two quickly established a mutual *ugh* relationship. Szilard told Byrnes he distrusted Compton, Conant, and Bush, who, Byrnes said, were to be consulted on bomb use. Byrnes then mentioned Oppenheimer and learned to his relief that Szilard did not distrust him also. Byrnes found he was able to break off an oppressive conversation about multitudes of civilian dead by saying that Oppenheimer too would be consulted.

Of several petitions circulated at Chicago against bombing Japan, the strongest was Szilard's. "If I had been there," said Allison, hesitating at the abnegation of moral responsibility implied in his *if*, "I would probably have signed it." Szilard wrote Teller requesting that he get signatures on the Mesa. Unintegrated soul that he was, Teller took the letter to Oppenheimer for his opinion. Oppenheimer made a few noncommittal comments and handed it back. A silence ensued. Teller did not go. "The matter is being dealt with at a higher level," said Oppenheimer in absent-minded dismissal.

The incident hardened Teller's dislike of him, but Oppenheimer was displaying ignorance rather than arrogance. By "a higher level" he meant that of statesmanship, which was still as much a mystery to him as top management had been before Groves took him in hand. In this area he was about to receive an education.

Groves was making bomb policy. Nothing better illustrates the vacuum created by Roosevelt's death than this appalling fact. "Groves was a tremendous lone wolf," says Major Ralph Carlisle Smith of the Mesa. "His importance has never been appreciated." With respect to Groves's motives and mental processes, his own statement seems clear but should be accepted with a charity and reserve which he does not ask for. "If the bomb hadn't been used," he explains, "in the first year after the war was over, the first Congressional investigation would have screamed that the government was responsible for the blood of our boys shed uselessly."

Groves's single significant ally—it is doubtful that he wanted even one—was Secretary of War Stimson. By melancholy coincidence, Stimson had been the Administration's first denouncer of Japanese imperialism and was now the highest surviving official to have been kept posted on bomb development. He philosophized that war is hell and took an unaccountably unreal view of the amount remaining to be got through in the Pacific.

Strong to mild distaste for full use of the bomb against Japan had been voiced on the one hand by General George Marshall and Admiral William Leahy and on the other by Bush and Conant. Those in Washington who knew much about the bomb did not know much about the military situation. Those who knew much about the military situation did not know much about the bomb.

President Truman did not know much about either. Around May 1, Stimson and Groves took him a twenty-four-page résumé on the bomb. "I don't like to read long reports," he told them. "Your present course is sound. Carry on as you are doing now." Stimson told Truman that a scheduled November invasion of Japan would cost a million casualties. Where he got this figure is a puzzle. Marshall estimated the cost at forty thousand. Leahy and Army Air Force General Henry Arnold did not believe an invasion would be necessary. But Truman took his advice from Stimson.

After his fashion each of these men was, of course, thinking not only of the war but of the coming peace. Bomb use was a question that each tried to fit into his strategy for putting his country into the strongest possible position vis-à-vis the Soviet ally.

With Truman's consent, Stimson and Groves on May 9 called together a mixed bag of eight government and science people, mostly bewildered about what was wanted of them. Stimson told them they were an Interim Committee to advise generally on many atomic matters, one of which was the use of bombs. He said he would be chairman. Groves, who like Stimson sat with them, seemed to take the cruder position that the use of bombs had already been decided and that they should rather concern themselves with such matters as news releases and future legislation.

"The whole thing was engineered by Stimson and Groves," says one of the members, Under Secretary of the Navy Ralph Bard. "We didn't know a damned thing about this business. For quite a while I couldn't tell what the hell was going on."

The committee met several times for large, windy discussions of

America's new atomic treasure-trove. Some of the members were hearing the peculiar, inverted-meaning word *atomic* for the first time. Groves preferred it to *nuclear*, which they could have looked up in any dictionary. On May 31 they got around to the detail of dropping bombs on Japan, devoting to it about an hour of a six-hour session.

It was to this session that Byrnes, one of the committee members, was looking when he assured Szilard that Oppenheimer would be consulted. He and Stimson had a different notion of what Oppenheimer was to be consulted about. Stimson had summoned Oppenheimer, Lawrence, Fermi, and Arthur Compton to Washington for the day as scientific advisers. Their function, he implied, would be to supply the committee more exact data than could be got from its scientific members, Bush, Conant, and Karl Compton, or from its guiding spirit, Groves.

"Gentlemen," Arthur Compton says Stimson began, "it is our responsibility to recommend action that may turn the course of civilization. In our hands we expect soon to have a weapon of wholly unprecedented destructive power. Today's prime fact is war. Our great task is to bring this war to a prompt and successful conclusion."

Thus, Stimson, whose grandiloquence Compton may have dressed up a little but not much, opened proceedings with a hint that he was not really asking anybody's opinion. Off in a corner George Marshall, who attended part-time, asked Ernest Lawrence whether an unused bomb could be kept a military secret after the war. Though not then aware of Security's tricks with Weinberg and Eltenton, Lawrence said no. Bard does not recall the incident. Lawrence impressed him as a fine man, but the only one of the four whom he remembers much contact with is Oppenheimer.

"Oppenheimer did the talking for them, as I guess he was supposed to do," says Bard. "At first I couldn't make out what he was saying, and then everything got clear. He told us the uranium bomb couldn't be tested, because material was being supplied too slowly. He said the plutonium bomb might be a dud and would have to be tested, but that even after that he couldn't guarantee the force of the explosion of the next one. He didn't say drop the bomb or don't drop it. He just tried to do his job, which was to give us technical background. I think he did it well. Certainly he didn't try to influence us in any way."

"After much discussion," run the official minutes of the meeting, "the Secretary [Stimson] expressed the conclusion, on which there was general agreement, that we could not give the Japanese any warning; that we could not concentrate on a civilian area; but that we should make a profound psychological impression on as many of the inhabitants as possible. At the suggestion of Dr. Conant, the Secretary agreed that the most desirable target would be a vital war plant employing a large number of workers and closely surrounded by workers' houses."

Having contributed their technical information, the four scientific advisers were theoretically not concerned with this agreement. But the human problem proved too much for Compton. "What shall I tell Szilard?" he asked plaintively as the session broke up. Oppenheimer, an idiot savant for the committee as he had once been for Groves, could produce no answer from his memory banks.

"We decided on dropping the bomb without warning," says Bard. "Stimson and Groves pushed it through. Afterward, I got to thinking.

"The Pacific war was a Navy war. The Army didn't know what the hell was going on there. The Navy had sewed up those islands so that nothing was coming in or going out. The Navy knew the Japanese were licked. The Army wanted to be in on the kill.

"The Japanese approached Russia and Switzerland for peace. The elements of peace were there. I thought we should give them a warning and approach them on terms of peace."

Bard wrote Stimson's subchairman Harrison a beautiful, lonely, unavailing protest, then demanded a White House appointment. Fearing Russia, Truman had begun to view Japan in terms of cold-war strategy. But in so far as his ruder language resources permitted, he echoed Stimson. "The question," he later summed up, "was whether we wanted to save many American lives and Japanese lives or whether we wanted to take a chance on whether we wanted to win the war by killing all our young men."

"For God's sake," Bard told Truman, "don't organize an army to go into Japan. Kill a million people? It's ridiculous."

Truman did not change. Bard resigned, the first nonscientist (Slotin was the first scientist) to understand that blind mass hysteria would not do in the new Nuclear Age.*

* To avoid a footnote clutter, several points on the bomb decision seem worth noting together. In the Interim Committee minutes, Conant's sugges-

Truman was preparing for a conference with Stalin and Churchill at Potsdam. While there, he meant to leave the bomb with carte
blanche in Stimson's hands. Overnervous, Stimson and Groves worried that even such a trifle as a clamor of physicists might dissuade
him from this arrangement. With Szilard's petition they dealt
effectively, making Szilard rephrase and recirculate it after Security censorship, then holding it back at internal transmission points
until Truman should leave the country. Thus they kept Truman
and the Interim Committee from considering it. ("I never *saw* the
petition," Bard declares, cursing.) Taking no chances, they also
bottled up in the same big brown envelope a paltering, equivocally
worded but still disturbing poll Compton had made of his subordinates' views at Chicago and Oak Ridge. Nevertheless, the most
tactful and best-loved of the refugees, James Franck, managed to
get a protest signed by seven physicists to the secretary of the Interim Committee. Stimson and Groves had to think of something
else to do with this one. With a flash of inspiration, they decided
to withhold it from the wobbling Committee by sending it to Oppenheimer at Los Alamos.

He had gone back there to push Fat Boy after one day in Washington. His directive was to assemble Fermi, Lawrence, and Compton to assess on technical grounds a protest got up on humane
grounds. Thus in theory the four had no need to wrestle with their
consciences. Like Truman, but with more excuse, they believed in
Stimson's million-casualty invasion. "We didn't know beans about
the military situation," said Oppenheimer. Even so, it was starting
to dawn on them that to say Fat Boy might fizzle at a prean-
nounced, fairly bloodless demonstration to watching Japanese was
tantamount to saying kill a defenseless multitude. And it was true;

---

tion was probably manipulated by Stimson from a weak qualm into the
ruthless appearance it has here. At the price of censorship on comments,
Fletcher Knebel and Charles W. Bailey obtained official permission to quote
this minute and other still-secret documents in a revealing article in *Look*
(August 13, 1963). For additional general background on the education Op-
penheimer was getting at this time, one should read also these authors' *No
High Ground* (New York: Harper, 1960) and Alice Smith's "Behind the
Decision to Use the Atomic Bomb: Chicago 1944–45," *Bulletin of Atomic
Scientists* (September, 1958). As for Bard, perhaps it should be added that
he knew the Army Air Force was destroying, with impunity, whatever in
Japan it wished to destroy.

Fat Boy might well fizzle; not even Little Boy could be positively guaranteed, since it could not be tested. Except for the Stimson-Groves maneuver, the long dilemma of the four men's war careers would never have become so explicit.

Each of the four reacted characteristically. Lawrence, who had the most life in him and the most instinctive love of life, fought longest against admission that a bloodless demonstration could not be relied on. Once Oppenheimer and Fermi had convinced him, his attitude began a massive total change, as it always did when he ran head-on into any dilemma. "He grew very impatient when people criticized the use of the bomb," says an intimate. "He thought it saved lives by ending the war."

Compton became sanctified. "He's more materialistic and pragmatic than anybody else about favoring bigger and bigger weapons," a mutual friend afterward complained of Compton to Fermi. "Why does he talk so much these days about God and philosophy and brotherhood?"

"Current need," Fermi replied. With his usual gusto in elucidating a subtle point, he summarized the nature of Compton's prominence in the public eye. "What did the country need most during the war? The bomb. What does it need now? Religion. He'll be leader again. I'm not surprised."

Fermi was a harder soul than Compton, less solaced by rationalizations. He and Oppenheimer, in his way equally hard, drew together. As the two on the spot, they took ultimate responsibility for answering the Franck protest. First they made nonsense of their assignment by saying that physicists were divided and without special competence on the moral question. Then they supplied what was wanted: a statement that technically the bombs could not be relied on to live up to a warning and that therefore, if they were used, they should be used without one.

On July 19, after the exaltation of the test night had left him, Oppenheimer wired Groves in Washington, requesting reconsideration on technical grounds of the schedule for bombing Japan—"Should like to be quite sure that the cost of going through with our present program is understood by you." The rest of the teletype deals with still-classified improvements in bomb design that had not been incorporated in Fat Boy and Little Boy. These improvements would, after a short delay, have yielded more and better bombs and might conceivably have justified revising the Interim Committee's objective of "a profound psychological impression" (*i.e.*, maximum civilian slaughter) from first bomb use. But Groves replied from Washington that it was now too late— "Factors beyond our control prevent us from considering any decision, other than to proceed according to the existing schedule for the time being." On August 6 Little Boy killed seventy thousand or more inhabitants of Hiroshima. On August 9 Russia entered the war on schedule, and Fat Boy killed thirty-five thousand or more at Nagasaki, where terrain and atmospheric conditions were less favorable.

Kistiakowsky saluted Japan's surrender with sixteen blasts of RDX outside the fence, and Mesa physicists danced a serpentine with clashing garbage-can lids. But their joy ebbed quickly and left a musty taste behind. On October 16, to a crowd watching the presentation of an Army certificate of commendation to the laboratory, Oppenheimer summed up the mood that had developed during the last two months. "If atomic bombs are to be added to the arsenals of a warring world or to the arsenals of nations preparing for war, then the time will come when mankind will curse the names of Los Alamos and Hiroshima."

The men in Omega showed they knew they were cursed already. Early in August, one low-grade Omega technician died in a chemical explosion and two were blinded. No further uranium bombs could be made for months, but a third plutonium bomb had been readied for the Dragon check. Slotin, sulking because Oppenheimer would not let him go see Japanese casualties at first hand, took a holiday, leaving his chief assistant, Harry Daghlian, to undertake it. Daghlian, also thin, dark, and morose, got an overdose of radiation and died on September 15. Slotin performed the check and several others, then next spring on May 21 gained what he seemed to long for. Poking the segments of the Bikini test bomb a little too close together, he set up a blue ionization glow in the room. Lunging from his chair, he covered the segments with his body until a half dozen observers could file out.

By that time it was too late for Slotin, but the most talented woman physicist on the Mesa, Elizabeth Graves, was asked by telephone to compute the chances of a man who had watched with his hand on Slotin's shoulder. Like McKibben, Elizabeth Graves was a no-nonsense type—Hiroshima, she used to say, was no worse than napalm. Methodically she began punching a calculator, then learned from another telephone call that the subject was her husband. "My mind went blank," she said. "I couldn't do the simplest sums in arithmetic." Graves survived with cataracts. Something like superstitious terror halted further necessary Dragon checks until entirely different methods could be devised from those Oppenheimer had kept going with complete safety during the war.

After Hiroshima, Oppenheimer lost the sense of purpose with which he had sustained the Mesa. "There was not much left in me at the moment," he said. Drifting, he let the Mesa drift and wanted to get away. The stillness some of his underlings sought in Omega —how could he be sure any longer that they were not right?—he looked for in a return to ivied halls and the study of cosmic rays. "Let the second team take over," Groves tactlessly or maliciously quoted him to the Mesa physicists. They swallowed loyally, feeling betrayed, sensing he was thinking of a darker betrayal he had led them into. "All right, it was all right," says Tuck. "The fellows who stayed *were* the second team. We couldn't compare at first with Oppenheimer, Bethe, Fermi, and some of the others who left. But they did good work here and it was not long before they were doing a *superb* production job." For his replacement as director, Oppenheimer hit on the fortunate choice of Bradbury, who for twenty years incredibly kept the Mesa steady while violent political storms broke over it. As well as he could with his own heart set on getting out, Oppenheimer joined Bradbury in urging Mesa physicists to stay.

October 16, the day Oppenheimer accepted the Army's commendation of the laboratory with a speech about mankind's curses, was also the day of his leaving. He drifted from one university to another.

First, there was Berkeley, where he and Kitty had built their new home just before the war. So big, so impersonal, Lawrence and his laboratory were hard to adjust to. "Everything was changed," said Sloan, who had also been away on war work. "I decided not to come back; I didn't want to change."

Lawrence's command, though more absolute, was more distant. He did not know all the people who worked for him. On inspection walks, instead of pausing for even the briefest, most uninformative conversations, he often merely checked on whether everyone looked busy. Once by mistake he fired a telephone company repairman who struck him as languid. Morale varied strikingly among the crews of different research projects. Inside the Laboratory, says the corporation physicist who had worked his way up from clean-up man in 1943, Lawrence was probably no longer the dominant personality.

McMillan, also back from Los Alamos, was trying to explain to Lawrence how one could actually get a hundred million volts of proton-acceleration from the big magnet Lawrence had converted to patriotic uses during the war. Incorporating a mysterious principle called phase-stability, the thing McMillan had in mind was not exactly a cyclotron. Lawrence was not wholly delighted. Proton flow, as distinguished from proton speed, was cut to almost nothing.* Two protons an hour, Lawrence philosophized, was what the sophisticated, alien, puzzling postwar generation of big machines was headed for.

Alvarez, also back from war work, was reviving interest in linear accelerators. Since Sloan had broken his back in 1937, these had been gathering dust. No one could think how to give their ion beams enough energy to penetrate the nucleus of the atom. Alvarez opened a new horizon. During a turn at the Boston M.I.T. Radiation Laboratory, he had helped develop metal-walled resonance cavities in which to tune radar waves. The idea could be applied to linear accelerators, he told Lawrence. Make the entire vacuum chamber a charged resonating cavity exactly tuned to a suitable radio-frequency wave, he said, and the linear accelerator would gain energy comparable with that of the cyclotron. On this principle Alvarez was developing the first so-called modern linear accelerators. (Ten years older, Sloan's are regarded by big-machine physicists as ancient.)

These machines—circular and linear accelerators—were no longer being built for medical-research purposes. Neutrons, it

---

* Machines incorporating the principle of phase-stability were called synchrocyclotrons. "The proton current of a synchrocyclotron is necessarily small when compared with that of a regular cyclotron," says a nuclear physicist. "On the other hand, the synchrocyclotron can go to *much* higher energy (speed) than can a cyclotron."

turned out, were not so good against cancer as X-rays. The idea behind the machines was to study the basic components of matter or sometimes, it seemed to physicists who looked on from outside Berkeley, simply to build big machines with unlimited government money.

Segré worked by himself independently in his own corner. McMillan showed strong tendencies to putter with inexpensive devices of paper and string in the old classic way of experimenters. Alvarez most nearly carried on the spirit of prewar Berkeley. Like Lawrence, Alvarez characteristically wanted to hurry and do big things, and he too tended to treat other scientists like servants. But he showed much more positive readiness to cause pain. "I watched him identify negative protons several years prematurely with a cloud chamber in 1938," says a frequent visitor to Berkeley. "Then, years later, after the war I had lunch with him at the Faculty Club while he was building a million-dollar bubble chamber. The project business manager came by and Alvarez started chewing him out in front of the whole table. I left and came back and Alvarez was still at it. Seemed needless to me. As well as I could tell, not the poor guy's fault at all."

Brilliant and capable, Alvarez divided his talent between experiments and public relations. "Frustrated," says another acquaintance. "He was the only one of those sunbathers who never got a Nobel prize, and they kept him reminded. Fantastic ego. Loved to tell how amazed the groups he lectured to were at how young he was. He would brag so openly you chuckled."

Accent on youth and hurry: this Berkeley tradition begun by Lawrence and extended by Alvarez became harder now to distinguish from mere grossness in the craving palate. "The library wanted to put up an oil painting of Lawrence where everybody could see it," says another out-of-Berkeley physicist. "I heard that Segré had advised against it, so I told him it seemed a nice idea to me.

" 'You don't understand,' he said. 'Do you know anything at all about paintings?'

"He took me up to the library to look at it. It was horrible. I don't see how anybody could help seeing it was horrible. Lawrence was vastly pleased."

"A matter of the taste buds," says still another physicist. "After the war I was with Lawrence and some of his crowd in a hotel room. They got out a bottle and offered me a drink. Rot gut. Terrible, terrible rot gut. Their faces fell apologetically when they watched me put it down.

" 'Something we've learned from recent researches at Berkeley,' Lawrence explained to me. 'They've studied the aging process of whiskey there and identified the chemical compounds that stimulate the taste buds on the tongue. This bottle contains all those compounds and it would be a shame to waste money on a really expensive brand that doesn't contain any more.' "

Lawrence impressed Oppenheimer as more nervous and irritable than before the war, and more what Oppenheimer thought of as very big-business in his manner. On the other hand, in Lawrence's conversation Oppenheimer was still "my theoretical physicist," expected to give advice as wanted and justify the machines by interpreting findings made with them as needed. A certain discomfort in relations between the two men was heightened by an instinct of the fickle public to make Oppenheimer a folk hero. "It was difficult for Lawrence to understand how things had changed," says Rabi. "Before Hiroshima he'd been the leader in science to the public mind and his laboratory had been the most famous. After the war Oppenheimer was hailed in print and talk as the great humanist, sage and wizard of the scientific world. His name carried magic. When he showed up in San Francisco, crowds gathered on the pavement around him."

Lawrence reacted not with jealousy but with a more urgent wish to enlist *his* theoretical physicist into his Radiation Laboratory projects. Oppenheimer's first impulse was to get as far away from Berkeley as he could. He committed himself to a professorship at Columbia in New York, then troubled by a sense of rootlessness, broke his promise. Late in 1945 he went to Pasadena and started teaching. "To Lawrence," Rabi observed, "Oppenheimer's leaving Berkeley seemed treason."

Cosmic rays began yielding secrets that from every point of view except life or death for the human animal were far more awesome than the bomb. Oppenheimer shared in identifying mesons of various kinds. In addition he helped define the new field of strange particles. ("It made me feel old," said Llewelyn Hughes, "to hear my graduate students begin burbling about strange particles.") But these studies required serenity, of which Oppenheimer had little.

"I hoped to stay put," he said of Pasadena. There the dean, his friend Richard Tolman, made everything serene for him except his telephone, which rang incessantly with calls from Washington. "I did actually give a course," he recalled afterward, "but it is obscure to me how I gave it now." Though he felt, as he put it, "sort of reluctant," unrest and guilt and hope all inclined him to try to respond to the questions of a new, imperious type of nuclear-physics student. "I was asked over and over both by the executive [branch] and the Congress for advice on atomic energy," he said. "I had a feeling of deep responsibility, interest, and concern."

The government had to decide what to do with its two-billion-dollar investment. Oppenheimer's involvement began with continued meetings of the Interim Committee to offer suggestions. These were sorely needed. "There was plenty of money but no direction," said a Washington observer, physicist Paul McDaniel. Through the winter of 1945–46, policy remained by default in Groves's hands.

A dam had broken, a limitation was gone on man's ability to kill his fellow man. Genuinely troubled, Congressmen reacted like molecules of water wanting to restrict themselves to old familiar Brownian movements, not willing yet to rush down through the sudden gap. Groves comforted them. Happily the thing was an American secret, or very nearly, he told a provisory Senate Special Committee on Atomic Energy. Russia could not build the bomb for twenty years. During this time our own work, continuing in compartmentalized secrecy, would keep us ahead. So at worst, after twenty years' dominance, this country would face only a stalemate in which no nation would try to change its relative position by war. Meanwhile the Senators could rest and be thankful for American know-how.

Scientists whom the Senators also called up before them sounded an uglier note. Urey said that, like it or not, they should first get an international agreement and then eradicate the whole horrible nuclear-fission industry root and branch. A famous old chemist, Irving Langmuir, estimated Russia could build the bomb in five years. Szilard said this country's effort, far from being inimitable as Groves had tried to make it seem, had been inferior: dithering in the first part, hobbled in the last part by Groves himself. On compartmentalization a Navy spokesman added his howls of complaint. The Senators told him to stop nit-picking. On the whole, they preferred to believe Groves. To support his position, Groves led in a parade of contract-corporation executives. They said the job could not have been done in Europe, much less Asia.

A big weather-beaten man, Senator Edwin Johnson (Democrat of Colorado), Elk, Oddfellow and Woodman, former section hand, sodbuster, and grain dealer, sat listening with a puzzled frown. It cleared up while a vice president of General Electric was testifying. Johnson had had a sudden illumination. He broke in to say that the secret behind our secret was the number of our technical schools plus our free-enterprise system together with our profit system. He spoke with real and touching modesty.

"The people in this part of the world may have what some folks call the creative mind or instinct, but don't you think that instead of having any advantage over other peoples just as men were born naturally, that it had been because of these conditions?" he asked.

"Yes," said the vice president.

It was in this state of mind that most of the Senators faced their star witness, Oppenheimer. Emotionally they could sense he had more at stake than the homeless wanderer Szilard, the prickly crank Urey, or the voice from the unfrightened past, Langmuir. A Jew to be sure, but still a native, he spoke to them with the hesitations that marked a sharing of their irrational pride, fear, and love.

Mostly he contented himself with answering questions. No, he could not guess how long the Russians would take, but the British could do it in two years. No, he did not like to think of a stalemate; this in fact was what kept him awake nights; nuclear armaments would mean nuclear war, against which there was no defense. Yes, Urey was right, we did need a treaty; even a treaty not watertight would still be better than the alternative. Yes, it would be worth destroying our bombs for. [The Senators had somehow failed to find out we had a supply of only one bomb, going on two.] No, he could not, simply could not, believe we should get entirely out of the nuclear business; there was more to it than just the bomb. Even now he thought it would do his friends at Los Alamos good to have something else to think of from time to time. For example? Well, the government meant to bolster Chiang Kai-shek with a power plant on the Yangtze River. In his opinion, this could well be supplemented with a power-producing reactor which scientists in this country could design.

"It seems to me," said Senator Johnson, "that this is the most reckless proposal I have ever heard made by anyone, scientist or politician or anyone else."

Johnson, it turned out, was outraged at an implied slur on Groves's second panacea, compartmentalization. The Russians, he believed, would steal the uranium and build a bomb of it, keeping the whole operation secret, by efficient compartmentalization, even from their own bomb makers. Oppenheimer's face turned weary and withdrawn, somehow a goad to further questioning, which developed as follows:

"Suppose the President comes to you and says, 'I want you to conceive of a plant where we can manufacture atomic bombs, utilizing diversified operations already in existence in such fashion that nobody making any part of the bomb will realize that the whole thing is to be assembled for that purpose.' Do you follow?"

"Yes."

"What would you do?"

"I would say, 'Better ask General Groves to do it.' "

"Do you think General Groves would have a fair chance of success?"

"No."

Laughter broke out in the hearing room, dissolving a little hysteric film from the Senators' eyes and earning from Groves a little resentment which Oppenheimer could ill afford to take on. People who knew him well doubt that he meant to be funny. Instead they guess that his more human parts had gone from that momentarily insufferable room, leaving behind only the idiot computer that had to stay and answer all questions, no matter how stupid.

Security agencies were then popularizing another fear that the Senators talked of a good deal. Under harmless commercial labels, enemy agents might import bombs into key industrial cities. This anxiety-surrogate, which could have roused a spree of vigilantism, Oppenheimer also dissolved in a burst of laughter. He could not answer the Senators' skeptical objections to a treaty outlawing bomb manufacture. But by continually holding up the alternative, he made one Senator, Brian McMahon of Connecticut, actually see it. After Bard, McMahon became the second nonscientist to move against the public wish and toward the public interest.

"In the winter of 1945–46," Oppenheimer recalled long afterward, "hysteria centered on our hypercryptic power and the hope of retaining it. I saw President Truman and he told me he wanted help in getting domestic legislation through. 'The first thing is to define the national problem,' he said, 'then the international.' "

This was a clear instruction to be fed into the marvelous computer which statesmen were tending to think they had in Oppenheimer. But by this time he was beginning to develop frayed circuits and untimely echo responses that did not erase satisfactorily from his memory banks. Truman looked at him with brisk inquiry that gradually turned into impatience. "Perhaps it would be best first to define the international problem," Oppenheimer said haltingly.

Even when thus viewed wrong-side-to, nuclear arms still seemed to Truman a bright spot in this country's position. He said something about our enormous advantage and his hopes that we could retain it. Oppenheimer got down to the business of trying to answer practical questions. Hesitant and cheerless, he seemed so different from his reputation that Truman wanted to know what was the matter.

"I feel we have blood on our hands," Oppenheimer mumbled briefly and waited for the next question.

"Never mind," said Truman. "It'll all come out in the wash."

On the international side, Truman was mostly concerned about working up a detailed proposition to put to the Russians through the United Nations. He assigned Oppenheimer to Secretary of State Byrnes, who in turn assigned him to Under Secretary Dean G. Acheson and a special consultant, David E. Lilienthal, chief builder of the T.V.A. These two were the star pupils in an odd little class of government officials to which Oppenheimer taught nuclear physics in hotel rooms and chartered airplanes while they toured this country's scattered nuclear installations. The class came to unanimous agreement—it always infuriated Oppenheimer's enemies to see how often his classes came to unanimous agreement—on what was called the Acheson-Lilienthal Report. None of the members felt teacher had dictated anything to them, all of them spoke gratefully of the help he had given with the mechanics of phrasing and sentence structure. Afterward he himself liked best to remember three passages:

International control implies an acceptance from the outset of the fact that our monopoly cannot last.

It is essential that a workable system of safeguards remove from individual nations or their citizens the legal right to engage in certain well-defined activities in respect to atomic energy which we believe will be generally agreed to be intrinsically dangerous because they are or could be made steps in a production of atomic bombs.

It therefore becomes absolutely essential that any international agency seeking to safeguard the security of the world against warlike uses of atomic energy should be in the forefront of technical competence in this field. If the international agency is simply a police activity for only negative and repressive functions, inevitably and within a very short time the enforcement agency will not know enough to be able to recognize new elements of danger, new possibilities of evasion, or the beginning of a course of development having dangerous and warlike ends in view.

Thus the world's nuclear plants and laboratories would become busy, peaceful, open places. Scientists from everywhere would constantly trek in and out, nuclear progress would be speeded, and purely negative gumshoeing kept to a minimum. "Inspection wouldn't get far if all the inspectors could do was snoop," Oppenheimer summarized.

To pay the Russians for their sacrifice of sovereignty (first they must agree to sacrifice theirs, then we would agree to sacrifice ours) this country could offer two inducements. In addition to dismantling our bombs we would actually share with them, under suitable inspection safeguards, small amounts of fissionable material for research purposes. Fascinating aesthetically, though of no real importance to the plan, was a thought Oppenheimer had for putting a little extra plutonium 240 in the samples of plutonium we gave them. What could *they* do with it? Something we could not?

Hysterically conditioned, our minds now skate away from the kind of war that is the alternative to these ideas, and therefore we find them bizarre. Afterward they were denounced as near treason. A saner criticism seems to be that there was small prospect the Russians would accept them. Still, 1946 was early nuclear times; we had not yet picked up much momentum downhill. Oppenheimer and his committee were sincere. One could make Oppenheimer's face grow slack and his eyes cloud with pain by accusing him of paltering then for mere propaganda advantage. "What do you mean, trying to fool people?" he said. "We went to Dumbarton Oaks house to take our proposal to Byrnes and Truman in a sort of moment of hope."

It did not last long. Byrnes at first raised his eyebrows at the report, then welcomed it as splendid ammunition for a stalwart new tongue he meant to enlist in the cold war. "The Secretary of State, without consulting me, appointed Bernard Baruch as our spokesman at the United Nations on March 16," said Oppenheimer. "That was the day I gave up hope, but that was not the day for me to say so publicly. Baruch asked me to be the scientific member of the delegation, but I said I couldn't. Then Truman and Acheson told me it might not look right if I got out now, so I said I would be present at meetings in San Francisco. Afterward I gave a talk at Cornell which you can call a sales pitch for the Baruch plan if you want to. But I only spoke of it as one of the analogues like the European Economic Union to a developing general concept of international cooperation."

Oppenheimer learned as well as taught while conferring on technical matters with the country's leaders. A moment of insight he could never forget came to him during a conference with Truman. Truman's face, as he remembered it, impressed him as serene, lit by mystic inner confidence. He felt that he was himself looking seedy.

"When will the Russians be able to build the bomb?" asked Truman.

"I don't know," said Oppenheimer.

"I know."

"When?"

"Never."

Baruch set the pattern for future international bomb negotiations by demanding so many preconcessions that no one of average intelligence could take him seriously. Even so a small chronic worry nagged at our top statesmen and military men: what if Russia should accept? They comforted themselves with a statement of Truman's that went far to set the worry at rest. The secret of the bomb, Truman announced, we would keep to ourselves as a sacred trust for humanity's sake.

"To the best of my knowledge, Oppenheimer never made any comment on this statement or any other statement by any politician," says William Higinbotham. "But I saw him pretty often around that time. From the way he looked, I think I could tell that Truman's statement and the incomprehension it showed just knocked the heart out of him."*

"That I may rise and stand, o'erthrow me," Oppenheimer had dreamed and, in his fashion, prayed on the Mesa. "Bend your force to break, burn, and make me new." This hope, mad or sane, had become basic to his existence, and now it was becoming clear that after the burning there was to be no renewal. "This atomic business is on for good and will cost us our freedom," he confided to an intimate or two and to Kitty, who lived these days on his nervous energy and was in no condition to bear such confidences. "I have seldom been as gloomy in my life; that even includes today," he reminisced in 1954 during the security proceedings which disgraced him.

One of the most frightful causes of war, Oppenheimer said in his lecture at Cornell, was "the fear which you don't know today, but which five years from now, eight years from now, you would otherwise know in the most terrible form, the fear that any day now an attack may be coming. . . . Mark my words, if there is no international control of atomic energy, the next war will be fought to prevent an atomic war, but it will not be successful."

While the international outlook for the bomb thus darkened, Congress worked at setting up an internal organization. Senator Edwin Johnson collaborated with Andrew May of the lower house, later imprisoned for stealing, to sponsor the first atomic-energy bill. "Most physicists hated it because it put everything under control of a military board," says Higinbotham. "Karl Compton, a saltier character than his brother, complained that it exempted [scientists from military control] only [when they were engaged in] contemplation and religion. Oppenheimer bewildered lots of people by refusing to join the public fight against it. But I think he had his reasons; he was on good terms then with General Mar-

* Released from Oppenheimer's spell on the Mesa, Higinbotham had come to Washington to run the central office of a new organization called the Federation of Atomic Scientists. Its policies, mild Szilard, sometimes ran with Oppenheimer's, sometimes opposed them.

shall and War Secretary Kenneth C. Royall, and he knew he could get modifications in detail from them. Anyway, the May-Johnson bill wasn't so bad. Its security provisions, for example, were less stifling than those we actually later got." Lansdale, who wrote the security provisions, felt there was not much need to enlarge existing statutes against treason. Security regulations, he reasoned, should be like traffic regulations; in both cases, the problem was primarily to prevent negligence, and for this purpose reasonable, limited penalties would be most effective.

Oppenheimer said he viewed the bill as a stopgap to prevent dissolution of Los Alamos and the other laboratories. The July 1946 Bikini exhibition shows why a change was needed at once. Groves and the confused planners had no real purpose but to give Russian observers a firsthand scare while complaining of the security breach in letting them watch. To get more blast from less mass, Mesa physicists during the winter had thought out many significant developments of the implosion principle. Groves would not let them test a single postwar advance in either of the two Bikini bombs. Consequently, they loathed their work on them. Groves thought of Los Alamos in terms of more Fat Boys and Little Boys. The production line he had in mind required artisans and engineers rather than physicists. Fences rusted, weeds grew high to invite the creeping saboteur, and the loyal second team wondered what they were there for. Not even Bradbury, who was proving a strong leader, could keep a good many of them from going home. Under these circumstances, the May-Johnson bill offered hope for some improvement in atmosphere.

At this dreary time Senator McMahon showed Oppenheimer he had despaired too soon. Very Celtic, McMahon was given to the second sight, and now he had a vision of himself and the rest of Congress on a long slide with Groves at the bottom of it. "He wants to keep control himself," said McMahon. "He would like it to end up in his lap."

Swimming against the hysteric tide, McMahon pushed through Congress the act that set up the present Atomic Energy Commission with its emphasis on civilian control and on unfettered research. Physicists generally hailed the McMahon Act as their deliverance. "I don't know," meditates Major Ralph Smith, an uncommitted observer. "Oppenheimer's backing that May-Johnson bill was the only thing he ever did that I couldn't have predicted he would do. But if you look close at the McMahon Act—nobody ever seems to—you see it permits complete military takeover in emergency. Maybe that's the only way McMahon could get it through. But since its main point is supposed to be the protection of civilian liberties, where's the difference?"

The nuclear dawn was wild with hope as well as fear. McMahon worried that his bill might put the country's coal mines and oil wells out of business. Higinbotham and Oppenheimer tried to set him right, but he and Truman could not help regarding the proposed Atomic Energy Commission as a sort of super T.V.A. With this view Truman in October of 1946 nominated Lilienthal to be chairman. Two of the commissioners, Lewis Strauss and Robert Bacher, were familiar with the government's science establishment. Strauss had been rear admiral in charge of Navy research during the war, and Bacher was the one physicist appointed. The other two members were Sumner Pike and William Waymack, a Des Moines, Iowa, newspaper executive. Pike distinguished himself particularly in raw-materials procurement. He resisted powerful mining interests and proved himself, in Smyth's words, a rock of integrity.

Congress had to confirm these nominations. To feel out political values in this new province, it began interminable hearings. Senator Kenneth D. McKellar (Democrat of Tennessee), smarting because Lilienthal had kept political patronage out of the T.V.A., took the lead. Senator Bourke B. Hickenlooper (Republican of Iowa) became chairman of the Joint Congressional Committee on Atomic Energy after the November election of 1946. He and another opponent of the Administration, Senator William F. Knowland (Republican of California), at first checked McKellar, then watched him thoughtfully, then supported him as they sensed he was catching the national mood. McKellar turned the hearings into an incredibly detailed canvass of subversives in government.

Meanwhile, Oppenheimer began feeling better. In December, Truman had appointed him one of nine technicians on a General Advisory Committee that was supposed to answer the Atomic Energy Commissioners' science questions. Since McKellar kept them too distraught to ask any, Oppenheimer with that peculiar simplicity that distinguished him had set the General Advisory Committee to doing the Commission's work. Once the ordeal of their confirmation was over in March, the Commissioners, particularly Lilienthal, Bacher, and Strauss, swung in behind him and gave him firm administrative support.

"This Washington business was my chief contact with history," says John Manley. "While Oppenheimer was on the General Advisory Committee, I had the job of part-time secretary. I took it because some physicist from the war project had to, and I expected it to be fairly dull, fairly routine. It wasn't. My curiosity and detachment gradually disappeared as my heart went out to Oppenheimer.

"In a sense, the General Advisory Committee was his committee, though he never played boss to it, and the Atomic Energy Commission was the Committee's agency, though they never gave it orders. Aside from Bob Bacher and one Commission executive, Walter Williams, who was in charge of materials production, this committee represented the only top-level people in the A.E.C. who who had had anything to do with the wartime project. So they had to take responsibility for decisions.

"Many who know Oppenheimer's service to the nation at Los Alamos do not know it continued at the same magnificent level for the next four or five years after the war. This second time around, everything he did had to be done against selfish and short-sighted hysterical pressures. They began with that McKellar business and mounted all the time."

Oppenheimer felt happy about his eight fellow General Advisory Committee members, who included Fermi, Rabi, Conant, and DuBridge. "Truman had made an extremely good choice," he said. The eight liked him too; before he could join them from a Christmas at Berkeley, they held their first meeting and unanimously elected him chairman. The nine were probably the best brains that the country has ever got to concentrate on a governmental problem.

"They were all individualists," says the A.E.C.'s present research director, Paul McDaniel. "Sometimes I watched Oppenheimer function as their chairman. He never dictated, he always apportioned time fairly to everyone, he always submitted himself and his opinions to theirs, he always drew from everyone a full and uninhibited expression of views. Afterward he faithfully reported the consensus to the Commission. The fact that under these conditions there always *was* a meaningful consensus on all serious issues is something that I just cannot explain, but it makes me think more rather than less of Oppenheimer."

"At the time of Oppenheimer's treason disgrace in 1954," says Manley, "there was a good deal of talk about how he had swayed or hypnotized or improperly influenced the General Advisory Committee. I was there and I knew he didn't do any such thing. I can't imagine any nine people who'd be more insistent on each making up his own mind for himself. What happened was that he at all times had the national interest at heart and never did anything or wanted to do anything except in the national interest as he saw it, and they could tell this as well as I could. He saw pretty clearly too. I realize this is a strong statement, but if I still had the files of the General Advisory Committee, I believe I could easily document it in detail."

For Rabi and DuBridge, then Cal Tech chancellor at Pasadena, sympathy with Oppenheimer's outlook probably came most spontaneously. Conant, educated by Groves and Stimson and by the test-night look on Allison's face, was no longer the man who had scorned the relativistic limit on the hundred-million-volt cyclotron. With Oppenheimer as an encyclopedia to consult, he got his science homework right, and he kept Oppenheimer comfortlessly reminded of the larger life-and-death implications of the technical questions that came before the Committee.

Fermi as always was the most interesting Oppenheimer associate. At the polls the two would have canceled each other's vote. "Immigrants are usually thought to be Democrats," says Segré. "Fermi hated to think of himself as an immigrant. He wanted to be as American as possible, and he thought one way to do it was to vote Republican." "Don't be too liberal," Fermi warned Wigner in 1947 (Wigner was swinging right anyhow). "You'll just be helping Uncle Joe." Fermi's share in the bomb decisions had shaken him up, but he was still capable of the hardest sort of utterances. "Some people," he remarked after Slotin's death, "accept the guilt in order to claim the credit." Was Fermi ruthless? "Cold and clear rather," says Manley. "Maybe a little ruthless in the way he would go directly to the facts in deciding any question, tending to disdain or ignore the vague laws of human nature. He admired

Oppenheimer's clarity, intelligence, and scientific ability, but the charge made in 1954 that Oppenheimer could control his thoughts strikes me as lunatic."

Still there was something to the charge. Fermi liked small, neat problems such as the behavior of neutrons and high-energy particles. Oppenheimer was by now possessed with a big sloppy one, the continued existence of the country and the human race. He could not control Fermi's thoughts, but he could set him thinking uncomfortably on uncongenial subjects. "It's because he'd seemed so prim and authority-respecting when I first met him back in 1940 that I was so impressed with the courage he showed at Los Alamos and most especially on the General Advisory Committee," said Oppenheimer. "Innate conservatism did not then blind him. He had as broad a view and as much concern as anyone. Not a philosopher. Passion for clarity. He was simply unable to let things be foggy. Since they always are, this kept him pretty active."

First, the Committee revived moribund existing installations. Hanford, which had burned out and stopped producing plutonium, they got going again under new management. At Oak Ridge they shut down vast needless electromagnetic plants. Under their guidance two laboratories that had been founded in 1946—Argonne and Brookhaven—rose to the stature of Los Alamos and Berkeley. From Los Alamos they removed the routine production line; freed to work at physics, the physicists there thought out bold, diverse advances in bomb design during the years 1947–49. Most important was an educational contribution. Along with another agency, the Office of Naval Research, Oppenheimer's committee pumped life into the nation's basic science establishment, its colleges, and assimilated them into the advancing edge of nuclear physics.

For physical scientists, at least, Oppenheimer and his committee made the nuclear age a millennium. Envious and hungry liberal-arts scholars saw their science friends get large grants, move out into the suburbs, and travel at will from dingy college laboratories to magnificent government ones. True, the spectacle was not pure joy. Too many physicists turned bourgeois found instrumentation —big, costly instruments to do what physicists had formerly done with a scrap of wire or with their fingers—easier than discovery. Too many peaceful uses of the atom were too comfortably explored.

Still, considering that the country had decided to stake its life on cherishing its secret, the expense was slight. Oppenheimer would not let would-be scientific empire-builders hide from the auditor's scissors behind "Science says" or "I cannot explain because this is classified top-secret." As for the estimable but tepid peaceful projects, they had a special justification. By drawing in a cadre of foreign scientists, they kept alive Oppenheimer's dream of an international science community vigilantly inspecting the world's laboratories to see that they studied war no more.

The committee and its secretary, Manley, saw this hope as the only way out for mankind; repeatedly Oppenheimer had to warn them that for the foreseeable future it was only a dream. But it gave them a high aspiration to keep them steady against hard shocks that were not long in coming.

"They were a distinguished group," says Bethe. "Farsighted, conscientious men dealing as practically as they could with a terrible, unique responsibility. It had been thrust on them, don't forget, and none of them had any ambition for power. Make that clear and I'll approve that phrase you keep trying to put into my mouth. The General Advisory Committee was a government of philosophers under a philosopher king. I'd say it another way. In those confused and deteriorating times they were a strong force on the side of the angels."

"Another point I could prove about Oppenheimer if I still had had the G.A.C. file," says Manley, "is that he saved the country from a lot of waste in manpower and money. I can't say the same for the other one you keep asking about. Lawrence had simply tremendous political influence, and in the time I'm talking about he had plenty of enthusiasm still. He kept coming to Washington to push some big new idea for radiological warfare or production of materials for bombs."

In both fields Lawrence's proposals at first sight looked thrifty, since in each field he wanted to make use of something from the scrap heap. At Hanford, for example, after the uranium slugs had been irradiated and the plutonium extracted, all sorts of deadly fission residues were left over. "To put it bluntly," says a distinguished former associate, "he got hot for the idea of gathering up the Hanford waste products [in a form which could be used in case of need] to dump on somebody we didn't like." From the General Advisory Committee, Lawrence got limited approval; from the military, unlimited enthusiasm. Radioactive "dusting" became a top-secret strategy that soon worked its way into folklore through science fiction. Should any dust ever be used, much would be needed. Realizing this, the General Advisory Committee still balked at Lawrence's expansive view of how much. Holding him down with respect to money, they wondered uneasily how well the military understood that if initiated against any but a primitive or defeated enemy, radiological warfare would be suicide.

Lawrence resented their coolness, but in these years before the Korean War his chief interest was in his other idea, which concerned bomb material. This was the one at which he drove heart and soul with most consuming urgency. Big is the word for it.

For practical production purposes, reactors and chemical engineering plants had outstripped his machines. He meant to restore the balance with a new machine, his biggest yet. Grotesquely simple to physicists, the thing he had in mind was an outgrowth of Alvarez' new-type linear accelerator. Lawrence said he meant to accelerate many, *many* protons. By their sheer quantity hitherto undreamed of, he declared he could add an undreamed-of resource to the country's nuclear armory. With them, once he got enough of them, he promised to turn the Oak Ridge waste product, uranium 238, into plutonium.

To accomplish this great purpose, which would relieve the country of dependence on foreign ore supply, he said he must build on the largest scale. He and Alvarez, his principal coadjutor in the enterprise, planned a pilot model of the machine, which would have a cylindrical vacuum chamber fifty feet high and a hundred feet long. Inside it floods of radio-frequency alternating current would have to be raised to an implausible voltage differential between the working parts. "The idea had possibilities," said Tuck, "if Lawrence had gone at it in an intelligent way. Instead he went at it baldheaded in the Berkeley way."

Lawrence code-named his project the Materials Testing Accelerator. Since he intended it not for testing but for manufacture, the title was deliberately deceptive. Everyone called it the M.T.A. To physicists now these letters evoke a gargantuan image limned with passion—the fullest extension of Lawrence's personality in its most violent conflict with men and nature. The voltage-differential required between the parts of the machine and the volume and intensity required in the beam were too great for twentieth-century technology.

"You can make anything defy the laws of physics, at least for a while, if you spend enough money on it," says Rabi. "The M.T.A. was silly." He formed an opinion because he had to; Lawrence would not rest until he had forced security-cleared physicists to line up for him or against him. Lamentably, the two lines were out of balance. On the one side were all Berkeley's top physicists except Segré, who ignored the M.T.A. at no matter what cost in rudeness to Lawrence. On the other side were the rest of the country's physicists. "The M.T.A. was a very ill-conceived thing," says Bethe. "Most of us predicted it would fail."

Even so, the fact that there *were* two sides is a puzzle that must be faced up to. Alvarez can perhaps be dismissed from consideration as an interested party. But if the M.T.A. was silly, how could Lawrence keep faith in it when surrounded by brilliant men like McMillan and sound men like Thornton? "That question," says Rabi, "shows you don't yet know Lawrence."

"I wasn't in favor of the thing," says Thornton, "but it wouldn't have been bad if there had really been a shortage of uranium ore." He was probably helped through solemn yea-saying conferences by an instinct for craftsmanship. As for McMillan, whatever helped him, possibly a wild sense of humor, helped him a little too much. To the general scientific body outside Berkeley, his support of Lawrence won him unenviable identification with what chemist Weissman calls "the whole damn California crowd." "Lawrence's group" is the term used by Smyth, involved in the controversy when he succeeded Bacher as Atomic Energy Commissioner. When asked to particularize, Smyth says, "Well, the best-known were McMillan and Alvarez."

To Lawrence, the disapproving murmur of the country's physicists was rather an exasperation than a handicap. "He was a man to ignore customary channels," says Manley. "He would bypass the Atomic Energy Commission and go directly to Congress." Especially but not exclusively Lawrence talked M.T.A. to the Joint Congressional Committee set up to keep the Commission under its wing.

His conservative outlook, his connections with the rich and mighty, his sincerity, and his reputation as founder of the Radia-

tion Laboratory created an overpowering impression on the Joint
Committee members. Some—like John O. Pastore (Democrat of
Rhode Island), who claims a place among the world's best scientists for "our late great Ernest Lawrence"—have not got over it
yet. Others, like Melvin Price (Democrat from Illinois), have got
over it. "My recollection of Lawrence?" he says, pursing his lips
wryly. "He was an operator, a promoter, a salesman."

Lawrence also talked M.T.A. to the generals in the Defense Department and set them afire with his optimism, so refreshingly
different from the incomprehensible deprecating meticulosities of
Atomic Energy Commission physicists. Probably Lawrence did not
stop here. "He went to Congress, he went to the Military," says
Paul McDaniel. "Did he also go to the President?"

High personages from Congress and the Defense Department,
glowing from a talk with Lawrence, repeatedly brought pressure
on the Atomic Energy Commissioners to push the M.T.A. The commissioners referred the matter to the General Advisory Committee.
"Like seeing the same bad movie again and again," said Conant.
On the first time round, Oppenheimer polled the committee and
wrote a report. The Atomic Energy Commission had a project time-
scale of priorities ranging from six months, most urgent, to forty
months, least urgent. Lawrence's grounds for urgency were that
the M.T.A. would yield substantial amounts of plutonium. "Promising and imaginative . . . ," wrote Oppenheimer. "Deserves vigorous support . . . fissionable material by new method . . . but
even if successful, cannot do what is expected of it . . . not significant as a source of supply . . . needs extensive testing . . .
many difficulties . . . recommend design and development schedule . . . of full forty months."

"Negative but not damning," an Atomic Energy Commission
official sums up Oppenheimer's report. When Lawrence saw it, he
made no such distinction but simply fell into his life's longest and
fiercest fury. He redoubled his sales effort, the Commission referred
the M.T.A. again to the Committee, and Oppenheimer replied
again with the same report. All the Committee signed it as before,
but Lawrence could not blame them all. Latimer too was a member of Lawrence's group and interested from the start in the for-
tunes of the M.T.A. Lawrence had him close at hand to whisper
ever more loudly that only Oppenheimer was responsible, since

changes like those in Conant between 1940 and 1947 showed Oppenheimer's chairmanship was not that of a natural man.

The Atomic Energy Commission official just quoted says it is important to know that Oppenheimer's stand on the M.T.A. was what made Lawrence his personal enemy.

"As for me," says Smyth, "when the M.T.A. kept coming up, I believed it was a waste of the taxpayers' money. This view was shared by at least one of the top members of the AEC staff directly concerned. But Lawrence and his group had such prestige that in the end we couldn't successfully oppose him."

In the face of Oppenheimer's adverse report which he could not get changed, Lawrence forced the Atomic Energy Commission to sign a contract putting the Standard Oil Development Corporation at his disposal. Near Livermore, a town in the wine country sixty miles northwest of Berkeley, a new laboratory rose at his bidding. There in a block-long building his scientists and Standard Oil's constructed the M.T.A. Beginning in 1947, work on it ran on into 1950.

Scenes worthy of science fiction took place inside the five-story vacuum chamber. Mostly Lawrence vaporized man-size copper bus bars in an effort to make them carry impossible voltages. Once for two whole hours he actually got the M.T.A. to produce a working beam. It merely melted down a succession of targets; no cooling arrangements could be devised to make them stand up long enough to undergo any significant transmutation.

These two hours were the final high point of Lawrence's life. By the end of the second hour, the M.T.A. had burned itself out. Because of engineering difficulties, he could never get it back into shape to repeat the performance.* Physicists at Livermore noticed

* "While the M.T.A. was a technical, engineering monstrosity, it did not defy the laws of physics," an uninvolved nuclear physicist sums up in retrospect. "In fact, Los Alamos is now [January of 1968] building a high current, high energy linac which is only about a factor of 50 lower in beam power than the M.T.A. was supposed to be. An even more ambitious, but serious, proposal is that of the Canadians who are designing a linear accelerator whose beam power is within a factor of 5 to 10 of that of the M.T.A. By 1980 we can build the equivalent of the M.T.A. if anyone wants it. The biggest problem yet to be solved is not the accelerator, or the ion source, but the target end. However, I agree that the M.T.A. looked silly to just about everyone outside of Berkeley, and Lawrence did try to bludgeon his way through without much finesse or deep understanding."

that in him too something vital seemed burning out. Most of them had come there unwillingly; they remembered a young Berkeley colleague who had attempted to refuse transfer on grounds that his calling was scientific research, not war production. "Pick up your pay," Lawrence had said and ripped off the identification badge pinned to the man's shirt. Lawrence drove them furiously as always, but more by telephoned orders from Berkeley than by personal contact. When he did see them, the tension he created had an ugly new edge to it. No longer shrugging off collapse of a detail when it became an obvious blind alley, he seemed rather to concern himself with fixing personal blame. His relation with Standard Oil science executives grew progressively embittered.

For the first time with any of his big machines—the cyclotron, the calutron, and now the M.T.A.—he was trying to beat forward against an official, authoritative prediction of failure. When he found himself fulfilling the latter part of Oppenheimer's forty-months schedule, it was his body that first accepted the prediction as truth. "Lawrence had no trouble with his health until the M.T.A. broke down," says Carrol Mills. "His hopes for the thing had been so enormous that I wouldn't be surprised if the failure—its effect came on gradually, mind you—was what killed him."

"For the physicists you are writing about," says Rabi, "make the point that their commitment to the work they found to do was total. It is in this sense that their lives ran parallel." Lawrence's trouble took the form of ulcerative colitis. Emaciated down to the bone, Oppenheimer had long been paying for his commitment with flesh; Lawrence now began to pay for his with bleeding that he could not stanch.

After watching the last red sparks of the M.T.A. in 1950, Lawrence lived for eight years more. Many other physicists who saw the change in his health and personality agree with Carrol Mills that his struggle first to promote the M.T.A. and then to make it work was what killed him. In any case it shaped his attitude toward Oppenheimer and everything he judged Oppenheimer stood for. The harder the M.T.A. became to defend scientifically, the more Lawrence tried to raise the Berkeley group into a center of opposition to Oppenheimer's governmental philosophy. "Among the tragic consequences of the M.T.A.," says Smyth, "don't forget its involving so narrow and naïve a man as Lawrence so deeply in political decision-making."

The issues confronting Oppenheimer during his chairmanship were too entangled to let him finish with one set of antagonists before encountering the next set. Untalked of at first because it might be a secret of real importance and then later because any mention threw Lawrence into rage, the M.T.A. permeated and inflamed all the other issues.

So did the issue of security, which began modestly for Oppenheimer in the spring of 1947. In those early nuclear times, security was for ambitious men still a tool rather than a religion. Groves used it to relieve seething, pent-up chagrin against his successor, Lilienthal. "He wanted nothing whatever to do with me," said Groves. "He thought I was the lowest kind of human being." So long as his dominion lasted, Groves kept Army Intelligence personnel files jealously in his own hands and out of J. Edgar Hoover's. Now, to prevent the possibility of Lilienthal's making political capital of them, Groves preferred to let Hoover inherit them. To Lilienthal, Groves sent a letter instead of the files. During the war, he wrote, for the purpose of actually getting work done he had hired security risks whom Lilienthal would need to fire in pursuance of the other purposes dictated by peace and the Atomic Energy Act. Next, to avoid sticky reminders that the war had been over for two years, Groves put himself out of reach by motoring down to Florida for his first vacation since taking over. At this time —the prearrangement cannot be proved—Hoover sent Lilienthal a file on Oppenheimer. Lilienthal was thus given the Hobson's choice of depriving himself of the bomb program's mainstay or else making himself vulnerable to ravenous Congressional wolves.

The file on Oppenheimer struck Lilienthal when it reached him as a typical F.B.I. file. Hoover had, in F.B.I. jargon, assimilated it —that is, struck out the names of the respondents and condensed their statements. Practically all of it was Manhattan District.

To study it, Lilienthal called a meeting of the Commissioners on the morning of March 10, 1947. For the rest of the day and most of the next day they handed it round to each other and exchanged puzzled looks. The superiority of Groves's system of not letting anybody assimilate *his* data for him is apparent in their reaction. "The information was like other information, and we had no way of determining whether it was true or false, and we did not see the people, and the informants were anonymous, and so on," Lilienthal recollected vaguely in 1954. "Well, I proceeded—we proceeded to try to evaluate it, some of it having the ring of veracity and some of it—for example, as I recall one of the reports, and I think it is in this report, the informant turned out to be a nine-year-old boy. If that is true in this case—it may not be—then obviously you could say, 'Well, this is probably not anything to rely on.' But in other cases the report would say that the informant 'X' is someone the Bureau has great confidence in, and you would assume that is true."

By three o'clock in the afternoon, the Commissioners felt they could get no more light from further study of Hoover's assimilation. Voluminous and derogatory, they decided, but either incomplete or else the graffiti from some sort of chronic incomplete past investigation. Obviously, Hoover himself or someone who had inspired him wanted them to do something with it. Lilienthal tried to telephone Groves but was told that he could not be reached.

Next they called in Bush, still chief administrator of the governmental science establishment and chairman of an Army and Navy Joint Research Development Board, of which Oppenheimer was a member. Bush did not remember, know, or care much about the case such men as Colonel Pash and Colonel DeSilva had erected against Oppenheimer during the war. Unhesitatingly Bush wrote out for the Commission a wholehearted recommendation of Oppenheimer's loyalty and service, acting shocked and disgusted that he had even been asked for one. Conant, also a member of the Army-Navy board and an early project administrator, did the same. Through Secretary of the Army Robert P. Patterson, the Commissioners dragged Groves out of hiding. Interrogated for the record, Groves expressed himself like Bush, but pointed out that the Atomic Energy Act, which he hated, concerned itself with past associations rather than with past and future usefulness. Patterson himself, Groves's direct superior, having no ax to grind, wrote out an unqualified Bush-type recommendation.

At this point, Lilienthal could have stopped, but he was a conscientious administrator, perhaps the country's best ever. Hoover would not let administrators make him divulge names of anonymous denouncers. Lilienthal did not attempt this, but he asked what Hoover thought of his own assimilation. Dismissing Colonel Pash's early romances, Hoover answered that the only reservation he felt was about the Chevalier incident, but that about this he felt strongly. Lilienthal talked of Oppenheimer's high services—he had noticed the assimilation made no allusion to these—and Hoover appeared to agree. Oppenheimer had been appointed to his Committee directly by Truman. Through White House aide Clark Clifford, Lilienthal learned that Truman did not want the dossier turned over to Congressmen on the Joint Committee, did not see cause for alarm, and would let Lilienthal know if his opinion changed. In case it might, the Commissioners waited through the spring to take final action.

Meanwhile the interplay between Groves and Hoover had brought Oppenheimer's brother Frank no such distinguished consideration. Lawrence fired him out of hand with a quick brutality that still alters the voices of physicists when they talk about it. Exactly how Frank's prewar Communist dossier got into Lawrence's hands is not clear; Hoover seems to have seen to it personally, since he afterward personally advised the Commissioners not to try to get Frank's clearance reinstated.

With respect to getting work done, Lawrence's act was a pity, since he drove away the one kindred spirit most likely after himself to make the M.T.A. go. Resentment over the issue of this machine was compounding itself in Lawrence's mind with anti-Communist mystique. "In politics after the war," says Bethe, "Lawrence's political ideas were straightforward: just hit the Russians hard with everything you can. Archconservative, he greatly disapproved of everything Oppenheimer did. I told you I loved them both. No. I cannot talk about Lawrence in a completely friendly way. One of Lawrence's most dedicated helpers with electromagnetic separation during the war was Oppenheimer's brother. Lawrence thought the world of him and had every reason to. Frank had every reason to look to him for help, but as soon as Frank had any difficulty, Lawrence forbade him even to come to the lab and visit. Do you understand how quite unusual a thing this is among scientists? Lawrence acted in a way I have not otherwise seen from any respected scientist."

Born to work on the M.T.A., Frank got a job teaching freshman physics at Minnesota. He had no vocation for it, which was perhaps just as well, since the House Un-American Activities Committee let him have only two years with the freshmen. During these two years Security and security grew progressively antithetical. While

Nazis took over our secret missile research ["Is it compatible with our moral standards?" asked Bethe. "Can the Army put any trust in them?"] native physicists lay awake nights wondering whether the F.B.I. had caught some former landlady in a spiteful mood. The House Un-American Activities Committee began a long, slow exposé of Communist espionage at Lawrence's laboratory during the war. They had one genuine physicist-spy, Joseph Weinberg. To make the most of him (no one ever seems to have thought of indicting him for treason), at the start they labeled him "Scientist X" and for six months strip-teased ponderously toward revelation of his name. Growing impatient, the Chicago *Tribune* labeled Martin Kamen, discoverer of Carbon 14, as Scientist X. Kamen had no Communist affiliations or sympathies, but he had relatives in Russia, and in 1944 to find out something about them had eaten a restaurant meal with the Russian vice-consul. Security agents in the next booth took down the conversation. Kamen, a leader in nuclear physics, made casual references to Fermi and to other colleagues outside Berkeley. These references did not fit Security's view that only information about calutrons should be permitted to the Russians. Stressing that no espionage or subversion was involved, Lansdale had got Lawrence to remove Kamen from war research. Now in 1949 Kamen decided to sue the *Tribune*.

Lansdale had given Lawrence a written report at the time. Kamen wanted Lawrence to clear up what it did and did not say, and to say something about his character and standing as a scientist. "Will you testify when the case is tried?" he asked.

To Kamen's astonishment, Lawrence replied that he had never read the report. As for mounting the witness stand, Lawrence required a peculiarly impossible commitment that characterized his position in those days. "I will not testify unless you can guarantee me immunity from cross-examination," he said.

The House Committee's publicity at Berkeley turned physicists' stomachs generally throughout the country. Lawrence's ex-student and old friend James J. Brady, on a visit from the Oregon State College at Corvallis, was surprised to learn it had not turned Lawrence's. "I used to think politicians were very so-so, run-of-the-mill people—not interesting," Lawrence observed to Brady. "Now I realize that where there's smoke there's fire. They're doing their job."

Later still when the Security cry had turned against Oppenheimer, Brady visited Berkeley once more. "Why is it that everywhere else they're for him and here they're against him?" Brady
asked Lawrence.

"That's an easy one," Lawrence answered. "This is the place
where we know him best."

The big point, Lawrence explained, was that Oppenheimer had
changed his story about whether Chevalier had talked with one,
two, or three physicists. "I can stand a lot," Lawrence said, "but
when a man lies to Security agents, that's it."

Brady was astonished at his intense, trembling bitterness and
wondered if the feeling was mutual. Afterward, Oppenheimer
stayed with Brady during a seminar at Corvallis.

"Like yesterday," said Brady. "It seems such a little while since
we were at Berkeley."

"Oh no," replied Oppenheimer. "To me it seems very long."

They talked of Lawrence. Brady searched Oppenheimer's face.
He could not detect much response. "There was a time when
Ernest liked to listen to theoretical physicists," Oppenheimer said
with mild melancholy, his mind perhaps running over the history
of the M.T.A. "Now he doesn't seem to listen to them any more."

Back in the summer of 1947 while the Atomic Energy Commission held off on Oppenheimer's formal clearance on the chance
Truman might change his mind, Security was still only a minor
impediment to bomb development. True, it had begun to cut from
the government payroll a swath of physicists like Frank Oppenheimer, except usually on flimsier grounds. But they were obscure
men. Taxpayers, as distinguished from physicists, could at least
philosophize that here was one set of government employees being
excised by another. As for Oppenheimer, the question before the
Commissioners was not one of protecting his job. As a consultant
paid only about a hundred dollars a month, he did not have any.
The question before the Commissioners was whether the country
needed Oppenheimer's services.

Lewis Strauss, despite assertions by a Congressional witness that
he had financed the Russian Revolution through his firm of Kuhn,
Loeb and Company, was the most conservative-minded Commissioner. After Bard had resigned from Stimson's Interim Committee, Strauss had taken his place to represent the Navy and there

had met Oppenheimer in the summer of 1945. "I was enormously impressed with him," said Strauss. "He was a man with an extraordinary mind, a compelling, dramatic personality, a charm for me that I suppose rose out of his poetic approach to the problem we faced together. I'm not his peer, of course."

Genuinely humble, genuinely in love with science—the Office of Naval Research, the best of the government's science-subsidy programs was his child—Strauss did not think of nuclear physics as a curse. "No, I would not wipe out any part of it, not the bomb nor any other part of it if I could," he said. "I believe everything man discovers, however he discovers it, is welcome and good for his future. In me this is the sort of belief that people go to the stake for."

Of all faiths, which by definition must be blind, faith in science (*i.e.*, knowledge) can lead us into the most violent contradictions. To have so impressed a man like Strauss was in the long run a bit of bad luck for Oppenheimer. Even in 1947 Strauss had begun to be torn, for to him Lawrence too was science, and Strauss's attachment to Lawrence was of longer standing. "The close personal association between Lawrence and me and between our families continued through the A.E.C. years," he said, his mind making inevitable comparisons. "Oppenheimer also had the ability to draw around him a large group of loyal, almost worshipful followers. But they did not include, it seems to me, men of the stature of Lawrence's group like McMillan and Alvarez."

In 1947 Strauss was friends with both sides. While he waited along with the other Commissioners to see whether Truman would change his mind, Oppenheimer's F.B.I. folder gave him no misgivings. Oppenheimer worried about being supposed to be teaching physics at Pasadena while actually spending most of his time en route back and forth to Washington. Strauss found a chance to help while serving his own ideal of science. On a bare knoll just outside Princeton was a group of buildings called the Institute for Advanced Study. Oppenheimer thought it bleakly landscaped but very highbrow. Privately endowed, it supported a faculty of mathematicians, scientists, and historians who were among the world's best. Strauss was one of the trustees and had been delegated by the others to seek a replacement for the retiring director. He took an opinion poll of the people who hung about the place and in accordance with it offered the directorship to Oppenheimer, who hemmed and hawed.

"Before I accepted the job," Oppenheimer testified in 1954, "a number of conversations took place. I told Mr. Strauss there was derogatory information about me. In the course of the confirmation hearings on Mr. Lilienthal especially, and the rest of the Commissioners, I believe Mr. Hoover sent my file to the Commission, and Mr. Strauss told me he had examined it very carefully. I asked him whether this seemed to him any argument against my accepting the job, and he said no, on the contrary. Anyway, no."

On August 17, 1947, the Commissioners formally voted Oppenheimer Q-clearance, the right to put on a badge emblemed with a big black "Q" and go as the need arose into the most secret recesses of the government's nuclear-materials laboratories. Assuming the directorship of the Institute in October, he turned it into a miniature analogue of the Acheson-Lilienthal plan, a retreat for scientists from everywhere in the world.

About the same time, Strauss ran into his first conflict with the philosophy Oppenheimer had diffused into the Atomic Energy Commission. The McMahon Act, blandly ignoring commitments by Roosevelt and Truman to the British, forbade any export of atomic energy or of secret information about how to produce it. The idiot phrase "atomic energy" meant nothing in itself.* Everybody defined it variously in accordance with his mood about se-

---

* Smyth is the guilty scientist who launched "atomic energy" into the world for people to argue about. He put it on the title page of the Smyth Report. "I knew better," he protests, "but General Groves told me 'fission' and 'nuclear' would look too technical." Smyth was the official historian of the Manhattan District. Groves had him write the report before Hiroshima and publish it on August 12, 1945, six days later. Groves's attitude, a mixture of hurry to see it in print and tizzy about its secrets, forecast the hysteria of the nuclear age. The brobdingnagian title-page title reads: *Atomic Energy for Military Purposes, the Official Report on the Development of the Atomic Bomb under the Auspices of the United States Government*. "Groves intended to call it *The Atomic Bomb* and make all this stuff the subtitle," Smyth explains. "But he was so used to being secretive about the words 'Atomic bomb' that he couldn't bear to think of putting them all alone up there at the top of the page for the printers to look at. So he decided to leave off the main title and stamp it on with a rubber stamp after the books were printed. Then after Hiroshima he felt there was no time for the rubber stamp. So the book came out with only that enormous subtitle, and everyone called it the Smyth Report."

curity, nationalism, and international cooperation. Oppenheimer took it to mean anything one could conceivably use to make bombs of. So did the General Advisory Committee and all the Atomic Energy Commissioners but Strauss.

Strauss by contrast talked of the term as pretty much the same thing as radioactivity, or at least any form of radioactivity that came out of the Atomic Energy Commission's plants and laboratories. A big peaceful by-product of Hanford and Oak Ridge was radioisotopes on a scale that put Lawrence's machines—all except the M.T.A.—out of the isotope-production business. The Commission sold small samples to qualified nongovernment researchers at cost. A French hospital asked for a sample for medical research. The other Commissioners felt happy to fill the request; it represented the innocent foreign aid they liked to associate themselves with. Strauss objected. He saw two dangers, both enhanced by the fact that France's best physicist, Frédéric Joliot, was a Communist. First, Strauss said, was the industrial danger: somehow the French might apply the isotopes to construction of an atomic-energy industry. (Persuaded by Groves's parade of corporation executives, Congress had vaguely intimated in the McMahon Act that industrial know-how was our fundamental atomic secret.) Second, Strauss said, was the danger the French might apply the isotopes to radiological warfare, which as Lawrence's friend he took more seriously than did the other Commissioners. He proposed that if the isotopes were to be supplied, an American be sent along to watch what the French did with them in the hospital.

All this was not exactly nonsense. It rationalized at a high level the feeling of the chairman of the Joint Congressional Committee on Atomic Energy, Senator Hickenlooper, and behind him that of Senators Edwin Johnson and John W. Bricker and Knowland and dim on the horizon Joseph McCarthy. These men, like Strauss, were obeying a profound wish of the American people: hire foreigners and marshal them to a holy war, but trust them with nothing. Strauss knew the isotopes were merely a token of trust, significant only as they implied willingness to move toward more meaningful trust hereafter. Blocking the movement was for him an act of faith to which even his love of science impelled him, since knowledge could be free only in a free world opposed at all points to the slave world and its dupes.

Though emotionally valid, this synthesis of ideas is hard to word convincingly. People who knew that Strauss had ended his formal education with high school and who heard his views at second hand suspected he was betraying mere ignorance about the nature of isotopes. People who saw his face when he talked had no such illusions: from genial and kindly it turned subtle, cold, hard, pitying and merciless as we imagine Torquemada's.

In 1947 the other Commissioners overrode his objections four to one. Henceforth they distributed isotopes widely abroad, and he watched in opposition, seeking a chance to prove how dangerous was their mania for extending to foreigners the fruit of this country's atomic labor. Toward Oppenheimer, the ultimate source of their mania, he began to bend a look of puzzled reappraisal.

Behind the scenes he saw Oppenheimer figure for the next two years in international negotiations about the bomb itself. There were two kinds of negotiation, in both of which the Departments of Defense and State used Oppenheimer as adviser. The first kind was a propaganda war with the Russians in the United Nations. On this, Oppenheimer's advice was urgent, unvarying, and simple: stop it. The speechmaking was dangerous, he said, because at any moment our spokesmen might blow too hot for caution and flourish themselves into commitments that could not be kept. Specifically he feared that to win a propaganda point they might agree to let the Russians learn much of our atomic activity while revealing little of their own. Such an agreement, he pointed out, would afterward have to be repudiated with useless damage to American prestige.

By contrast, the other kind of negotiation, that with the British, carried lethal voltage. "The bitterest problem after I came in," it was called by George F. Kennan, Deputy Secretary of State for policy planning from 1947 to 1950. The British wanted collaboration from us in the construction of power-producing reactors. Roosevelt and Truman had pledged such collaboration. Congress had forbidden it. With reactors one could make plutonium for bombs. But unless the M.T.A. worked, this country then knew of no source of uranium that could keep us from being dependent on the British Commonwealth's ores. To get allies, we were giving billions in foreign aid, much of it to the British, and simultaneously outraging the British by gross repudiation of our word.

Happy men, says Chekhov, are those who keep their eyes shut, and this is what Congress was doing. A *secret de Polichinelle* which they would not learn was that in the matter of bombs we had no secrets from the British. No one, for example, knew more about fission bombs than James Tuck, then at Oxford. Every significant advance made before 1951 toward the super, fusion, or thermonuclear bomb was summed up in a top-secret "Disclosure of Invention" or patent by von Neumann and Klaus Fuchs, who was then at Harwell. Involving security, such facts as these could be talked of only at executive Congressional sessions. At open sessions, Congressmen could forget them in the sheer happiness of demanding tighter security and narrower patriotism from the guardians of our secret.

True, every copy of the Smyth Report printed after October of 1945 told in an addendum the story of the British and Canadian wartime contribution. As events in 1949 will show, no one could make Congress see it. Hickenlooper and Bricker and Knowland, with Strauss as their most sympathetic link to the Atomic Energy Commission, made softness to the British political death. "The source of my alarm and concern about this matter," observed Kennan, "was the conviction that if we failed to solve this problem, the Russians would be the gainers."

"In the early months of 1949," said Oppenheimer, "a set of conferences were held here in Princeton by the Departments of State and Defense. I was an adviser. General Lauris Norstad was the chief representative for Defense and Kennan for State. General Kenneth Nichols, who had been Groves's number two during the war, also sat in for the Army, and there were a number of other government leaders.

"The purpose of the conference was to restore the partnership with the United Kingdom and Canada. There was no provision for this in the McMahon Act. No one had had the courage to admit the existence of the United States' dependence on the British [Commonwealth] for raw material.

"It seemed to me the first business of the conference was to recognize that the English and Canadians had played a vital role in the development of the bomb. Kennan and Norstad were quick to see a real glint of nobility in the way they had worked for us and then borne their exclusion. These two men responded with a nobility of their own."

How much the conference accomplished is an open question. "We were successful in tiding relations over the crucial period 1948–49," said Kennan in 1954, giving much of the credit to Oppenheimer. At that time such a tribute was perilous to receive. "You might just as well have asked Leonardo da Vinci to distort an anatomical drawing," Kennan added in an effort to take the sting out, "as expect Robert Oppenheimer to speak responsibly to the questions we were talking about and speak dishonestly."

Oppenheimer in 1954 called the negotiation abortive. "I had better not say why, because I was not in the politics of the abortion. But I have always regretted that failure, and I am not sorry for the effort I made."

Success would have required the conferees to resist the prevailing mood of Congress and the nation. General Nichols tended rather to share the mood than to resist it. "He was a nice guy," said Norris Bradbury, "but his mind had been so long in the Army straitjacket that the range of Oppenheimer's thought made him uneasy and resentful."

Even so, the conference progressed with slow, reluctant acceptance of facts by men like Nichols. In Washington, the Cabinet decided the stakes were high enough to justify a call on the one revered national figure who could make the country understand the British partnership. "By the summer of 1949," said Oppenheimer thirteen years later, "the Executive was quite ready to push things. They recruited Eisenhower, then Chief of Staff, and he sat in with us. When he saw the intense hostility toward the proposal, he began shifting about restlessly in his chair, then looked at his watch, said, 'My golly,' and beat it."

The British tried hard to make electricity economically from fission. Had we backed them, no one can say for sure they might not have accomplished something. But while they sank from ally to hireling, the American voter grew ever more suspicious of those in high places who might be unsound about keeping our secret.

The House Un-American Activities Committee, gnawing away inside Lawrence's laboratory, discovered how to make Oppenheimer help. They got hold of transcripts which Lansdale, the decent bloodhound, had made of conferences with Oppenheimer early in the war. Lansdale had then some reason to ask questions and Oppenheimer some reason to trust him. Now, as Lansdale himself remarked, it was old stale stuff rendered meaningless by the swing of the pendulum away from the mood of the Thirties. The House Committee did not care. First at a secret session they would read Oppenheimer an answer he had made to Lansdale, then ask, "Now, Doctor, is it true or false you believed so-and-so was a Communist?" Afterward they would trickle bits of Oppenheimer's brand-new testimony to the papers. In this way they made news and used Oppenheimer to ruin the career of one of his ex-students, Bernard Peters.* Physicists throughout the country, especially those who did not understand the mechanics of the inquisition, were shocked and disgusted with Oppenheimer. "The harshest criticism I ever heard spoken about him," says Frederick Seitz, president of the National Academy of Sciences, "was for his part in what happened to young Peters. Some physicists who didn't know him as well as I did thought he had done it to save his own hide."

Meanwhile Senator Hickenlooper, the Joint Atomic Energy Committee's opposition party leader, was pecking away hostilely at the Atomic Energy Commission. Hickenlooper found out that indirectly through the National Academy of Sciences and the National Research Council, the Commission had given a twenty-two-year-old Communist $1,600 with which to study graduate physics at the University of North Carolina. He called Academy and Council leaders to the witness stand and urged them to change their award system. Why, he asked, should they not reassure the shaken nation by getting an F.B.I. dossier on all scholarship applicants before considering their science qualifications?

At this point on May 14, 1949, Oppenheimer decided to put his oar in. "My colleagues and I," he wrote to the Joint Committee,

---

* As a boy in his native Germany, Peters had participated in organized street fights against the Nazis. In the late Thirties at Berkeley, Oppenheimer understood him to say that he had fought as a Communist party member and that American Communists were too tame to understand the need for violence. Upon inquiry by Security, Oppenheimer at Los Alamos said Peters had been "dangerous and quite a red." The House Committee in secret session read this back to Oppenheimer and asked him to confirm that he had said it. The Committee then leaked this testimony to a conservative newspaper in Rochester, New York, where Peters was teaching at the University of Rochester. Resulting headlines caused Peters to be fired. Oppenheimer tried to help Peters with a letter to the liberal Rochester *Democrat*. In it he emphasized the changes that had taken place both in Peters and in the political climate since the Thirties. Oppenheimer commended Peters' integrity, brilliance, and teaching ability. Nevertheless Peters could not get another job in this country and was obliged to go to India.

"attach a special importance to restricting to the utmost the domain in which special secret investigations must be conducted. For
they inevitably bring with them a morbid preoccupation with con-
formity and a widespread fear of ruin, that is a more pervasive
threat precisely because it arises from secret sources. Thus, even if
it were determined, and I do not believe that it should be, that on
the whole the granting of fellowships, or more generally of Federal
support, to Communist sympathizers were unwise, one would have
to balance against this argument the high cost in freedom that is
entailed by the investigative mechanisms necessary to discover and
characterize such Communist sympathizers. That is what we all
have in mind in asking that these intrinsically repugnant security
measures be confined to situations where real issues of security do
in fact exist and where, because of this, the measures, though repugnant, may at least be intelligible."

Hickenlooper frightened the Commission into stricter security
measures with the graduate students. But as for Oppenheimer,
Hickenlooper said he was disappointed he had not come in person
instead of just writing a letter. "I would have liked to question
him," he complained.

During the next thirty days, Hickenlooper got his chance. He
and Senator Edwin Johnson began a campaign to amend the
Atomic Energy Act. As a first step, Hickenlooper denounced Lilienthal spectacularly. An alarming quantity of uranium 235 had been
lost at Argonne Laboratory, Hickenlooper declared (this later
proved mistaken), money was being wasted on community projects
at Hanford, Los Alamos, and Oak Ridge, personnel turnover was too
high, and the security-clearance system inadequate. "Terrible, incredible mismanagement," Hickenlooper charged, but his implicit
grounds were more shocking. Lilienthal the hand and Oppenheimer
the remote brain required a day's work for a day's pay from anyone
contracted to the Atomic Energy Commission. This broke the pattern of the military-industrial complex that Eisenhower long afterward, when he was leaving office, warned against. How could the
rich remain patriotic if one did not keep them rich? Congress voted
Hickenlooper an investigation and joined in it with a whole heart.
Inevitably it too turned into a security hunt.

Hitherto, the Administration had kept F.B.I. dossiers out of
Hickenlooper's hands. It had also kept them from the House Un-

American Activities Committee. But this Committee was now acting as though somebody had passed on to it a good deal of the dossiers' contents. It made no sense to withhold from anybody what
the House Committee had got hold of. In a letter deprecating slan-
der, Lilienthal wrote Hickenlooper he would let him have any
dossier he asked for by name. Hickenlooper asked for a large number. With delighted horror, he discovered how many scientists had
been pinks in the Thirties. Making sensational charges, he grilled
a host of them, often to their ruin, but mostly he concentrated on
Oppenheimer.*

The trouble for Hickenlooper was that he had to do it all in
secret session, thus throwing away priceless newspaper headlines.
If he had done it in open session, the physicists would have had
a chance to reply. They might demand names and—horrible
thought—even ask to cross-examine the F.B.I.'s informants.

The result, declared McMahon, chairman again since the 1948
Democratic victory, would be irreparable damage to the reputation
of the F.B.I. The solution, replied Hickenlooper, was easy: hold
partly secret, partly open sessions and trickle out bits of damaging
testimony. This was what the House Committee was doing already.
But Hickenlooper had fuller, newer dossiers and meant to bring
down bigger, livelier game. He might thus have saved the world
by putting out of work those few of his countrymen who could
actually make bombs. But our leaders still had in them dregs of
restraint and sanity. McMahon and a young lawyer-Congressman,
Henry Jackson from Washington State, insisted the security ses-

* In ten secret sessions of the Joint Committee, Hickenlooper quoted
F.B.I. dossiers to denounce thirty-six A.E.C. employees. Twelve dossiers reflected on character, i.e., sex-and-drinking habits, twenty-four on loyalty
and associations. Sex-and-drinking, which mostly concerned stenographers
and plant workmen, did not make so good a show as might have been expected. Of the twenty-four loyalty-and-associations cases, three were fired
or forced to resign in the course of the year; three were reassigned to non-
secret work, and the rest, including Oppenheimer, retained in their previous
work. Like him, however, they became vulnerable to a resurrection of the
Hickenlooper-F.B.I. case against them any time they should be on the
losing side of the in-and-out power struggles going on inside the atomic
energy establishment. Probably half of them eventually lost their clearance.
In addition, emergency clearance, which had been given 3,317 new or
temporary employees while the F.B.I. investigated them, was withdrawn
from four new employees upon completion of the F.B.I.'s investigation of
them.

sions be all open or all closed. On the advice of his most powerful and intelligent ally in Congress, Senator Knowland of California, Hickenlooper decided to spare the F.B.I. and forgo such headlines as he could not get by vague public denunciations of Scientist A, Scientist B, *et cetera.*

Strauss seems to have put him on the track of his Scientist A, a secret-documents librarian at Los Alamos who had once been a Communist. In the next month such strong forces gathered behind the campaign that Hickenlooper became only its embarrassingly boorish front-runner. These forces included, besides Strauss and Knowland, who had the support of the Hearst interests, all that spectrum of big business whose organs of printed expression were to the right of *Fortune* magazine. New Dealers on the Joint Committee, uneasily sniffing the political air, deduced that the Air Force had also begun covertly pushing Hickenlooper.

The generals behaved so slyly that it was not easy to tell. Congressman Chet Holifield (Democrat of California) watched the magazine articles of William Bradford Huie, a sort of Ayn Rand at that point in his career. *"Reader's Digest* calls him a close confidant of several of the ablest U.S. generals," said Holifield at a Joint Committee meeting, "and says he is well known for his studies of air power. He is a ghost writer for men in high places and important positions." Yes, agreed Congressman Melvin Price; and he remarked that from praising the Commission, Huie had abruptly switched to denouncing it—a sign that the powers behind him had reversed their stand.

The Air Force generals could not afford to tell the public their grievance. The nearest they could come, observed Price, was a plaintive cry by Huie in the June 1949 issue of *Nation's Business:* "How can the Air Force practice detonating atomic bombs when they can't get any to practice with?" What this meant was that in accordance with the Atomic Energy Act and the advice of Oppenheimer's Committee, Lilienthal firmly kept bomb tests under his control, authorizing them only to verify new scientific developments. The Air Force hated to drop dummies and hated Lilienthal for making them do so.

Toward Oppenheimer the Air Force attitude was ambivalent. On the one hand they regarded him as the brain behind Lilienthal, distrusted him thoroughly, and maintained a curious practice with respect to him. As early as 1947 at the very time of the Air Force's creation, they had got hold of his F.B.I. file and started telling its contents to any officer or civilian employee who might conceivably ever come into contact with him. On the other hand the Air Force regarded him as their chief source of bombs: valuable when watched, much more valuable still if he could be controlled. To get control of him, the generals felt they only had to strike down Lilienthal. This, in the opinion of Price, they were attempting to do through Huie's writings. "I am very much disturbed," said Price, "by what appears to me to be a concerted campaign . . . to destroy public confidence . . . in our national security . . . by distorted statements, misrepresentations and lies, and I think it was done for the purpose of discrediting this Commission."

All these forces gathered rather suddenly behind Hickenlooper in early June of 1949. Their public cry was Security. To keep it going they needed something newer than the political missteps that a Los Alamos librarian had made in the Thirties. Strauss offered them a genuine live, current security issue.

During the past two years Strauss had watched the Atomic Energy Commission fill two thousand requests for research isotopes to uncleared applicants here and abroad. Steadily his distrust and resentment had mounted. He had protested to the Secretary of State without avail. The Norwegian Embassy sent in the 2,001st request or thereabouts on March 28, 1949. Dr. I. T. Rosenquist of Norway's Royal Defense Research Establishment wanted a millicurie of iron 59 to trace its diffusion through molten steel. Routinely but painstakingly, Atomic Energy Commission officials ascertained that the research was good physics and that Rosenquist and his research team were good physicists. Strauss, on the other hand, discovered that one of the Norwegians in the research team was, had been, or by American security standards might be termed a Communist.

"Wonderful," says Paul McDaniel, who inside the Commission had shared in the checking. "I still have no idea how Strauss did it. So far as we knew or cared, those Norwegians might have been crypto-Martians. But I was glad we'd made sure they had a reputation for fundamental scientific research, since that was all they could do with their millicurie of iron except throw it away."

To Strauss the thing did not look so simple. Norway, as he elaborated his point, wanted better turbines and therefore wanted better steel for turbine blades and therefore wanted more fundamental knowledge on the nature of steel and therefore wanted us to give her atomic energy for industrial purposes and we had done it and she was a foreign nation and we were forbidden by law to give foreign nations atomic energy for industrial purposes. And this was not all (here the reasoning becomes involved): Norway might use her ill-gotten know-how about turbines to build plants to build reactors to build bombs. "A clear violation of the Atomic Energy Act," Hickenlooper told reporters and summoned Strauss to an open Joint Committee hearing to prove it by a recitation of the above.

Hickenlooper then called Oppenheimer to the witness stand. He tried to get him to admit the shipment was proof of terrible mismanagement or worse in the Atomic Energy Commission. Along with other Commission officials responsible, Paul McDaniel watched intently. So did Strauss.

"No one can force me to say you cannot use these isotopes for atomic energy," said Oppenheimer. "You can use a shovel for atomic energy. In fact you do. You can use a bottle of beer [he probably meant a can of beer] for atomic energy. In fact you do. But to get some perspective, the fact is that during the war and after the war these materials have played no significant part, and in my knowledge no part at all."

A little laugh buzzed through the caucus room. Hickenlooper persisted. He enumerated the vital uses of radiation, including the biological and medical. Foreigners, he told Oppenheimer, must get nothing, nothing at all from us to help them develop atomic energy. How could we best make sure?

Keep them from unirradiated American man, Oppenheimer replied.

Laughter buzzed louder in the room. Knowland took over suavely and asked Oppenheimer to assess the general military-industrial value of research isotopes. "Far less important than electronic devices," Oppenheimer answered. He paused and seemed to contemplate the question drearily. "But far more important than, let us say, vitamins. Somewhere in between."

Laughter broke out for the third time. Hostility in that room was too intense for it to be healing. McDaniel wondered whether Oppenheimer knew the effect he was making.

"To understand the laughs, you'd have to understand the way

he looked," says McDaniel. In unconscious mimicry, McDaniel's own face sags and turns blank when he tries to describe the impression Oppenheimer gave of a suffering computer. "His face seemed to say, *I might have put this time in on something connected with science. How strange, how cruel you people are to make me even comment on these weary, far-out fancies.* As best I can put it, this was the suggestion in his manner that turned the hearing into comedy. I don't know whether he intended it or just felt that way."

At the close came the usual questions of that time about giving more authority to Security personnel. "Morbid," said Oppenheimer. He stared about the room with no pretense of good will, and the atmosphere of comedy slipped away.

He had it in him to wonder why he was there, to experience a moment of sickness at the small, wordy triumphs he was winning. Knowland and Hickenlooper and their myrmidons, being already wholly committed, did not count for him so much as Strauss, who had sat through ridicule of his position with face impassive but eyes ominously gleaming. Was it possible to communicate anything to Strauss? In his mind Oppenheimer had a story he wanted to tell Strauss, but which he did not tell him until long after all issues and Oppenheimer's own fate had been settled. Fermi had told him the story, perhaps made it up out of the same puzzlement about Oppenheimer that Oppenheimer felt about Strauss. The story as Fermi had planted it in Oppenheimer's mind ran as follows:

"What makes you go fishing?" Fermi said he had asked Segré.

"Oh, I can't explain it."

"Why not walk?"

"You wouldn't understand."

"Yes. I have figured it out. You like the contest of wills."

Bleak and cynical, Fermi could not understand what Oppenheimer hoped for from such contests as this in the caucus room. Oppenheimer could not understand why Strauss seemed determined to ride with the politicians down so clear a road, viewing all warning signs as mere occasions for belligerence.

"The best guarding is simply to lock everything up and not let anybody in," Oppenheimer told them. By this procedure they might have instinctively protected themselves and the human race. What he had come for was to show them that it was too late for this, that they must know where they were headed. "The best security is in the grave," he said.

At this hearing Oppenheimer killed the isotope issue and set back security's advance a little. "He had been pretty rough on the politicians, but they were used to it," says McDaniel. "Strauss wasn't. On his way to the door I saw Oppenheimer stop in front of Herbert Marks, the Commission's legal counsel, and ask something. Marks was looking at Strauss and seemed to be shaking his head. Later on I learned the exchange at the door had gone this way:

" 'How did I do?'

" 'Too well, Robert, too well.' "

Next day, June 14, 1949, perhaps by no coincidence, the House Un-American Activities Committee publicly exposed Frank Oppenheimer. "For a long time they'd had that Manhattan District stuff on Frank—everybody seemed to have that stuff—and they'd asked him at a secret session if he'd been a Communist, and he'd said no, I think to protect his brother," said William Higinbotham. "I'd helped him get a lawyer who told him he'd have to say yes, and he did at another secret session. Then they called him up before an open session."

Under oath before a full press gallery, Frank readmitted his prewar Party membership, but positively refused to name other former members whom he had known. He showed even more determination when asked to name the physicist on whose terrace garden he had twice met with the notorious Steve Nelson. "Those occasions had nothing to do with politics," he insisted. Having moved up from playing cat-and-mouse with him to playing cat-and-mouse with his brother, the House Committee did not push the question to the point of a contempt citation.

A few months earlier, during the winter, Frank had bought a bit of the high range of the Blanco basin in southwest Colorado, meaning to spend his summers there. Now, as Lawrence had done before, the University of Minnesota fired him. Having nowhere else to go, he took his family to Colorado.

After his public testimony, Oppenheimer collided again with Hickenlooper in a furious secret Joint Committee session on security, then he too left Washington. After teaching six weeks at Pasadena, he joined Frank in the mountains.

Unable to get another college job, Frank said he was going to try to use the new place to raise cattle. Oppenheimer doubted he was cut out for the life. "Very beautiful," Oppenheimer thought, looking at the mountains, and suspected this was the reason Frank had got the place.

To keep his brother in touch, Frank had subscribed to *The New York Times* by mail. "Something in the August 20 issue you might like to see," said Frank. "Something about a conference Truman held with Senate leaders. Look how it says the Senators carried on when they came out of Blair House."

"I picked up the paper and read what the Senators told reporters," says Oppenheimer. " 'The situation is far worse than we thought,' they said. 'So dreadful we can't even talk about it. Oh, if what we have just learned of had never happened!'

"What they had finally learned of was how much the British had contributed to our bombs. Carson Mark, Canada's chief physicist at Los Alamos, probably had a good deal to do with their teaching. A British-Canadian plan, which Mark had submitted to Truman, called for us to collaborate with the British or else let them build bombs on their own."

"The paper says the Senators came out of Blair House holding their hands to their heads," Frank observed with naïve interest. Oppenheimer regarded him pensively. Frank's whole career of service to and reward from his country had been compressed into the short time since 1941. To Oppenheimer it seemed longer. Frank was lucky not to be in jail for contempt, but, pale-green 1937 Communist membership card and all, if he had testified against his brother, the government would probably have let him keep on teaching freshmen physics. Long ago among similar red mountains Oppenheimer had watched Frank play the flute and make up his mind on physics as a career. Now that the wheel had come full circle, Oppenheimer could not view Frank's prospective future of unsuccessful cattle raiser without a touch of envy. "Absolutely away from this nightmare which has been going on for many, many years," thought Oppenheimer.

In early September he went back to Princeton. "I had just got in the house," he said, "when I heard the phone ringing. It was to tell me that our surveillance network had picked up evidence the Russians had detonated an A-bomb."

9

THE PHILOSOPHER KING

DETECTION HAD COME about irregularly, almost improperly. Officially it was the Air Force's responsibility, carried out with surveillance flights around and over Russia. The Air Force kept them secret even from the Navy. Consequently Navy chemist Peter King did not know he was poaching when he too had the idea of maintaining a systematic check on fallout. He improved on delicate tests invented by Anthony Turkevich at the Metallurgical Laboratory and recommended by Oppenheimer to the Army at the end of the war. King's procedure was to analyze rainwater samples routinely collected for him on ships and bases all over the world. Evidence of the Red bomb came to him as micromicrocuries of cerium 141, yttrium 91, and other telltale fission products in the water.

Chagrined, Air Force spokesmen at first gave King's bad news no support. Government leaders were incredulous. In their hearts they found it absurd that so little cerium and yttrium should be expected to outweigh so much faith in the uniqueness of American industrial know-how. Oppenheimer himself had unconsciously absorbed enough such faith not to look for the news for three or four more years. But he had looked for it then. By the time he had finished scrutinizing the data, Truman called him to Blair House and asked him if it was true. He said yes, but Truman simply could not believe him.

The Joint Committee on Atomic Energy called him to a secret session. Over and over again he repeated that the fallout was in-

deed Russian. Half-convinced, most of the Congressmen decided
that the news if true confirmed what they had known all along:
Security should have been given tighter control over scientists.
Only Senator Arthur H. Vandenberg had the sudden vision that
lets a man feel lost and open. "Doctor, what shall we do now?" he
asked as Oppenheimer was leaving the stand.

"Stay strong and hold on to our friends," Oppenheimer replied.
The expression on Vandenberg's face burned into his memory.
Afterward he interpreted it as accusing. He wished he had said,
"I don't know."

Both answers would have been fairly honest and very unspec-
tacular. To put over either answer, one had first to release the ques-
tioner from the grip of hysteria. Oppenheimer could do it by virtue
of the quality in him that Strauss called poetic and Latimer unnatural. To stay released, a politician like Vandenberg would have
to pay with his head. Oppenheimer's weakness was that he never
had any idea how much political sacrifice he was demanding. The
first intimation of human nature's way out of this particular crisis
came to him in an excited telephone call from Teller on the night
of September 23.

A decision of Truman's had inspired the call. Truman did not
believe in the Red bomb, but he earnestly believed that the Russians and Hickenlooper would try to make propaganda advantage
of it. To forestall them, he gave the news to the reporters that day,
and Teller saw it in the paper. "What shall we do? What shall I
do?" Teller asked excitedly.

Teller was then spending about three fourths of his time at the
University of Chicago and the rest at Los Alamos. "Just go back
to Los Alamos and keep working," Oppenheimer answered. Plainly
disappointed, Teller asked if that was all. After a long offensive
pause, Oppenheimer got out another bit of advice. "He told me to
keep my shur-r-rt on," Teller used afterward to complain to sympathetic listeners in a fascinating Hungarian accent and in the
tones of a wounded child.

Teller went back to Los Alamos, but not very cheerfully. Bradbury and his Tech Board of senior physicists suited Teller no better
than Oppenheimer and his Board had suited him during the war.
They were working hard at Los Alamos on new bombs, they were
interested in Teller's specialty, the Super or hydrogen-fusion bomb,
but they too wanted him to keep his shirt on.

By 1949 bomb development at Los Alamos had reached a stage that is still classified and perhaps in some aspects still truly secret. After reluctantly stimulating the Russians with the unimproved Bikini bombs, physicists had been happy to get down to business under the new regime without Groves. An obvious speculation is that their work on bombs moved in the direction toward which Oppenheimer had tried to push Neddermeyer—thinner and more complicated shells, more difficult geometries, more neutron initiator, less chemical detonator, harder push, completer fission, more heat, and smaller critical mass. The result was many more, and more violent, bombs per kilogram of plutonium. As for size, Los Alamos had by this time designed a half-megaton bomb big enough to destroy by itself any of the country's cities except the five largest, which would need two. Toward litle bombs using only a fraction of what had formerly been thought critical mass, physicists worked with special energy. They hoped to get something that instead of being a mere population killer would be effective against combatants on the battlefield. As for production volume, Lilienthal seemed to quote with approval a statement in the Hearst newspapers that Sandia, the production facility, could turn out two bombs a day.

All this was germane to Teller's specialty, the Super. Here the problem was to raise deuterium suddenly enough and to a temperature high enough to make the thermonuclear reaction go. In 1942 the outlook had been thought good. In 1943 the need for tritium and the impossibility of producing enough had killed hopes the Super might play a part in the war. In 1944 calculations suggested heat from fission could induce significant added heat from thermonuclear reactions in deuterium even where the thermonuclear reactions were unsustained. In 1945 further calculations indicated this hope was mistaken. In 1946 the best hope was to coat the fastest possible fission bomb with successive layers of frozen tritium and deuterium to the amount of one cubic meter. Then, according to this design, the whole was to be encased in a uranium-238 tamper that would itself fission violently and produce enormous fallout.

As a weapon, this device had an obvious insuperable drawback. The thing would have to be manufactured on the site where it was to be exploded. The enemy would have to provide workshops where frozen deuterium and tritium could be complexly molded for immediate use. We might as well have asked the Russians to let us mine the Moscow subway system. In addition to this practical difficulty, there remained the basic problem of getting enough heat from the fission-bomb fuse. Hydrodynamics calculations on the Mesa's I.B.M. machines did not look good, and when Neumann explored them further in 1947–48 with his new digital computers, they looked even worse.

All these ups and downs Oppenheimer faithfully reported to various administrative superiors over the years. At his security trial in 1954, Roger Robb, the prosecutor, used these reports in a curious way. He adduced shifts in outlook as mutually contradictory lies treasonably intended to keep this country from protecting itself with the new weapon. (The Security Board let him do this, because they had put themselves and the conduct of the trial in Robb's hands from the start. "I think the reason Robb had things his own way was because Gordon Gray, the chairman, was a college-professor type," said John Lansdale, rationalizing disgust at the questions asked him into support for a lifelong disdain. "You know what I mean, one of these young-old, yes-and-no, talk-nice college-professor types.")

It was true, of course, that few physicists looked with pleasure toward the prospect of a world armed with Supers. By reason of a tacit agreement between the American and Russian governments, hard news about fallout is still not easy to come by. What Oppenheimer, Bethe, Fermi, and von Neumann told each other on the subject in 1946, as distinct from what was later told to the public, is still worth thoughtful attention. The once top-secret but now declassified *Manhattan District History, Project Y, the Los Alamos Project (Technical and Administrative)* digests their views on fallout from a ten-megaton Super:

The most world-wide destruction could come from radioactive poisons. It has been estimated that the detonation of 10,000 to 100,000 fission bombs would bring the radioactive content of the Earth's atmosphere to a dangerously high level. If a Super were designed containing a large amount of U-238 to catch its neutrons and add fission energy to that of the thermonuclear reaction, it would require only in the neighborhood of 10 to 100 Supers of this type to produce an equivalent atmospheric radioactivity. Presumably Supers of this type would not be used in warfare for just this reason.

Subsequent "dirty" tests have negated this last sentence and have carried us into the neighborhood mentioned in the preceding sentence. "It would have been wrong in 1946, it was wrong in 1949, it is wrong in the Sixties to deny the horror of the thing," says Bethe.

"You talk of the dreadful situation we have got into," says Teller, "and it is worse than you realize. Produced by the superficial, facile, unintelligent, selfish approach of the American people. We are behaving like spoiled children, we are talking about the end of the world. There is *no* chance the human race or even mechanical civilization should disappear. The danger has been invented to scare us. The bomb is more the symbol of our fear than the cause of it. If we continue to behave as I have watched us behave in the last fifteen to twenty years—and if the British outdo us as they are doing now—in ten years more the world will be Communist."

When Teller speaks of Communism, his face freezes like Strauss's into a mask so stylized and inhuman that one thinks all conversation must be over. But, like Strauss, he is a kindly man. He knows people have the whim to regard scientific discovery, not Communism, as his forte. For Teller, work means discovery. Many scientists never discover anything except routine elaborations and refinements. Oppenheimer had told Teller in September of 1949 to get back to work at Los Alamos. How would one go about the work of discovery? Is it the same for the scientist as for the artist, an irrational fit of excitement in which one spins gold from straw? Does the excitement come for the scientist, as it does for the artist, before the gold? How much does environment count? Can one do it with one's shirt on?

"This is so stupid," says Teller. "I wish I could make you understand. I am talking about new ideas. You sense the problem and then begin to think around it and about it. In a scientist's work, excitement and elation can come from all sorts of sources including success. There is no such thing as inspiration. Insight and understanding come from long familiarity."

Many scientists gain the long familiary. Why does only one here and there also gain the insight that produces new ideas? Accident, Teller has said in many public statements, lucky escape from the urging of the child in the home, of the boy in the school, of the man in the laboratory not to be one-track, difficult, obsessed. Without a break, no one can hold out against the urging. "There is no such thing as genius," says Teller. "I would guess you think of Oppenheimer as a genius, and this shows what I mean. He knew more, but Fermi could do more. In a positive sense, Fermi had the character of a child. Others like Oppenheimer surpassed him in knowledge; Fermi knew this and was not bothered by it, for he rightly understood that character is much more important than intelligence. But you must not think his firmness and self-reliance as a scientist were born with him. There was a time he thought seriously of giving up physics. [The Germans had snubbed him and discouraged him, says Segré.] Then he had the luck to meet a great teacher, Ehrenfest, who persuaded him and managed him into feeling that he was all right."

Teller speaks these last words with a special tenderness ("Worshiped Fermi," said Oppenheimer), which beclouds his thesis that creative physicists differ from creative artists in needing no inspiration. In 1949 the thing that waited on the Mesa to be born still had long to wait. It demanded a new idea. When Teller went back, subsequent events began to turn on the question of how much inspiration he felt was in the Mesa's crisp October air.

Bradbury wanted to push research on the Super, but he would not reorganize the entire laboratory around it without a directive from above. Even so, he had many physicists giving time to theory and experimentally measuring energy levels of deuterium and tritium. Though not in charge of all this, Teller had a full-time crew of his own when he wanted one. In another able Hungarian physicist, Frederic de Hoffmann, he had a dedicated collaborator whom he dealt with exactingly. ("Getting married today," de Hoffmann is said to have once told him and got the following reply: "Freddy, does this mean you will not be at work in the lab tonight?")

Since the war, Bethe, von Neumann, and Fermi had periodically come to the Mesa to confer with Teller on the Super. Always the conclusion, verified by endless calculations of heat gain and loss fed into von Neumann's digital computers, was that the thermonuclear reaction would not go in any practicable hardware they could design. A necessary fundamental idea was missing, and Fermi did not seem sorry. "I am by no means sure the human race is going to survive," he told the Mesa's chief resident mathematician, Stan Ulam, a progressively more important figure at the conferences.

Ulam is the only scientist mentioned here besides Oppenheimer who uses the word *beauty* unself-consciously. Like Oppenheimer, he projects the intensity and awareness of the poet. His eyes are his most commanding feature; when he speaks they seem to well with green light; one must look again and again at the irises to keep in mind that they are not quite green. Physicists quote him on the Mesa as they once did Oppenheimer, especially on subjects otherwise too grim for social conversation. Fermi in 1954, for example, commented on the last stage of his cancer as follows: "They put dogs out of the way. Why must I go through this?" But the Mesa prefers to remember Fermi's deathbed as Ulam saw it: "The serene Doric. He talked to me smiling. For me it was reliving Plato's *Phaedo*." After the shock of Oppenheimer's treason disgrace that same year the Mesa also found some comfort in Ulam's comment: "What he believed in, he held to. He willingly exchanged his victor's laurel for a crown of martyrdom." To distinguish between Ulam's turn of speech and Oppenheimer's, one must note that what stirs and kindles Ulam is always in the past. Oppenheimer's most moving words have been concerned with hope. Of this there is never a trace in Ulam, perhaps because he is a later twentieth-century type.

Even before the war ended, Ulam had been caught up in the conferences with Teller and the others about the Super, but in 1946 his participation had been interrupted. He showed symptoms of an unusual illness. "When he was well, I would guess you'd put his I.Q. at about 180," says a Mesa associate with medical connections. "First it went down to average; he couldn't solve problems any better than I can. It kept on going down, and he seemed to have difficulty articulating his thoughts. Then lower still, and he couldn't talk at all. They took him to a hospital where he had to be fed and cared for like a baby. In spite of what people say about a brain tumor, there was absolutely no physical cause. After a while he recovered and came back to the Mesa, perfectly sound, just the same as before, except that he could hold his own a little better with Teller. I don't think they liked each other too well. They got on each other's nerves. In my opinion what Teller would consider a favorable atmosphere for work would be one where everybody revolved around him."

If what had made Ulam ill in 1946 was recoil from a glimpse of the missing idea, he was still able to keep it buried in his psyche in 1949 and for two years more. "I don't believe he would ever have come out with it if Teller hadn't got him angry," says Frederick Seitz. Meanwhile in the bright, shortening days of early October in 1949, Ulam kept talk about the Super centered on the unsolved problem of hydrodynamics. Excited by the White House announcement of the Red bomb, Teller fretted at Ulam's cool dispassion and wondered whether the Mesa had been the right place to come to.

Elsewhere the announcement had stirred more flurry. On October 5, Teller had a long-distance telephone call that showed him he, not the Mesa, was in step with the nation's mood. In a voice crackling with urgency, Lawrence told him action had to be taken at once, massively, with no delay. Did Teller also believe the Super the only answer? "Yes!" Teller responded with his whole heart.

Earlier that day, Latimer had kindled Lawrence. At least Latimer believed it was he who had kindled him. Latimer had started worrying about the Super earlier than most people, he said, and on October 5 had looked for Lawrence among the crowded lunch tables in the Berkeley Faculty Club. "I got hold of Ernest Lawrence," he said, "and I said, 'Listen, we have got to do something.' "

Hardest to swallow of all the odd facts about Berkeley is that such a man as Latimer should have been head of chemistry and later dean, to say nothing of being assistant director of the Radiation Laboratory. By now Latimer's deep, gabbling, unmodulated voice was in perfect tune with the times. Lawrence listened, then after a while went up the hill behind the campus to confer with Alvarez in the Radiation Laboratory's administrative office. The three formed a plan to team the Livermore M.T.A., which was not dead yet, with a vast new reactor installation on the Bay. Lawrence believed he could use the M.T.A. to produce neutrons that would convert lithium to tritium. The reactors he meant to be of a specialized type that would supplement the M.T.A. The two systems were to be used together much as steam is used with water power. With their joint product, which he talked of as a bucket of neutrons, he meant to supply Teller plenty of tritium with which to build the Super.

Not much could be said for the scheme from the point of view of physics. The connection with the M.T.A. was difficult to defend, and Lawrence was also disadvantaged in knowing little of reactor design. The reactors he and Alvarez envisaged were, by compari-

son with designs of the Commission's reactor specialists, primitive
and unproductive. Though unversed in reactors and hydrodynamics, Alvarez was a good physicist. He was also a tense and ambitious man, tired of being overshadowed by Berkeley's Nobel prize
winners and hungry for command, in which he seemed to find special release when he could use it to cause pain. Lawrence promised
him the directorship of the proposed Bay installation, and he accepted.

The three packed their bags and left for Washington on October
6, stopping at Los Alamos to share mutual enthusiasms with Teller.
By now Lawrence was in a mood to give away Atomic Energy
Commission installations as though he owned them. Teller was not
happy at Los Alamos. Perhaps then, perhaps the following year,
the thought first crossed Lawrence's mind of giving Teller a laboratory of his very own where he would be happy. By doing so in
1952, Lawrence partly filled up an aching void left in him by what
he regarded as Oppenheimer's desertion in 1946. "I've got as good
a theoretical physicist as Oppenheimer ever was," he asserted to
Brady after he had installed Teller in a new home.

By an irony too bitter for Lawrence to think about, this new
home turned out to be the great building at Livermore that he had
constructed to house the M.T.A. Naturally the M.T.A. was no
longer there. By 1952 not even the ghost of it was there, insofar as
Lawrence had power to exorcise it after its failure in 1950. "A
stupid object, but it should have been kept," says a Mesa physicist,
pretending flippancy to conceal his own bitterness at the abject and
ugly story he was being asked about. "That monstrous vacuum tank.
They could use it now at Livermore. We could use it now like crazy
here at Los Alamos. Lawrence was too cute for this. He had it ripped
out and broken up to dispose of the *corpus delicti*; he cleverly engineered matters so the odium didn't shock so much. So they had
the empty building, and that's what Teller moved into at Livermore. Then after what he did to Oppenheimer, Teller felt they
didn't like him so much here, and so when he came back to visit,
it was often for weeping sessions in which he would protest, 'I'm
not a heel!' "

"Do you or do you not believe that Dr. Oppenheimer is a security risk?" Robb, the prosecutor, asked Teller in the Gray Board's
dingy, narrow, crowded, jerry-built hearing room in 1954. Every-

one caught his breath, for under the security-jargon camouflage of
the proceedings, everyone knew this was the top moment in the
century's most famous treason trial.

Robb had laid the ground by carefully dissociating the evil of
disloyalty from the evil implied in "security risk." To simplify the
issues, he had told Teller, it would be best to dispose of the question
of Oppenheimer's loyalty first and separately. "I have always assumed, and I now assume that he is loyal to the United States,"
Teller had said as soon as Robb had assured him the big question would come later. When it came, Teller took his time about
answering.

"In a great number of cases I have seen Dr. Oppenheimer act—
I understand that Dr. Oppenheimer has acted—in a way that is
for me exceedingly hard to understand," Teller said. "I thoroughly
disagreed with him in numerous issues and his actions frankly
appeared to me confused and complicated. To this extent I feel that
I would like to see the vital interests of this country in hands
which I understand better and therefore trust more. In this very
limited sense I would like to express a feeling that I would feel
personally more secure if public matters would rest in other
hands."

So vague and unresponsive, so violently twisted into a mood
piece about the way he would like to feel, Teller's answer looks
like a mere fit of petulance that could hurt no one. "But it wasn't,"
says Rabi. "It was brilliantly thought out to meet the needs of
Robb and those twerps on the Board." This is the view which Teller
discovered Los Alamos also took; hence the weeping sessions on his
visits there. That it was the correct view Teller himself could not
help demonstrating in a low-voiced gloating to Oppenheimer after
the hearing was over: "I knew I'd have to fight you, Robert, and
now I've won."

As for the new home Lawrence provided him at Livermore, Teller was surrounded by fledgling Ph.D.'s, all twenty years younger.
He was happy in it, but, in comparison with the years when he
and Ulam got on each other's nerves at Los Alamos, uncreative.

All these events, of course, were far in the future though not
unpredictable on October 6, 1949, when Lawrence, Alvarez, and
Latimer broke their eastward flight with a stopover to see Teller at
Los Alamos. The three flew on to Washington next day, arriving in
the afternoon. "We started talking the best we could," says Lati-

mer, "to present our message to various people in Washington."

They had just time for a call at the Commission offices before they closed. The Research Division then had a director named Kenneth Pitzer. As a former graduate student of Latimer's, a chemistry professor on leave from Berkeley, and a consultant of Lawrence's at the Radiation Laboratory, he had enough close ties with Lawrence to be generally considered another member of the Lawrence group. He listened with approval to Lawrence's plans for the Super and for the new Bay reactor laboratory. Then he called in his administrative assistant, Paul Fine, and the conference turned sour.

Assistant or not, Fine was a theoretical physicist. He saw the Super as an unsolved problem and he took a dim view of Lawrence's reactor designs. "No imagination," Alvarez judged. Pitzer could not make Fine stop criticizing. "A chemist doesn't have much influence with theoretical physicists," reflected Latimer, scenting Oppenheimer behind Fine's behavior, as he always did behind anything he did not like.

Lawrence as usual decided to forget physicists and go to the real seats of power. His two awed companions he took to dinner that night at a hotel suite maintained in Washington by his millionaire friend Alfred Loomis. With Loomis he mapped his strategy.

The political right needed another rallying cry to go with security, preferably one that would rouse the military. The next day Lawrence set off on a round of visits to Congressmen and to Army and Air Force generals. Clear and galvanic as Pavlov's bell, Lawrence's message pulled them out of their stunned confusion over the Red bomb.

Strauss he had already enlisted, probably by long-distance telephone on October 5, when Latimer had first set him moving. On that day Strauss wrote a memo to Senator McMahon, urging the Super and paving the way for a visit by Lawrence. At Lawrence's urging, General Hoyt Vandenberg, Air Force Chief of Staff, went before the Joint Congressional Committee on October 14. "Having the Super weapon," Vandenberg summarized for Lawrence, "would place the United States in the superior position it had enjoyed up to the end of September by having exclusive possession of the weapon."

Lawrence's point was easy to grasp. With expressions of relief on their faces, Congressmen and generals fell in line behind him, even Senator McMahon, who had been trying to think for himself. By converting McMahon, Lawrence stripped the Atomic Energy Commission of its last political champion. Lilienthal, when Lawrence got around to seeing him, stared moodily out the window and talked like Paul Fine. The other Commissioners tried to be at once agreeable and noncommittal. For them the situation was the same as that which Lawrence had forced them into with the M.T.A., when, in Smyth's words, "we couldn't oppose him."

In mid-October, Lawrence returned to California satisfied that he had reoriented the country's nuclear establishment and become its center of power. To check, he lunched in San Francisco with another multimillionaire right-wing leader, John Neylan, his official spokesman on the University Board of Regents. Neylan told him that he had done well in Washington, that the Joint Congressional Atomic Energy Committee was already unblocking additional funds for him. On the strength of this assurance, Lawrence formally appointed—hitherto he had only promised to appoint—Alvarez to the directorship of the new Bay Reactor Laboratory. With a simple faith that seems to justify an opinion of Segré's that he was a hero-worshiper at heart, Alvarez cleaned out his old desk and waited to be assigned an executive suite.

He and Lawrence and Latimer got from most of the Radiation Laboratory's leading figures except Segré a vague promise to "join" (as Alvarez wrote in his diary, choosing his words carefully) the new project. They also had long talks with a consultant of Lawrence's from the University of California at Los Angeles—David Griggs. Griggs's technical field, the flow and breaking of rocks under high pressure, had little to do with nuclear physics. His importance was as a link to the Secretary and Chief of Staff of the Air Force, which had made him one of its principal scientific advisers. The Air Force was aggrieved because Oppenheimer and Lilienthal kept A-bombs out of its hands. On receiving the appointment, Griggs had been officially warned not to trust Oppenheimer. Griggs was what Alvarez called an enthusiastic person and Oppenheimer called paranoid. Griggs hardly knew Oppenheimer personally, but he and Latimer came to total agreement that the Air Force and the Radiation Laboratory alike owed their humiliations to something peculiar and sinister in Oppenheimer's personality.

To mark Lawrence's rising national influence, one of his laboratory staff members, Glenn Seaborg, had recently been appointed to the General Advisory Committee. A chemistry professor under Latimer, Seaborg had been throughout his career a protégé of Latimer's and Lawrence's. Thus he now caught an intense dose of anti-Oppenheimer persuasion. "I certainly worked hard on Seaborg," said Latimer.[1] He and Lawrence wanted Seaborg to speak for them the next time the Committee met, which they knew would be around the end of October. As a good scientist and a nervous, irritable, indecisive sort of man, Seaborg was in a difficult position. Fortunately for him, he had scheduled a trip abroad that would keep him from the Committee meeting. He wrote Oppenheimer a long, tormented letter saying that he deplored Lawrence's Super program but would need to hear good arguments before he could take on sufficient courage to oppose it.

Neylan was then planning a purge of leftist college professors at Berkeley that was to drive away every last one of Lawrence's remaining theoretical physicists. Meanwhile, however, Lawrence still had Serber. In Washington, Lawrence had not felt it worthwhile to see Oppenheimer. Now from Berkeley he had Serber, who he judged would be his most sympathetic contact, call Oppenheimer and present his message.

Serber proved a poor salesman, unclear on the vital connection between pushing the Super and building the new Bay laboratory. Worse still, from Argonne Laboratory and Oak Ridge came a series of long-distance telephone replies from the Commission's reactor authorities. Chief of these was Walter Zinn, secure in his position, famous for his contribution to reactor development, a sharp and tactless man. He termed Lawrence's reactor designs backward and inefficient, and he expressed puzzlement as to why Alvarez, who knew comparatively nothing about the field, should be in charge. Zinn had himself outlined a project for more advanced neutron-producing reactors. He made it explosively clear that he felt they should be built on the Savannah River in the Oak Ridge region rather than on the north recesses of San Francisco Bay near the M.T.A. "Apparently Zinn has thrown a lot of doubts into people's minds about the wisdom of our program," Alvarez wrote in his diary.

Back pressure was building up, Lawrence decided. He phoned Strauss long distance from Berkeley. "Don't weaken!" he urged, and Strauss said he would not. Newspapers began to rumor that an internal struggle was going on in government circles about

whether to make a bomb that worked on the principle of thermonuclear fusion of hydrogen atoms. For these leaks, which constituted a frightening breach of security, nobody was ever prosecuted.
By taking his case to the politicians, Lawrence had made them
inevitable.

Lawrence had not worried too much about physicists on his
Eastern sales trip, because by prearrangement Teller was to take
care of these. A week after their conference at Los Alamos on October 6, Teller too started east. "Rode out of here like a white knight
going to do battle against the wrongs of the world, which in his
case was a pretty small world, being mostly just him," said a Mesa
physicist.

Fermi was then due back from a trip to Italy. Had he returned
earlier, his friendship with Strauss and Teller might have modified
their initial movements as a tree may stop the first rockfall of
an avalanche. Teller met his plane at the Chicago airport and
found him tired and somber. Disgust at Teller's implied alliance
with the Hickenlooper-Knowland faction, whose designs on the
Atomic Energy Commission he had publicly denounced, made
Fermi curtly unsympathetic.

Teller continued on east to Ithaca to see Bethe, then director
of the Institute of Nuclear Studies at Cornell. He appealed to Bethe
to give up his job there, at least temporarily, and work full time
on the Super at Los Alamos. Since Bethe did not like to think of
a world armed with Supers, Teller said cunningly, he could come
and try to prove positively that the Super could never be made.
Idealism was the best lure to use on Bethe. This last argument won
him, and he said he would come. At that moment the phone rang
and Oppenheimer invited him to Princeton for a conference. Teller
came along fearing the worst. "He'll change your mind for you,"
Teller warned Bethe.

Oppenheimer expected that the Commission and the members
of his Committee would be called by Truman to a conference at
the White House on what to do about the Red bomb. On October 21
he wrote Conant a letter which he afterward said was as measured
and honest a review of the situation as any he could ever make:

DEAR UNCLE JIM:

We are exploring the possibilities for our talk with the President on
October 30th. All members of the Advisory Committee will come to the

meeting Saturday except Seaborg, who must be in Sweden, and whose general views we have in written form. Many of us will do some preliminary palavering on the 29th.

There is one bit of background which I would like you to have before we meet. When we last spoke, you thought perhaps the reactor program offered the most decisive example for the need for clarification. I was inclined to think that the Super might also be relevant. On the technical side, as far as I can tell, the Super is not very different from what it was when we first spoke of it more than seven years ago: a weapon of unknown design, cost, deliverability, and military value. But a very great change has taken place in the climate of opinion. On the one hand, two experienced promoters have been at work, i.e., Ernest Lawrence and Edward Teller.

The project has long been dear to Teller's heart; and Ernest has convinced himself that we must learn from Operation Joe [the Red bomb] that the Russians will do the Super, and that we had better beat them to it. On the technical side, he proposes to get some neutron-producing heavy-water reactors built, and to this I think we must say amen, since [other classified military applications] and many other things will all profit from the availability of neutrons.

But the real development has not been of a technical nature. Ernest spoke to Knowland and McMahon, and to some at least of the Joint Chiefs. The Joint Congressional Committee, having tried to find something to chew on ever since September 23rd, has at last found its answer: We must have a Super, and we must have it fast. A subcommittee is heading west to investigate this problem at Los Alamos and in Berkeley. The Joint Chiefs appear informally to have decided to give the development of the Super overriding priority, though no formal request has come through. The climate of opinion among competent physicists also shows signs of shifting. Bethe, for instance, is seriously considering return on a full-time basis; and so surely are some others. I have had long talks with Bradbury and Manley, and with von Neumann. Bethe, Teller, [Major General] James McCormack [A.E.C. military applications] and [Robert] Le Baron [chairman, Military Liaison Committee] are all scheduled to turn up within the next thirty-six hours. I have agreed that if there is a conference on the Super program at Los Alamos, I will make it my business to attend.

What concerns me is really not the technical problem. I am not sure the miserable thing will work, nor that it can be gotten to a target except by ox cart. It seems likely to me even further to worsen the unbalance of our present war plans. What does worry me is that this thing appears to have caught the imagination, both of the congressional and military people, as the answer to the problems posed by the Russian advance. It would be folly to oppose the exploration of this weapon. We have always known it had to be done; and it does have to be done, though it appears singularly proof against any form of experimental approach. But that we become committed to it as the way to save the country and the peace appears to me full of dangers.

We will be faced with all this at our meeting; and anything that we do or do not say to the President will have to take it into consideration. I shall feel far more secure if you have had an opportunity to think about it.

I still remember my visit with gratitude and affection.

ROBERT OPPENHEIMER

When Bethe and Teller came to see him at Princeton, Oppenheimer talked mostly about reactors for producing plutonium and neutrons. On the Super he did not say much, but he showed the two a letter from Conant replying to his own. It said the Lawrence-Strauss-Knowland reorientation of the Commission would go into effect "over my dead body." This was not the same thing as opposing research on the theoretical barrier to the Super. "You see my mind is not changed. I'll still come," Bethe told Teller when the conference was over.

Unspoken in Bethe's mind, Teller knew, was a money question. Oppenheimer and Lilienthal had set salaries for Commission scientists at a level comfortable but not lavish. Stars of the bomb story like Bethe could command at a place like Cornell a salary almost as high as the football coach's. By returning to Los Alamos, Bethe would therefore lose money. To remind Bethe where the big money truly was, Teller took him to see Strauss, who offered to make up the difference out of his own pocket, much as one tips a waiter. Bethe expressed thanks, but by this time both his idealism and his hard physics sense were having second thoughts. A day or two later these were hardened for him by two fellow theoretical physicists, Georg Placzek and Victor Weisskopf in New York, and he called Teller up at Strauss's apartment to say he was not coming after all.

Since Bethe had been the chief recruit he wanted, Teller was shaken and angered. He blamed Oppenheimer. Such skittish mavericks as theoretical physicists, he reasoned, had no common reverence but Oppenheimer, and therefore when they misbehaved in a group, Oppenheimer must be responsible. "Incredibly devious," Teller calls him. "Essentially one virtue: a really intelligent man. Also a dreadful fault: extremely vain. Vanity is his vice. The amount he has is excessive. An exceedingly great influence on the politics of the country and on the thinking of the physicists, a tremendous influence. Note, before the bomb on Hiroshima, he rejected and repressed the movement not to drop it, he used precipitation, he favored acting violently at a time when the war was already won. Afterward, when we were in a losing struggle for survival he argued, 'We are guilty, we must not trust these dreadful instruments of war.' That's what he told the Press, that's what he told his friends: 'We are guilty, we are guilty.' "

Teller's hurt was very personal. One cannot help thinking that he viewed guilt in terms of status denied him. Though no match for Teller as a scientist, Latimer was more acute in human relations. "Dr. Oppenheimer is a very modest man," Latimer said at the 1954 hearing, clearly perceiving that he must establish a worse motive than vanity. "People who didn't work with him on the Mesa get the idea he wanted to take too much credit for the A-bomb," says Major Ralph Smith, director of the documents division at Los Alamos; "I don't think he wanted to take *any* credit." "No, he didn't want the credit," says Bradbury. "I think he just wanted to serve his country. Anyhow, about the Super. He and I didn't see eye-to-eye about that after the money started flowing in. But he had to give his opinion. My God, that's what they were paying him for."

The ghastly light Oppenheimer had seen on the Jornada del Muerto had instantly convinced him the world would never be the same again. But for four years more he had kept on progressively learning how it would be different. Jocular and sheepish, Bainbridge had turned to him with a grin at zero plus one minute and said, "Well, we're all sons of bitches now." Oppenheimer was a simpler man than Bainbridge, so simple that people like Strauss, Teller, and Lawrence kept looking for the hidden convolution in his character. They could not believe, the politicians could not believe, and the public could not believe what nevertheless seems stark fact: that all he wanted was just not to be any more of a son of a bitch than he could help, and not to encourage the other poor sons of bitches in their hopes of frying and poisoning themselves utterly. As it grew in him, this motivation took the form of pain. A man in pain, in comparison with men who are not, may behave with more, less, or equal intelligence. But in any case his behavior will be subtly different. It is this difference that constitutes Oppenheimer's aesthetic interest, his claim on the attention of the sophisticated. By October of 1949 when, as he put it, "It had become clear to me that we would tend to use any weapon we had," the pain was fully developed.

The Joint Chiefs of Staff in late October, at last, defined their response to the Red bomb. General Omar N. Bradley, their spokesman, did so in an official report. Only United States bomb supremacy, said Bradley, had matched Russian army supremacy, and to meet the new threat we had no recourse but more bombs. As a comment on the spirit of the times, Bradley's report seemed to Oppenheimer strange and sad.

Pain, which was his index of realization, mounted in him as he watched pressure for the Super build up throughout October. Contrary to his expectations, Truman did not confer with the Commission and Advisory Committee members in a body. Instead, Truman asked Lilienthal to do it and report to him. Lilienthal had Oppenheimer schedule the Advisory Committee to meet on Saturday and Sunday, October 29 and 30.

Unconsciously Oppenheimer began looking forward to when he could ease himself of an intolerable burden. "I knew we just couldn't let things go as a matter of course," he says. "I knew something had to be done." As he left his office Saturday morning, a slang phrase from his youthful years at Cambridge, England, crossed his mind. "I'm going to spend a penny," he told a secretary.

On the other side, all factions that had joined to grasp control of the Atomic Energy Commission also regarded the meeting as crucial. Despite his enormous political influence, Lawrence was not entitled to a seat at the Commission's formal deliberations. To avoid the indignity of waiting outside the door, he sent Alvarez to do it for him.

By now Zinn had made Alvarez uneasy about his directorship. Standing hungrily in the marble lobby of the Commission building on H Street, Alvarez greeted the Commissioners as they walked by him; he learned they were to be present at the start of the Advisory

Committee session. The Joint Congressional Committee's staff director, William Borden, whom Senator McMahon had sent to push the Super, stopped to talk for a moment; Lawrence and Alvarez had converted him during Lawrence's promotional trip. Afterward Generals Bradley and Norstad passed by, a tantalizing reminder to Alvarez of how close he was to the big time. "I saw the famous military men whom I recognized from their pictures follow along," he says wistfully. Then the lobby became empty and silent; for between two and three hours Alvarez waited on the hard stone floor for his directorship.

As a legislative-branch employee, Borden could not attend the meeting either. But before it got under way, he looked up Manley, the Advisory Committee Secretary, to make him a sales pitch. The two talked a long time. A twenty-eight-year-old Air Force enthusiast, Borden had written a book to prove that future military operations must be airborne and nuclear. With no knowledge of physics, he had no way to challenge Lawrence's confident, easy optimism. Manley explained to him that the cost of enough tritium for the hypothetical Super would pay for many, many hundreds of additional plutonium bombs. Borden nodded at appropriate times and seemed to listen intelligently.

"I had the sense I had practically convinced him the big bang wasn't worth it militarily," says Manley. "Just on the basis of cost in fissionable material, I felt I had convinced him." But in fact Manley had only proved how hard it is to recognize even the grossest hysteric. Borden dismissed what he heard as the parroting of a zombie. Three years later he wrote to J. Edgar Hoover labeling Oppenheimer not a mere ordinary traitor but an enemy agent "under a Soviet directive" to abort the Super. Of all Oppenheimer's enemies, only Lawrence could stomach this. When Lawrence and Strauss were in control after the Gray Board hearing, Strauss mentioned to Lawrence in Ralph Smith's presence that the Atomic Energy Commission needed a new general manager. "Let's get Borden for it," Lawrence said.

"God, Ernie, you wouldn't hire that ———," said Smith, and he made a spitting movement with his lips.

Lawrence looked surprised. "Since Mr. Borden is now otherwise employed, the question of his employment by the Commission does not arise," Strauss interposed with silken tact.

Foreseeing none of this and having as he thought deconverted Borden, Manley took his place in the Committee conference room. Lilienthal opened the meeting. The President, he said, had told him to ask whether the Commission's activities should be supplemented as a result of the Red bomb. First, there was the general question of expanding the Commission's normal A-bomb production. Second, there was the particular question raised by one of the Commissioners, Admiral Strauss, whether the Commission should undertake an all-out program toward the Super.

Lilienthal said "all-out program." The fashionable jargon phrase of the day was "crash program." Were they the same? It was a very important point, said Gordon Gray at the 1954 security hearing, because he could not satisfy himself that the issue put before Oppenheimer and on which Oppenheimer took an adverse stand was a crash program rather than just any program. By such melancholy subtleties Gray crept toward his little niche in history.

After Lilienthal had spoken for the Commission, Oppenheimer turned to the generals. Norstad was there for the Air Force, the most pugnacious of the three services, the most determined to dictate bomb policy. But Norstad was not like his juniors, the new breed of generals in the Strategic Air Command. To their subsequent bitter regret, he let Bradley do most of the talking. There are grounds for suspecting Norstad had some inkling of the unsolved basic physics problems of the Super, or, as the Strategic Air Command would have put it, was soft toward Oppenheimer.

Bradley repeated the no-recourse-but-the-bomb statement from his report. Oppenheimer estimated the cost of an all-out industrial effort toward the Super in terms of additional plutonium bombs. Half-megaton sizes were already designed and scheduled for production, he reminded Bradley. As compared with these, he asked, what military advantages could Bradley see for the hypothetical Super?

Bradley thought visibly, then made an answer that was to win him expressions of contempt from Oppenheimer's enemies. "Only psychological," he said.

During Saturday morning the Advisory Committee listened to its outsiders, the Commissioners and the generals, let them go, and then itself recessed for lunch. Downstairs Alvarez scanned each departing face and felt farther from his directorship. When the

Committee came down for lunch, it had had very little time yet to decide anything. But if Lawrence's reactor proposals, instead of going with a whoop, were to be subjected to cold-blooded comparison with Zinn's, the outcome was dismally predictable. Besides, Alvarez was not very patient. To the knot of Committee members who stepped out of the elevator, he addressed one short question: "Yes or no?"

Oppenheimer took him to lunch and tried to intimate disarmingly that the answer was No. As always in really sticky situations, the conversation had absurd overtones. Alvarez had made himself in a sense Lawrence's messenger and junior partner. The M.T.A. was not dead yet. "This was one of many things tied into the question of the Super," says Bethe. "It seemed obvious that Hanford and the Savannah River project were the places to get the plutonium and. the lithium-tritium. Lawrence claimed the M.T.A. would compete with them, which was obviously wrong." For Oppenheimer to cancel the proposed Bay installation, whose director sat opposite him glumly chewing, was to heap another insult on the M.T.A., for which the Bay installation was to be a standby.

The trickiest of all explanations to have to make to an ambitious man is that his ambitions are ridiculous. Skating nervously over the point, Oppenheimer made an effort—he had a good deal of respect for Alvarez—to communicate something of his deeper feelings about the crash program toward the Super. M.T.A., backward and inefficient reactor designs, and unsolved hydrodynamics problems were not what Alvarez testified he remembered of the conversation. "He said that he did not think the United States should build the hydrogen bomb," Alvarez testified, "and the main reason he gave for this, if my memory serves me correctly, and I think it does, was that if we built a hydrogen bomb, the Russians would build a hydrogen bomb, whereas if we did not build a hydrogen bomb, then the Russians would not build a hydrogen bomb."

How unconscious and uncontrived is the implication here that the Super was the hydrogen bomb and that it could be built? Five scientists, all from California, swore in 1954 that they thought Oppenheimer a security risk: Teller, Alvarez, Latimer, Pitzer and Griggs. Teller was most famous, but Alvarez, though considered hard-headed and brutal to people dependent on him, was probably most trusted by other physicists.

One of the leaders in the atomic establishment says that he was appalled by an intimation he caught in 1954 of the way anger and frustration had affected Alvarez' mind: "I remember a shocking conversation I had with Alvarez. It was before the Hearings. I want to make it clear that I am not giving his words but trying to reconstruct his reasoning. What he seemed to be telling me was 'Oppenheimer and I often have the same facts on a question and come to opposing decisions—he to one, I to another. Oppenheimer has high intelligence. He can't be analyzing and interpreting the facts wrong. I have high intelligence. I can't be wrong. So with Oppenheimer it must be insincerity, bad faith—perhaps treason?' "

As for his lunch on that October Saturday in 1949, said Alvarez, it showed him "the program we were planning to start was not one that the top man in the scientific development of the A.E.C. wanted to have done." Without waiting to hear the decisions of the Advisory Committee, he went back to California and put his papers back in his old desk, correctly convinced he would never be director.

For Oppenheimer, the lunch, though he could not get through it without hurling mortal defiance at Lawrence's California group, came near being his comic relief for that grim day. A suspicion that will not go away is that in touching on the more grotesque parts of the California plan, he let his face sag into the lines of the suffering computer. "Did he finally get to the point of making jokes about the M.T.A.?" says Bethe. "I don't know. He may have. I can well imagine that he may have."

Oppenheimer went back to the Committee room, empty now of all faces except those that could see and share his pain. "You want to know how they looked?" says Manley. "I can't tell you, except that I think they all looked as though they felt the way I did. The issue they had to decide cut so far into them, I think, that even the functions of the subconscious were disturbed. I was so overwhelmed myself, my memory is almost a blank.

"Fermi? Cold affability, I would say. Not detachment, since all his attention and energy were being directed to the issue that had been forced on us. Pretty well worked up, I would guess, for one of the few times of his life."

Oppenheimer began the session by asking Fermi to assess the Super's technical feasibility. Fermi had always tended to view the thermonuclear reaction as a measureless grave; he had expected, however, that humanity would wait for science to open it before they tried to crowd in. He did not confine his remarks to the technical problem. "As far as I could see the situation," he said in 1954, "I had the concern that the pressure for this development was extremely inordinate. Or so it seemed to me. I was concerned that it might weaken the development of conventional atomic weapons which was then picking up, and essentially set it back for what seemed to me a not quite decided advantage on the other side."

"Fermi was very circumspect, very reserved when he testified before the Gray Board," said Allison. By that time, the late spring of 1954, Fermi had begun showing symptoms of cancer recognized only in retrospect three months later. "I just sit at my desk and don't move around much any more," he told another friend, physicist John Marshall. Other changes had come over him. In 1950 he had refused reappointment to the Advisory Committee when his term expired, but had not thus escaped continued involvement. He watched control of the Atomic Energy Commission pass to Hickenlooper, whom he had denounced, and Strauss, a warm personal friend and benefactor, and Lawrence, whom he despised, and Teller, whose obstreperousness he alone had in the past been able to check with a fatherly, deprecating "Edward! *Edward!*"

"I'm a fatalist by nature," Fermi used to say. Power was a fact he had always respected to the extent of keeping his mouth shut about its follies. "Nobody could influence *his* thinking," associates assert as a confident axiom. But with the aura which Latimer had noted, Oppenheimer had begun to radiate pain. Until 1950 Fermi was exposed. The effect was to dissolve in Fermi's mind the normal barriers with which as a discreet skeptic he was wont to separate thought from action. Afterward he looked back with trouble and wonder. "When I was on the Advisory Committee," he told Wigner about the end of 1952, "I took stands which I wouldn't now. I feel they were too close to Oppenheimer's."

By then Oppenheimer and the science community he spoke for were plainly on the losing side of a power struggle which the Mesa viewed as between Lawrence and Strauss on the one side and Oppenheimer, Bradbury and themselves on the other. To tilt against windmills was not in Fermi's nature, and yet when he was around Oppenheimer it was clear to him that this was what he should do. He was the century's best problem-solver. But this problem, like Slotin's

Dragon earlier and his own cancer pain later, he could deal with only by exclusion.

"During our large and ill-managed bout with the Super," said Oppenheimer, "Fermi was as good as anyone. A year or so after the thing had carried, the Defense Department wanted to build up its Research and Development staff. Fermi by then had been out of the Advisory Committee for some time. I was asked to see if he could be persuaded to join this other group. 'I think it's important,' he said to me, 'but I can't do it. I have lost confidence in the validity of my judgment.' This remark struck me because during most of his life he had had unlimited confidence. Afterward, when he and I drifted out of touch, I thought about it a good deal, and now I treasure it."

Fermi's last sharp view of the two roads came to him on his deathbed. Strauss brought him twenty-five thousand dollars, a medal, and word that the Commission would henceforth periodically honor its best scientists with a similar award to be called the Fermi award. At the same time the newspapers and magazines in which Fermi sought divertisement from his cancer kept annoying him with a persistent nonfact. By then Teller and Ulam had discovered the principle of the hydrogen bomb. ("Couldn't have been done without Ulam," says Bethe. "Certainly couldn't have been done without Teller.") Faithful to the right-wing interests then in power in the government, newspapers and magazines kept saying the discovery and the thing itself had been made at that wonderful new laboratory, Livermore. At Livermore, Teller's young crew had in fact confined themselves to freezing and studying tritium, which the discovery dispensed with. Fermi issued the last of the few statements he ever made to the newspapers. It was short. First he cleared his throat with a perfunctory compliment to Teller, then got to the point. "The Los Alamos Laboratory," he said, "has deserved the gratitude of this nation for its development of both A and H weapons." It is hard to be sure why he wanted to say this. "Because it was true and he was a truthful man," says Segré. But against the background of that year's events, this reason seems trivial. "Wanted to clean up a little after what the country had done to Oppenheimer," says William Higinbotham. "After all, Oppenheimer *was* Los Alamos." But this reason, if true, suggests a sophisticated indirection in Fermi departing far from what Ulam calls the Fermi Doric.

Oppenheimer was probably the simpler man. On Saturday afternoon, October 29, 1949, he faced his fellow Committee members with no pretense of liking the pressures the Commission had channeled down upon him.

Oddly, neither he nor anyone else there had any hesitation about exploring the possibility of the Super to its absolute end. Blocking the step would have been easy. To cut off the necessary raw materials, he had only to let Lawrence build his inefficient neutron-producing reactors and gear them to the M.T.A. To dry up the necessary fundamental research, he had only to let Lawrence enshrine Teller in some new laboratory (Livermore was not yet available) or, better still, make Teller director of Los Alamos. Thus he could have won thanks and at the same time kept us thermonuclearly harmless. Instead, with the fatal smoothness that made him the most nightmarish figure in the nightmare he knew he was living, he guided the Committee through the only meaningful steps that could be taken toward the Super. These were, first, to recommend a huge outlay for Zinn's Savannah River reactors and, second, to let Bradbury do what he wanted, which was to try hard to get as much fundamental research as he could from Teller, von Neumann, Ulam, and the other brains at Los Alamos. All this part of the Committee's business, together with recommendations for further expanding plutonium production, went as a matter of course.

The issue he could not let go as a matter of course was quite different. All factions—Lawrence's group, the politicians, the Air Force—which had previously cried security and now cried crash program meant at the very least a public program. They wanted the Commission to confess sin and advertise to foreigners what we would like to be able to do to them. Oppenheimer and his fellow physicists on the Committee gave the point close, bleak attention. The passage in their report dealing with this, Lilienthal said in 1954, much impressed him. Groping in his memory, he reconstructed the passage as follows: "To announce publicly, as apparently it was necessary, the building of a weapon of almost unlimited size would be in conflict—would put us in the eyes of our friends and potential friends in an unfavorable light without compensating advantages."

More truly than he knew, General Bradley had called the Super a psychological weapon; it was less bomb than bluster. All countries that could manage it would have to, as a matter of course, continually and secretly explore the possibility of the thermonuclear reaction by such steps as the Savannah River project. Nothing could stop this but the Acheson-Lilienthal plan, whose open laboratories were a wrecked dream of almost every nuclear physicist outside California. ["The failure of this plan was the greatest tragedy of the postwar world," says Bethe.] But a public program would be a senseless sanction of the prevailing mass death-oriented hysteria. Why the United States should wish to start rather than deter an overt international competition passed the understanding of every scientist gathered around Oppenheimer's big polished committee-room table. "That's because they could all see beyond their noses," says Bethe. "It's a pity so few other people in the country could."

Oppenheimer polled them all painstakingly. "Gave them perfect opportunity to express their views," said Fermi. "Consumed an ungodly amount of time," said Conant. But at this point Oppenheimer made his first slip. He did not circulate Seaborg's letter around the table. "What of it?" says Bethe. "Try to see what those people had on their minds." The indecisive letter could not have had much effect on the Committee's deliberations. But by not circulating it Oppenheimer laid himself open to personal enemies if they should ever get control of the Commission. He may have forgotten the letter; by 1954 he showed visible awkward surprise when it was suddenly exhibited to him at the hearing after having been carefully preserved for five years in his own files. Seaborg himself afterward said he was glad not to have been involved one way or another in the Committee's October responsibilities.

On the crash program toward the Super, it turned out they all felt the same. "A decision that it was not the right time to go in an absolutely overriding way in that direction was as far as I remember unanimous," said Fermi. Dread rather than hope, in their view, was the only motive for probing the unsolved hydrodynamics problem. They doubted the Super as then conceived would prove to be the way. But they all agreed in a guess that five years' concerted and imaginative effort was likely to reveal a way. The world, they said, would then be in a situation they wished to prevent. "We believe a Super bomb should never be produced," their report concluded, a statement that was afterward adduced as evidence that Oppenheimer had brainwashed them. The minority, Fermi and Rabi, added a qualification to the effect that this country should not start the program without first trying earnestly to get an agreement with the Russians to leave it alone. Since the Russians were then regarded as our only nuclear rival, this minority statement was a distinction without a difference.

"I sort of had the view at that time that perhaps it would be easier to outlaw by international agreement something that did not exist," Fermi explained. He had always said governments would use anything they could, but that this was their business, not the scientists'. Now an unwonted word, a concept dim and discomforting as the faces he saw reflected in the table top, forced its way to his tongue: evil. "The fact that no limit exists to the destructiveness of this weapon makes its very existence and the knowledge of its construction a danger to humanity as a whole," he said in his minority coda. "It is necessarily an evil thing, considered in any light."

These conclusions of the General Advisory Committee Oppenheimer reported to Lilienthal, who, after conferring with his fellow Commissioners, reported them to President Truman. "No crash program toward the Super" ran the shocking word among the insiders. "It just makes me sick," McMahon said, condoling with Teller, who also was sick.

So, after a little consideration, were the generals of the Air Force. In November, Lilienthal, against whom they had a grievance, won a nine-to-six vote in the Joint Committee to shut down Hickenlooper's investigation, then resigned. At Truman's insistence, Lilienthal consented to stay on until February. But since he thus became politically a dead soldier, the Air Force transferred its grievance to Oppenheimer.

Ironically, the Air Force was angry because Oppenheimer wanted it to maintain a strong capability not only for strategic bombing but also for air combat and for tactical bombing in which atomic weapons might or might not be used. This was a balanced-force concept the Air Force could not tolerate, because in tune with the hysteric demand of the times for cheap, safe solutions, it was becoming madly unbalanced in favor of its own Strategic Air Command.

As always, Oppenheimer reflected the majority view of scientists

whom the government consulted on any military-scientific problem. "You need a very strong Strategic Air Command," said one of
the Air Force's principal scientific advisers, Norman Ramsey, a
physics professor at Harvard. "I believe, however, that Oppenheimer felt that too large a fraction of the Air Force's monies were
going to that, as compared with the very small amount that was
going to the problem of Air Defense. I must admit I agree with
him." The question, Ramsey insisted, was not tactical versus strategic air power, but whether to have at least a little of both. "I don't
know of any scientist concerned with military things who thinks
we should drop the Strategic Air Force. Almost all I know, and it
is my impression that Dr. Oppenheimer would also agree, agree
that it should be the biggest part of the Air Force, but not the
whole thing."

Major General Roscoe Wilson described himself to the Gray
Board as a dedicated airman and a big-bomb man. To show how
much, he started to denounce the Navy's spokesmen by name until
Gray pulled him up. Wilson glanced at Oppenheimer, who was
looking at him with astonishment. "Well, this is a little embarrassing to me," he said and then spoke the mind and heart of the Strategic Air Command:

I believe in a concept which I am going to have to tell you or my testimony doesn't make sense.

The U.S.S.R. in the airman's view is a land power. It is practically independent of the rest of the world. I feel that it could exist for a long time
without sea communications. Therefore it is not really vulnerable to attack by sea. Furthermore it has a tremendous store of manpower. . . .
My feeling is that the men in the Kremlin cannot risk the loss of their
base. This base is vulnerable only to attack by air power. . . . I further
believe that whereas air power might be effective with ordinary weapons,
that the chances of success against Russia with atomic weapons or
[thermo] nuclear weapons are far, far greater.

It is against this thinking that I have to judge Dr. Oppenheimer's
judgments. Once again, his judgments were based on technical matters.
It is the pattern I am talking about.

I have jotted down from my own memory some of these things that
worried me.

First was my awareness of the fact that Dr. Oppenheimer was interested in what I call the internationalizing of atomic energy, this at a time when the United States had a monopoly, and in which many people, including myself, believed that the A-bomb in the hands of the United States with an Air Force capable of using it was probably the greatest deterrent to further Russian aggression. This was a concern. . . .

To do this [monitor the Russian nuclear effort] the Air Force felt that it required an elaborate system of devices. Some were relatively simple to produce, some of them were very difficult to produce, and some of them were very costly. Dr. Oppenheimer was not enthusiastic about two out of three of these devices or systems. I do not challenge his technical judgment in these matters, but the over-all effect was to deny the Air Force the mechanism which we felt was essential to determine when the bomb went off. In our judgment, this was one of the critical dates, or would be at that time, for developing our national-defense policy.

Dr. Oppenheimer also opposed the nuclear-powered aircraft. His opposition was based on technical judgment. I don't challenge his technical judgment, but at the same time he felt less strongly opposed to the nuclear-powered ships. The Air Force feeling was that at least the same energy should be devoted to both projects. . . .

The approach to the thermonuclear weapons also caused some concern. Dr. Oppenheimer, as far as I knew, had technical objections, or, let me say, approached this with conservatism for technical reasons, more conservatism than the Air Force would have liked.

The sum total of this, to my mind, was adding up to that we were not exploiting the full military potential in this field. Once again it was a matter of judgment. I would like to say that the fact that I admire Dr. Oppenheimer so much, the fact that he has such command of the English language, has such national prestige, and such power of persuasion, only made me nervous, because I felt if this was so, it would not be to the interest of the United States, in my judgment.

It was for this reason that I went to the Director of Intelligence to say that I was unhappy.

Each of General Wilson's items disappeared when looked at directly. On the three detection systems, his remarks can be interpreted as follows: For the one that really worked, analysis of stratospheric fallout, Oppenheimer was enthusiastic; for flying over Russia with airscoop and camera, not so much. Asked to be specific on Oppenheimer and the nuclear airplane, Wilson amplified: "He had a time-scale. As I recall, it was the orderly development of these things in series that appealed to him." Asked if he could have designed an effective bomber to deliver the 1949-concept Super, Wilson said "Yes," then floundered trying to qualify the absurd lie without taking it back.

It was the pattern that was significant, General Wilson insisted, safe in the knowledge that the Air Force Chief of Intelligence also looked only with peripheral vision and therefore saw the pattern too. "We imagine hell as vast," says Dostoevsky. "But what if it's one little grimy room with spiders in every corner?" Oppenheimer had prestige enough to handle Lawrence's group, and Strauss, and the Hickenlooper-Knowland wing of Congress. All these people flaunted patriotism to get their way, but as fighters the Air Force made them look clean.

During the last two months of 1949, the government took the official position that its primary answer to the Red bomb would not be a Super bomb. To their mournful astonishment, after a few weeks Oppenheimer and his committee saw their conclusions rehashed in the newspapers. Before Hiroshima, no one had decided anything. The scientists had assumed the government would decide, the government had assumed the military would decide, and the military had assumed they were expected to fry Japanese. Against this natural falling motion no one had interposed himself wholly except Bard, too minor a figure to stop it. Now the falling motion had begun again, but someone had looked into the thermonuclear grave, taken thought, and stopped the motion into it. Someone had decided—and must pay.

Oppenheimer stood more nearly alone than one might think. True, his committee supported him unwaveringly. So did Lilienthal, but it has been denied that Lilienthal had a Commission decision behind him when he took Oppenheimer's report to the President. "There was no such Commission decision," says one of the Commissioners. "My point here is that the Commission never formally voted yes or no." Instead of a vote, what Lilienthal seems to have had was an expression of views: against the crash program and in favor of Oppenheimer's report, himself, Sumner Pike, Smyth, and a new Commissioner, Gordon Dean; for the crash program and against Oppenheimer's report, Strauss.

This consensus of four—not to call it a decision seems hairsplitting—held good only during the first week of November, then melted. By November 9 Gordon Dean reported to the President through Lilienthal that he now sided with Strauss. Smyth too modified his position, though less decisively. Only a minority of the Commission—Lilienthal, who was resigning, and Sumner Pike, a rock of integrity but not a scientist or politician—continued firm behind Oppenheimer's report.

"I think Oppenheimer underestimated the effect of the continuing low-level attacks on Commission policy," said Manley. "I think he overestimated his strength to resist the pressures exerted in Washington. Partly the pressures had taken the form of those damned Congressional hearings. (I never heard him comment on foolishness like McKellar's and Hickenlooper's.) Partly the pressures were exerted more quietly by the military. I had thought that civilians would be consulted about employment of the weapons, that the McMahon Act would provide civilian control over military uses. But the Department of Defense would present its demands, and all we were expected to do was to meet them. What bothered me most was seeing the Commission undermined down to a manufacturing department for the Department of Defense. I realized I had been watching an interesting experiment toward sensible civilian control of a vital government activity. It had been a rather grand concept of a government agency, and it was sad to see it go to pieces."

"A strong force on the side of the angels," Bethe called Oppenheimer's committee. While in January of 1950 it spent itself trying to stay the national death wish, research toward the Super went on unaffected by the overt struggle. Further calculations proved more flatly than ever that as a weapon the Super was impossible. Since the issue had shifted from physics to psychology, no one cared much. More exciting was a development from London that shook up both sides, though which side it favored was hard to say. The British reported they had caught Klaus Fuchs giving bomb data to the Russians and had got a confession from him that he had been doing it for years.

All security-cleared scientists in the country thought at once of the Fuchs-von Neumann patent. To check on how much it contained about the Super, Bethe in New York telephoned Ralph Smith, director of the documents division at Los Alamos.

"Is it all there?" Bethe asked.

"All," said Smith.

"Oh," replied Bethe in a tone Smith found hard to distinguish from the moaning of the long-distance wires.

Bethe was in New York to attend a convention of the American Physical Society. Many of its other members had a right to know, and when he told them they all looked equally desolate. "We were a pretty glum bunch," said Oppenheimer, then commuting between New York and Washington.

After conferring with him, Bethe began to think. Since this government now knew it shared the secret of the Super with its principal ally and with its principal enemy, an international agreement to ban the thing looked more obviously advantageous. One could not tell the American public why, of course, since Security was still functioning effectively against them. Still, it might be possible to tell them something in the way of sanity. Bethe and eleven other physicists who were not bound to silence by membership on Oppenheimer's committee held a press conference in a Physical Society office.

At the beginning Bethe acted as spokesman. He said that we should pledge not to use the thing first, and tried to explain why. The reporters wanted to hear only about traitors, preferably unarrested. What was the affinity between atomic science and treason? Flustered, Bethe lost the thread of his argument. "Not handling them well," thought Allison, and intervened to bring the discussion back to the point. "Allison couldn't do it," says Wheeler Loomis, the Physical Society president. "The reporters were hyenas. They made fools of Bethe and Allison, and then I stepped in and they made a fool of me."

Loomis is lean, elegant, intolerant of bombast, not the kind of man who likes to kick a dead horse. "The newspaper accounts of that conference looked to me like the handwriting on the wall. You could see what Oppenheimer was going to get for holding his finger in the dike. You could see where the human species wanted to go. How much more time do they have, I wonder? Twenty years? Thirty years? Anyhow, that interview showed me there was nothing I could do to stop them."

Teller and Lawrence had also come east for the convention. At Los Alamos Smith had a call from Teller. Up to Smith's "All," in answer to the von Neumann-Fuchs patent question, the conversation developed as it had done with Bethe. Then it took a different turn.

"I don't believe it," said Teller. If it was true, his bomb—*his* bomb—was a thing the Russians thoroughly understood and perhaps laughed at. Seeming momentarily frantic at the thought, Teller cast about for nearer enemies. Smith's job was to see that patent registrants made their disclosures of invention intelligible and complete; could it be Smith's fault that Fuchs and von Neumann had written all of Teller's ideas into their disclosure as subsidiary information? "If it's all there," Teller told Smith, "it's because *you* put it there."

When Teller regained his composure, he and Lawrence worked out an opposite construction of the news from Bethe's. "High councils" became their unifying phrase. Fuchs had penetrated this country's high nuclear councils, in which, therefore, drastic change must be made with great haste. To urge the point, the two addressed a secret session of the Joint Congressional Committee. The Committee needed little persuasion; it was already on their side. Their purpose was to whip it into action, to make it executive instead of legislative. The date was probably Monday, January 30, 1950. "I shall never forget," Senator Bricker reminisced to Senator Pastore a decade later. "I think you were not there that day, when Dr. Teller and Dr. Lawrence testified on this subject. I say that they were the two most convincing from the outside [that is, except the Congressmen themselves]. It was a most impressive thing. They said . . . we had to move ahead with it —the information had been carried by Fuchs and he sat in high councils in this country—and that if we didn't, the thing Senator Scott mentioned a moment ago might happen [that is, the Russians might be first, as in fact they were in 1953; Bricker slid over this point]. Dr. Teller, I remember well, said, 'If you give me eight or ten scientists'—and he named a part of them—'we will make it.' And Dr. Lawrence was just as strong in his support. Unfortunately Dr. Lawrence is gone now. Dr. Teller is continuing his great service. And the testimony of these two witnesses first as to the danger of not doing it, second as to the possibility of the accomplishment, and to the ways and means of doing it, I think had as much to do with strengthening our position, Senator, as anything could have done."

"The one boast of the members of the Joint Committee on

Atomic Energy," Pastore reminisced in his turn, "is that they disputed the recommendation of the General Advisory Committee under the leadership of Mr. Brian McMahon and Mr. Hickenlooper. They marched down to the White House (I was not there) and said to the President, 'You have got to overrule this; Mr. Teller says there is a possibility here.' "[2]

Earlier on that same Monday, January 30, Oppenheimer reported to Truman that Fuchs knew all about the Super. For advice on what to do, Truman at once convened a committee of three—the Secretary of Defense, Louis A. Johnson; the Secretary of State, Dean Acheson; and Lilienthal. With Lilienthal opposing, they voted two to one formally to inaugurate the crash program toward the Super. Next, giving the final ineluctable evidence of the nation's hysteric death-orientation, they wrangled over how Truman should announce it. Acheson wanted Truman to apologize to citizens of allied countries, Johnson did not. Truman on Tuesday afternoon, January 31, issued a simple, dignified statement drafted by Johnson. The Super was then known to be a device which, if it could be made to explode at all, could only be made to explode on the site where it had been fabricated. As easily read between the lines in foreign chancelleries, Truman's statement said that by way of a symbolic gesture we were going to spend billions on an impossible weapon which, if it were not impossible, would put us in a position to kill everybody.

Oppenheimer on that Tuesday afternoon was answering questions at another secret session of the Joint Committee. "A few minutes after I testified, I believe, or shortly after I testified, the Presidential announcement came out, and I knew what it was going to be," he said at his security hearing. With no hope of altering the event, he still thought the Congressmen would be wiser if they could share some of the October mood of his committee of scientists. "I testified in order to explain as well as I could the grounds for the advice, the color of the advice."

Senator Bricker, being a Hickenlooper man, later made no sympathetic restatement of Oppenheimer's remarks on the occasion. But as he listened, his mind went back to a statement he had heard from Oppenheimer at an earlier session of the Committee: "I hope and pray we will never make the Super." Something of the *color*—Oppenheimer's word for "pain"—came through to

Bricker. "I began to get a glimpse of tremendous power," he said.

Oppenheimer, for his part, watched the politicians' faces with inveterate hopefulness. Here and there in a room heady with political triumph, he was encouraged by an indrawn breath, a mouth momentarily bleak. His inculcation of the sane, hard thought bore curious fruit. Taught by him to reason out consequences, McMahon secretly in 1952 proposed a peace of widening deserts: the United States must get the Super first, then progressively destroy each nation about to do so. Expecting national survival, McMahon never quite came to live with Oppenheimer in his nightmare. Congressman W. Sterling Cole (Republican of New York) came closer. "Cole let me know in 1949–50 that he shared our misgivings about the Super," said Oppenheimer. "Then at my security hearing in 1954 I had the feeling that if there had not been such heavy political pressure he would have spoken out." Leaving Congress in 1957, Cole received as his political reward the directorship of the American-subsidized International Atomic Energy Agency. By then three nations had the true hydrogen bomb. At a grim conference in Vienna, Cole remembered Oppenheimer. "I had a dream you came here and said you'd like to help me," Cole wrote him. "If the dream was true—if you see any hope left—let me know. If not, you don't need to write."

On January 31, 1950, his fifty-fourth birthday, Strauss too was expecting Truman's announcement. His term as Commissioner had been a long contest of wills with the rest of the Commission. In every one of its dozen non-unanimous decisions, he had been one-to-four on the losing side. The Commission's last such decision, to uphold Oppenheimer against the crash program, had plunged him into what he later let a newsman-protégé term his Gethsemane. Truman's reversal brought him out. It was the highest triumph he could hope for against his four present fellow Commissioners. His plans already laid, he went to the White House and resigned, then staged a celebration at the Shoreham Hotel. Congressmen, generals, government officials, and, of course, newsmen came to rejoice with him over the country's dedication to the way of the Super.

While Strauss circulated among his guests and gracefully threw back to them their congratulations on the fight just won, he grew continuously more aware of one unsmiling face. Oppenheimer stood off in a corner, looking to Strauss's mind tense and unre-signed. He turned to another guest, Strauss afterward heard, and quoted Woodrow Wilson: "A battle is never won or lost."

Similar celebrations, but minus the birthday pretext and the intrusive specter, were being put on by Lawrence and Latimer at Berkeley and by Teller with less éclat at Los Alamos. Strauss's un-failing good manners made it impossible for him not to invite to his celebration the country's principal atomic adviser. Thus Strauss was the first to discover how precariously weak was the joint victory of which he had been strategist. Oppenheimer had no sense of expediency. Ghastly-simple, he would ignore person-alities and spread the desolation of his outlook wherever he was invited to go. Neither Lawrence nor Teller could counter his influ-ence. Lawrence's weakness was internal. Even while he cele-brated, he was bleeding over the difficulties of the M.T.A. Teller's weakness was external; he wanted admiration and subservience at Los Alamos but instead got antagonism.

Strauss at the time had little further power to help them. But three years later, as personal adviser to a President whom Oppen-heimer had galled with demands for impolitic statesmanship, Strauss was to have unlimited power. For Teller's separate labora-tory, there would be lavish funds and inordinate publicity. For Lawrence there would be much more. First the Atomic Energy Commission's highest accolade, the Fermi Award. Next, person-ally from Eisenhower's hands, the Sylvanus Thayer Award, a special new one devised by the Army. Last, after both this and the Fermi medal together proved inadequate to stanch Lawrence's bleeding, a post-mortem commemoration equal to Fermi's, an annual medal and award to be given by the Commission to young scientists in Lawrence's name.

All these great gifts Strauss was able to channel to his friends after he remade the Atomic Energy Commission in 1953–54. Chairman then, and with all the former commissioners replaced but Smyth, he commanded four-to-one majorities instead of losing by them as before.

To remaking the Commission he gave careful attention. Carroll Wilson, its general manager or chief executive, steadily resisted the new policies Strauss and Hickenlooper tried to force upon it. Truman had talked of making Wilson Lilienthal's successor but was dissuaded by political advisers. Denouncing the pressures that were changing the commission, Wilson resigned but retained full access to Commission secrets (Q-clearance) and much influence in the industrial atomic establishment. When Strauss came back as chairman, physicist David L. Hill told a Congressional committee, "He apparently started to work on a few of the people who had dared to disagree with him in the past. The first to receive his attention was Carroll Wilson. . . . Immediately after Strauss's appointment an unusually intensive investigation of Wilson was suddenly initiated. At the same time his employer, the Climax Uranium Company, of which Wilson was an officer, received a strong indication that Strauss felt he should have been consulted before such a man as Wilson had been hired."* For his own general manager Strauss as chairman appointed General Kenneth Nichols, long hostile to Oppenheimer.

Thus, it was as an intrusive specter that Oppenheimer presented himself at Strauss's feast of canapés at the Shoreham on January 31, 1950. Ernest K. Lindley, the newspaper columnist, noticed the contrast between Oppenheimer's face and most of the other faces there.

"You don't look jubilant," Lindley remarked to him.

Oppenheimer respected Lindley. For a minute the two stood silently looking round at the statesmen and generals whom Strauss had brought together. Urbanely muted scraps of conversation floated to them from here and there in the room.

A posh party, Oppenheimer was thinking, but somehow with the same lack he had sensed in every other government group he had seen assemble over a question of nuclear arms. He felt it urgent to define the lack, but was a long time locating the words for it. His best try he made at a seminar ten years later, after megatons of blast had become commonplace, but before gigatons: "I

---

* Senate Interstate and Foreign Commerce Committee Hearings, March to May, 1959, Nomination of Strauss to Commerce Secretary (Washington: U. S. Government Printing Office, 1959), p. 731.

The committee never asked Hill to name his source. Hill was acting as spokesman for the Federation of American Scientists (membership 2,200) to oppose Strauss's nomination.

"I did not personally order any investigation of Mr. Wilson so far as I can remember," Strauss told the Committee and added, "I am curious to know why you think the charges [that Strauss had done so] are serious." *Ibid.*, p. 826.

find myself profoundly in anguish over the fact that no ethical discussion of any weight or nobility has been addressed to the problem of atomic weapons. . . . What are we to make of a civilization which has always regarded ethics an essential part of human life, and which has always had in it an articulate, deep, fervent conviction, never perhaps held by the majority, but never absent: a dedication to Ahimsa, the Sanskrit word that means doing no harm or hurt, which you find in Jesus and simply and clearly in Socrates, what are we to think of such a civilization, which has not been able to talk about the prospect of killing almost everybody, except in prudential and game-theoretic terms?"

One reason Oppenheimer considered himself complex was his seminar-habit of complex sentences. Stripped down to its successive stimulators, this utterance seems to reveal the stream of consciousness of a very simple man: "Myself in anguish . . . they talk . . . civilization . . . Ahimsa . . . Jesus . . . they talk . . . about killing almost everybody."

At a party, not even Oppenheimer was capable of freezing a fellow guest with such an outcry. But he was thinking hard on the subject, so hard that in Lindley's opinion he had lost track of whom he was with before he finally replied to the comment on jubilance.

"This is the plague of Thebes," he said.

Long afterward he also worked out a reply to the implied question of why he did not resign and get out, of why, as Fermi would have put it, he persisted in going fishing: "Humanity must have some room to hope."

10

REVENANT

By his announcement President Truman formally initiated humanity's lemming march toward the thermonuclear bomb. All nations responded, but at first principally the keepers of the Super's secret—ourselves, the Russians, and the British.

The State Department sent Oppenheimer word that for him to resign in protest would aggravate foreign misgivings, and the government began its crash drive toward the Super. "Scientifically nonsense," Oppenheimer heard physicists call it and decided in the summer of 1950 that all technical prospects for the bomb were sour. He went to Smyth and the new Commission chairman, Gordon Dean, and asked if the time had come for his resignation, but they dissuaded him.

Mesa physicists were loyally trying to obey President Truman's directive to build the Super. The best plan they could think of was to ship the half-megaton bomb designed in Lilienthal's day to the Pacific atoll of Eniwetok and assemble the Super around it. Construction began at the start of 1951 and a test date was scheduled for mid-May. As the Super took shape, it overspread the atoll like a small factory town. Psychologically, Oppenheimer judged, the project was good for Mesa physicists, because it would give them a chance to verify their mathematical prediction that the giant fission bomb would be hot enough to kindle thermonuclear reactions in frozen tritium. But these reactions, though of scientific interest, promised no lead to the construction of a transportable bomb. In February and March of 1951, Oppenheimer and his committee repeatedly reminded the Mesa that it had not yet thought of any way to make a thermonuclear weapon.

On the Mesa, Ulam in turn reminded Teller, who viewed the coming Eniwetok test as a personal fulfillment and was in ecstasy about it. The two men angered each other until from a frozen deep inside Ulam spilled the missing and still-classified fundamental idea for a thermonuclear weapon. Teller listened to it disdainfully but after a night's sleep assembled it into ideas of his own to make this country's first important thermonuclear advance since 1942.*

In June of 1951, after the Eniwetok test proved fruitless, Oppenheimer called a conference on weapons at Princeton. Teller there described the radical new kind of bomb he had worked out from Ulam's suggestion. "But this is not the Super," demurred an Atomic Energy Commissioner, Thomas E. Murray. Murray asked if the thing Teller had in mind could be developed without a new directive from Truman. Oppenheimer lit with the flashing comprehension that once had electrified the Mesa. "That's it," he declared, meaning that Teller had moved the thermonuclear bomb out of the impossible stage. The overt international competition to build it had been going on for over a year. Oppenheimer had now no thought except of the scientific steps this country must take to win. "Sweet and lovely and beautiful," he called the Teller-Ulam invention, and said Truman would be glad to change his directive.

The Super's uselessness had been due to its gargantuan machinery for refrigerating and reconcentrating tritium. The Teller-Ulam plan was to detonate not tritium but a solid stable compound of light lithium and deuterium (Li^6H^2). Though exciting, the plan did not provide a manufacturable bomb design, but only opened an avenue for research and development.

Out of dread that some other country might have the idea and develop it first, Oppenheimer pushed it as hard as he could. Impressed, Teller asked him to come back to the Mesa and direct the

* The Mesa Documents Division later drew up a patent (Disclosure of Invention) and invited Teller to come and sign it. Teller read it, frowning. "Insufficiently accurate," he said, threw it down on the table, and stamped angrily out. The Mesa had put Ulam's name first. Ulam knew nothing of Teller's refusal; to avoid exacerbating relations between the two men, Mesa authorities decided not to tell him.

work from there. Oppenheimer investigated, found that Teller had
a foolish quarrel with Bradbury and refused. "I would have been
an ancient and not on my toes," he explained afterward. The
Mesa, Oppenheimer judged, was better off in Bradbury's hands.
Bradbury was free from the troubling realizations that made Oppenheimer feel ancient with respect to this late grim stage of
weapons research. "No, it doesn't bother me," Bradbury would
say with utterly convincing sincerity. "Someone has to do it."

The Super died too slowly. During the next few years test devices for the Teller-Ulam invention were so encumbered with an
addition of refrigerated tritium that they could not be considered
bombs. No one has ever said who caused the new development to
be impeded by the clinging vestiges of the Super. Perhaps the interests who had originally promoted the enormously expensive
Super program were unwilling to see it wholly eliminated. Perhaps the conservative military mind, knowing that tritium had
already been thermonuclearly kindled and that lithium deuteride
had not, insisted on retaining tritium as a fail-safe component.

In the summer of 1952, the Mesa at last submitted to Oppenheimer's committee a workable though long-range research program that would clearly lead to an unrefrigerated droppable H-
bomb. The part of him that was a death-dedicated technician, the
part that loved the lithium-hydride idea, could finally rest. The
other part, which had once believed nuclear physics could further
Ahimsa, took over. He announced he would not accept reappointment to his committee and on September 17, 1952, received the
following letter:

DEAR DR. OPPENHEIMER: Having in mind your strong desire, which
you expressed to me last month, to complete your service on the General
Advisory Committee to the Atomic Energy Commission with the ex-
piration of your present term, I note with a deep sense of personal regret
that this time is now upon us.

As Chairman of this important committee since its inception, you may
take great pride in the fact that you have made a lasting and immensely
valuable contribution to the national security and to atomic energy progress in this Nation. It is a source of real regret to me that the full story
of the remarkable progress that has been made in atomic energy during
these past 6 years, and in which you have played so large a role, cannot

be publicly disclosed, for it would serve as the finest possible tribute to the contribution you have made.

I shall always be personally grateful for the time and energy you have so unselfishly devoted to the work of the General Advisory Committee, for the conscientious and rewarding way in which you have brought your great talents to bear upon the scientific problems of atomic energy development, and for the notable part you have played in securing for the atomic energy program the understanding cooperation of the scientific community.

As director of the Los Alamos Scientific Laboratory during World War II, and as chairman of the General Advisory Committee for the past 6 years, you have served your country long and well, and I am gratified by the knowledge that your wise counsel will continue to be available to the Atomic Energy Commission on a consultant basis.

I wish you every future success in your important scientific endeavors.

Very sincerely yours,

HARRY TRUMAN

The Departments of Defense and State continued to consult him. In late 1952 the State Department toyed with an idea it called Operation Candor and invited him to speak for it at a secret conference. He advised three kinds of candor. First, candor to the public about the limitations of nuclear arms as a tool of diplomacy. Second, candor to our allies about how we would use nuclear arms in war. Third, candor among government leaders about the need for supplementing big bombs with an expensive fighting establishment and a system of radar and interceptor defenses.

In early 1953 the new President, Eisenhower, canceled Operation Candor. The general belief, said physicist David Hill, was that Eisenhower acted upon the counsel of his personal atomic adviser, Strauss. In July of 1953, Eisenhower appointed Strauss chairman of the Atomic Energy Commission to succeed Gordon Dean, whose term was up. In August of 1953 the Russians set off their first detectable thermonuclear explosion. Hints about it from Georgi Malenkov, the Soviet premier, were confirmed by fallout analysis. Instead of detouring through the Super, they had on this first explosion tested a true H-bomb, droppable and unrefrigerated.* Eisenhower summoned Strauss. How long, Eisenhower asked, would we take to catch up? Seven months, Strauss answered.

The only published report of this interchange is by James Shepley and Clay Blair, Jr., in a book which they prepared the following year with Strauss's help—*The Hydrogen Bomb*. The book is a polemic against Oppenheimer and the Mesa and an adoration of Teller.† The authors said Strauss meant he would have a prototype in seven months, but they failed to add that neither this prototype nor any of the others produced before 1956 would be a usable bomb.

In 1953 Oppenheimer, who as General Advisory Committee chairman had established the research program on which Strauss relied, was no longer consulted by the Commission. In the late fall he went to England and delivered a lecture series on the B.B.C. "We are today anxiously aware that the power to change is not always necessarily good," he said. "As new instruments of war, of newly massive terror, add to the ferocity and totality of warfare, we understand that it is a special mark and problem of our age that man's ever-present preoccupation with improving his lot, with alleviating hunger and poverty and exploitation, must be brought into harmony with the overriding need to limit and largely to eliminate resort to organized violence between nation and nation. The increasingly expert destruction of man's spirit by the power of police, more wicked if not more awful than the ravages of nature's own hand, is another such power, good only if never used."[1]

Reality in 1953, physicist David Inglis observed, was the rapid

* Thermonuclear explosions, being large, were easy to detect and analyze at great distances. Possible components of a test device were: fission-bomb core, lithium to be converted by heat into tritium, refrigerated tritium, deuterium, uranium-238 wrapper, and "environment" materials such as stainless steel. The presence and amount of these components could be determined with astonishing accuracy and clearly showed whether the other side had exploded a bomb or a stationary device.

† *The Hydrogen Bomb* (New York: David McKay, 1954). On Oppenheimer (p. 27): "When he was called to work on the atomic bomb in World War II, he insisted that Communists be allowed to come with him." On Teller (p. 228): "It was an accident bordering on the miraculous that the nation had working in its atomic weapons laboratory, where he could pit both his knowledge and determination against Dr. Oppenheimer, a man like Edward Teller."

horrible fruition of the bomb.[2] As a nation we escaped into dreams. "More effective, less costly security," Secretary of State John Foster Dulles explained to justify the new military policy of massive retaliation. Presumably he alluded to H-bombs which the Russians had and we did not. A Chicago firm, Henry Regnery Company, published a three-hundred-page book by Medford Evans purporting to prove the Russians did not manufacture their plutonium but got it shipped to them by Communists in the Atomic Energy Commission. Back in 1946 Oppenheimer had set Congressmen laughing at the fear security agencies were trying to promote over the atomic saboteur (see page 257). Now J. Edgar Hoover, persistent, revived the saboteur and explained how to recognize the gun-type or implosion bomb he would be equipped with. "In the first case we would look for some kind of gun-barrel," Hoover wrote to all sheriffs, village constables, and city policemen. ". . . In the second case we would look for a device using high explosive to squeeze fissionable material. . . . Pieces which might be smuggled would probably be of a size that could be carried on the person." Senator Joseph McCarthy effectively halted radar bomb-defense research by charging thirty-one scientists at the Army's Signal Corps Laboratory in Fort Monmouth, New Jersey, with espionage.

"There is the dreadful problem, obvious from the beginning, of atomic defense," observed Harold Urey. "But, in addition . . . perhaps the most remarkable and discouraging feature is the nearly hysterical popular clamor about this espionage problem. . . . Reputations of innocent people are destroyed with almost no protests from the public. Accusations are accepted as proof of guilt. The morale of a vital military laboratory is nearly destroyed, and our most mature and respected leaders of science do not protest. The Bill of Rights of our Constitution is violated in fact daily, without arousing any really effective protest from anyone."

Around the beginning of December 1953, Oppenheimer finished his English lecture series and saw some of his peers in science on the Continent, among them Niels Bohr, Pierre Auger, and Francis Perrin. They received him with a sort of compassion for his country's sick imaginings. "We looked bad," he recollected long afterward. "I was abroad then, so I know. They told me,

'America is where you're in trouble if you don't have faith in bigger and bigger bombs.' "

An American in Paris, Haakon Chevalier, had learned his travel plans through Bohr and written a request to see him. "We still have a friend of whom it has been said that he is a communist," Kitty Oppenheimer told her husband's Security Board interrogators next year, then added, "I called his wife and said we would like to see them. . . . I think I looked it [the number] up. . . . On the other hand I may have had a note from Haakon in my purse with the telephone number. . . . I think Haakon wrote us."

It was Haakon Chevalier who a dozen years before at a Berkeley dinner party had carried to Oppenheimer the engineer George Eltenton's offer to transmit secrets to the Russians. Since then Chevalier had suffered one occupational setback after another. In 1943 he took a leave from the University of California, applied for a position in the Office of War Information, and was rejected. Having obtained leave before making sure of the O.W.I. job, Chevalier could not expect to return to the university payroll until the fall of 1944. He filled up this time with translations and writing for magazines. In the fall of 1944 he took an additional half year's leave to build an extension on his house and to plan a novel that, when published in 1949, proved financially disappointing. He resumed teaching at the start of 1945, then took the winter of 1945–46 off to work as a translator at the Nuremberg war-crimes trials. Returning to the university in the fall of 1946, he resigned after being denied a promotion he thought he deserved and left the campus in December. At the end of 1950, after a long, unremunerative effort to live by writing and translating, he went to Paris and there succeeded in obtaining a job with UNESCO. Now, in 1953, he felt he was about to lose the UNESCO job and wanted Oppenheimer's help in retaining it.

His career thus somewhat resembled that of Frank Oppenheimer, who in 1949 risked a contempt citation by refusing to tell the House Un-American Activities Committee whether he personally knew Chevalier to have been a member of the Communist Party. Leading the nation in folly, California maintained a state Senate Fact-Finding Committee on Un-American Activities, which in its Sixth Report printed a résumé on Chevalier as follows:

Professor Haakon M. Chevalier was one of the most ubiquitous figures in the Communist set at Berkeley. He had been a student at the University of California, and taught romance languages there from 1927 until December, 1946.

Miles G. Humphries, who was secretary for the Communist Party of Alameda County in 1934, has testified that Rudy Lambert was even then working with Communists who were members of the faculty at the university, and he stated, "Lambert reported to me that Haakon Chevalier was, in 1934, the faculty unit organizer for the Communist Party in Alameda County, and that meetings of the faculty unit were regularly held in Chevalier's home and were frequently attended by Lambert. This University of California unit was handled with extreme secrecy, the members being unknown to the regular Party members and handled only by Lambert, who reported directly to the District Committee of the Party. * * * I drove Rudy Lambert to Chevalier's home twice to these faculty meetings, but was never allowed to go inside where the meetings were being held."

Chevalier testified before this committee in November, 1947. He admitted affiliation with Communist front organizations, including the American Committee to Save Refugees, the American Council for Soviet Relations, with two Communist-controlled publications known as *Black and White* and *Dynamo*, with the League of American Writers, the Writers' Congress of 1936, and the Joint Anti-Fascist Refugee Committee. He also admitted acquaintance with . . . [long list of souls whom the California committee considered damned].[3]

Public employment comes hard in our witch-hunt times for a man who can be thus impugned. The California Committee, the House Un-American Activities Committee, and the F.B.I. joined hands to harry him off California and Federal payrolls. Chevalier, who thought of himself as a tormented character out of Kafka, said that after 1946 he had no source of income but writing, which paid poorly. In 1947 the House Committee published, in what he considered an unfair way, his part in Eltenton's 1943 effort to get bomb data for the Russians. He complained uninhibitedly to his friends. Oppenheimer, who saw him occasionally, tried to undo the damage in 1949. He testified to the House Committee that Chevalier had not carried Eltenton's feeler to anyone but himself, had expressed outrage about it, and had behaved innocently throughout. The newspapers published this testimony. Somewhat rehabilitated, Chevalier went to Paris in 1950 and obtained his position as a UNESCO translator.

There in 1953 after Kitty's telephone call, she and Oppenheimer had dinner with him ("A fool thing for Oppenheimer to do," says an A.E.C. authority who regarded himself as neither Oppenheimer's friend nor enemy). Oppenheimer listened to Chevalier's UNESCO difficulties. "He understood that if he continued this work as an American citizen, he would be investigated, he would have to be cleared for it, and he was doubtful that he would be cleared," Oppenheimer said upon interrogation in 1954. "He did not wish to renounce his American citizenship [and become a French citizen]. He did wish to keep his job."

A few days before, Oppenheimer had lunched at the American Embassy with one of its attachés, a Harvard classmate. Oppenheimer suggested to Chevalier that he take his questions to the attaché. Later Oppenheimer learned to his unpleasant surprise that Chevalier wrote the attaché that Oppenheimer had urged him to make use of the attaché as a personal confidant-assistant. "Not anything I communicated," Oppenheimer said at his hearing when confronted with the gushy, intimacy-demanding letter.

Chevalier was a man of immense social charm and much literary ambition. First to Oppenheimer in many letters, then to the public in many articles and in his book *Oppenheimer: The Story of a Friendship*, Chevalier attributed his troubles exclusively to the report Oppenheimer made in 1943 to Security about the Eltenton incident. The report, Chevalier complained, had hounded him, plagued him, wreaked untold havoc on his life. In his writings Chevalier partly implied and partly asserted that the report was the specific cause of each of his job disappointments. The report, he further implied, was the one truly damaging thing in the F.B.I.'s Chevalier dossier. Enough other obvious material, of course, was available for the dossier to preclude him from job clearance even if he had never heard of Oppenheimer. This point he avoided noting, and in telling of each disappointment he juxtaposed exclamations about the F.B.I. dossier. *Oppenheimer: The Story of a Friendship* describes a scene at the Office of War Information in 1943, when Joseph Barnes of that agency rejected Chevalier's application. By Chevalier's account, the F.B.I., contrary to its wont, had showed Barnes its Chevalier dossier and Barnes said somberly that the allegations there were fantastic, utterly unbelievable.[4] "I have never seen an F.B.I. dossier in my life," Barnes comments. "All I told Chevalier was that we had failed to clear his name through the Civil Service Commission. I had not the slightest idea why."

As for the Chevalier-Eltenton incident, such interest as it has is in the fact that it provided the only substance to the case that the Eisenhower Administration worked up against Oppenheimer. Three accounts should be compared.

1. Chevalier's, which is unsworn, is that Eltenton talked to him in vague terms about the desirability of seeing whether so eminent and liberal a scientist as Oppenheimer might not wish to help Russia against the common enemy by supplying her with scientific data of military value. Chevalier says that he said No, he would not convey Eltenton's feeler, but that he conveyed it anyhow in a very disapproving way and that Oppenheimer was shocked. He declared that after the war he and Oppenheimer did not have the "slightest recollection" of what they had said to each other. (Haakon Chevalier, *Oppenheimer: The Story of a Friendship*, pp. 45–47.)

2. Oppenheimer's to Pash in August of 1943 (quoted on page 205 above): "An interview could be arranged with this man Eltenton, who had very good contacts with a man from the [Russian] Embassy who was attached to the consulate who was a very reliable guy—that's his story—and who had a lot of experience with microfilm work, or whatever the hell."

3. The Atomic Energy Commission's official bill of charges against Oppenheimer, as written by General Kenneth Nichols in 1954, gives the following account: "It was reported that prior to March 1, 1943, possibly three months prior, Peter Ivanov, secretary of the Soviet consulate, San Francisco, approached George Charles Eltenton for the purpose of obtaining information regarding work being done at the Radiation Laboratory for the use of Soviet scientists; that George Charles Eltenton subsequently requested Haakon Chevalier to approach you, either directly or through your brother, Frank Friedman Oppenheimer, in connection with this matter; and that Haakon Chevalier finally advised George Charles Eltenton that there was no chance whatever of obtaining the information."

Nichols added new data from some source other than Oppenheimer, who did not tell Pash and was never alleged to have told anybody what Chevalier "finally advised" Eltenton. Only Chevalier or Eltenton could have supplied this "finally advised" part. Chevalier says he did not supply it, and since he was always hoping to clear himself enough with Security to get government employment, he would almost certainly not have damned himself with the "finally."

"Finally advised" is also significant because the dating of the Eltenton-Chevalier and Chevalier-Oppenheimer exchanges is not satisfactory in the records. Chevalier wrote that he could not recall any dates, Eltenton so far as the records show was never asked, and Oppenheimer told Pash the incident had occurred "several months" before. By Nichols' official statement, Oppenheimer may have waited as many as nine months or as few as five to report the incident to Security. Groves, by Lansdale's account at the hearing (see page 207), may have waited as many as three months to report to Security the names of Chevalier and Frank Oppenheimer. General Nichols' information on what Chevalier "finally advised" Eltenton and on what the Russian Peter Ivanov said to Eltenton when getting the business started, it may be deduced, must then have come from Eltenton himself. When charging Oppenheimer with being too slow in reporting on Chevalier, General Nichols was also vague about dates. Even in 1954 the Eisenhower Administration did not wish to illuminate the dreary, complicated rat's nest that Security had been running in 1943.

Was Eltenton supplying the F.B.I. the precise dates of all these exchanges on a day-to-day basis? The likelihood is that he was doing so unwittingly as a Confidential Informant or Highly Confidential Informant. As used in assimilated F.B.I. reports, these terms denote, respectively, a person whose telephone is tapped and a person whose home or office is bugged with a listening device. "That Eltenton was an informant in this sense is not unlikely," says Lansdale. In this way the F.B.I. could have made Eltenton a sufficiently useful tool without ever formally enlisting him or gaining his consent.* "To suggest or indicate that he was a conscious

---

* To monitor its own suspects, Army Intelligence rented a house in Berkeley and set up a busy telephone switchboard. The F.B.I. was even more energetic. Eltenton and Chevalier were talkative types much easier to trap electronically than was the hard-bitten Steve Nelson, who neverthe-

informer of the Bureau," Lansdale judges, "seems to me an attempt
to read too much into the facts as known."

Groves testified at the hearings that he wanted the espionage
group to be at Shell and called Eltenton the key man in it. Chevalier pictures himself as a cat's-paw in a scheme of Groves's to
involve Oppenheimer in something discreditable that would put
Oppenheimer irrevocably under Groves's thumb (*Oppenheimer:
The Story of a Friendship*, page 177). By this conjecture Chevalier
overestimates his own significance and that of the "Chevalier incident" to Groves, who could hardly have known Chevalier would
carry the tale from Eltenton to Oppenheimer with such eager,
bustling, outraged innocence. Eltenton's basic usefulness—the reason Groves kept him at Shell—seems rather to have been the monitoring of information that traitors like Weinberg might feed to
Peter Ivanov and to keep the information misleadingly concentrated on the calutron (see page 202).

Aside from dates, the chief question about the Chevalier affair
is to how many scientists Chevalier conveyed Eltenton's feeler. Oppenheimer let his original "two or three" be turned by Pash into
three, then according to Lansdale told Groves there were only two
(himself and Frank), then, after Chevalier had begun to beg him
frantically not to ruin his life, told the House Un-American Activities Committee that there was only one, himself. On this number—one—he stood at the 1954 hearings even when Roger Robb,
the prosecutor, told him it was a felony to have lied to Pash. The
relevance to the security hearings of his having exaggerated the
number of people approached by Chevalier, if he did exaggerate
it, was never explained. No one at the hearing, not even Robb, im-
puted any other purpose to Oppenheimer than to make Security
open its eyes to a security danger. "I was an idiot," Oppenheimer
said to cut short the interminable questioning. Ostensibly he meant
for what he had said to Pash. More fundamentally he was perhaps
expressing disgust at the Oppenheimer who had imagined the
bomb could teach Ahimsa to mankind.

A blank wall: this is what Oppenheimer discovered had been
built around him when he came home in December of 1953. Its

less in a tapped telephone conversation with Weinberg gave the first clue
to the latter's treason. After the war Eltenton returned to his native England
and has since refused comment.

bricks were from F.B.I. folders, its builder was Eisenhower. A formal statement about this December action was issued three months later by the Atomic Energy Commission: "The President in consultation with the Chairman of the Commission, the Secretary of Defense, and the Director of Defense Mobilization directed that pending a security review of material in the file a blank wall be placed between Dr. Oppenheimer and any secret data."

On December 21, Strauss summoned Oppenheimer and told him of the President's order. Oppenheimer had then only a token link with the Commission—a consultant's contract which would expire in July and of which the Commission had made no use since September. This was not the link that Eisenhower meant to break with his order, but rather the link of respect and confidence that bound the scientific community to Oppenheimer. He was their rallying point against the government's sick, unreal reliance on a yet unbuilt H-bomb. To break this link, the government had to force Oppenheimer to concur in his own repudiation. Strauss gave him twenty-four hours to do so or face security proceedings. The next day Oppenheimer wrote Strauss as follows:

You put to me as a possible desirable alternative that I request termination of my contract as a consultant to the Commission, and thereby avoid an explicit consideration of the charges on which the Commission's action would otherwise be based. I was told that if I did not do this within a day, I would receive a letter notifying me of the suspension of my clearance and of the charges against me, and I was shown a draft of that letter.

I have thought most earnestly of the alternative suggested. Under the circumstances this course of action would mean that I accept and concur in the view that I am not fit to serve this government that I have now served for some twelve years. This I cannot do. . . .

On the following day, December 23, the general manager of the Commission, General Kenneth Nichols, replied:

As a result of additional investigation as to your character, associations, and loyalty, and review of your personnel security file in the light of the requirements of the Atomic Energy Act and the requirements of Executive Order 10450, there has developed considerable question whether your continued employment on Atomic Energy Commission work will endanger the common defense and security and whether such continued employment is clearly consistent with the interests of national security.

General Nichols set April 12 as the date for a personnel security board to conduct formal hearings. The board, specially created for the purpose, consisted of one public figure, Gordon Gray, until recently Secretary of the Army in the Eisenhower Administration; one financier-industrialist, Thomas A. Morgan, former chairman of the board of Sperry Corporation; and one scientist, Ward Evans, from Loyola University in Chicago.

Nichols stated two basic accusations. The first was a portmanteau accusation of Communist associations put together from what Lansdale at the hearings called a rehash of old stuff from the Manhattan District security files.[5] The second accusation was stated by Nichols as follows:

It was further reported that in the autumn of 1949, and subsequently, you strongly opposed the development of the hydrogen bomb: (1) on moral grounds, (2) by claiming that it was not feasible, (3) by claiming that there were insufficient facilities and scientific personnel to carry on the development, and (4) that it was not politically desirable. It was further reported that even after it was determined, as a matter of national policy, to proceed with development of a hydrogen bomb, you continued to oppose the project and declined to cooperate fully in the project.

On March 1, 1954, according to a statement by Strauss at a press conference, we set off a fifteen-megaton H-bomb. Since the Russians' had been only one megaton, the public assumed that ours was fifteen times better. A secret of state ruthlessly guarded was that ours was still not a usable bomb but only an experimental device. It was a psychotic secret, since there was no reason to doubt that the Russians could analyze fallout as well as we could.

When the hearings began on April 14, Nichols' second or H-bomb accusation was interminably discussed by witnesses, by the prosecutor, and by the security board chairman. Not being under contract to the Commission, Oppenheimer's lawyers were uncleared to hear its secrets. Consequently except when they were sent out of the room, all this discussion was carefully meaningless doubletalk. So were the we-pass-over-his-disturbing-behavior findings of the board majority. Evans, the dissenter, on the other hand summarized clearly: "He did not hinder the development of the

H-bomb and there is absolutely nothing in the testimony to indicate he did."

To support Nichols' primary accusation of Communist associations, Robb looked remotely back to the time before the war. Houses Oppenheimer had been in, people who had been in his house, names and places hard for him to remember—these Robb disinterred hour after hour. To more recent times he would periodically return with a form of questioning that ran: Have you since met with any of these others as you have with Chevalier, about whom you have lied to us here or to Security in 1943?

For additional contemporaneity, Robb relied on the testimony of California scientists. He summoned the five who next to Lawrence had been Oppenheimer's sharpest antagonists and asked them if they thought Oppenheimer a security risk. Teller and Alvarez, comparatively famous, and Latimer, Pitzer, and Griggs, comparatively obscure, all swore they thought so.

More than a dozen physicists, chemists, and engineers appeared for the defense.* Evans knew them all by reputation. "A considerable segment of the scientific backbone of our nation," he adjudged them as he listened, and wished they would stop mistaking him for a lawyer. Collectively they made the adverse California group look insignificant, and they were often eloquent, as for example Vannevar Bush:

I had at the time of the Los Alamos appointment complete confidence in the loyalty, judgment, and integrity of Dr. Oppenheimer. I have cer-

---

* They were: Robert F. Bacher, physicist at California Institute of Technology and former Atomic Energy Commissioner; Bethe; Bradbury; Oliver E. Buckley, former director of research, president, and chairman of the board of the Bell Telephone Laboratories; Bush; Karl T. Compton, retired president of Massachusetts Institute of Technology; Conant; Lee DuBridge, president of California Institute of Technology; James B. Fisk, vice-president of the Bell Telephone Laboratories; T. Keith Glennan, president of Case Institute of Technology; Mervin J. Kelly, president of the Bell Telephone Laboratories; Charles C. Lauritsen, physicist of California Institute of Technology and leader of the country's rocket research during World War II; Manley; Rabi; Norman F. Ramsey, Jr., Harvard physicist and consultant to the Defense Department on atomic energy; John von Neumann; Walter G. Whitman, head of the Chemical Engineering department at Massachusetts Institute of Technology; Harry A. Winne, electrical engineer, former vice-president of General Electric and subsequently chairman of the Defense Department's Technical Advisory Panel on Atomic Energy; Jerrold R. Zacharias, director of the Nuclear Science Laboratory at Massachusetts Institute of Technology.

tainly no reason to change that opinion in the meantime. I have had
plenty of reason to confirm it, for I worked with him on many occasions
on very difficult matters. . . . My faith has not in the slightest degree
been shaken by that letter of General Nichols' or anything else. . . . But
I think this board or no board should sit on a question in this country of
whether a man should serve his country or not because he expressed
strong opinions. If you want to try that case, you can try me. I have expressed strong opinions many times, and I intend to do so. They have
been unpopular opinions at times. When a man is pilloried for doing
that, this country is in a severe state.

A dismal room—so thought another of them, Rabi, on entering
and looking it over. "The board were stationed in front, then Robb,
then Oppenheimer in the back. It made me rather indignant to
see him there," he reflected afterward. Near the end of his testimony he remarked that he had consistently thought the whole
proceeding beginning with Strauss's suspension of clearance had
been most unfortunate.

"What was that?" Evans broke in.

Rabi assumed he was talking to a packed court. ("I had no idea
Evans would come out against the majority," he said afterward.
"I still can't guess how they came to pick him.") "A very unfortunate thing and should not have been done," he repeated mechanically for the record. Then something took hold of his throat.
His voice, normally a liquid baritone, choked and turned guttural
with anger. "In other words, there he was," he heard himself
testifying incoherently. "He is a consultant, and if you don't want
to consult the guy, you don't consult him, period. Why you have
to then proceed to suspend clearance and go through all this sort
of thing—he is only there when called—and that is all there is to
it. So it didn't seem to me the sort of thing that called for this kind
of proceeding at all against a man who had accomplished what
Dr. Oppenheimer had accomplished. There is a real positive record,
the way I expressed it to a friend of mine. We have an A-bomb
and a whole series of it * * * and what more do you want—mer-
maids? This is just a tremendous achievement."*

* "You can't fill in those asterisks yet," Rabi says upon inquiry. "All
you can do is footnote that Oppenheimer made further contributions in
addition to those publicly known."

After high tributes of this sort, Robb would refocus the hearings on people and places of Oppenheimer's teaching days and dwell with formless iteration on what he called Oppenheimer's lie or pack of lies about Chevalier. This was the part of the case that most newspapers, following through leaks, played up in faithful reflection of the public mood.

"As for the Board and the prosecutor," says Rabi, "I've always assumed that nobody but Strauss had anything much to do with picking them." Robb had been legal counsel of Fulton Lewis, Jr., a radio propagandist for Senator Joseph McCarthy.

"Do you think scientists are screwballs?" Evans asked Lansdale, who explains that out of disgust at the way the Board let Robb dominate them he answered yes. "But then I looked at Evans," said Lansdale. "For the first time I noticed his eyes, bright and quizzical. He gave me an impression of great shrewdness. I decided Robb was not going to have it all his own way." By dissenting, Evans cut the guilty verdict against Oppenheimer to two-to-one. "To damn him now and ruin his career and his service, I cannot do it," Evans declared.

Evans is dead. Conjecture on whether he fell short of what had been expected of him depends on the parallels one sees between the Board and the Commission. Each contained one scientist, and each registered one dissent from the verdict. Strauss himself held the whole matter to be a mere consensus of individual decisions. "Fate threw Oppenheimer and me into the situation in which I stood with the majority in a four-to-one vote that he was unfit to serve his country," Strauss explained. "It put a great strain on our relationship, but we continued on a first-name basis and I retained him in the academic position he holds by virtue of the fact I had invited him to take it."

The Institute at Princeton kept its internal quarrels strictly private. Outwardly it seemed so serene as to encourage an impression that all its trustees were of one mind and that therefore any one trustee might depose its director. Internally there was a deep division like that in the Atomic Energy Commission. In 1952 the mathematics faculty voted to invite to membership for the year 1953–54 a brilliant young mathematician, Felix Browder. His father was the notorious Communist Party leader Earl Browder, and his mother was fighting a deportation order to her native Russia. Oppenheimer stood unyielding behind the appointment and staked his directorship on the principle that here Communist associations were not a matter of concern. Insiders felt little doubt that Strauss opposed Oppenheimer and the Board's majority on the issue and would have deposed Oppenheimer as director if he could have.

Smyth had as little doubt that Strauss would have liked the Commission's verdict against Oppenheimer to be unanimous. "During the Board hearings I often wondered if I could have prevented them," says Smyth. "But I had thought the choice was between a McCarthy investigation or a Commission investigation. I had thought a Commission investigation was more likely to be orderly and objective. My dissenting opinion I think contained the implication that it wasn't as objective or orderly as it should have been. And, of course, I think the verdict was wrong."

Evans and Smyth were not the only scientists who failed to come up to the mark in the security proceedings. Bradbury, asked to recount his differences with Oppenheimer over thermonuclear policy, insisted at passionate length that these differences implied nothing malevolent or subversive, that they did not make Oppenheimer a security risk. "When I got through with that speech, there was a long silence," Bradbury recollects. "I had the feeling that I'd said something that wasn't what they expected and that they didn't quite know what to do next."

Lawrence left Berkeley to appear at the hearing, came as far east as Oak Ridge, then sent a telegram to Robb that he was turning home again because of ill health. "His illness was psychological," says a distinguished former associate. "For him to hang back and send his lieutenants in to attack was dastardly." This judgment overlooks the fact that it was Lawrence's body, not his mind, that flinched from cross-examination. "I saw him just before he left Berkeley," says Brady. "He was keyed up to testify against Oppenheimer and he meant to do it, but he was really ill. He was bleeding badly."

Physicists who regard Strauss as the master architect of the case against Oppenheimer believe that in the last analysis Strauss was sincere. In the hysteria of 1954, his anti-Communist mystique fulfilled a deep national demand. His worship of science as Lawrence and Teller embodied it and his Hamiltonian theory of government looked respectable. A more personal motivation, in the opinion of physicists who had followed the earlier isotope controversy, was vindictiveness at the laughter then raised against him.

It is possible that Strauss had another motivation more deeply personal still. "Intimate . . . most intimate," the Gray Board majority gloated in their official findings on Oppenheimer's connection with Jean Tatlock, a decade in her grave. Why they should have thus disgraced themselves and why General Nichols should have disgraced himself by putting such an irrelevant word in his bill of charges is a puzzle. Sexual fantasy is often grossest in those who rise in the world by puritanical hard work and self-denial. During the secret proceedings, the Commission's Washington scientific staff listened attentively to Lewis L. Strauss, Jr., who had touchingly fulfilled an ideal of his father's by becoming a physicist. "On the day the five Commissioners were considering their yes or no vote," says a high Government official, "young Strauss kept talking about how shocked he was at what he called Oppenheimer's infidelity with 'that woman.' He implied it was a heavy consideration against Oppenheimer. I got the feeling he was echoing a dinner conversation he'd heard the night before at his father's table."

The board majority announced they had found Oppenheimer to be a security risk. Their declaration was so befuddled with protests about their own decency and their faith in Oppenheimer's loyalty, discretion, and deep moral convictions as to obscure what they actually meant. No such obscurantism cloaks General Nichols' letter concurring with their findings and transmitting them to the Commission on June 12, 1954:

The record contains no direct evidence that Dr. Oppenheimer gave secrets to a foreign nation or that he is disloyal to the United States. However, the record does contain substantial evidence of Dr. Oppenheimer's association with Communists, Communist functionaries, and Communists who did engage in espionage. . . .

In my opinion, Dr. Oppenheimer's behavior in connection with the Chevalier incident shows he is not reliable or trustworthy; his own testimony shows that he was guilty of deliberate misrepresentations and falsifications either in his interview with Colonel Pash or in his testimony

before the Board; and such misrepresentations and falsifications constituted criminal, * * * dishonest * * * conduct. . . . *

The Board found that, following the President's decision, Dr. Oppenheimer did not show the enthusiastic support for the Super program
which might have been expected of the chief adviser to the Government
under the circumstances; that, had he given his enthusiastic support to
the program, a concerted effort would have been initiated at an earlier
date, and that, whatever the motivation, the security interests of the
United States were affected. In reviewing the record I find that the evidence establishes no sinister motives on the part of Dr. Oppenheimer in
his attitude on the hydrogen bomb, either before or after the President's
decision. I have considered the testimony and the record of this subject
only as evidence bearing upon Dr. Oppenheimer's veracity. In this context I find that such evidence is disturbing.

Smyth dissenting, the Commission concurred with Nichols. On
June 29 it passed a never-revoked judgment that Oppenheimer
was, in Strauss's words, unfit to serve his country.

When the proceedings were over, Oppenheimer commented
once more on the Chevalier affair, then held his peace about it for
the rest of his life. In July of 1954, while he was digesting his conviction and disgrace, he received another letter from Chevalier. It
contained the usual you-have-ruined-my-life-so-do-something plea.
At this time Chevalier was selling a publisher a précis of a vi-
tuperative fictional biography of Oppenheimer—*The Man Who
Would Be God*. Even an idiot, as Oppenheimer termed himself in
this matter, could sooner or later have enough of Chevalier. He
wrote Chevalier for the last time. His letter, unlike those from
Chevalier to him, was intended only for the addressee and not for
the reading public. Chevalier's anguished printed reflections upon
the letter, however, tell a good deal about its contents. An easy in-
ference is that Oppenheimer wrote that the relation of anything he
had ever done or said to Chevalier's sufferings was not clear.

Clamorous but insignificant, Chevalier's writings, like the hearings themselves, show that Oppenheimer's life can stand inspection
down to the last senseless detail. One must, finally, put all this
damned nonsense, to use Oppenheimer's term for the hearings, into

* The asterisks here seem not an ellipsis but a stylistic device of General
Nichols' for emphasis.

its proper, dismally small perspective in order to gain any comprehension of Oppenheimer as a scientist, American, or human being.

Thus ended Oppenheimer's strong, often successful seven-year endeavor to turn the country to sane nuclear courses. Spent behind his blank wall, he saw Lawrence dominant.

Lawrence's Fermi award and Sylvanus Thayer award together amounted to the greatest recognition ever given to a scientist by the government. Lawrence dictated appointments at will to the governmental scientific establishment maintained by the Defense Department and the Atomic Energy Commission. Congress gave him unlimited money for his programs and for his laboratory, including the laboratory branch he provided for Teller at Livermore. But the M.T.A. and the Super, the most gigantic of the programs to which he was committed, defied all his energy to make them go. The strain and the failure coincided with worsened bleeding from his ulcerative colitis. During the mid-Fifties the driving force drained from him. By 1956 he too was spent. No longer imperious, he became the philosophical master tinkerer again who had long ago inspired graduate students at Berkeley. "Why, fellows, you don't want a big machine," he told a group of them who had taken root at the University of Illinois and were redesigning the cyclotron there. "There's too much emphasis these days on sheer size for its own sake. Build something small and precisely suited to the research information you want from it."

For a decade Berkeley had built big accelerators of many kinds for the Atomic Energy Commission. The Brookhaven Laboratory, where Stanley Livingston was a chief designer, had consistently run second in competition for government funds. By 1956 Lawrence no longer cared much about the competition, but his laboratory was still fiercely driven on by a Lawrence of the past. "I want to get out of the machine-design field," said the head of a design group at Berkeley. "We are hag-ridden by a superstition that everything our lab does must be the biggest and the best."

During this decade Livingston went often to Berkeley to compare new ideas and to keep the programs of the two laboratories complementary. Cooksey watched anxiously. "I think Cooksey felt I was a threat to Lawrence's reputation," Livingston says. At Berkeley the two pioneers of American big-machine physics found few chances to talk together except under Cooksey's eye.

Livingston felt that Cooksey was creating and guarding a Lawrence legend that did Lawrence no service. "There was greatness in the man, but it wasn't the kind of greatness Cooksey wanted for him," Livingston reflects. "On my trips to Berkeley we never really got together. But in 1956 Lawrence went to an international physics convention in Switzerland, and I was there too. I had a beer with him by Lake Geneva and we reminisced about the early days. Neither of us could forget the violent conflicts behind us, but we sat and looked at the water and talked quietly, and we remembered our friendship. I was glad. It was my last talk with Lawrence."

National hysteria about security and the bomb, though never disappearing, grew quieter. Democrats regained control of Congress and began saying fallout was a needless increment to human ills. For a long time the Administration protested there was a difference between clean American and dirty Russian bombs, then in early 1958 acknowledged the need for a test ban. To pave the way for a meeting of statesmen with powers to sign a tentative treaty, it was announced that American, Russian, British, and French scientists would confer at Geneva on whether detection measures were technically reliable. Two American scientific representatives were appointed—James Fisk and Robert Bacher—and they in turn selected a panel of specialist-consultants headed by Bethe. All three had spoken for Oppenheimer at the 1954 hearings.

Preparations for the technical conference went briskly forward in the spring of 1958. Strauss, whom proliferating enemies in Congress had weakened politically, looked on with hostility and suspicion. "I was very much concerned about the negotiations with the Russians," he explained afterward. "I didn't trust certain of the advisers. I had enough influence left to have Ernest appointed [third scientific representative]. He was not well, but I prevailed on him to go. I believe if he had had his health and strength he would have come back and said, 'This thing is just a fraud.' "

An even older friend of Lawrence's, physicist James Brady, at this time had an impression of a Lawrence much farther removed from the issues on which physicists had been so long and so fiercely divided. "I saw him at Berkeley just the day before he took off for

Geneva," Brady recalls. "I think the last thing he did at Berkeley was something for me. My daughter wanted to do summer work at the Radiation Laboratory. 'Get a job for Mary Anne,' he said to Cooksey. That was like him, never to overlook a chance to do a kindness.

" 'You're going to have a very tough time with those Russians,' I told him.

"He seemed very tired but hopeful, not cynical or bitter. 'No, I don't think so,' he said. 'Not at all. We've got a good chairman in Jim Fisk, we've made sound technical studies, and I don't think we'll have any trouble with the Russians.' "

At Geneva, Lawrence supported Fisk and Bacher. But his bleeding rapidly increased and he grew more silent each day. After two weeks he left the conference, came home and died a month later on August 27. "He spent his last resources at Geneva," said Strauss. "The cost was his life. He wouldn't have refrained if he had known it would be. That was his way."

President Eisenhower, in response to a proposal initiated by Strauss, wrote to the Atomic Energy Commission in September:

I strongly agree that the memory of Dr. Lawrence, as well as his great contributions, should be commemorated. To that end, I request that you initiate action to establish a memorial award bearing his name, for especially meritorious contributions in the broad field of atomic endeavor.

Such an award would seem to me to be the most fitting both as a recognition of what he has given to our country and to mankind, and as a means of helping to carry forward his work through inspiring others to dedicate their lives and talents to scientific effort.

The Lawrence award, the Atomic Energy Commission announced in December, would differ from the Fermi award in being specially intended for young scientists and would

consist of a medal, a citation and up to $25,000. It will be made to not more than five recipients in any one year in the amount of not less than $5,000 each, but not necessarily every year, and will be presented in the spring of the year, to men or women who are not more than 45 years of age. . . .

In 1963 a fresh new wind began to blow through the recesses of the Atomic Energy Commission. On the morning of November 22, the White House announced that President Kennedy would personally present Oppenheimer the Fermi award in a public ceremony the following month. The science community took this to be Kennedy's first step in a plan to quash the Commission's 1954 verdict and clear Oppenheimer completely. On the afternoon of November 22, Kennedy was assassinated.

Political advisers warned President Johnson that it might be safer to have the award presented by a committee. But he said he would do it himself because, as he explained to Oppenheimer at the White House ceremony, "One of President Kennedy's most important acts was to sign the award."

The ceremony took place on December 2 in the Cabinet Room, which was packed with dignitaries and reporters. When Johnson handed him the Fermi citation, Oppenheimer stood looking at it for a long moment of reflective silence. "In his later years, Jefferson often wrote of 'the brotherly spirit of science which unites into a family all its votaries . . . ,' " Oppenheimer said in a rapid low personal voice to Johnson, seeming to forget there was anyone else in the room. "We have not, I know, always given evidence of that brotherly spirit of science. This . . . is in part because . . . we are engaged in this great enterprise of our time, testing whether men can . . . live without war as the great arbiter of history . . . I think it is just possible, Mr. President, that it has taken some charity and some courage for you to make this award today. These words I wrote down almost a fortnight ago. In a somber time I gratefully and gladly speak them to you."

Senator Hickenlooper called the award ceremony shocking and revolting. Republicans of the Joint Committee on Atomic Energy boycotted it in a body.

The Commission had offered Oppenheimer a new hearing a year before, but Oppenheimer had felt no impulse to go through that sort of nonsense again. The Commission, even in the wake of the Fermi award, would not simply quash the 1954 verdict. ("I believe this would have been legally impossible, but I'm not sure," says an ex-Commissioner.) The government took no further steps to clear his name, and on February 18, 1967, he died an official security risk.

In their last years Lawrence and Oppenheimer alike removed

themselves from the deep quarrels that still divide both scientists and statesmen. But the passions of their lives had been the passions of the science of their time. "You cannot separate their scientific side from their human side," Rabi says. "What paints the one paints the other." Their contributions to physics as experimentalist and theoretician, body and mind, seem accurately delineated in their Fermi award citations:

. . . to Ernest O. Lawrence for his invention and development of the cyclotron and for his many other contributions in nuclear physics and atomic energy.

. . . to J. Robert Oppenheimer for his contributions to theoretical physics as a teacher and originator of ideas and for leadership of the atomic energy program during critical years.

"How can I tell you whether I expect to be happy?" Oppenheimer said in his late years at Princeton. "There's a sort of joy that's hard to be intelligible about in watching discoveries in physics—an example for me is the work Yang and Lee have done on Parity. I think this may be enough—watching and sharing a little —to entitle a man to be called happy. I don't expect anything else, except I'd like to be proved wrong about what will come of this atomic business. I was quite wrong in believing it would cost us our freedom. Our lives are fairly good, fairly peaceful. We seem to go on almost untouched except as the arms race gives employment to many. Overt hysteria has declined since the fifties. Perhaps people will have time to think. No one should say there is no hope."

NOTES

CHAPTER 4

1. *In the Matter of J. Robert Oppenheimer, Transcript of Hearings* (Washington: Government Printing Office, 1954), pp. 9, 49, 101–102, 115, 117, 186–187, 873.

CHAPTER 5

1. Pearl Buck, "End of the World? One Nobel Prize Winner Interviews Another," *The American Weekly*, March 8, 1959, p. 11.

CHAPTER 6

1. The quote is from General Kenneth Nichols' letter to Oppenheimer embodying the Atomic Energy Commission's official bill of charges against him (p. 343).
2. *Oppenheimer Transcript*, pp. 131, 882, 883.
3. *Ibid.*, pp. 660–664, 668–672.
4. Their names were eventually exposed in HUAC *Hearings Regarding Communist Infiltration of Radiation Laboratory and Atomic Bomb Project at the University of California* (Washington: Government Printing Office, 1949), Vols. I, II.
5. Arthur H. Compton, *Atomic Quest* (New York: Oxford University Press, 1956), p. 130.

CHAPTER 7

1. *Oppenheimer Transcript*, p. 275.
2. *Ibid.*, p. 961.

3. Friedman's refusal, on grounds of self-incrimination, to say whether he had been a Communist was not followed by a court indictment. Bohm and Lomanitz were indicted for contempt of Congress in December of 1950. Upholding their right against self-incrimination, a federal court acquitted them in 1951. Weinberg on May 11, 1951, was held in contempt by the Federal District Court in Washington for refusing to answer questions put to him by a federal grand jury investigating espionage activities. On May 17 the court upheld his right against self-incrimination and dismissed the contempt charges against him. In 1952 Weinberg was indicted for perjury to HUAC about Communist Party membership. He was tried in Washington Federal District Court. Judge Alexander Holtzoff, who presided, remarked on February 27, 1953, that unless HUAC released secret records, he might have to acquit Weinberg. On March 5 the jury acquitted Weinberg. Holtzoff disagreed, telling the jury, "I disapprove of your verdict." Weinberg commented that he was happy to prove his innocence. Apparently he alluded to the perjury charge. Search of available published materials reveals no subsequent denial of other allegations that had been made against him, including Lansdale's: "We proved to our satisfaction that he gave information to Steve Nelson for money." (*Oppenheimer Transcript*, p. 268)

4. *Oppenheimer Transcript*, pp. 118, 128, 852, 875-876, 880, 882-883.

5. *Ibid.*, p. 846. The most serious allegations about Eltenton were those made by Groves (p. 207 of this narrative) and by General Nichols (p. 340 of this narrative) and by Lansdale, as follows: "Eltenton was well known to us as a Communist, active in the Communist apparatus on the west coast and a member of this laboratory group, this F. A. E. C. T." (Lansdale, *Oppenheimer Transcript*, p. 263) Search of published material reveals no testimony, denial, or other comment by Eltenton on these allegations.

CHAPTER 9

1. *Oppenheimer Transcript*, p. 665.
2. Senate Interstate and Foreign Commerce Committee Hearings, March to May, 1959, Nomination of Strauss to Commerce Secretary (U.S. Government Printing Office, 1959), pp. 413–414, 646–647.

CHAPTER 10

1. J. Robert Oppenheimer, *Science and the Common Understanding* (New York: Simon and Schuster, 1954), p. 97.

2. *Bulletin of Atomic Scientists*, February 1954, p. 41.

3. *Sixth Report, Un-American Activities in California* (Sacramento, 1951), p. 235. Miles G. Humphries is mentioned at length in the First Report but not in the Second through the Fifth, and only on this page of the Sixth. He therefore probably made his contribution about Chevalier to hearings held in 1943.

4. Haakon Chevalier, *Oppenheimer: The Story of a Friendship* (New York: George Braziller, 1966), p. 49.

5. *Oppenheimer Transcript*, p. 270.

GLOSSARY

Alpha radiation. A stream of positively charged particles each consisting of two protons and two neutrons and each therefore constituting the nucleus of a helium atom. Emission by radioactive elements of alpha radiation is a sign of their radioactivity or nuclear disintegration.

Atomic reactor. When fissionable materials, usually uranium but sometimes thorium or artificially produced plutonium, are assembled in sufficient quantity, their unstable fissioning atoms emit enough neutrons to sustain a chain reaction from other atoms in the assembly. The first successful reactor, Fermi's pile of uranium slugs and graphite blocks at the Metallurgical Laboratory (see page 125), achieved a sustained reaction in December of 1942. The graphite was used to slow or moderate the speed of neutrons to increase the likelihood of their being captured by uranium-235 atoms and lead to more fission and thus a chain reaction. Heavy water was used as a moderator in other reactors like the Water Boiler (see page 226). Reactors in which the fissionable material is a mixture of the uranium isotopes 235 and 238 transmute part of the uranium 238 into plutonium and were used to produce plutonium during World War II. Bombs were sometimes called fast-fission reactors. The uranium 235, or plutonium, was very pure and no moderator was used to slow the neutrons. Design of bombs had to be based on calculations of the fissions caused by neutrons moving at a range of speeds that could be ignored by designers of moderated reactors.

Beta radiation. A stream of electrons moving at about the speed of light with energies up to several million electron volts. Beta radiation is created naturally in some decaying radioactive elements by a complex process worked out by Fermi in his Theory of Beta Decay.

Chain reaction. Fission or splitting of the uranium or plutonium nucleus is caused by the capture, by the nucleus, of a neutron. When each fission releases more than one neutron that is subsequently captured by other nuclei, the number of fissions will multiply and the result will be a self-sustaining chain reaction.

Deuterium, heavy water, and tritium. Most hydrogen atoms have a nucleus consisting of one proton. Every five-thousandth hydrogen atom, however, has both a proton and a neutron in its nucleus and is called a deuterium atom. Deuterium is a stable isotope of hydrogen. Heavy water is water in which most or all of the hydrogen is deuterium. Tritium, which has two neutrons, is an unstable isotope of hydrogen that emits beta radiation and has a half-life of twelve years.

Dirac Theory. One of the three or four major foundations of quantum mechanics, this theory furnished an explanation of electron spin and magnetic moment, predicted the existence of the positron, established the creation and annihilation of matter in the form of positive and negative electron pairs, and defined empty space as negative electrons with imaginary velocity—that is, with negative kinetic energy.

Electrons. Elementary particles that constitute the periphery of the atom outside the nucleus and have a negative charge to match the nucleus' positive charge. Free electrons moving through a wire constitute an electric current.

Electron-volt. A unit of energy equal to the amount of energy acquired by an electron when it falls through a potential difference of 1 volt. An electron volt is equal to 1.6×10^{-12} erg. To lift a gram one centimeter against earth's gravity takes about 980 ergs of energy.

Fission. A naturally occurring disintegration of an atomic nucleus in which the nucleus breaks into two main fragments and emits neutrons that cause fission of additional atoms.

Fissionable material, manufacture processes for. Fissionable material for bombs was manufactured during World War II by four processes. One process produced plutonium in reactor piles (see page 108). The other three processes separated uranium 235 from ordinary uranium; they were the calutron or electromagnetic process (pages 116-117), the gas-diffusion process (pages 109-110), and the thermal-diffusion, or steamplant, process (pages 209-210). Two other separation processes, abandoned after a considerable preliminary effort, were the centrifuge process (pages 110-111; page 139) and the isotron process (pages 137-138).

*Focusing in cyclotrons.** *Electric focusing.* "The gap between Dee faces

* From *Particle Accelerators* by M. Stanley Livingston and John P. Blewett (New York; McGraw-Hill, 1962). Copyright 1962 by McGraw-Hill Book Company, Inc. Used by permission of McGraw-Hill Book Company.

can be considered a cylindrical lens. In the diagram below a schematic cross section of the Dee gap is shown, indicating the lines of electric field and the direction of forces on a particle crossing the gap. We note that there are convergent forces on entering the gap and divergent forces on leaving.

"The first effect noted is a net displacement toward the median plane. This is equivalent to the 'thick-lens' displacement of off-axis rays in an optical lens system. As for the optical case, it can be shown to be proportional to the displacement Z from the median plane. . . . It will be most significant for the first few gap crossings when ions are at low energy. . . .

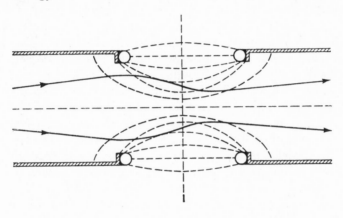

Cross section of the electric-field pattern between the Dees of a cyclotron. A typical ion path (exaggerated) illustrates the mechanism of electric focusing.

"Two mechanisms in electric focusing can be isolated and discussed. First, since the ion is being accelerated to higher velocity during its passage across the gap, the time spent in the convergent field is longer than that spent in the divergent field. This 'energy change' effect is most pronounced in early accelerations when ion energy is low. . . .

"Second, particles crossing the gap will experience an electric field which changes during the time of transit. In that portion of the rf cycle when the rf field is decreasing in magnitude, the convergent force on entering the gap will be larger in magnitude than the divergent force on leaving, so the net result is convergence. . . .

"The net result of these two major effects is an effective focusing only during early stages of acceleration. . . . Electric focusing is strong enough to be significant only in the first few accelerations." (Livingston and Blewett, *Particle Accelerators*, pp. 148–150).

*Magnetic focusing.** "The feature which makes the method of multiple acceleration practical is the focusing resulting from the shape of the magnetic field. Ions making 100 or more revolutions in a cyclotron traverse a path hundreds of meters in total length. In a uniform magnetic field, in which field lines are strictly parallel, there would be no vertical deflections and no focusing. Ions traveling at a small angle to the median plane would follow a helical path and would strike against the top or bottom surfaces of the Dees; the probability of an ion reaching the collector at the periphery would be vanishingly small.

"Magnetic focusing results from a small decrease in magnetic field with increasing radius, so that lines of magnetic flux are concave inward. This shape of field exists naturally near the periphery of cylindrical poles as a result of 'fringing.' In the central region an adequately decreasing field can be obtained by shaping the pole faces so that the gap widens slightly with increasing radius, or the effective gap length in the center can be shortened by inserting disk-shaped iron shims in gaps between the vacuum chamber and the magnet poles. At any point off the median plane in such a concave field the field has a radial as well as an axial component (see diagram below). Deviant particles traversing such a field experience restoring forces due to the radial field component tending to return them to the median plane. The direction of forces acting on orbiting particles is also illustrated in the figure below. The magnitude of the radial component of magnetic field, and thus of the restoring force, is proportional to the displacement from the equilibrium orbit."

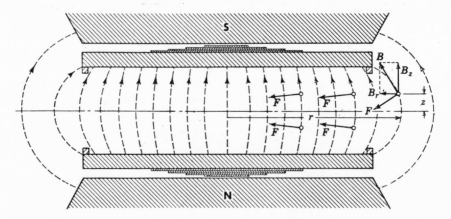

Radially decreasing magnetic field between poles of a cyclotron magnet, showing shims for field correction.

* [*Ibid.*, pp. 143–144]

Gamma rays. Extreme high-energy nonmaterial radiation unlike other radiations in that it comes from the nucleus of the atom and not from the peripheral electrons that are the source of light rays and X rays.

Ions. Atoms that have taken on an electric charge showing that the negative charge of their electron periphery no longer matches the positive charge of their nuclei. Positively charged ions are atomic nuclei with one or more of their peripheral electrons stripped off.

Isotopes. All the atoms of a chemical element have the same number of protons in their nuclei but may not have the same number of neutrons. If they do not, they are different isotopes of the element. Some isotopes are unstable; that is, they decay into other elements over a period of time ranging from a fraction of a second to millions of years. In decaying they emit alpha or beta radiation and are called radioactive.

Neutrons. Elementary particles that, unlike protons and electrons, have no electric charge and can move freely through matter, whose bulk or volume is produced largely by electrons, until stopped by collision with an atomic nucleus. The mass number of an element is the number of protons and neutrons in its atomic nucleus added together. Elements that fission emit neutrons from their disintegrating nuclei.

Nucleus. This is the central part of the atom. Its mass consists of protons, and, except for hydrogen, of neutrons. In the atom the nucleus carries a positive charge equal to the negative charge in its attendant periphery of electrons.

Proton. An elementary particle with a positive charge matching the negative charge of an electron, but with a mass over a thousand times greater. The number of protons in the nucleus of an atom determines the chemical identity or atomic number of the atom. A hydrogen atom is an atom with one proton in its nucleus, helium an atom with two protons, lithium an atom with three protons and so on through the periodic table of increasing atomic numbers.

Quantum mechanics. The twentieth century's most fundamental new comprehension of nature began with the concept of the quantum, the discrete unit of energy or momentum of a subatomic particle, and the principle of uncertainty. To define and measure the interaction of these units is the work of quantum mechanics. All theoretical physicists of the century, including Einstein, have dedicated themselves to this work. It has revolutionized man's perception of the physical world and of his subjective mental processes.

Radioactivity, artificial. Joliot's initial discovery (see page 60) within a few years led to the creation of radioactive isotopes of all elements. Other biological uses besides those described in Chapter 3 have been the tracing of metabolic processes by which organisms ingest food and of photosynthesis in plants. A chief use in chemistry has been a study of chemical bonds, valences, and exchange reactions. Industry uses artificial radioisotopes to follow products and impurities through production processes, to test for leaks, to measure diffusion and distillation, and in metallurgy.

X rays. Waves of energy like gamma rays and light rays. Compared with light, they are of extreme high energy, though less than that of gamma rays. Soft X rays have relatively low energy and long wave length; hard X rays have relatively high energy and short wave length.

BIBLIOGRAPHY

Alsop, Joseph and Stewart, *We Accuse: The Story of the Miscarriage of American Justice in the Case of J. Robert Oppenheimer*, New York: Simon and Schuster, 1954.

Alsop, Stewart, and Lapp, Ralph E., "The Strange Death of Louis Slotin" in *Man against Nature*, ed. by Charles Neider, New York: Harper & Brothers, 1954.

Barrett, Edward L., Jr., *The Tenney Committee*, Ithaca, N.Y.: Cornell University Press, 1951.

Birge, Raymond T., "Physics and Physicists of the Past Fifty Years," *Physics Today*, May, 1956, pp. 20–28.

Boorse, Henry A., and Motz, Lloyd, *The World of the Atom*, two volumes, New York: Basic Books, 1966.

Brode, Bernice, *Tales of Los Alamos*, published in the bi-weekly *LASL Community News*, Los Alamos, New Mexico, June 2, 1960, through September 22, 1960.

Bulletin of the Atomic Scientists, December, 1945, to present. Published monthly except during the summer, the basic information source on the views and activities of the science community with respect to questions concerning atomic energy. It is astonishingly readable.

Byrnes, James F., *All in One Lifetime*, New York: Harper & Brothers, 1958.

Cahn, Robert, "Behind the First A-Bomb," *Saturday Evening Post*, July 16, 1960, pp. 16–17, 72–75.

California, State of, Joint Fact-Finding Committee on Un-American Activities of the California Legislature (1943 through 1949) and Senate Fact-Finding Committee (1951), Sacramento. *First Report*, 1943; *Second Report*, 1945; *Third Report*, 1947; *Fourth Report*,

1948; *Fifth Report*, 1949; *Sixth Report*, 1951. This is the egregious "Tenney Committee."

Cameron, Frank, *Cottrell: Samaritan of Science*, Garden City, N. Y.: Doubleday, 1952. A brilliant and entertaining biography.

Carlson, J. F., and Oppenheimer, J. R., "Multiplicative Showers," *Physical Review*, February 15, 1937 (Vol. 51), pp. 220–231.

Chadwick, James, "The Cyclotron and Its Applications," *Nature*, October 8, 1938, pp. 630–634.

Clark, Ronald W., *The Birth of the Bomb*, New York: Horizon Press, 1961.

Compton, Arthur H., *Atomic Quest*, New York: Oxford University Press, 1956.

Feinberg, J. G., *The Atom Story*, London: A. Wingate, 1952.

Feis, Herbert, *Japan Subdued: The Atomic Bomb and the End of the War in Europe*, Princeton, N. J.: Princeton University Press, 1961.

Fermi, Enrico, "Genesis of the Nuclear Energy Project," *Physics Today*, November, 1955, pp. 12–16.

Fermi, Laura, *Atoms in the Family*, Chicago: University of Chicago Press, 1954.

————, *Atoms for the World*, Chicago: University of Chicago Press, 1957.

Goldwin, Robert A., editor, *The Case of the Impenetrable Cloud*, Chicago: American Foundation for Political Education, 1957. A collection of documents on the decision to use the atomic bomb against Japan.

Goudsmit, Samuel, *Alsos*, New York: Henry Schuman, 1947.

Groueff, Stephane, *Manhattan Project: The Untold Story of the Making of the Atomic Bomb*, Boston: Little, Brown, 1967.

Groves, Leslie R., "Development of the Atomic Bomb," *Military Engineer*, June 1946 (Vol. 38), pp. 233–243.

————, *Now It Can Be Told*, New York: Harper & Brothers, 1962.

Hawley, Gessner G., and Leifsen, Sigmund F., *Atomic Energy in War and Peace*, New York: Reinhold, 1945.

Hewlett, Richard G., and Anderson, Oscar, Jr., *The New World, a History of the Atomic Energy Commission, Volume I: 1939–1946*, University Park, Penn.: Pennsylvania State University Press, 1962.

Institut Solvay. Structure et propriétés des noyaux atomiques. Rapports et discussions du septième conseil de physique tenu à Bruxelles du 22 au 29 octobre, 1933, Paris: Gauthier-Villars, 1934.

Irving, David, *The German Atomic Bomb*, New York: Simon and Schuster, 1968.

Jaffe, Bernard, *Men of Science in America,* New York: Simon and Schuster, 1944.

Jungk, Robert, *Brighter than a Thousand Suns,* New York: Grove Press, 1958.

Knebel, Fletcher, and Bailey, Charles W., *No High Ground,* New York: Harper & Brothers, 1961.

————, "Secret: The Fight over the A-Bomb," *Look,* August 13, 1963, pp. 19–23.

Lamont, Lansing, *Day of Trinity,* New York: Atheneum, 1965.

Land, Barbara, "Dr. Paul C. Aebersold, Mister Isotope," *Science World,* May 4, 1960, pp. 1–2.

Lang, Daniel, *Early Tales of the Atomic Age,* New York: Doubleday, 1959.

————, *From Hiroshima to the Moon,* New York: Simon and Schuster, 1959.

————, *The Man in the Thick Lead Suit,* New York: Oxford University Press, 1954.

Laurence, William L., *Dawn over Zero: The Story of the Atomic Bomb,* New York: Alfred A. Knopf, 1947.

————, *The Hell Bomb,* New York: Alfred A. Knopf, 1951.

————, *Men and Atoms,* New York: Simon and Schuster, 1959.

Lawrence, Ernest O., "The Biological Effects of Neutron Rays" (lecture), *Radiology,* September, 1937, pp. 313–322.

————, "The Growth of the Physics Department" (lecture), *Symposium on the Physical and Earth Sciences,* Berkeley, 1958.

————, "High Current Accelerators" (lecture), *Science,* December 9, 1955, pp. 1127–1132.

————, "Nuclear Physics and Biology" (lecture), *Rutgers University, Publications of the 175th Anniversary Celebration, Number 4,* New Brunswick, 1942.

Lawrence, Ernest O., and Edlefsen, N. E., "On the Production of High Speed Protons" (talk by Lawrence), *Science,* October 10, 1930, pp. 376–377.

Lawrence, Ernest O., and Livingston, M. Stanley, "A Method for Producing High Speed Hydrogen Ions without the Use of High Velocities," *Physical Review,* June 15, 1931 (Vol. 37), p. 1707.

————, "The Production of High Speed Light Ions without the Use of High Voltages," *Physical Review,* April 1, 1932 (Vol. 40), pp. 19–35.

————, "The Production of High Speed Protons without the Use of High Voltages" (letter dated July 20, 1931), *Physical Review,* August 15, 1931 (Vol. 38), p. 834.

Livingston, M. Stanley, "The Production of High Velocity Hydrogen Ions without the Use of High Voltages," thesis submitted in partial satisfaction of the Ph.D. requirements, University of California, May, 1931. (Ms. in University of California Library.)

Livingston, M. Stanley, and Blewett, John P., *Particle Accelerators*, New York: McGraw-Hill Book Co., 1962.

Livingston, M. Stanley, and McMillan, Edwin M., "History of the Cyclotron," *Physics Today*, October, 1955, pp. 18–34.

Mann, Wilfrid B., *The Cyclotron*, New York: Chemical Publishing Company, 1940.

———, "Recent Developments in Cyclotron Technique," *Nature*, April 8, 1939, pp. 583–585.

Masters, Dexter, and Way, Katharine, editors, *One World or None*, New York: McGraw-Hill Whittlesey House, 1946.

McClelland, Charles A., *Nuclear Weapons, Missiles, and Future War*, San Francisco: Chandler Publishing, 1960.

McMillan, Edwin M., *The Transuranium Elements: Early History*, Les Prix Nobel, Stockholm: Kungl. Boktryckiert P. A. Norstedt & Söner, 1952.

Millikan, Robert A., *Autobiography*, New York: Prentice-Hall, 1950.

Oppenheimer, J. Robert, *The Flying Trapeze: Three Crises for Physicists*, London: Oxford University Press, 1964.

———, *The Open Mind*, New York: Simon and Schuster, 1955.

———, *Physics in the Contemporary World*, Cambridge, Mass.: Harvard University Press, 1947.

———, *Science and the Common Understanding*, New York: Simon and Schuster, 1954.

Oppenheimer, J. Robert, and Snyder, H., "Continued Gravitational Contraction," *Physical Review*, September 1, 1939 (Vol. 56), pp. 455–459.

Rouzé, Michel, *Robert Oppenheimer, the Man and His Theories*, New York: Fawcett Publications, 1965.

Segré, Emilio, Biographical Introduction to *Collected Papers of Enrico Fermi*, Chicago: University of Chicago Press, 1960.

Shepley, James R., and Blair, Clay, Jr., *The Hydrogen Bomb*, New York: David McKay, 1954.

Sloan, David H., "A Radiofrequency High-Voltage Generator," *Physical Review*, January 1, 1935, pp. 62–71.

Smyth, Henry D., *Atomic Energy for Military Purposes, the Official Report on the Development of the Atomic Bomb under the Auspices of the United States Government*, Princeton, N. J.: Princeton University Press, 1945.

Stewart, George R., *The Year of the Oath: The Fight for Academic Freedom at the University of California*, Garden City, N. Y.: Doubleday, 1950.

Strauss, Lewis L., *Men and Decisions*, Garden City, N. Y.: Doubleday, 1962.

Teller, Edward, and Latter, Albert L., *Our Nuclear Future*, New York: Criterion Books, 1958.

U. S. Atomic Energy Commission publications.

Allardice, Corbin, and Trapnell, Edward R., *The First Pile*, A.E.C. Report TID-292, March, 1955.

Hawkins, David; Truslow, Edith C.; and Smith, Ralph Carlisle, *Manhattan District History, Project Y, The Los Alamos Project*, two volumes, 1961.

In the Matter of J. Robert Oppenheimer, Transcript of Hearings before Personnel Security Board, 1954.

In the Matter of J. Robert Oppenheimer, Text of Principal Documents and Letters of Personnel Security Board, General Manager and Commissioners, 1954.

In the Matter of J. Robert Oppenheimer, Statement of the Atomic Energy Commission, June 12, 1954, 1954.

Living in Los Alamos, informational brochure including an 18-page "Short History" of the community, Los Alamos, N. M., 1960.

Los Alamos Scientific Laboratory, informational brochure including a 17-page "Brief History" of the laboratory, Los Alamos, 1960.

Semiannual Reports of the Atomic Energy Commission, January, 1947, through July, 1956.

U. S. Congressional Committees—Hearings, Reports, and Committee prints.

Disarmament Subcommittee of Senate Foreign Relations Committee, *Hearings on Disarmament and Foreign Policy*, 85th Cong., 2nd Ses., January 28 to February 2, 1958.

House Committee on Un-American Activities, 81st Cong., 1st Ses. *Hearings Regarding Clarence Hiskey Including Testimony of Paul Crouch*, May 24, 1949.

Hearings Regarding Communist Infiltration of Radiation Laboratory and Atomic Bomb Project at the University of California, Berkeley, April 22, 1949, through September 27, 1949. Two volumes.

Hearings Regarding Steve Nelson, June 8, 1949.

Testimony of Paul Crouch, May 6, 1949.

Testimony of James Sterling Murray and Edward Tiers Manning, August 14 through October 5, 1949.

Joint Committee on Atomic Energy.

Atomic Energy Fellowship Program, *Hearings before the Joint Committee*, May 16 through May 23, 1949.

Biological and Environmental Effects of Nuclear War, *Hearings before the Special Subcommittee on Radiation*, 86th Cong., 1st Ses., June 22 through June 26, 1959.

Confirmation of Atomic Energy Commissioners and General Manager, *Hearings before Senate Section of the Joint Committee*, 80th Cong., 1st Ses., January 27 through March 4, 1947.

Confirmation of A.E.C. Commissioners, *Hearings*, March 29, 1950, June 29, 1950, August 16, 1950, January 29, 1952.

Confirmation of A.E.C. Commissioners, June 1953 to March 1955, *Hearings before the Senate Section of the Joint Committee*, 84th Cong., 1st Ses., June 27, 1953, through March 8, 1955.

Fallout from Nuclear Weapon Tests, *Hearings before the Special Subcommittee on Radiation*, 86th Cong., 1st Ses., May 5 through May 8, 1959. Three volumes.

The Hydrogen Bomb and International Control: Technical and Background Information, Joint Committee Print, 1950.

Investigation into the U. S. Atomic Energy Project, *Hearings before the Joint Committee*, 24 parts, May 26 through July 11, 1949.

Report on Investigation into U. S. Atomic Energy Commission, 81st Cong., Report No. 169, October 1949.

Providing Radioisotopes for Medical Research, Report of the Subcommittee on Research and Development, August 1954.

Radioactive Fallout and Its Effects on Man, *Hearings before the Special Subcommittee on Radiation*, 85th Cong., 1st Ses., May 27 through June 7, 1957. Two parts.

S. 3323 and H. R. 8862, To Amend the Atomic Energy Act of 1946, *Hearings before the Joint Committee*, 83rd Cong., 2nd Ses., May 10 through June 18, 1954. Two volumes.

Soviet Atomic Espionage, Joint Committee Print, April 1951.

Uranium Inventory at Oak Ridge, *Hearings before the Joint Committee*, June 20, 1949.

Senate Committee on the Armed Services.

Satellite and Missile Program, *Hearings before Preparedness Investigating Subcommittee of the Senate Committee*, 85th Cong., 1st Ses., November 25, 1957, through January 23, 1958.

Senate Committee on Interstate and Foreign Commerce.

Hearings on Nomination of Lewis L. Strauss to Be Secretary of Commerce, 86th Cong., 1st Ses., March 17 through June 14, 1959.

Senate Special Committee on Atomic Energy.

Hearings from November 27, 1945, to February 15, 1946, on Development, Use and Control of Atomic Energy, 79th Cong., 2nd Ses., 1946. Five parts.

Hearings, January 22 through April 8, 1946, on S. 1717, 79th Cong., 2nd Ses., 1946. Five parts. (Separate from the November 27, 1945, through February 15, 1946, Hearings.)

U. S. Patent Office, February 20, 1934, Patent No. 1,948,384, 7 pages (the cyclotron patent).

University of California publications in addition to budgets, bulletins of the colleges, employee directories, and annual reports by the president to the governor of California. *The Californian* (student magazine), 1930-1932; *Chronicle* (faculty magazine), 1929-1932; *Science in the University*, 1944; *The 1939 Nobel Prize Award in Physics to Ernest Orlando Lawrence*, 1940.

INDEX